ANTONIO GRAMSCI
AND THE REVOLUTION THAT FAILED

ANTONIO GRAMSCI

AND THE REVOLUTION

THAT FAILED

MARTIN CLARK

YALE UNIVERSITY PRESS

NEW HAVEN AND LONDON

1977

For my Parents

Designed by John Nicoll and set in Monotype Bembo

Printed in Great Britain
by Robert MacLehose & Co. Limited, Glasgow

Published in Great Britain, Europe, Africa, the Middle East, India and
South-East Asia by Yale University Press, Ltd., London.
Distributed in Latin America by Kaiman & Polon, Inc., New York
City; in Australasia by Book & Film Services, Artarmon, N.S.W.,
Australia; in Japan by Harper & Row, Tokyo.

Library of Congress Cataloging in Publication Data
Clark, Martin.
  Antonio Gramsci and the revolution that failed.

  Bibliography: p. .
  Includes index.
    1. Gramsci, Antonio, 1891–1937. 2. Trade-unions – Italy – Political
activity – History. 3. Communism – Italy – History. 4. Italy – History –
1914–1945.
  I. Title.
HX288.G7C52 1977   335.4'092'4 [B]   76-49754
ISBN 0–300–02077–5

'We have no experience whatever of how we can and should lead the struggle for Socialism in a regime of advanced capitalism . . . there do not exist even implicit indications in the classics of our doctrine'

(Palmiro Togliatti, in *L'Unità* 13 February 1962)

PREFACE

THIS book has evolved over several years. It started out as a specialised monograph, indeed as a Ph.D. thesis written for the University of London, concerned with the Turin labour movement during and after the First World War. Inevitably it came to focus also on the figure of Antonio Gramsci and on his early activities in Turin, and in so doing became partly biographical. Gramsci in those years was discussing matters of perennial interest in political theory and sociology, and this fact again extended the scope of the book. Moreover, the Turin labour movement at this time was faced with the rise of Fascism, and it seemed right not to ignore this major historical issue altogether. Finally, Gramsci and his colleagues have exercised great influence on the later history of the Italian Communist Party, an influence which is still noticeable today. Thus my original monograph has become illustrative of wider themes. In the process it may have become too diffuse, so I offer the following Reader's Guide. Those interested in the 'eternal questions' of political theory should concentrate on the Introduction and on Chapter Three; those interested in Gramsci should read Chapter Three and the Conclusion; those interested in the rise of Fascism, Chapter One and the Conclusion; those interested in the Italian Communist Party, Chapter Eleven, the Conclusion and the Postscript. Those interested in history should read everything, as usual.

Many people have helped me write this book. In particular, I should like to thank Denis Mack Smith, who first interested me in Italian history, and first suggested I should write about Gramsci; and Eric Hobsbawm, who tolerantly supervised my postgraduate studies, and was always generous with his time and learning. I also welcome this opportunity of thanking Dr. Costanzo Casucci, who guided me through the Central State Archives in Rome, and all the helpful staff of the State Archives, the Gramsci Institute in Rome, the National Library in Florence, the Feltrinelli Institute in Milan, the British Library, the Library of the London School of Economics, the National Library of Scotland and the Edinburgh University Library. I am grateful to the Director of the Gramsci Institute and to Giulio Einaudi Editore s.p.a. of Turin, for permission to quote from Gramsci's works, and to the Centre for the Advanced Study of Italian Society, University of Reading, for permission to reproduce material that first appeared in a booklet published by the Centre in 1973. I have derived much benefit from talking to knowledgeable people over the years, and perhaps especially from Sergio Caprioglio, Stefano Merli and Emilio Soave in Italy, from Victor Kiernan, Adrian Lyttelton and Stuart Woolf in Britain, and from Guido De Meo peripatetically. Professor Gwyn Williams provided an essential stimulus for publication, and James Cornford, Denys Hay and Ivor Guild, W. S., provided advice and help at a difficult time. Mrs Joan Ludvik cheerfully volunteered to type much of the manuscript, quite outside the normal course of duty. My wife Ruth has had to tolerate both my absence while researching and my presence while writing. She includes proof-reading among her many talents. I owe a particular debt to John Nicoll of the Yale University Press office in London; without his initiative and enthusiasm this book would not have appeared. Finally, and perhaps unusually, I should like to thank an anonymous publisher's reader at Yale for his helpful and constructive suggestions.

CONTENTS

A2

COMMON TERMS

Consiglio di Fabbrica

I have translated this term throughout the book as 'Factory Council'. Strictly speaking, it signified the entire body of 'Workshop Commissars' (*Commissari di Reparto*), and so the Factory Council at the main Fiat works had about 250 members. However, the term was also used to indicate the 'Internal Commission' (*Commissione Interna*), usually of five members, elected by the full Factory Council; and this usage was particularly current during the 'Occupation of the Factories' in September 1920. I hope that the meaning will always be clear from the context.

Controllo

The Italian word *controllo* has been translated as 'control'. Thus *controllo operaio* is 'workers' control', *controllo sindacale* is 'Trade Union control', etc. However, the Italian word is weaker than its English equivalent, and in some cases 'checking' or 'supervision' might be a better translation.

Interventista

The word *interventista* has been translated as 'interventionist'. It refers to those people who, during the period of neutrality in 1914–15, had agitated for Italy's entry into the First World War. By extension, it came to mean 'militarist' or 'warmonger', and was applied more widely. Also 'interventionism', etc.

Sindacato

Sindacato and its derivatives (*sindacalismo*, *sindacalista*) has normally been translated as 'Trade Union' (Trade Unionism, Trade Unionist), especially when it refers to the moderate 'reformist' Socialist-led Trade Unions affiliated to the General Confederation of Labour. However, the same word is used in Italian for bodies that are obviously 'syndicalist', and I have therefore translated it as 'syndicate' ('syndicalist', 'syndicalism') when it refers to anarcho-syndicalist organisations of various kinds, or to the Fascist syndicates.

ABBREVIATIONS

C.G.I.I.
Confederazione Generale dell' Industria Italiana, General Confederation of Italian Industry (national employers' organisation).

C.G.L.
Confederazione Generale del Lavoro, General Confederation of Labour (reformist Socialist Confederation of Trade Unions).

F.I.O.M.
Federazione Italiana Operai Metallurgici, Italian Federation of Metal-Mechanical Workers (reformist Socialist Trade Union, affiliated to the *C.G.L.*).

P.C.d'I.
(later *P.C.I.*)
Partito Comunista d'Italia, Communist Party of Italy (founded 1921. It later changed its name to *Partito Comunista Italiano*, Italian Communist Party).

P.P.I.
Partito Popolare Italiano, Italian Popular Party (Catholic but 'non-confessional' party, founded in 1919 by Don Luigi Sturzo and others).

P.S.I.
Partito Socialista Italiano, Italian Socialist Party.

U.I.L.
Unione Italiana del Lavoro, Italian Union of Labour (a small 'interventionist', 'syndicalist' body based on Parma).

U.S.I.
Unione Sindacale Italiana, Italian Syndical Union (anarcho-syndicalist organisation, strong in Liguria and the Marches).

INTRODUCTION

The Question of Workers' Control

THE end of the First World War saw attempts in nearly all the belligerent countries to revitalise the various Labour movements. These efforts often amounted to 'grass-roots' revolts against official Socialist Party or Trade Union organisations, and they were particularly important in the various munitions centres, from Petrograd to Turin. Men believed that revolution was both possible and imminent, but that it was unlikely to be achieved by existing left-wing bodies working through traditional means. New institutions had to be set up, to 'prepare' or carry through the revolution; and the form these new institutions normally took was that of Workers' Councils, based either on geographical units or on the factory.[1] The new movements opposed the conventional Socialist doctrine that the new order could be set up only *after* the capture of political power by political means. They also (although this remained everywhere in the realm of theory) rejected the idea that a Socialist economy involved State ownership of the means of production, and administration of them by professional managers responsible to the State. These movements all failed in their main aims, although they often had considerable impact on national politics, and their leaders were often instrumental in setting up new labour organisations (e.g. Communist Parties) that survived after the

[1] For Russia, see especially P. Avrich, *The Russian Anarchists* (Princeton U.P., 1967), and his 'The Bolshevik Revolution and Workers' Control in Russian Industry', in *Slavic Review* vol. xxii (1963), pp. 47–63; F. Kaplan, *The Bolshevik Ideology* (Owen, London 1969); M. Brinton, *The Bolsheviks and Workers' Control* (Solidarity, London 1970); R. Daniels, *The Conscience of the Revolution* (Harvard U.P., 1960); and O. Anweiler, *Die Rätebewegung in Russland, 1905–21* (Brill, Leiden 1958). For Germany, see E. Kolb, *Die Arbeiterräte in der Deutschen Innenpolitik 1918–19* (Droste Verlag, Dusseldorf 1962); A. J. Ryder, *The German Revolution of 1918* (Cambridge U.P., 1967); and A. Mitchell, *Revolution in Bavaria* (Princeton U.P., 1965). For Britain, see B. Pribicevic, *The Shop Stewards' Movement and Workers' Control 1910–22* (Blackwell, Oxford 1959); and J. Hinton, *The First Shop Stewards' Movement* (Allen and Unwin, London 1973). cf. also M. Tronti (ed.), *Operai e Stato* (Feltrinelli, Milan 1972).

original movements had collapsed. Their very lack of success is extremely revealing of the general nature and structural defects, both of official contemporary Socialism and of unofficial left-wing movements.

This book is a study of one of these movements, the Factory Council movement in Italy. The movement in Italy presents many of the features found elsewhere, but in some ways it was the most interesting case of all. It reflected, and contributed at least a little, to the decline of the Liberal parliamentary system in Italy, and is thus of interest to political scientists concerned with the topical question of why democratic regimes fail.[2] Moreover, the Italian movement produced one of this century's leading Socialist theorists (Gramsci), and one of its outstanding practical politicians (Togliatti). For this reason it has acquired 'mythological' characteristics which have survived to this day, and which have had a considerable impact on the ideology and policies of the largest and least bureaucratic Communist Party in Western Europe. I hope, therefore, that this book will be useful not only for labour historians interested in spontaneous working-class movements and factory organisations. It can be read also as a modest contribution to the growing literature on political crisis, and as a study in the origins of a major Communist Party.

Much of the book (especially Chapter Three) deals with the ideas and activities of Antonio Gramsci, the leading writer and journalist involved in the Factory Council movement. In recent years Gramsci has become a well-known figure even outside Italy. His writings while in prison, on literature and Marxism, on Italian history and intellectuals, above all on cultural 'hegemony' – i.e. how the ruling classes control the media and education – have been widely discussed.[3] His earlier ideas about 'workers' self-management' in industry, and his emphasis on 'participatory democracy', have received less attention. This book therefore aims to clarify and set in context one of the most important episodes in Gramsci's intellectual biography. The 'Revolution that Failed' in 1919–20 was a constant theme in Gramsci's later writings (see Conclusion, p. 225), and

[2] See the forthcoming volume edited by Juan Linz and R. A. Stepan, *Crises and Breakdowns of Democratic Regimes* (Yale U.P.); J. Linz, 'La Caduta dei Regimi Democratici', and P. Farneti, 'La Crisi della Democrazia Italiana e l'Avvento del Fascismo: 1919–22', both in *Rivista Italiana di Scienza Politica*, anno V (1975), n. 1, pp. 7–43 and 45–82.

[3] Two selections of Gramsci's Prison Notebooks have been translated into English: A. Gramsci, *The Modern Prince*, translated by Louis Marks (Lawrence and Wishart, London 1957); and *Selections from the Prison Notebooks of Antonio Gramsci*, translated by Q. Hoare and G. Nowell Smith (Lawrence and Wishart, London 1971). I have outlined my views of the Prison Notebooks' importance in a review of the Hoare and Nowell Smith edition, in *Political Studies*, vol. xx, December 1972, pp. 492–6. A complete critical edition has recently been published in Italian: A. Gramsci, *Quaderni del Carcere*, 4 vols (Einaudi, Turin 1975).

led to many of his reflections about why revolutions fail, how political parties should be organised, and the role of ideology.

Indeed, it is unusual for a social theorist to become so deeply involved in 'unofficial' political activity in the way Gramsci was in the Factory Council movement. Many of his ideas may be seen as emerging from the industrial society of his time, and in that sense this book is an essay in the 'sociology of ideology'. Certain strands of social thought may be applicable only in certain societies at certain periods. On the other hand, Gramsci was a good enough thinker to transcend his own time and place, and many of his themes are ours today – the nature of cultural revolutions, the importance of education and the media, the need for workers' self-management. Above all, there is his fascination with the role of intellectuals in bringing about social and political change. In our alleged 'post-industrial society' this theme could hardly be more fashionable, especially as Gramsci was well aware of the tensions between meritocratic elitism, the needs of production, and the interests of ordinary workers. He knew all about the argument that Marxism was merely an ideology of the discontented intelligentsia, trying to replace the old privileged groups and form a 'New Class' which would oppress the proletariat in its turn.[4] Gramsci's activities in the Factory Council movement were an intelligent, yet realistic, attempt to prevent this outcome – or, if the outcome were inevitable, to mitigate its consequences through new 'participatory' institutions. Gramsci's struggle with these problems gives the Italian movement enduring interest for political theorists.

The Factory Council movement in Italy, like similar movements elsewhere, also raises some of the classic questions of political and industrial sociology. A young, educated radical intelligentsia is found leading a 'Socialist', factory-based political movement. How did this come about, and was their leadership effective? The mass support for the movement was given by skilled engineering workers. Why were they so militant? Obviously a book on this theme must consider the leadership, but it cannot concentrate entirely on the leaders, even when they are of Gramsci's stature; it must also seek to 'explain' the collective militancy of unknown workers. This is more difficult than might appear. Industrial workers – especially skilled engineering workers – are rarely militant, and in Italy itself there were few major outbreaks of industrial unrest between 1920 and 1968. Moreover, many of the available sociological 'theories' of working class militancy seem inadequate. Explanations in terms of 'increased class-consciousness' or 'greater solidarity' among workers

---

[4] This idea was commonplace among anarchists and syndicalists, and is also of course found in Mosca, Michels, Pareto and Machajski.

are often circular – the 'militancy' is said to be caused by the 'class-consciousness', and yet the only evidence for the 'class-consciousness' is the 'militancy'.[5] In any case, measuring the class-consciousness of workers fifty years late is an even more hopeless task than trying it *in situ*. Other kinds of 'explanations', especially those in terms of rapid economic and social change, seem to me more plausible. Clearly the World War, industrial expansion, urbanisation and inflation had important, if unquantifiable and indirect, effects, and I therefore discuss these matters more fully in Chapter One.[6] Rapid social changes should affect the composition of the working class – its age, skills, regional origins and the like – although this appears to have been less significant in the Italian engineering industry, where the Factory Councils flourished, than in other industries (or than in the engineering industries of other countries, notably Britain). Working class traditions are also important. Every country, indeed every city, has its own folk-memories of deeds performed by heroes long ago, and in the Italian case there were recognised forms of social protest (especially the riot and the strike) 'available', together with the appropriate attitudes.[7] There were also, of course, non-militant workers' institutions, which also had their own customs and their own group-loyalties. Much of this book is concerned with attempts to evolve new institutions (Factory Councils) and new types of collective action, from within a labour movement that often remained obstinately attached to the old ways.

But the 'explanation' for 'militancy' that seems to me most convincing, and which I have implicitly adopted throughout this book, rests mainly on considerations of power.[8] The periods of greatest popular agitation in Italian history do not correlate particularly well with rapid social change or industrial break-down,[9] but they were all periods of great *State* weakness, when the whole political structure was being radically changed or at least seriously threatened. The techniques of social control available

---

[5] cf. C. and L. and R. Tilly, *The Rebellious Century, 1830–1930* (Dent, London 1975), p. 8.

[6] The Tillys have argued (*ibid.*, p. 6) that such explanations are false, since violent protest and collective extremism does *not* come from the groups worst affected by social change (e.g. immigrants). But it is probably more a question of power – unskilled migrants cannot protest effectively, skilled workers can.

[7] cf. A. Pizzorno, Introduction (pp. 7–27) to A. Pizzorno (ed.), *Lotte Operaie e Sindacato in Italia (1968–72)*, vol. i (Il Mulino, Bologna 1974).

[8] I am indebted to the concept of 'latent power' developed by Michael Poole in his excellent book *Workers' Participation in Industry* (Routledge and Kegan Paul, London 1975).

[9] C. and L. and R. Tilly, *The Rebellious Century* cit., pp. 245–6. The periods considered are 1843–9, 1859–63, 1868–70, 1893–4, 1897–8, 1913–15 and 1919–22. I would add, as the Tillys tentatively do, 1944–7 and 1968–72.

to the old ruling elites were no longer effective. In these conditions 'militancy' pays – although it should be said that often the militancy is defensive in character, and designed to protect traditional rights at a time when the State is manifestly incapable of doing so, when everything is up for grabs and the currency is collapsing. This explanation in terms of political power is not circular, for there is plenty of evidence concerning, and good explanations for, the State's weakness, quite apart from the visible popular militancy; and it is not trivial. Government action, or inaction, was a crucial factor in 1919–20, as this book will show.

Of course, workers' power does not derive solely from the formal political system. Workers have greater power if there is full employment, if they work in expanding industries, if they have rare skills, if they are well organised, and so forth. Job-security (or its absence) is arguably the most important theme in any 'explanation' of working class militancy in terms of power. But job-security is itself a political matter. It depends on the possibility of victimisation against individuals or particular groups of workers, on government willingness to use troops to break strikes, on government willingness to rescue ailing industries with public funds, on the level of social security payments etc. In Italy, these factors had their customary importance in 1919–20. Working class militancy collapsed in 1921, along with job security and the reformist Giolitti government.

This emphasis on 'working class power' as the main explanation for 'working class militancy' may strike some readers as unduly hard-nosed, even unduly pessimistic about the human condition. I do not suppose that all readers will share these views, but it seems right to make them explicit in the Introduction. I am assuming that workers will be 'militant' if they get a chance. This is not to deny the existence of such old sociological favourites as the 'deferential worker', mindful of his proper station, nor of his rather more plausible successor, the 'privatised worker', anxious only to collect his wages and go back home to his family.[10] But I regard these gentlemen as *responses to* a situation of powerlessness, rather than as 'explanations' of it. Nor do I wish to deny that workers' values and attitudes can be important. The influence of local traditions has already been mentioned, and it is clear that workers may have very different perceptions of their power. They may be optimistic, pessimistic, realistic or brainwashed. In addition, the values and attitudes of employers, governments, consumers and the citizenry in general may prove very

[10] M. Poole, *Workers' Participation in Industry* cit., p. 92.

influential, often more so than those of shop floor workers. I am merely arguing that it is sensible to regard 'militancy' as the *natural* outcome when workers enjoy some real power in industrial societies (which is not often). Much of this book, especially its emphasis on factory institutions and their role in industrial conflicts, should be read in the light of these remarks.

However, even if workers' attitudes do not satisfactorily explain why workers are militant, they are very relevant to how workers' power is *used*. I have assumed so far that 'militancy' involves securing concessions within the existing industrial system, which is taken as being one of necessary conflict.[11] However, militancy may well provide only short-term or illusory benefits, and it certainly does not normally imply the ability to impose some other preferred political or economic structure. Gramsci saw this problem clearly. Like most Socialist thinkers, he was a moralist. He assumed that capitalism was collapsing; the task was, there-fore, to 'educate' workers to use their power 'reasonably', so as to build a New Order. They needed to develop technical and managerial skills, they needed to be better educated generally, above all they needed self-confidence and ability to take a broader, long-term view of their own interests. Militancy was not enough; on the contrary, it was useless in constructing Socialism, and might easily provoke a right-wing reaction which would destroy workers' power. Hence Gramsci's life-long efforts to 'educate' the working-class away from 'militancy', and to train a new working class elite. 'Real' workers' power meant the ability to organise production. It would be exercised in practice through workers' institu-tions, based initially on the work-place, and these Factory Councils would also have major educational functions. The whole aim of the movement – at least for Gramsci – was to use workers' power for constructive, 'non-militant' purposes.

The Factory Council movement raised very sharply, therefore, many of the issues that most concern democratic industrial nations today. If rational industrial production is desirable (and 'productivist' ideas were widespread in this period, as is shown in Chapter One), presumably some kind of industrial discipline is needed. Yet when workers and their institutions enjoy great political power, discipline cannot be provided by the traditional means – force, the market, or fear of unemployment. So what happens to industrial production? Gramsci and the Factory Council leadership answered that the workers must discipline themselves, and

---

[11] The classic statements of this position are in R. Dahrendorf, *Class and Class Conflict in Industrial Society* (Routledge and Kegan Paul, London 1959), and H. A. Clegg, *A New Approach to Industrial Democracy* (Blackwell, Oxford 1960).

regarded genuine 'workers' control' as the only method whereby continued industrial production could be guaranteed.

These ideas obviously ran completely counter to more traditional 'militant' views of working-class action. They also ran counter to the traditional 'oppositionist' labour institutions. Whether 'reformist' or 'revolutionary' these were essentially 'militant', engaged in fighting within the existing society rather than in attempting to build a New Order. Much of the opposition to the Factory Council movement came from the established labour institutions, jealous of their prerogatives of 'opposition' within the existing economic system. Moreover, the movement relied mainly on *skilled* engineering workers – the labour aristocracy of the time – and had little appeal for others. The problems of 'workers' self-management' proved intractable. Industrialists and managers were also hostile, needless to say, and insisted on maintaining the principle of 'authority in the workplace'. In 1921 they succeeded, mainly because of a rapid decline in skilled workers' power. There was a sharp economic recession, government policy changed, and assembly-line manufacture was extended, reducing the demand for craft skills. In these circumstances managerial authoritarianism seemed to provide the best long-term solution to the problem of industrial discipline.

Even so, this issue will not go away. Wherever workers have real power the same problems recur. The current debate on 'workers' participation in industry' is concerned with much the same themes as was Gramsci, although of course from a different political angle. It is not surprising that the demand for greater 'participation' seems to come mainly from technicians and highly skilled workers,[12] or that some very eminent writers see this issue as a major area of conflict in the future[13] – both in capitalist and 'socialist' societies. Workers' 'participation', in all its various forms, is the alternative to 'militancy'. It is an attempt to guarantee industrial discipline in a period of workers' power, and to secure the assent of skilled and well-educated workers to managerial criteria and the needs of production. Clegg and Mandel have argued that workers' 'participation' would mean that workers would acquire managerial views. This is indeed

---

[12] J. H. Goldthorpe *et al.*, *The Affluent Worker: Industrial Attitudes and Behaviour* (Cambridge U.P., 1968), pp. 20–21 and 108–9. 61 *per cent.* of craftsmen, but only a third of non-craftsmen, wanted a say in management. Similar findings are reported for Yugoslavia (e.g. D.S. Riddell, 'Social Self-Government – the Background of Theory and Practice in Yugoslav Socialism', in *British Journal of Sociology*, 1968, pp. 47–75). cf. S. Mallet, *La Nouvelle Classe Ouvrière* (Seuil, Paris 1963) and A. Touraine *La Conscience Ouvrière* (Seuil, Paris 1966).

[13] D. Bell, *The Coming of Post-Industrial Society* (Heinemann, London 1974), p. 8; R. Dahl, *After the Revolution?* (Yale U.P., 1970), pp. 135–6.

the whole point, and Gramsci would have greatly despised anybody who thought that such an outcome was undesirable.[14]

The debate on 'participation' is necessarily focused on the Trade Unions, as their traditional 'oppositionist' role is challenged. Trade Unions need some kind of factory organisation, if only to ensure that national agreements are implemented; but they do not want any workers' 'participation' *outside* the official Union structure, nor do they want the Union weakened as a 'militant', 'resistance' organisation.[15] Trade Unionists are uneasily aware of the dangerous paradox inherent in 'participation' schemes. Such schemes aim to reduce workers' 'militancy', which *may* involve weakening the Unions, reducing workers' power and thus ultimately making 'participation' less necessary from the management's point of view. Moreover, Trade Unionists are often anxious to avoid any split between skilled, active, 'participatory' workers and the rest, for their whole justification, and much of their rhetoric, rests on working-class 'solidarity'. Here again, these arguments are not new, and were frequently heard in Italy in 1920.

Two frequent outcomes of these debates deserve special mention. There have been many schemes for worker 'participation' in decision-making on a limited range of issues, usually of a fairly technical kind, on the shop floor. Often this 'participation' is only consultative, but it may involve setting up more or less genuinely autonomous work-groups, with real responsibilities for their own work. This outcome can be very useful to higher managers, as it frees them from a host of petty disputes, maintains morale and production, and does not seriously question managerial authority on key issues. It has occurred in 'State-socialist' countries like Poland, and may be regarded as a kind of 'administrative deconcentration' comparable to the efforts of bureaucracies everywhere to avoid the evils and delays of excessive centralisation.

The second group of schemes has been termed 'pseudo-participation', or 'participation as a means of persuasion',[16] and is a familiar feature of progressive management in advanced capitalist societies. People like to

[14] H. A. Clegg, *A New Approach to Industrial Democracy* cit., p. 23; E. Mandel, 'The Debate on Workers' Control' (esp. pp. 354–5), in G. Hunnius, G. D. Garson and J. Case (eds), *Workers' Control* (Random House, New York 1973), pp. 344–73. Clegg (*op. cit.*, pp. 104–5) discussing Yugoslav self-management, complains that the Workers' Councils aim to win the agreement of workers to a heavy rate of capital investment at the expense of consumption: 'It is by such a route that the Communist comes full circle to agree with reactionary businessmen, at the expense of the values of the free labour movement.' Quite so.

[15] M. Poole, *Workers' Participation in Industry* cit., p. 119; see also G. Merritt, 'France's Shop-Floor Directors', in *Financial Times* 14 February 1975; G. Turner, 'Workers on the Board', in *Sunday Telegraph* 16 and 23 November 1975.

[16] S. Verba, *Small Groups and Political Behaviour* (Princeton U.P., 1961), pp. 219–25.

feel they have a hand in a decision, whether they do or not. Consultative bodies, joint management-workers committees, liaison groups etc. – this is the machinery whereby an organisation's goals can be communicated downwards. This reduces the visibility of the control that is needed in an industrial society, and increases the acceptability of decisions. Clearly both these forms of 'participation' can enhance managerial authority. On the other hand, both of them presuppose fairly 'enlightened' managers, especially at the lower levels – men who are more interested in securing industrial efficiency than in retaining their own hard-won status. Such men are rare, and in the real world the temptation to revert to authoritarian methods is ever-present.

Gramsci recognised and accepted the possibility of both outcomes. The Factory Council movement *was* important mainly in the primary work-group. As for 'pseudo-participation', the question scarcely arose, for Gramsci was unwilling to admit that the 'real' aims of managers and of workers might differ. Workers were 'mature', and capable of running the factories competently; workers and managers were both 'producers', and as such should ally against the parasitic classes – financiers, bureaucrats and the like. In short, Gramsci accepted the tenets of 'productivism'. He tried energetically to enlist the support of engineers, technicians, foremen and white collar employees for the Factory Council movement. His efforts failed. Industrialists insisted on retaining their prerogatives and refused to accept that workers might have equal status as 'producers'. Furthermore the application of Taylorist schemes for 'scientific management' – assembly line production, detailed time and motion studies, the elimination wherever possible of individual initiative – dealt a mortal blow to the industrial power of skilled craftsmen. The Factory Council movement was about the nature of industrial management, among other things, and arguably it was here that Gramsci made his greatest mistake. He welcomed the 'Scientific Management of Labour' in the name of productivity, but it was incompatible with 'pseudo-participation'.

Many of these arguments apply, of course, to the wider political system as well as to industrial management. The Factory Council movement in Italy, like Guild Socialism in Britain, put forward ideas for a new representative structure, ultimately for a new kind of State, as well as for different factory management. Both Gramsci and G. D. H. Cole firmly believed that 'training for subservience' took place in authoritarian industry; and it is worth remembering that more recently a famous survey found a correlation between perceived ability to share in decisions at work, and people's sense of political competence.[17] In the present crisis of

[17] G. Almond and S. Verba, *The Civic Culture* (Little Brown, Boston 1965), pp. 294–7.

representative democracy these 'participatory' ideas are very apposite. Indeed, the modern State shows many of the familiar features of the industrial scene. On the one hand, increased claims by the citizenry for a share in decision-making – usually the most educated citizens, and often organised in small, 'unofficial' groups; on the other, serious efforts by governments and central bureaucracies everywhere to introduce 'administrative deconcentration' and 'pseudo-participation', so as to secure more ready acceptance of their goals.[18] An added problem for governments is that their 'goals' are ill-defined and even less generally accepted by citizens than are industrialists' goals by workers. The authoritarian temptation is again ever-present.

Nowhere is this seen more clearly than in Eastern Europe. The main themes of this book recur in every discussion of Socialism, and in many of the available models of a 'Socialist society' – centralist-administrative, 'cybernetic', 'regulated market' or 'self-management'.[19] It is noticeable that Workers' Councils have arisen wherever there have been popular protests against the regime (Hungary 1956, Czechoslovakia 1968), and that these Councils have embodied a temporary 'Gramscian' alliance between ordinary workers and the technical intelligentsia, against Party and bureaucracy. The obvious tactic for the Party, apart of course from repression, is to make material concessions to workers (especially less skilled workers), in order to win them away from the reformers, and to play on the rivalries and jealousies between workers and managers. This tactic has every chance of success. After all, any real 'workers' self-management' implies workers' control of investment, pricing, wage incentives, distribution of profits etc., and it implies that rigid production targets are *not* laid down by the central planners. It thus necessarily means some kind of market economy, and consequently greater rewards for the successful, greater inequality between firms, industries and regions, greater mobility of labour, more redundancies and ultimately greater unemployment. Obviously in this situation the Party can expect some working-class support in re-establishing central control. Moreover, the Party has every incentive to do so, since a 'market economy' may well create pressure for *political* changes. The end result has usually been 'administrative deconcentration' of low-level decisions, and an authoritarian form of 'pseudo-participation' – too authoritarian, however, and too pseudo, to convince many members of the educated elite.

[18] cf. James Cornford (ed.) *The Failure of the State* (Croom Helm, London 1975), in which I have a chapter on Italian public administration. The issues are well discussed in Carole Pateman, *Participation and Democratic Theory* (Cambridge U.P., 1970).

[19] For an excellent summary of recent debates, see David Holloway, 'Models of Reform in Eastern Europe', in James Cornford, *The Failure of the State* cit., pp. 141–73.

The partial exceptions – or perhaps extreme examples – have been Hungary and Yugoslavia. The New Economic Mechanism in Hungary relies heavily on the market for many purposes, and attempts to defuse worker unrest by operating price controls over consumer goods, and above all by hindering redundancies. Workers' participation is minimal (there are no Workers' Councils) and the main beneficiaries of this 'market' system appear to be managers, either official or unofficial ('Nepmen').[20] The Yugoslav experience, on the other hand, shows that 'participation' need not always be 'pseudo'. Although, no doubt, reality does not always measure up to ideals – Warner remarks that all men are influential, but some are more influential than others – nevertheless the Workers' Councils in Yugoslavia discuss real issues, have real powers and take real 'managerial' decisions.[21] Unfortunately, Yugoslavia is also a classic example of how 'self-management', a market economy, and social inequalities are intertwined. As Sharon Zukin laments, 'it seems a travesty of the ideals of Socialist humanism, a mockery of claims to "democracy and equality" to appropriate the concept of self-management to patch up a capitalist system.'[22] This is not quite what the Yugoslavs have done, but one can see what she means. Yet perhaps only a strong, authoritarian centralised State can enforce equality; and perhaps the price is too high. And it is worth remembering that however limited 'workers' power' may be in a market economy, it has certainly been one of the first casualties in the centralised administrative economies.

I cannot claim that Gramsci – any more than the Yugoslavs – has the answer to these problems. What I do claim is that the Factory Council movement in Italy was concerned with many of the issues that are still relevant today, and that Gramsci was one of the few Socialist thinkers to worry about the very presuppositions of Socialism. He thought 'workers' self-management' was essential, both on moral grounds – it rescues men from serfdom – and on economic grounds – it alone can produce a sober,

---

[20] cf. D. Granick, 'The Hungarian Economic Reform', in *World Politics*, vol. xxv, 1973, pp. 414–29; Alec Nove, 'Economic Reforms in the U.S.S.R. and Hungary, a Study in Contrasts', in A. Nove and D. Nuti (eds), *Socialist Economics* (Penguin Books, London 1972), pp. 335–62.

[21] On Yugoslavia, I have found the following most useful: Jaroslav Vanek, *The Participatory Economy* (Cornell U.P., 1971); Sharon Zukin, *Beyond Marx and Tito* (Cambridge U.P., 1975); G. Hunnius, 'Workers' Self-Management in Yugoslavia', in G. Hunnius, G. Garson and J. Case (eds), *Workers' Control* cit.; D.S.Riddell, 'Social Self-Government – the Background of Theory and Practice in Yugoslav Socialism', in *British Journal of Sociology*, 1968, pp. 47–75; M. Warner, 'Whither Yugoslav Self-Management?', in *Industrial Relations Journal*, Spring 1975, pp. 65–72; and E. Pusic, 'Intentions and Realities – Local Government in Yugoslavia', in *Public Administration*, Summer 1975, pp. 133–52.

[22] S. Zukin, *Beyond Marx and Tito* cit., pp. 74–5.

disciplined, industrious skilled labour force. He has not been proved wrong yet. However, the questions whether 'self-management' might not depend on 'workers' power', whether 'workers' power' is compatible with the discipline of the market place, and whether a market system is compatible with 'social solidarity', will no doubt prove as troublesome in the future as they did for Gramsci in the 1920s. So, too, will the appeal of authoritarianism, and perhaps above all the tenacity of old institutions and old bureaucracies. With all their failings, regimes collapse much less often than one would expect.

CHAPTER ONE

The Great War and its Impact

THE Factory Council movement in Italy, like its counterparts in other countries, was a product of the First World War. This Chapter will therefore consider in turn the effects of the war on industry, on the activities and role of the State, on living standards and popular discontent, and on the existing labour movements.

The effect on industry is the easiest to assess: it produced a war boom. A guaranteed market, at guaranteed prices, led to a rapid growth of the war industries. One estimate is that Italy spent 13,761 million pre-war (gold) *lire* on arms, munitions and means of transport in these years.[1] Italian industry produced six times as many pieces of artillery during the war as the Italian army had possessed when it started;[2] on Armistice Day there were 7,709 cannons in the field, more than the British had.[3] Aircraft production started virtually from scratch, yet in 1918 6,523 planes were built, and 14,820 engines (many were exported to Britain).[4] As for vehicles, the army had an insatiable need for lorries, trucks, ambulances and the like. The Turin firm of Fiat increased its capital from 25½ million *lire* in 1914 to 125 million *lire* by the end of the war,[5] absorbing many of the smaller metal-works in the city, including the car manufacturers Diatto. By 1918

---

[1] The estimate is by F. Zugaro, quoted in A. Caracciolo, 'La Grande Industria nella Prima Guerra Mondiale', in A. Caracciolo (ed.), *La Formazione dell' Italia Industriale* (Laterza, Bari 1969), pp. 197–8. He divides the expenditure into artillery, shipping, aircraft, etc.

[2] L. Einaudi, *La Condotta Economica e gli Effetti Sociali della Guerra Italiana* (Yale U.P. and Laterza, Bari 1933), p. 67.

[3] R. Romeo, *Breve Storia della Grande Industria in Italia* (Cappelli, Bologna 1961), p. 119.

[4] L. Einaudi, *La Condotta Economica e gli Effetti Sociali della Guerra Italiana* cit., p. 69; R. Romeo (*Breve Storia della Grande Industria in Italia* cit., p. 120) gives the figure as 14,280. Fiat alone made 15,830 aircraft engines during the war (see *Fiat – a Fifty Years' Record*, Mondadori, Milan 1951, p. 171), and in 1918 1,500 of them were exported to Britain – see A. Caracciolo (ed.), *La Formazione dell' Italia Industriale* cit., p. 212.

[5] A. Caracciolo, *La Formazione dell' Italia Industriale* cit., p. 212.

Fiat produced over 90 *per cent*. of all vehicles made in Italy, and had
become the leading vehicle producer in Europe, producing about 75
four-wheeled vehicles a day[6] – 25,000 a year – in addition to its aircraft
and artillery production. In 1914 Fiat had made about 3,300 vehicles;
during the four years of war, the firm produced 70,862 vehicles, of which
more than 60,000 were for the Armed Forces of Italy or her Allies.[7]

This rapid expansion naturally benefited a few sectors only. The army
needed woollen garments, for example, but not silk. Indeed, it mainly
benefited a handful of large firms – Ilva, Ansaldo, Breda, Fiat, Pirelli and
a few others. Only the large firms had the technical skills, and the financial
support, to transform their production quickly enough and on a large
enough scale; and only a few firms had the political contacts to ensure
regular supplies of coal and other raw materials. In any case, government
officials preferred to place orders with 'reliable', well-connected large
firms rather than with a host of smaller ones. The result was industrial
'concentration'. The war industries were centred on a few firms, and on a
few regions – Piedmont, Lombardy and Liguria; the war greatly increased
the relative backwardness of the South. These firms engaged in both
vertical and horizontal integration, so as to guarantee supplies and to
'rationalise' production. Integration could be dangerous as well as bene-
ficial, and some of the firms – notably Ansaldo – became vast shaky
'conglomerates' with few industrial interests in common.[8]

The war not only stimulated – and distorted – Italian industry, but did
so in particular *ways* that undermined many of the assumptions of the
pre-war Liberal regime. Italian industry had always been a tender plant,
nurtured by State orders and tariff protection; yet during the war, in
Arturo Labriola's words:

By forcing the capitalist to produce its requirements, by providing him
with the raw materials, by fixing prices, by preventing him from selling
how, when and to whom he might wish, by forcing him to make
specific agreements with his workforce and to accept special supervision
by public officials, by requisitioning and compensating him as it saw

[6] This was the normal production. 176 were finished in a single day, 31 December
1917 (G. Prato, *Il Piemonte e gli Effetti della Guerra sulla sua Vita Economica e Sociale*,
Yale U.P. and Laterza, Bari 1925, p. 101).

[7] A. Caracciolo, *La Formazione dell' Italia Industriale* cit., p. 212; V. Castronovo,
Giovanni Agnelli (U.T.E.T., Turin 1971), p. 153.

[8] L. Einaudi, *La Condotta Economica e gli Effetti Sociali della Guerra Italiana* cit.,
pp. 264–6; R. Romeo, *Breve Storia della Grande Industria in Italia* cit., pp. 122–4; L. De
Rosa, *La Rivoluzione Industriale e il Mezzogiorno* (Laterza, Bari 1973), pp. 149–61;
F. Chessa, *La Concentrazione delle Industrie e la Guerra* (Athenaeum, Rome 1920),
pp. 65–76.

fit – often not compensating at all – in these ways the State made a frontal attack on the whole principle of private property and authority.[9]

State intervention on this scale required a large bureaucratic apparat, even though much of the work was done by Special Commissions (297 of them for industry alone, advising the various Ministries) on which prominent industrialists sat. Of the Ministries, the new Under-secretariat (later Ministry) of Arms and Munitions had the most power over industry. It employed over 5,000 people by the end of the war, and was responsible for placing most of the contracts and, above all, for supervising the system of 'Industrial Mobilisation'.[10]

'Industrial Mobilisation' was the key to Italy's war effort. The system rested on a Central Committee in Rome, on which the leading arms manufacturers sat – Agnelli of Fiat, Breda, Pio Perrone of Ansaldo, Caproni – and a number of Regional Committees. The Regional Committees consisted of a high ranking army or navy officer as President, two representatives of the employers, two workers' representatives, and two 'civilian' economic experts. A further decree on 16 July 1917 enlarged the composition of the Regional Committees, which thenceforth had a President, 4 to 6 civilian experts, and 2 to 5 representatives from each side. Below the regional level, there were also 'groups' of firms, in which one industrialist acted as 'group leader' and exercised authority over competing firms in the same sector.[11] The various committees negotiated the arms contracts, distributed the coal and raw materials to firms, and ensured transport for deliveries. The opportunities for abuse were clearly immense, at a time when normal accounting procedures had been waived for the duration of the war, and some notorious cases were revealed by the post-war Commission of Enquiry.[12]

Perhaps the most important feature of the 'Industrial Mobilisation' system was its impact on labour relations. All firms that produced, or might conceivably produce, military supplies, were liable to be declared 'auxiliary', and in this case all personnel became subject to military

[9] Arturo Labriola, 'La Dittatura del Proletariato ed i Problemi Economici del Socialismo', in *Nuova Antologia* 16 November 1920, pp. 103–4.

[10] For details, see A. De Stefani, *La Legislazione Economica della Guerra* (Yale U.P. and Laterza, Bari 1926); also L. Einaudi, *La Condotta Economica e gli Effetti Sociali della Guerra Italiana* cit., pp. 99–130; and A. Caracciolo, *La Formazione dell' Italia Industriale* cit., pp. 174 ff.

[11] A. Caracciolo, *La Formazione dell' Italia Industriale* cit., pp. 187–8.

[12] Camera dei Deputati, *Relazione della Commissione Parlamentare d' Inchiesta per le Spese di Guerra* (Rome 1923), esp. vol. ii. Note that the State normally paid some of the costs of production in advance. The whole issue of 'excess profits' and how they should be taxed was much debated – see, especially, L. Einaudi, *La Guerra e il Sistema Tributario Italiano* (Yale U.P. and Laterza, Bari 1927), pp. 129–229.

discipline, with the workers being supervised by armed soldiers. It was also prohibited to leave or change one's job without written permission from the local Regional Committee.[13] Thus firms had every incentive to agree to be made 'auxiliary'. Not only did they secure raw materials and favourable contracts, they also kept their workers out of the army, and could call on the military authorities to discipline their workers if necessary. By the end of 1918, there were 1,976 'auxiliary' firms in Italy, 762 of them engaged in the metal-working or engineering industry.[14] Moreover, a decree of October 1916 set up a kind of subsidiary *ausiliarità*, whereby workers in industries that had not been declared 'auxiliary' could also be obliged to observe military discipline if a decree to that effect were issued by the local Committee of Industrial Mobilisation. Industrialists may have lost their competitive birthright, but they certainly gained their mess of pottage – sanctified, too, by the thought of patriotic duty nobly done. Conversely, those who detested the 'Industrial Mobilisation' system – and much of its impact was disciplinary – came to hate their employers and the State with equal ferocity. I will discuss the impact of the system on workers and their organisations below (pp. 24–6), but I wish to emphasise here that a formidable 'military-industrial complex' was set up (or rather, greatly expanded) during the war.[15]

Thus during the war Italy acquired a 'regulated economy'. The State controlled prices and incomes, the State distributed raw materials, the State controlled foreign trade, the State directed labour, the State rationed consumption, the State was the only market for most industrial goods, and the State banned strikes.[16] All this was quite contrary to the competitive, small-firm atmosphere of pre-war Liberal Italy – although it was not quite so contrary to the pre-war *practice* as it seemed, especially as far as the steel industry was concerned. Even so, many of the assumptions of the old Italy had been undermined, and some obvious questions then arose. When the war was over, would Italy – could Italy – simply give up regulating its economy in this way? Might that not lead to economic collapse, and betray the hopes of millions of patriots? Was not a State-directed economy inevitable, even desirable, after the war? Many indus-

[13] Article 20, Royal Decree of 22 August 1915.

[14] L. Einaudi, *La Condotta Economica e gli Effetti Sociali della Guerra Italiana* cit., p. 104; A. Caracciolo, *La Formazione dell' Italia Industriale* cit., pp. 178–9 – Caracciolo gives a break-down of these firms by sector and region.

[15] Mario Abrate, detailing the composition of the Piedmontese Regional Committee in November 1917, points out that even the 'civilian' members were industrialists: 'obviously the (Industrial) League had taken over the Piedmontese Committee' (M. Abrate, *La Lotta Sindacale nella Industrializzazione in Italia*, Angeli, Milan 1967, p. 163).

[16] R. Romeo, *Breve Storia della Grande Industria in Italia* cit., p. 115.

trialists were fearful of what might happen if foreign trade were resumed without tariff protection, or if wages were freed of control.[17] But if the war meant the end of the market economy, who would allocate resources? Who would choose what to produce? And what new State institutions would be needed to do these things, to mobilise support and enforce compliance? Economic regulation was clearly incompatible with existing Parliamentary and social institutions, especially the existing Trade Unions. In short, a new regime would replace Liberal Italy. What would be its nature? – and who would be in charge of it?

Thus in the latter stages of the war, and in the years immediately after it, there was a confused and acrimonious debate about political and economic first principles. The most fashionable theories were vaguely 'productivist', and claimed to extend to the whole of society the ideas of Frederick Taylor on factory organisation.[18] The men in charge should be 'experts', 'engineers', 'producers'; there was one optimal solution to social problems, and only technical experts could find it; and there was a natural alliance of all 'producers' (entrepreneurs, managers, and workers) against all 'parasites' (rentiers, old ruling elites and politicians). The 'white-hot heat of the technological revolution' had created a new ruling class, and these new men could be guaranteed to solve all social problems by their skill at management and at increasing production. Hence the old Parliament was obsolete – what would its members talk about, when all policies were decided by experts? The old capitalism was also obsolete, for the modern economy would be planned and centralised, with industrial production carried out by vast cartels, small firms abolished, and foreign trade at a minimum.[19] Obsolete, too, was the class war; the real problem was not how to divide up the proceeds of industry, but how to increase them. These 'productivist' ideas were new then, however familiar they may have become in our day; they were compelling, in the war-time context of

[17] Luigi Einaudi wrote that 'by this time men thought and acted like Communists. The industrialists more than the workers.' (L. Einaudi, *La Condotta Economica e gli Effetti Sociali della Guerra Italiana* cit., p. 146).

[18] On 'Taylorism', see C. S. Maier, *Recasting Bourgeois Europe* (Princeton U.P., 1975), and the same author's 'Between Taylorism and Technocracy', in *Journal of Contemporary History*, vol. v, no. 2 (1970), pp. 27–61, esp. pp. 40–4; C. Pellizzi, *Una Rivoluzione Mancata* (Longanesi, Milan 1948), Chapter One; A. Aquarone, 'Aspirazioni Tecnocratiche del Primo Fascismo', in *Nord e Sud*, April 1964, pp. 109–28; G. Belluzzo, *L'Organizzazione Scientifica delle Industrie Meccaniche in Italia* (Bertero, Rome 1917); R. Vivarelli, *Il Dopoguerra in Italia e l'Avvento del Fascismo* (Istituto Italiano per gli Studi Storici, Naples 1967), pp. 270–1; R. De Felice, *Mussolini il Rivoluzionario* (Einaudi, Turin 1965), pp. 492 ff.

[19] These ideas, expressed in Walter Rathenau's books *Von Kommenden Dingen* (1916) and *Die Neue Wirtschaft* (1917) were very influential in Italy. An Italian edition of the latter book appeared in 1919.

rapid economic growth and social change; and they promised a way out of social tensions.

Taylorism, therefore, was important as an 'explanatory' ideology, at a time when the economy had undeniably been 'engineered' and 'rational-ised' along 'progressive' lines. It was even more important as a 'self-justifying' ideology for those who saw themselves as leading the war effort – the 'interventionists', the volunteer officers, the patriotic and the young. Pre-war Liberal Italy seemed hopelessly old-fashioned, and bereft of moral authority over large numbers of young people; and these young people were the ones who were winning the war. Taylorism offered the better educated young men of Northern Italy a place in the sun, in a new regime. Mussolini was quick to see the possibilities. His newspaper, *Il Popolo d'Italia*, appeared from 1 August 1918 with the sub-title *The Combattents' and Producers' Daily*;[20] and even previously he had seized on productivist ideas as being more 'progressive' than Socialism and as offering scope for propaganda among working people – even for Trade Unionism of a new kind.[21]

Indeed, much of the debate on the 'New Industrial State' turned on the role of Trade Unions, and on the relationship between them and the State machinery. 'Productivism' obviously implied that the Unions – or some other kind of workers' organisations – would have a vital role in the future. They would, of course, no longer be fighting the class war; but they would represent the 'producers', they would collaborate in planning, and above all they would have the technical expertise to enable the State to carry out its tasks. In Alfredo Rocco's view, the Unions were to be 'assimilated' into the State machinery, in return for guarantees of full employment, social welfare, and mass production of consumer goods.[22] Rocco, who had been a nationalist pre-war and was later to introduce the major constitutional innovations of the Fascist regime, regarded industrial concentration (national cartels) and Trade Unions as together heralding some kind of 'corporatist' State. 'Corporations', of workers and employ-ers, should together organise the whole of production within a general framework planned by the State.

---

[20] Previously it had been a 'Socialist Daily'. R. De Felice, *Mussolini il Rivoluzionario* cit., p. 406.

[21] R. De Felice, *Mussolini il Rivoluzionario* cit., pp. 411–12; F. Cordova, 'Le Origini dei Sindacati Fascisti', in *Storia Contemporanea*, anno 1, n. 4 (December 1970), pp. 925–1009, at pp. 930–1.

[22] A. Rocco, 'Il Momento Economico e Sociale', in *Politica* 24 April 1919; and his speech to the University of Padua 15 November 1920, given in A. Lyttelton (ed.), *Italian Fascisms* (Jonathan Cape, London 1973), esp. pp. 280–4. cf. also F. Chessa, *La Concentrazione delle Industrie e la Guerra* cit., pp. 132 ff.

Rocco was perhaps unusually coherent in his views, but a quasi-syndicalist, quasi-nationalist outlook was surprisingly common by the latter stages of the war.[23] The Republican Party Congress in December 1918 heard many calls for 'syndicalism' of this kind;[24] the Futurists wanted self-government by 'technical bodies', and the interventionist (i.e. pro-war) syndicalists of the Italian Union of Labour called for a 'Government of Syndicates', with workers running their own factories for the benefit of society.[25] Even the reformist-Socialist leaders of the General Confederation of Labour (*C.G.L.*) climbed on the bandwagon. The *C.G.L.*'s Directive Council called at the end of the war for 'the transfer of deliberative powers on the technical aspects of social legislation and the regulations concerning it from Parliament to suitably transformed Trade Union consultative bodies' – a kind of 'Professional Parliament'.[26] The discussions in the Parliamentary Commission on Post-War Problems in 1918, and on the setting-up of a Constituent Assembly in 1919, (see below, pp. 32–4) were also much concerned with these issues.

Naturally, all these ideas were firmly rejected by the dominant Liberal school of economists (Luigi Einaudi, Pareto), and indeed by many industrialists. Those who had not been deeply involved in the war effort, or those who could foresee prosperity in the post-war period *provided they were left free* to export their products, remained committed to older free-trade principles. Those involved in international trade, as well as many smaller businessmen, called for an immediate dismantling of the 'war restrictions'. Giovanni Agnelli of Fiat drew from his war-time experiences very different conclusions from those of other armaments manufacturers. Another European war had to be avoided at all costs, and the way to do this was to set up a Federal Europe, or at least a Customs Area – 'After the initial period of reorganisation, the effect of the tremendous change from separate national markets to a single continental market will create such possibilities of trade that industries will receive the same rousing stimulus

[23] See, for example, V. Scialoja, *I Problemi dello Stato Italiano dopo la Guerra* (Zanichelli, Bologna 1918), pp. 113 ff, calling for a continuation of the 'Industrial Mobilisation' system post-war (Scialoja was chairman of the economic sub-committee of the Parliamentary Commission on Post-War Problems); and Senator E. Ponti, 'Il Sindacato Industriale ed il Nuovo Orientamento Economico', in *Nuova Antologia* 1 & 16 December 1918. Other examples are given in A. Lyttelton, *The Seizure of Power* (Weidenfeld & Nicolson, London 1973), p. 203.

[24] R. De Felice, *Mussolini il Rivoluzionario* cit., p. 442.

[25] F. Cordova, 'Le Origini dei Sindacati Fascisti' cit., p. 935. For the Italian Union of Labour, see note 86, p. 34.

[26] Resolution of the Directive Council of the *C.G.L.*, published in *Battaglie Sindacali* 22 January 1919. cf. also International Labour Office *Studies & Reports*, Series B, no. 9, pp. 10–16.

which American industry experienced after the Civil War'.[27] The parallel with events after the Second World War is obvious, and arguably Agnelli saw more clearly than did Rocco the nature of the emerging modern economy. But Fiat was exceptional, in that it could convert from military to civilian vehicles fairly easily – and even Fiat kept a high level of production in 1919 and early 1920 only because of continuing military orders for trucks and lorries.[28]

Industrialists were, therefore, divided among themselves, and uncertain about what ought to be done. In December 1918 the President of the Turin Industrial League spoke in favour of a rapid return to liberty, a dismantling of State controls, etc. – or, as a second best, a system of cartels and syndicates among employers, to distribute raw materials and rationalise production.[29] As for many other middle-class people – civil servants, rentiers and pensioners – their main worry was about inflation. Civil servants, too, were unwilling to see the existing machinery of State replaced by a new 'syndicalist' network. Clearly Mussolini – and other politicians – had to tread warily.

In practice, most of the war-time controls were abolished in 1919, and very little was done (before 1925) to set up a controlled corporate State. Although a new, more protectionist tariff came into force in 1921, a 'self-sufficient' economy, and full State control of foreign trade, did not emerge until the mid-1930s. Even so, the 'productivist' discussions of 1918–19 were important. They helped to focus public attention on the need for a new kind of State, and thus made the general 'crisis of the Liberal regime' more acute. In 1919, that regime was further undermined by the advent of mass organised political parties – the Socialist Party and the new Catholic Popular Party – exploiting the new proportional representation system to win 156 and 100 seats respectively in the new Parliament (see p. 78). In these circumstances, the idea of a State responsive to 'technical', rather than popular, demands seemed even more compelling.

The fundamental feature of 'productivism' was, of course, the need to discipline labour; and perhaps the fundamental reason why some of the new ideas were not applied in 1919–20 was that labour was still too powerful, and too alienated, to be drawn into the State network – yet not powerful enough to overthrow it. If the war had been popular, or if it had provided some obvious benefits for working people – or if it had been lost – then all might have been different. Pre-war Italy had a long tradition

---

[27] G. Agnelli & A. Cabiati, *Federazione Europea o Lega delle Nazioni?* (Bocca, Turin 1918), p. 108; the translation is from *Fiat – A Fifty Years' Record* cit., p. 120.

[28] V. Castronovo, *Giovanni Agnelli* cit., p. 173. They were desperately needed in the newly acquired Alpine regions.

[29] M. Abrate, *La Lotta Sindacale nella Industrializzazione in Italia* cit., p. 201.

of popular protest and militancy,[30] and these traditions were exacerbated in the urban areas by the effects of war-time expansion on living standards, hours of work, and factory discipline, as well as by the general unpopularity of the war itself.

As far as living standards were concerned, the well-known economist Antonio Fossati estimated that 'in the war years the purchasing power of real wages went down to levels a quarter below that of real wages in 1913';[31] and recently Sergio Ricossa has produced a very similar calculation, showing real wages down from 100 in 1913 to 73.0 in 1917 and to 64.5 in 1918.[32] It is revealing, in fact, to compare the increase in the cost of living with available figures for the increase in money wages. Bachi's cost of living index for the whole of Italy (1913 = 100) shows figures of 132.7 for 1915, 199.7 for 1916, 306.3 for 1917, and 409.1 for 1918.[33] Meanwhile the average daily earnings in industry had risen merely from 3.54 *lire* in 1913 to 4.03 *lire* in 1916, 4.90 in 1917, and 6.04 in 1918.[34] However, all these figures cover a wide range, from female textile workers to skilled engineers. Redenti estimated that men in the key metal-working and mechanical industries were earning 9 *lire* a day at the end of 1917, including piece-rate earnings and cost-of-living allowances; the highest 'categories' could reach 27.42 *lire* per day. Pre-war rates had averaged 3.90 *lire* a day in these industries.[35] It is reasonable to conclude that skilled labour in engineering was scarce during the war, that its wage rates rose accordingly, and that more industrial jobs were available generally, especially for women. On the other hand, the evidence for a *general* decline in real wages seems convincing,[36] and even the skilled men had real

[30] See, especially, G. Manacorda, *Il Socialismo nella Storia d'Italia* (Laterza, Bari 1966); S. Merli, *Proletariato di Fabbrica e Capitalismo Industriale* (La Nuova Italia, Florence 1973); and R. Del Carria, *Proletari senza Rivoluzione* (Oriente, Milan 1966).

[31] Quoted by P. Spriano, *Torino Operaia nella Grande Guerra* (Einaudi, Turin 1960), pp. 187–8. Fossati's figures, taking 1913 = 100, are: 1914, 99.7; 1915, 93.45; 1916, 85.0; 1917, 73.07; and 1918, 64.6.

[32] S. Ricossa, 'Italy 1920–70', Chapter 5 of C. Cipolla (ed.), *The Fontana Economic History of Europe*, vol. vi (Fontana, London 1973), p. 13.

[33] Quoted by G. Prato, *Il Piemonte e gli Effetti della Guerra sulla sua Vita Economica e Sociale* cit., p. 184.

[34] *ibid.*, p. 93.

[35] Data in the *Bollettino del Comitato Centrale della Mobilitazione Industriale*, October 1918, quoted in L. Einaudi, *La Condotta Economica e gli Effetti Sociali della Guerra Italiana* cit., p. 118; G. Prato, in his *Il Piemonte e gli Effetti della Guerra sulla sua Vita Economica e Sociale* cit., p. 132, gives average daily earnings for all workers at Fiat as 7.61 *lire* in 1916, and 9.81 *lire* in 1917; piece-rate workers at Fiat earned 7.10 *lire* in 1914, 7.60 in 1915, 8.25 in 1916, 10.63 in 1917, and 14.48 *lire* in 1918.

[36] Although it has recently been disputed by Piero Melograni, in his excellent *Storia Politica della Grande Guerra* (Laterza, Bari 1971), pp. 359–69. I remain unconvinced that the figures he quotes are any more reliable than the ones more generally used. Melograni is no doubt correct in saying that the war provided extra employ-

problems. Daily wages may have increased, but so had the hours (and intensity) of work. A 70-hour week was compulsory at Fiat by March 1916, and nearly all workers in fact put in 75 hours.[37] These long hours particularly affected women, who lacked the time for shopping; and public transport and food were scarce.

Popular discontent focused on food and housing. In Milan, where average daily earnings in industry were 6.71 *lire* in 1918, it was found in May 1918 that an 'average working-class family' – two adults, one child aged between 10 and 15, and two children under ten years of age – was spending as much as 75.35 *lire* a week on 'prime necessities', and would be spending 99.75 *lire* a week on them if consumption of foodstuffs had been maintained at 1913 levels.[38] It is clear that working-class households depended for vital necessities on there being at least two wage-earners in the family. At Turin, the situation was comparable; to take just two basic foods, the average annual consumption of meat per inhabitant fell from 68.16 kg. in 1912–14 to 47.72 kg. in 1918; sugar consumption fell from 16.45 kg. to 8.24 kg.[39] Rationing was introduced for bread and *pasta* in mid-1917. Sometimes a municipal council applied it to other foods as well, but usually there was no need to ration meat or sugar, for most people did not eat enough of them to make it worth while.[40] As for housing, the shortages in most big cities were acute. Building virtually stopped during the war;[41] and the 1921 Census found 45 *per cent.* of the population of Turin, and 51.9 *per cent.* of that of Milan, living in one or two-room dwellings.[42] Of the other major cities in Italy, only Naples and Messina were more crowded.

ment opportunities (especially for women), and that this factor cushioned many working-class families from a fall in consumption; but the long hours worked by women, and the absence of opportunities for shopping, were themselves a powerful source of discontent (e.g. during the Turin bread riots).

[37] V. Castronovo, *Giovanni Agnelli* cit., p. 106.

[38] *Bollettino della Cassa Nazionale Infortuni*, May 1918.

[39] G. Prato, *Il Piemonte e gli Effetti della Guerra sulla sua Vita Economica e Sociale* cit., p. 177. P. Spriano, *Torino Operaia nella Grande Guerra* cit., pp. 188–93, gives a more detailed analysis of the rise of the cost of living in Turin during the war. R. Bachi, in *L'Alimentazione e la Politica Annonaria in Italia* (Yale U.P. and Laterza, Bari 1926), p. 103, gives different figures for the falls in consumption per head at Turin: meat down from 64.6 kg. in 1912–14 to 41.9 kg. in 1918; sugar from 15.5 kg. to 7.1 kg.

[40] R. Bachi, *L'Alimentazione e la Politica Annonaria in Italia* cit., p. 274; S. Somogyi, 'Cento Anni di Bilanci Familiari Italiani', in *Annali dell' Istituto Giangiacomo Feltrinelli* anno I (1959), pp. 121–263, esp. pp. 170 ff.

[41] Rooms completed and declared inhabitable fell in Milan from 15,436 in 1913 to 312 in 1919; in Turin, from 12,725 to 616 (U. Giusti, *Le Grandi Città Italiane nel Primo Quarto del XX Secolo* (Venturi, Florence 1925), p. 51).

[42] *ibid.*, p. 50; A. Capodiferro, 'Abitazioni', in *Annali di Statistica*, series VIII, no. 17 (1965), pp. 259–93, esp. p. 273.

Popular discontent was heightened by an awareness that industrial profits had reached unprecedently high levels. The Socialist daily newspaper *Avanti!* regularly published the balance sheets of the leading industrial firms, with appropriate comments. The widespread belief in industrialists' profiteering was only strengthened by recurrent financial scandals,[43] and by the various attempts of the leading industrial firms to gain control of the main banks.[44] Illegal profits were also made on the black market, which kept prices high and made certain foodstuffs unobtainable; in Turin, for example, the Giolittian paper *La Stampa* waged a fierce campaign against the Shop-Keepers' Co-operative, and freely alleged widespread corruption.[45] By the end of the war, as the result of all these factors, class antagonism in the cities had become acute.

This whole process was exemplified by the riots at Turin in August 1917.[46] The riots, in which about fifty people were killed,[47] were the most serious expression of popular discontent to occur during the war; barricades were raised, troops had to be rushed in. They were not 'revolutionary' in the sense of being a serious attempt to overthrow the government and seize power, or even in the sense of being an attempt to end Italy's participation in the war, but arose as a result of a local bread shortage, coupled with discontent at the long hours being worked in the city's munitions factories. The rioting appears to have been completely spontaneous – there is no evidence of it having been organised by the local or national Socialist Party, or by any other groups. Such rioting, and such discontent, remained of course within the traditional context of the Italian constitutional system; it may even be said to have formed part of that system. The riot was the traditional means of drawing the authorities' attention to grievances. It did not represent even an inchoate attempt to overthrow the existing political order, nor did it amount to a coherent

[43] Several big industrialists were arrested in March 1918 for their part in exporting silk by-products to Switzerland, whence they were re-exported to Germany and used for munitions. It was also rumoured that Pirelli tyres had been found on Austrian trucks after the capture of Gorizia in August 1916.

[44] These attempts failed, but were renewed in 1920. See L. Einaudi, *La Condotta Economica e gli Effetti Sociali della Guerra Italiana* cit., pp. 272–73.

[45] See, in particular, *La Stampa* 28 March 1918.

[46] The fullest account of the riots is in P. Spriano, *Torino Operaia nella Grande Guerra* cit., pp. 206–69. cf. also R. De Felice, 'Ordine Pubblico e Orientamenti delle Masse Popolari Italiane nella Prima Metà del 1917', *Rivista Storica del Socialismo*, no. 20 (1963), pp. 467–77; R. Del Carria, *Proletari senza Rivoluzione* cit., vol. ii, pp. 35–47; A. Monticone, 'Il Socialismo Torinese ed i Fatti del Agosto 1917', *Rassegna Storica del Risorgimento*, anno xiv (1958), f. 1, pp. 57–96; and (a critique of Monticone) D. Zucàro, 'La Rivolta di Torino nel 1917 nella Sentenza del Tribunale Militare Territoriale', *Rivista Storica del Socialismo*, no. 10 (1960), pp. 437–69.

[47] The figure is Monticone's estimate, confirmed and accepted by Spriano (Monticone, *op. cit.*, p. 86, note 3; Spriano, *op. cit.*, p. 255).

social movement designed to secure radical innovations within that order. The Turin riots are important mainly as an indication of the extent of popular discontent in the cities with the conditions brought about by the war. Similar riots occurred in the immediate post-war period, particularly the food riots of June–July 1919,[48] which were provoked by a sudden sharp rise in food prices.

Urban discontent was, therefore, fairly ineffective, and part of its ineffectiveness during the war lay in the fact that industrial workers were normally exempt from military service, and were regarded by front-line soldiers as contemptible *imboscati*, or shirkers. The troops' antagonism was accentuated by stories of fabulously high wages being paid to industrial workers (at a time when combat troops received 50 *centesimi* a day), and it is true that in 1917 the troops' rations of such foods as meat and sugar were much less than the average consumption at Turin.[49] Thus urban discontent was never a real threat to the established order. The workers were without weapons, and were faced, at least until the completion of demobilisation in 1920, by a hostile army consisting largely of peasants.[50] Moreover, urban workers had virtually no combat experience, and were imbued with an anti-militarist spirit that prevented them from making any serious attempts to secure arms or form military units, even after the war.

Nor could urban discontent be effective *within* the factories. I have already outlined briefly the system of 'Industrial Mobilisation', applied to most large firms during the war, and shown how workers in them were subject to quasi-military discipline. Within the 1,976 'auxiliary' firms, workers came to be divided into four separate groups: the 'military', or 'commanded' workers – i.e. men who were actually in the Forces, but who had been seconded to munitions factories; 'exempted' workers, who would have been in the Services but for their skilled trade; 'civilian' workers, with no military liability; and, finally, women and youths under 18. Of the 905,000 workers in 'auxiliary' industries at the end of

[48] See below, pp. 75–6.

[49] See footnote 39, p. 22, for consumption at Turin. Soldiers not in the front line received 600 gr. of meat a week (i.e. 31.2 kg. p.a.) and 75 gr. of sugar (3.9 kg. p.a.) in 1917. (G. Zingali, *Il Rifornimento dei Viveri dell' Esercito Italiano durante la Guerra*, Yale U.P. and Laterza, Bari 1926, p. 535; this book is bound into the same volume as R. Bachi, *L'Alimentazione e la Politica Annonaria in Italia* cit.).

[50] On demobilisation, see G. Rochat, *L'Esercito Italiano da Vittorio Veneto a Mussolini* (Laterza, Bari 1967), pp. 169–87. A. Serpieri, *La Guerra e le Classi Rurali Italiane* (Yale U.P. and Laterza, Bari 1930, p. 49) estimates that 46 *per cent.* of the men called up into the army during the war were peasants or agricultural workers. The peasant-infantry felt great resentment towards the industrial workers exempted from military service.

the war, only 331,000 (36 *per cent.*) were either 'military' or 'exempted' workers, the remaining 574,000 being divided into 304,000 without military obligations, 196,000 women, 60,000 youths, and 14,000 prisoners of war or colonial workers.[51] The proportion of 'exempted' workers was not high, and the popular impression that all armaments workers were *imboscati* (shirkers) was false. Nevertheless, the total increase in the number of workers employed in the munitions factories ensured that the majority of *engineering* workers, at least at Turin, retained their jobs throughout the war[52] – a factor of considerable importance in estimating the impact of Industrial Mobilisation.

The main impact of 'Industrial Mobilisation' on the lives of the workers was disciplinary. The fact that workers were forbidden to leave their posts without permission from the Regional Committee ensured that employers could retain their workers whatever the conditions of employment, for in practice the local Committee almost never granted permission in the face of employers' opposition. The factory regulations in operation at the beginning of the war were left intact, and Union leaders complained that the military officers appointed to judge disciplinary infractions always accepted the employers' views, being themselves inexperienced in such matters.[53] In addition, dismissal became the most effective of all punishments. For the 'military' or 'exempted' workers it could mean being sent to the front; and even for the others, it meant exclusion from all other 'auxiliary' factories and the consequent necessity of working for lower wages in some small workshop. Abandonment of one's job, or any kind of insubordination, was liable to be punished by a spell in a military prison; and during the ten-month period from January to October 1918, 19,018 workers were in fact sentenced to terms of hard labour, while a further 9,522 suffered spells in an ordinary prison.[54] These measures were undoubtedly effective in enforcing discipline, despite the great discontent they caused; the only important agitation during the war was the Turin rioting of August 1917, and absences from work were sharply reduced

[51] L. Einaudi, *La Condotta Economica e gli Effetti Sociali della Guerra Italiana* cit., p. 111. His figures are based on those given in the *Relazione della Commissione Parlamentare d'Inchiesta per le Spese di Guerra*, vol. 2, p. 408. G. Prato, *Il Piemonte e gli Effetti della Guerra sulla sua Vita Economica e Sociale* cit., p. 82, divides the 36 *per cent.* of the labour force that was either 'military' or 'exempted' into 17 *per cent.* 'military' and 19 *per cent.* 'exempted'.

[52] P. Spriano, *Torino Operaia nella Grande Guerra* cit., p. 150.

[53] M. Guarnieri, *La Mobilitazione Industriale* (Tipografia Co-operativa, Turin 1918), p. 9. cf. also *Avanti!* (Milan ed.) 12 March 1918.

[54] L. Einaudi, *La Condotta Economica e gli Effetti Sociali della Guerra Italiana* cit., p. 114. These figures, however, total only 0.0188 *per cent.* of the total war-time labour force.

from their pre-war level.[55] Nevertheless, the iron discipline imposed upon
a reluctant working population, who regarded themselves as working in
intolerable conditions in order merely to swell their employers' profits,
seriously exacerbated class hatred in the big industrial cities.

There were also other sources of grievance. 'Dilution' was one, as
women found unskilled industrial jobs, and as peasants flooded into the
industrial cities to relieve the labour shortages. At the end of the war,
22 *per cent.* of the workers in 'auxiliary' factories were women – less than
in Britain, but still a big increase; only the oldest and best organised Union
in Italy, the printers', managed to keep them at bay. As for rural immigrants, the data is more limited. The Censuses of 1911 and 1921 failed to
reflect war-time conditions – many peasants had returned to the land or
had emigrated by Census Day in December 1921, because of the industrial
recession of that year – and were in any case notoriously unreliable.[56]
Even so, it seems clear that most big cities (but not Genoa) had population
influxes in these years; that Liguria and Rome attracted their immigrants
from other regions of Italy, whereas the Piedmontese and Lombard cities
did not; and that the increase in population of Turin was accompanied by
an absolute decline of population in many rural zones of Piedmont.[57]
Non-Census data, such as official registrations of population movements,
show that in Turin the big influx of peasants took place in the early years
of the war (42,933 net in 1916), that the city's population reached a peak
of 518,423 in 1918, and then declined until 1921.[58] In July 1918, an
unofficial census in Turin by the city's Rationing Office (*Ufficio Tessere
del Servizio di Annona*) found 185,587 'wage-earners' in Turin; the 1911
Census had reported 79,223 industrial workers, including transport and

[55] L. Einaudi (*op. cit.*, p. 113) gives the percentage of days lost as 8.4 before militari-
sation; 4.88 after it.

[56] The 1911 Census seriously understated the rural population; cf. F. Coletti,
La Popolazione Rurale in Italia (Fed. Ital. Consorzi Agrari, Piacenza 1925), and
Coletti's remarks in his Chapter on 'La Emigrazione Italiana', pp. 3–19, in R. Acca-
demia dei Lincei, *Cinquant'Anni di Vita Italiana*, vol. iii (Hoepli, Milan 1911). The 1921
Census was regarded as especially defective in its figures for the resident population.

[57] The 1921 Census (*Censimento Generale della Popolazione*, 1921, vol. xix, publ.
Rome 1928) shows the population of Rome as rising from 542,123 to 691,661 from
1911 to 1921; Milan, 599,200 to 718,800; Turin, 427,106 to 502,274 (p. 106). Only
74.1 *per cent.* of the male population of Liguria in 1921, and 75.9 *per cent.* of that of
Latium, was born in the region; the comparable figure for Piedmont is 92.3 *per cent.*,
and for Lombardy 93.7 *per cent.* (*ibid.*, pp. 188–9). The population of all rural areas
(i.e. in communes of less than 15,000 inhabitants) in Piedmont fell by 4.74 *per cent.* in
these years, compared with a national *rise* of 4.01 *per cent.* – but the traditional
European outlets for temporary migration from Piedmont were still available in 1921,
and this probably accounts for most of the decline (*ibid.*, p. 33 and pp. 47–50).

[58] G. Prato, *Il Piemonte e gli Effetti della Guerra sulla sua Vita Economica e Sociale* cit.,
p. 140; P. Gabert, *Turin – Ville Industrielle* (P.U.F., Paris 1964), pp. 8 and 138.

building (both figures include women).[59] Turin had become a 'proletarian city', with nearly a third of its population involved in industry; the number of industrial workers had probably doubled since 1913.

If it is difficult to estimate the exact extent of these changes, their impact is even harder to assess. Valerio Castronovo has recently stressed the *differences* among Turin workers during the war, ranging as they did from skilled engineering craftsmen with years of industrial experience and considerable knowledge of Trade Union organisation, to women employed in textiles (but also by Fiat, in the stores and radiator shops), to unskilled ex-peasant labourers.[60] The craftsmen often felt swamped – Fiat, after all, employed four times as many people at the end of the war as at the beginning. Moreover, Taylorist methods of factory production were not merely being discussed. They were being introduced, even before the war, and Fiat was a pioneer in this field. Giovanni Agnelli had visited Henry Ford in 1912, and had installed the first assembly line on his return. Initially, the innovations were welcomed, as skilled men easily secured jobs as foremen, or as supervisors of assembly line workers, or else retained specialised positions in parts of the factory that required skilled labour.[61] But the whole issue became a source of much friction during the post-war transition, and even during the war the constant disputes over piece-rates and bonuses owed much to the skilled craftsmen's desire to protect their status and secure the benefits of any technical improvements.

Both the existing labour movements and the State authorities were, of course, well aware of all this discontent. The usual remedy was simple: increased pay. A circular issued on 19 July 1917, by General Dallolio, the Minister for Arms and Munitions, to all the Regional Committees of Industrial Mobilisation, spoke of 'the critical period that the war industry is now going through, because of the signs of unrest, ill-feeling, and weariness among the working masses, which continually disturb life in the workshops'. Dallolio went on: 'Since the ferment among the workers almost always originates from conflicts of an economic nature, the Committees should always bear in mind the policy of this Ministry on the

[59] G. Prato, *Il Piemonte e gli Effetti della Guerra sulla sua Vita Economica e Sociale* cit., p. 140 and p. 70. cf. also P. Spriano, *Torino Operaia nella Grande Guerra* cit., p. 142.

[60] V. Castronovo, *Giovanni Agnelli* cit., p. 119. In 1922 Agnelli revealed that Fiat employed 7,600 workers in 1914, but almost 30,000 in 1918. Of the 30,000, 6,000 were 'military', 700 were Libyans, and 1,300 were prisoners of war (*Ordine Nuovo* 22 February 1922).

[61] V. Castronovo, *Giovanni Agnelli* cit., p. 320; L. Bonnefon-Craponne, *L'Italie au travail* (Roger, Paris 1916), pp. 119–20; and M. Abrate, *La Lotta Sindacale nella Industrializzazione in Italia* cit., p. 110.

matter: concede as much as possible, rather than be forced to yield.'[62]
Throughout the war, the Committees helped to settle 948 conflicts, and
issued orders to settle by decree 458 others.[63] A further large number was
settled with the aid of one or more members of the Committees, acting
individually; for example, in Milan alone, between June 1916 and
December 1917, 161 conflicts were resolved by individual members, as
compared with 46 by the whole Committee and 74 settled by decree.[64]

Thus the Committees of Industrial Mobilisation were not *only* disciplinary bodies (see p. 25); they also resolved wage conflicts, in order to
prevent any halt in production, and it was in helping to reach these
settlements that the Union members of the Committees played an important role in the war effort, and came in for some bitter criticism as a result.
As one leading Trade Unionist proclaimed at the end of the war, the
Committees of Industrial Mobilisation were not in themselves arbitration
committees, but they did 'serve excellently as organs of conciliation, and
have made an undoubted contribution in getting a greater number of
industrialists and workers used to the idea of negotiating on all the issues
that divide them.'[65] Trade Union leaders had been longing for some kind
of conciliatory body which could step in when negotiations broke down.
They therefore welcomed the new bodies as a step forward in industrial
organisation, even though they still preferred, whenever possible, to
settle matters without recourse to them. Thus the attitude to Industrial
Mobilisation of the leading Trade Unionists – in particular, those belonging to the Socialist Trade Unions affiliated to the General Confederation of Labour (henceforth referred to as the *C.G.L.*) – was one of
qualified approval. Bruno Buozzi, the secretary of the Metal-workers'
Union, *F.I.O.M.*, described the new regulations as 'a fairly successful
document'.[66] The Unions could not defend their members from disciplinary measures, but they could and did secure wage improvements,
safeguard hygiene and safety standards, assist in the granting of exemption
from military service to members, and give invaluable advice on the most
efficient and economic use of their manpower. The decision to join the
Regional Committees brought the Unions tangible benefits in increased
influence, and this can to some extent be measured in increased

[62] *State Archives*, Ministero dell' Interno, Direzione Generale Pubblica Sicurezza,
Affari Generali e Riservati, A 5 (Guerra), b. 53, 'Agitazioni Metallurgiche'.
[63] L. Einaudi, *La Condotta Economica e gli Effetti Sociali della Guerra Italiana* cit.,
p. 116.
[64] *Bollettino del Comitato Centrale di Mobilizzazione Industriale*, February 1918.
[65] M. Guarnieri, *La Mobilizzazione Industriale* cit., pp. 15–16.
[66] 'Un documento abbastanza felice'. Report of Buozzi's speech to the National
Meeting of *F.I.O.M.* 25 June 1916, in *Il Metallurgico* 18 July 1916.

membership: *F.I.O.M.* in December 1914 had 11,471 members, but this figure had risen by December 1917 to 32,482, and by September 1918 to 47,192[67] – and this increase had been achieved at a time when Union propaganda was impossible.

On the other hand, the Union leaders also became very closely associated with some of the evils of the Industrial Mobilisation system, and were bitterly attacked by their own members for 'collaborationism'. In 1921 Gramsci wrote that during the war some workers in Turin were horrified to find, when they went on behalf of their 'nascent factory organisation' to negotiate with the official bodies set up to control industry, that these bodies contained, 'sitting next to the bosses' delegates, comrades belonging to the Party, the very people who were proclaiming the impossibility of breaking off the class struggle because of the war, and yet by their Trade Union activities were renouncing the most elementary principles of class activity.'[68] Thus by the end of the war the Union leaders affiliated to the *C.G.L.* had grown accustomed to playing an influential role within the existing structure of society; on the other hand, many ordinary workers were very discontented, and more 'intransigent' than ever in demanding a Socialist revolution.

The same factors that affected the Unions also influenced the Socialist deputies in Parliament, the Co-operatives, and Socialist-controlled local government bodies. Even for those theoretically most opposed to the war, some forms of 'collaboration' proved inevitable. Co-operatives assisted their members to withstand rises in the cost of living and to secure a more equitable distribution of foodstuffs. Socialist deputies sat on Parliamentary Commissions and Enquiries, and helped prepare social legislation. After the military defeat at Caporetto, the most respected of the parliamentary Socialists, Filippo Turati (leader of the Party's reformist wing) worsened the potential split in the Labour movement by proclaiming that the fate of the nation was at stake on Monte Grappa. Although such patriotic views were not typical of most of the deputies or 'reformists', they were largely responsible for the vote of condemnation of the Parliamentary Group's conduct in the war, carried at the Socialist Party Congress in September 1918. In short, by the end of 1918 almost all the traditional organs of Socialist authority – economic as well as political – were pursuing moderate, 'collaborationist' policies which were resented and rejected by many Socialist Party members.

[67] Interview with 'some leaders of *F.I.O.M.*', in *Avanti!* (Milan ed.) 6 April 1918. The September 1918 figure is from Buozzi's report to the Rome Congress of *F.I.O.M.* in November 1918, reported in *Avanti!* (Milan ed.) 3 November 1918.

[68] 'Forza e Prestigio', in *Ordine Nuovo* 14 January 1921 (now in A. Gramsci, *Socialismo e Fascismo*, Einaudi, Turin 1966, p. 43).

The main exception was the Directorate of the Socialist Party. The Italian Socialist Party (henceforth *P.S.I.*) had been divided, at least since 1901, between a policy of 'collaboration' with the State, in order to secure limited reforms, and a policy of revolutionary 'intransigence'.[69] The intransigents were finally victorious at the party's Reggio Emilia Congress in 1912. This fact, combined with the disastrous experience of the Libyan war, and the period of nine months' neutrality preceding Italy's entry into the World War, during which much of the early war enthusiasm had evaporated, ensured that the Italian Socialist Party adopted from the outset a consistent policy of opposition to the war – the only Socialist party in Western Europe to do so.[70] This policy had, of course, considerable tactical advantages for the *P.S.I.*: as the war continued, and conditions became more and more intolerable, the *P.S.I.* attracted increasing support in the country as the only political party in Italy openly committed to peace. On the other hand, its attitude isolated it from virtually all other sections of public opinion and condemned the party to merely sterile opposition, for under the stringent war-time censorship there was normally no way of making its opposition effective.[71] Furthermore, opposition to the war became the touchstone of left-wing virtue, and 'interventionism' the greatest of sins.[72] 'Intransigent' Socialists detested the reformists as being soft on militarism, and detested most other 'radical' political groupings even more strongly, for the same reason.[73] War-time conditions helped to strengthen the 'intransigent' wing of the Socialist Party: unable to give a lead to popular opinion, it was nevertheless forced to act as a mouthpiece for popular discontent and increasingly revolutionary aspirations. The Director General of Public Security wrote in

[69] For details of the conflict between the various factions of the *P.S.I.* before the war, see W. A. Salomone, *Italy in the Giolittian Era* (Univ. Pennsylvania Press, 2nd ed., 1960), pp. 42–85.

[70] For details of the period 1914–15, see L. Valiani, *Il P.S.I. nel Periodo dalla Neutralità all' Intervento* (Feltrinelli, Milan 1963).

[71] For the *P.S.I.*'s activity during the war, see A. Malatesta, *I Socialisti Italiani durante la Guerra* (Mondadori, Milan 1926); and L. Ambrosoli, *Nè Aderire nè Sabotare* (Edizioni Avanti!, Milan 1961). 'Neither adherence nor sabotage' was the formula drawn up by the Party's secretary, Lazzari, to define the Socialist attitude to the war. The only effective step taken by the *P.S.I.* in opposition to the war was the printing of the Zimmerwald manifesto in the party newspaper, *Avanti!*, on 14 October 1915.

[72] See note on Common Terms, p. xi; and G. Berti, 'Appunti e Ricordi 1919–26', in *Annali dell' Istituto Giangiacomo Feltrinelli*, anno VIII (1966), p. 12.

[73] Indeed, they even blamed the Republicans, Radicals, pro-war syndicalists, reformist Socialists and the like for Italy's entrance into the war, and it is true that these groups had agitated for it in 1914–15, had unreservedly supported the decision to intervene and were proud to claim the credit for having forced a reluctant government to declare war.

March 1917 that 'the moderate Socialist elements have lost all influence over the masses, and the whole subversive movement is now being led by the most extreme revolutionaries.'[74] The *P.S.I.*'s 'intransigent' attitude, which was usually known as 'maximalism' after 1917, was forced on it during the war as the only possible response to war-time political conditions. Throughout the war the Directorate of the Party – elected by the constituency party members at Party Congresses – remained in the hands of the 'maximalists' and continued to advocate a policy of revolutionary 'intransigence', as did the Party's daily newspaper *Avanti!*.

An excellent illustration of this development within the *P.S.I.* was provided by the Turin rioting of August 1917. Although, as has been seen, the Socialists were not responsible for it, they felt they ought to be; and Serrati, the editor of *Avanti!*, made the journey post-haste from Milan to Turin, arriving just in time to be arrested as an instigator, together with most of the leaders of Turin Socialism. The Turin riots, and the subsequent military disaster of Caporetto, for which the Socialists were also blamed, confirmed the damaging effects of Socialist propaganda in the eyes of the government and indeed of all supporters of the war, and provide a clear example of the need to follow popular opinion strengthening the 'maximalist' attitudes of the *P.S.I.*

It is clear, too, that the Russian Revolution must have been important in determining an 'intransigent' attitude towards existing society. Although the impact of the Bolshevik Revolution is not measurable, how far events in Russia were followed in Italy was shown in August 1917, when the Kerensky government's two emissaries, Smirnov and Goldenberg, were greeted at Turin with shouts of 'Viva Lenin!'. The Italian government allowed public meetings on this occasion, and at Turin Serrati seized the opportunity to provide a very free translation of Goldenberg's speech, calling for an end to the war and an Italian revolution.[75] The Russians had shown what could be done, and after October 1917 their example provided, for party members, an ideological counterattraction to the 'bourgeois' ideals of democracy and self-determination associated with President Wilson.[76]

The most striking evidence for this conflict within the labour movement occurred in the summer of 1918, over the issue of the so-called

[74] Director General of Public Security to Prefect of Turin, 13 March 1917 (quoted by P. Spriano, *Torino Operaia nella Grande Guerra* cit., p. 179).

[75] P. Spriano, *Torino Operaia nella Grande Guerra* cit., pp. 225-8.

[76] These ideals were common to many Italians in 1918–19, especially servicemen and ex-servicemen, and the *P.S.I.*'s rejection of them merely accentuated its isolation from much of the rest of public opinion. cf. P. Melograni, *Storia Politica della Grande Guerra* cit., p. 560.

Commissionissima – the 'Commission for the Study of Measures for the Post-war Period' – set up by the Orlando government to study and draft proposals to deal with the economic and social situation likely at the end of the war.[77] To the left-wing of the *P.S.I.*, the constituency parties, and the Party Directorate, the idea of such a Commission was anathema; and their views were strengthened by the fact that publication of the proposals for the Commission coincided with preparations for the trial of leading Socialists for their alleged part in the Turin riots of August 1917, and also with the government's refusal to allow the *P.S.I.* to hold a Congress during the war.[78] To the right-wing of the party, the Parliamentary Group and the Unions, the Commission seemed to be merely the logical continuation of war-time collaboration in Industrial Mobilisation, and an opportunity to effect some valuable structural reforms, in particular those called for in the 'minimal programme' drawn up by the *P.S.I.* and the *C.G.L.* in May 1917. This programme had urged: abolition of the Senate, universal suffrage with proportional representation, tax reforms, the eight-hour day, a State insurance scheme, civil service reform, the socialisation of land, and the subjection of foreign policy to parliamentary control. Consequently, when the *C.G.L.* was invited by the government to take part in the Commission, its national secretary, Rigola, eagerly accepted; but this decision was overruled in July by the *P.S.I.* Directorate, which forbade party members to have anything to do with the government's Commission. Rigola therefore resigned, after failing to persuade his fellow Union leaders to ignore the Party's directives.[79] He later wrote:

> It will be understood that it was not merely the question of the 'Commissionissima' that persuaded me to insist on resigning, this was merely the last straw. There had been discontent in the executive committee for some time, because of the eternal problem of independence. This is so true that when I was gone my successors went and drew up the 'Pact of Alliance' with the Directorate, which was the source of so much evil [di tanto mal fu matre].[80]

The whole incident is the clearest possible indication of the fact that

[77] The Commission was set up by a decree of 21 March 1918, and was divided into two sub-commissions, one to deal with legal, administrative and social issues, under Scialoja, and the other to discuss economic questions, under Pantano. The debate in the *P.S.I.* centred on the question of 'collaboration' with the second of these.

[78] The trial began at Turin on 10 July. The refusal to allow a Congress was later withdrawn, and the 15th National Congress of the *P.S.I.* took place at Rome in the first week of September 1918.

[79] *Avanti!* (Milan ed.) 26 July 1918.

[80] Rigola to Bertero, n.d. (Tasca Archives, Feltrinelli Institute).

Unions and Party were pursuing different paths, and that it was essential to hammer out some kind of compromise, or for one to control the other.

Rigola's place at the head of the *C.G.L.* was taken by Ludovico D'Aragona, whose first task it became to negotiate a 'Pact of Alliance' with the *P.S.I.* This Pact, signed on 29 September 1918, stated that national economic strikes were to be proclaimed and led by the *C.G.L.*, after hearing the views of the Party Directorate, which pledged itself not to hinder or obstruct the carrying out of the *C.G.L.*'s decisions; whereas political strikes were to be proclaimed and led by the Party Directorate, after hearing the opinion of the *C.G.L.*, which also pledged itself not to hinder or obstruct the carrying out of the Party's decisions.[81] It is important to emphasise that this 'Pact', which was to prove a vital issue during the 'Occupation of the Factories' in September 1920, was signed in September 1918 as the only possible defence by the *C.G.L.* against dominance by the Party Directorate, and was a direct answer to the veto on the *Commissionissima*. Nevertheless, the distinction between economic and political strikes was clearly an artificial one; and even after the Pact had been signed, the conflict between the *C.G.L.* and the Party Directorate had still to be fought out, and could not be avoided.[82]

The same basic conflict between the Socialist Party leadership and its mass support on the one hand, and the other official Socialist organisations – Unions, Co-operatives, and deputies – on the other, may be seen in the debate on the issue of the 'Constituent Assembly' at the end of the war. The 'Constituent Assembly' was supposed to draw up a new Constitution, embodying such structural reforms as the abolition of the Senate (and possibly also of the monarchy), proportional representation with universal suffrage, abolition of arbitrary legislation, etc. The idea was widely supported at the end of the war,[83] and in November 1918 the *C.G.L.*'s Directive Council enthusiastically endorsed it – although it hoped that the Assembly would be elected by 'professional categories'.[84]

[81] The text of the Pact of Alliance was printed in *Avanti!* (Milan ed.) 30 September 1918.

[82] In July 1920, Serrati admitted that the Pact would not prevent conflict if there were not a 'sincere desire to reach agreement by both parties'; and Bianchi, of the *C.G.L.*, wrote that the Pact was unrealistic and that in fact all decisions were taken jointly by the *C.G.L.* and the Party (see *Professional'niye Soyuzi v Italii*, by D'Aragona, Bianchi, Dugoni and Serrati, Izdaniye Tsentral'novo Sovieta Professional'nikh Soyuzov, Moscow 1920, pp. 43 and 20). These statements are a measure of how completely the situation had changed by the summer of 1920, but it is worth noting how both writers emphasised the unreal nature of the Pact, just two months before the 'Occupation of the Factories'.

[83] cf. P. Nenni, *Il Diciannovismo* (Ed. Avanti!, Milan 1962), pp. 19–20; and A. Tasca, *Nascita e Avvento del Fascismo* (La Nuova Italia, Florence 1950), pp. 18–20.

[84] The full *C.G.L.* proposals were published in *Battaglie Sindacali* 8 March 1919.

The Party Directorate, on the other hand, at a meeting held on 7–11 December, committed itself to a programme of immediate 'institution of the Socialist Republic and the dictatorship of the proletariat';[85] with the outbreak of revolution in Germany and Hungary, there could be no doubt of the correct path for Italy to follow. This was, in fact, the most expedient policy for the party to adopt. The idea of the Constituent Assembly was being strongly supported by former 'interventionists' like Mussolini, and indeed the various former 'interventionist' groups were the most vocal in support of it. The 'Constituent Assembly' was regarded as collaborationism, just as the 'Industrial Mobilisation' system and the 'Commissionissima' had been; for politicians, as opposed to Trade Unionists, to accept the idea was unthinkable.

Nor did all Trade Unionists accept the idea. Although the reformist C.G.L. was the largest Trade Union organisation in Italy, it was not alone.[86] The revolutionary syndicalists of the Italian Syndical Union (henceforth U.S.I.) had opposed the war throughout, and thus, like the Socialist Party, derived increasing support from popular anti-militarism and discontent. The U.S.I. had been founded in 1912 after a split away from the C.G.L., and had close links with the Italian anarchist movement led by Errico Malatesta. It was particularly strong in Liguria and the Marches; in August 1919 it claimed 30,000 members in its metal-workers' Union alone, 12,000 of whom were said to be in Sestri Ponente.[87] The syndicalists of the U.S.I. were genuinely revolutionary, were enthusiastic for mass action in unison with the more extreme wings of the Socialist Party, and had genuine mass support in certain areas. The U.S.I. syndicalists remained important throughout 1919 and 1920 – indeed, their importance has been much underestimated by most historians. They

---

[85] cf. A. Malatesta, *I Socialisti Italiani durante la Guerra* cit., p. 201.

[86] The C.G.L. had claimed 320,000 members in 1914, and almost 250,000 in 1918 (M. Neufeld, *Italy: School for Awakening Countries*, Cornell U.P., Ithaca 1961, pp. 362–4). In 1919 its membership leaped to $1\frac{1}{2}$ million, and to over 2 million in 1920. The other main Union organisations were the Catholic Italian Confederation of Workers (C.I.L.), which claimed half a million members in 1919 and nearly 1,200,000 in 1920, mainly in textiles and agriculture; the Italian Syndical Union (U.S.I.) – see text above; and the Italian Union of Labour (U.I.L.), centred on Parma and led by Alceste De Ambris and other former syndicalists. It claimed 162,000 members in January 1919. The U.I.L. pursued an 'interventionist' nationalist policy and was associated with D'Annunzio and with Mussolini (until January 1920). See F. Cordova, *Le Origini dei Sindacati Fascisti* (Laterza, Bari 1974) and his article with the same title, in *Storia Contemporanea* anno 1, n.4 (Dec. 1970), pp. 925–1009; B. Uva, *La Nascita dello Stato Corporativo e Sindacale Fascista* (Carucci, Assisi 1973); R. De Felice, *Sindacalismo Rivoluzionario e Fiumanesimo nel Carteggio De Ambris–D'Annunzio* (Morcelliana, Brescia 1966).

[87] *Guerra di Classe* 6 September 1919.

acted as a revolutionary pressure-group, seeking to influence the Socialist Party and *C.G.L.* Trade Unions in a revolutionary direction.

This chapter has shown, I hope, that many of the necessary conditions for labour militancy and conflict were present in Northern Italy by the end of the First World War. There was a tradition of working-class militancy pre-war, severe factory discipline that was suddenly relaxed at the end of hostilities, continued high inflation, fairly full employment and shortages of skilled labour, a general 'crisis of regime' that emphasised the fragility of all existing political and social institutions, class hatred ('the bourgeoisie as war profiteers'), and little national solidarity – on the contrary, a vast gulf between those who had supported the war and those who had opposed it. All this was superimposed on a society undergoing rapid urbanisation and industrialisation, in which existing labour institutions were widely regarded as inadequate, in which there was resentment at intensified exploitation, and in which there were pockets of skilled workers needing to defend their established positions against technological change.[88] It is a text-book picture. In the immediate post-war period the inevitable explosion occurred. However, this picture is incomplete without noting the formidable weaknesses in the Northern workers' position: the isolation of the cities (from rural areas, and from each other); an intelligent entrepreneurial class enjoying State support; young middle-class activists who felt they had won the war *despite* the 'sabotage' or 'defeatism' of urban workers; and an army that could easily be used to repress industrial or political militancy. There would clearly be limits to what might be achieved.

[88] A. Pizzorno, Introduction (esp. pp. 7–8) to A. Pizzorno (ed.), *Lotte Operaie e Sindacato in Italia* (1968–72), vol. i (Il Mulino, Bologna 1974).

CHAPTER TWO

The Rise of the Internal Commissions

THE conflict within the Italian labour movement (p. 29 ff.), and the growth of the engineering and metal-working industry, stimulated another important development. During the war many armaments factories had set up workers' 'Internal Commissions' (*Commissioni Interne*). The Commissions were a kind of grievance committee elected by the Union members on the shop floor to ensure effective application of local and national wage agreements, and to bring grievances to the notice of management, Union leaders, and if necessary to the Regional Committee of Industrial Mobilisation. They had begun in the early years of the century as temporary, ad hoc committees to put forward complaints concerning punishments, dismissals, and the like – the big issues of wages and hours being left to the Unions. In October 1906 came the first official recognition of a *permanent* Internal Commission, in the agreement signed between the Metal-workers' Union, *F.I.O.M.*, and the Turin car firm Itala. Article 19 of the agreement ran: '[The Internal Commission] will consist of 5 workers from the factory, and will remain in office throughout the three years of the agreement.' At the same time a closed shop was set up in the factory. All conflicts (including wages and hours) arising from application of the contract were to be discussed in the first instance between the Internal Commission and the management; only if they failed to reach agreement was the Union to be called in.[1] The Itala agreement did not last long, being ended by the bitter industrial struggles of 1907–8, and the Commissions then became once more temporary bodies for specific grievances, with very limited functions and well under the control of the Unions. In a further agreement between *F.I.O.M.* and

[1] See M. Abrate, *La Lotta Sindacale nella Industrializzazione in Italia* (Angeli, Milan 1967), pp. 67–8; P. Spriano, *Socialismo e Classe Operaia a Torino 1892–1913* (Einaudi, Turin 1958), pp. 175–8; and M. Guarnieri, *I Consigli di Fabbrica* (Edizioni 'Il Solco', Città di Castello 1921), pp. 18–19.

the Turin automobile industry in 1913, separate arbitration bodies were set up within the factories, containing representatives of both employers and workers, and the Internal Commissions tended to be subordinated to these, or in some cases identified with them.[2] This was the situation at the outbreak of the war, but the sweeping changes brought about by the Industrial Mobilisation system revived the need for some kind of purely workers' body to represent grievances (especially disciplinary ones) to management. The expansion of industry in war-time conditions also ensured that employers would be more likely to make concessions on minor matters, in order that production might be continued. The existence of a workers' body within the factory was an advantage to management as well as to the workers themselves.

Thus very shortly after Italy's entry into the war, the institution appears to have been virtually ubiquitous in the metal-working factories of Lombardy. *Il Metallurgico*, the journal of *F.I.O.M.*, the reformist Socialist Metal-Workers' Union affiliated to the *C.G.L.*, consistently reported successful negotiations – usually on disciplinary matters – carried through by Internal Commissions, often with the aid of a local Union leader. Even official recognition of the Commissions was some-times obtained: at the factory of Sesto Abramo Valsecchi, in Sesto S. Giovanni near Milan, an agreement signed in December 1915 included a special article affirming that 'the Firm formally pledges itself to the recognition of an Internal Commission appointed by the workers, charged with negotiations with the Firm on all conflicts that may arise at work.'[3] Even where such official recognition was not achieved, the number of disputes to be resolved, and the over-riding necessity of resolving them, soon broke down the distinction between ad hoc com-mittees appointed for specific purposes, and permanent workers' repre-sentatives within the factory. The way this distinction broke down may be seen from events at the Diatto Bros. factory in 1917: 'At the end of the conflict, the Workers' Commission was given a mandate to stay in office so as to check on complaints received and ensure that the agreement obtained is observed.'[4] The leaders of the Turin metal-workers, Emilio Colombino and Mario Guarnieri, emphasised the importance of these bodies by early 1917. They wrote that most conflicts were resolved without a decree of the Regional Committee of Industrial Mobilisation – 'the majority of conflicts brought before the Committee was later dealt

[2] The agreement is printed in M. Abrate, *La Lotta Sindacale nella Industrializzazione in Italia* cit., pp. 117–8. cf. also P. Spriano, *Torino Operaia nella Grande Guerra* (Einaudi, Turin 1960), p. 154.
[3] *Il Metallurgico* January–February 1916.
[4] *La Squilla* 8 June 1917.

with by the same Workers' Commissions, in the presence of delegates from the (Regional) Committee. The Committee's ordinances were few.'[5]

Internal Commissions were normally elected by Union members only. Sometimes the dues-collectors and leading workers agreed on a list, and the 'election' was merely a mass meeting held to give formal approval to the list; the meeting was held in the presence of a representative of F.I.O.M.[6] Very often the Internal Commissions remained impermanent, and were almost always restricted to minor conflicts. Union leaders felt that the Internal Commissions could be useful and effective only if backed by strong Union organisations, and they insisted on retaining control over them.[7] By the summer of 1918 the Commissions had achieved recognition by the management in most factories, and the demand for recognition, when this had not already been achieved, became a normal item included with wage claims.[8] It was also high on the agenda at the Congress of F.I.O.M. in Rome at the beginning of November 1918. Nevertheless, there were signs that an alternative role for the Internal Commissions was beginning to be considered in some circles, probably as a direct result of the antagonism to F.I.O.M.'s 'collaborationist' policy that became apparent in 1918. It is interesting that as early as September 1918 a group of workers at the Farina factory in Turin wrote to the Socialist Party newspaper Avanti!, asking whether the Internal Commission should represent the working class or the Union; and three members of the Commission replied that they represented the workers in the Farina plant, not F.I.O.M., since they were elected by the workers, not the Union.[9] The great expansion in Internal Commission activity in the war, the semi-recognition they achieved, and the growing divergences between the Trade Union leaders and their workers, represented at least a potential threat to Union control of the Commissions.

Many of these issues were debated at the national Congress of F.I.O.M., the engineering and metal-workers' union, held in Rome in November 1918, just a few weeks after the signing of the Pact of Alliance. There

[5] E. Colombino & M. Guarnieri, 'La Mobilitazione Industriale e l'Organizzazione', in La Squilla 15 February 1917.

[6] A. Jaccia, 'Vita Operaia', in Ordine Nuovo 12 July 1919 (now in P. Spriano, ed., Ordine Nuovo, Einaudi, Turin 1963, p. 181).

[7] M. Guarnieri, I Consigli di Fabbrica cit., p. 22.

[8] In May 1918 para. 6 of the memorandum put forward by the workers at the Industrie Metallurgiche factory at Turin was headed 'Recognition of the Internal Commission'. Article 3 at the Molle Factory, and Article 5 at the Ferrando Bros. works, contained the same request (La Squilla 8 August 1918 and 19 October 1918).

[9] Avanti! (Turin ed.) 21–3 September 1918, quoted by P. Spriano, Torino Operaia nella Grande Guerra cit., p. 299.

was much opposition from the floor to the Union's policy of 'collaboration' in the Industrial Mobilisation system, to its general lack of militancy, and to the attitude of the Union's secretary, Buozzi, to the *Commissionissima*.[10] More significant, perhaps, was the fact that the delegates from Turin went to Rome with a manifesto programme calling for greater participation by the workers in deciding the policy of each local branch, or 'section', of the Union.[11] It included the passage: 'We wish to state openly that the leaders should follow the tactics and the paths laid down and desired by the masses; otherwise they should leave their posts in favour of men better able to interpret the needs and wishes of the masses.'[12] The opposition of the Turin delegates to the official Union leadership was vital, given the city's heavy concentration of engineering workers. At the Rome Congress, the first signs of this opposition appeared; and it is interesting that it crystallised round the issue of the functions and role of the metal-workers' Internal Commissions.

Similarly, the Union leaders put forward proposals at the Rome Congress for the Internal Commissions to become permanent organs of 'workers' control', dealing with all problems of wages, discipline, etc. under the guidance and leadership of the Unions. Colombino proclaimed:

We must aim at the maximum degree of democracy within the factory, at transforming our old Internal Commissions into permanent organs of control, with powers to concern themselves with the whole running of the factory, wages, discipline, and the whole complex series of problems that affect, directly or indirectly, the interests of the working class.

Only in this way can relations between capital and labour be improved, by making the workers conscious of industrial and productive arrangements, and by raising them from their present role of automata to that of citizens entrusted by society with one of the highest functions of civilisation, labour . . .

We are in favour of conquering the factory. Meanwhile, we seek more control, through which we hope to attain a degree of maturity and experience necessary for running the industrial system . . .

[10] See *Avanti!* (Milan ed.) 5 and 6 November 1918; and *Il Metallurgico* 27 March 1920.

[11] Printed in *Avanti!* (Milan ed.) 17 October 1918.

[12] This criticism referred mainly to the row in Turin over Buozzi's support for the *Commissionissima*. A meeting of Turin metalworkers on 8 August had condemned Buozzi, especially for acting without consulting the workers. On 22 September Buozzi replied to his critics by claiming that 'the Unions and their secretaries, even when they seem to be not very militant or class-conscious, are always far more so than the anonymous masses' (*Avanti!*, Milan ed., 10 August and 25 September 1918).

We want to put the Internal Commissions and the Union workshop representatives to good use. We want to watch over the whole activity of the industrialists, so as to be able to create the Union leaders and administrators of tomorrow.[13]

Colombino was clearly aware that the Union had lost contact with the shop-floor, and seems to have realised the potential danger of the Internal Commissions becoming an instrument used against the Unions by the left-wing Socialists; his proposals were an intelligent attempt to stop this happening. The extended functions to be attributed to the Internal Commissions had thus become an important part of reformist, in particular of Union leaders', thinking by the end of the war, an element in their general political strategy. A prominent Socialist deputy, Modigliani, commenting on the *F.I.O.M.* Congress, wrote that 'these Internal Commissions, which appear today to the short-sighted to be a collaborationist instrument, useful for the defence of wages within the workshop, are regarded by those who set them up and organise them as the nuclei of the technical body that will carry through, in the first place, administration, and later expropriation, by the workers.'[14]

When the Industrial Mobilisation system was abolished in March 1919,[15] labour relations and factory discipline became a more important issue, both for industrialists and workers. Employers were anxious for the transition to peace-time production to be as smooth as possible, and this required considerable investment and some guarantees of 'social peace'. The collaboration of skilled workers was needed, and employers sought it by concessions to the Unions on pay and hours, and by concessions at factory level (incentive schemes and piece-rates). This naturally enhanced the importance of the Internal Commissions, and their role soon became a national issue. Official recognition of the Commissions was rapidly secured at Milan, where an agreement signed in November 1918 included a 55-hour week (i.e. the Saturday half-day, known as the 'English Saturday'), an Unemployment Fund, and recognition of the Internal Commission's right to deal with disputes over the application of wage agreements, hygiene, etc.[16] At Turin, negotiations proceeded rather differently. The workers at the Turin car firm Scat urged the workers' representatives in

---

[13] His speech was reprinted in pamphlet form: E. Colombino, *Relazione* (Tipografia Co-operativa, Turin 1918). Reports also appeared in *Avanti!* (Milan ed.) 6 November 1918, and in *Battaglie Sindacali* 27 March 1920.

[14] Modigliani's article on the *F.I.O.M.* Congress, in *Critica Sociale* 1–15 December 1918.

[15] Decree-Law of 18 March 1919, n. 648. In practice the system stopped earlier.

[16] Details of the agreement were published in *Avanti!* (Milan ed.) 16 and 17 November 1918.

the negotiations to 'pay special attention to the detailed functions to be carried out by the Internal Commissions, particularly in regard to disciplinary matters',[17] and detailed regulations for their functioning were in fact drawn up before any agreement was signed. Article One of the regulations emphasised that the Internal Commissions were to be 'regarded as the fiduciaries and mandatories of the Union signatory to the agreement'. Members of the Commissions were to be elected at a meeting of all Union members (Article Three). The Commission was to meet normally for two hours every Saturday to receive complaints, and would be allowed to see all necessary documents. A member was to be present in future at work-tests held to determine piece rates.[18]

The Turin regulations were, in fact, more detailed than those embodied in the national metal-workers' agreement signed on 20 February 1919. The national agreement established an 8-hour day at last – i.e. a 48-hour week, instead of the previous 55, 60 or even 70 hours; the Saturday half-day, the 'English Saturday', was given up. There were also substantial pay rises. But the most important provisions concerned the Internal Commissions. They could negotiate with the management on any collective grievances, as well as on individual ones arising from application or interpretation of the agreement. Their members were to hold office for a year; they were to be given a special office for their own use in the factory; and they were to fulfil their tasks only outside working hours. The other significant feature of the agreement concerned the various stages of negotiation to be gone through before a strike could legitimately be called. If no agreement were reached between the Internal Commission and the management, the dispute was to be referred to a Commission of Six, three from the employers' Federation and three from *F.I.O.M.* This in effect ruled out unofficial strikes, for failure to observe the somewhat cumbersome procedure meant, according to the terms of the agreement, loss of a week's pay; however, 'political' strikes were exempted from these provisions, in accordance with the 'Pact of Alliance'.[19] In short, the natio-

---

[17] *Avanti!* (Turin ed.) 6 January 1919.

[18] Prefect of Turin to Ministry of the Interior 31 January 1919 (in *State Archives, Min. Int., Dir. Gen. P.S., Aff. Gen. e Ris., 1919, b. 54, 1° Fascicolo, 'Agitazioni Metallurgiche').

[19] The agreement was published in full in *Battaglie Sindacali* 8 March 1919. For the Pact of Alliance, see p. 33. See also (on the February 1919 agreement): M. Abrate, *La Lotta Sindacale nella Industrializzazione in Italia* cit., p. 211; M. Neufeld, *Italy: School for Awakening Countries* (Cornell U.P., Ithaca 1961), p. 370; G. Maione, *Il Biennio Rosso* (Il Mulino, Bologna 1975), pp. 9–10; and R. Rigola, *Storia del Movimento Operaio Italiano* (Domus, Milan 1946), p. 438. Rigola wrote that the employers granted the eight-hour day in order to secure Union support for Taylorism and the scientific organisation of labour.

nal agreement gave the employers a firm promise of a reasonable degree
of industrial calm at a time of great political and industrial unrest, and at a
time when they were anxious to introduce new methods of production;
in return, they had to concede the 8-hour day. The agreement gave
F.I.O.M. all the prestige accruing from the 8-hour day, as well as apparently
ruling out all the dangerous possibilities inherent in the system of Internal
Commissions.

The agreement, significantly, aroused considerable protest among the
metal-workers, especially in Turin and in the syndicalist strongholds of
Liguria. At Turin, it was criticised on the grounds that the conquest of the
8-hour day had been nullified by obligatory overtime, that the 5 or 10
minutes' lateness 'tolerated' at the start of work had been abolished, and
that – worst of all – the *immediate* freedom to strike had been thrown away.
The new piece-rates (increased by 16 *per cent.* in the national agreement,
and extended to other groups of workers, including labourers) were seen
as a plot by employers to increase production, to divide the working class
and to reduce basic wages. Union leaders at Turin soon decided it was
necessary to negotiate with the automobile employers to change the system
of payment, so as to reduce piece-rates and increase basic pay; and they
also felt it necessary to call a meeting of the Internal Commissions to
approve their work.[20] Some workers also urged that the Internal Commissions should have deliberative functions on all disciplinary matters –
'no order should be valid unless discussed and approved by the Internal
Commissions.'[21]

There were more protests in Liguria, and numerous strikes in the
Ansaldo and other plants there in early March 1919. At Sestri Ponente, the
U.S.I. Metal-Workers' Union denounced the agreement as the end of the
class struggle. The sense of grievance there was enhanced by the fact that
the syndicalist leaders had signed a local contract three weeks previously,
giving them the 'English Saturday' and a 44-hour week, which they were
now forced to renounce.[22] The *U.S.I.* metal-workers, meeting at Bologna
in June 1919, denounced the national agreement in the strongest possible

[20] *Avanti!* (Turin ed.) 30 May 1919. An agreement was reached between the local
branch of *F.I.O.M.* and the Turin Automobile Manufacturers on 12 June 1919, and it
was published in *L'Italia Industriale* Jan.–March 1920, pp. 16 ff. Piece-rates were
limited to 50 *per cent.* of basic pay in automobile factories, and to 40 *per cent.* in other
metal-mechanical firms (these other local engineering firms had accepted the agreement in principle). Thus basic pay was higher in Piedmont than in other regions.
For the consequences, see p. 81.

[21] For details of the Turin opposition to the agreement, see *Avanti!* (Turin ed.)
15 March 1919; and G. Maione, *Il Biennio Rosso* cit., pp. 12–14.

[22] The *U.S.I.* had been excluded from the national negotiations, and were thus left
isolated and helpless at their conclusion. See *Guerra di Classe* 19 April 1919.

terms, and decided to initiate a general agitation throughout Italy for its abrogation. The syndicalists' complaints, interestingly, concentrated on the Internal Commission issue. That the Commissions could only function outside working hours made them inoperative; management was left free to avoid discussing any given issue, because it could refuse to fix a time to meet the Commissions; and the machinery preventing strikes was, in the view of the *U.S.I.*, worse than the penal code.[23]

The value of the new machinery in preventing strikes was soon shown in practice. The negotiations in each factory on piece-rates were largely left to the Internal Commissions, as were the practical arrangements involved in introducing the 8-hour day. At Fiat the Internal Commission had the important task of 'reviewing' all piece-rates in the factory so as to work out the exact amount of the increase.[24] It was also largely instrumental in persuading the workers back to work after a brief stoppage caused by a piece-rates dispute.[25]

The role of the new institutions in Turin's industrial life by the end of the war is most clearly shown by the important agitation of the 'technicians' in the metal-working factories, which began in February 1919 and culminated in a technicians' strike in April. The strike forced the employers to close the factories and thus to lock out almost all the Turin metalworkers. Hence the ordinary workers and their immediate superiors, the technicians, found themselves in necessary alliance against their employers; and Union leaders were quick to seize their opportunity. Colombino proclaimed that the technicians' co-operation represented a great opportunity to 'create among the workers the technical competence necessary for the direct management of the factories . . . meanwhile we wish, by means of our workshop delegates, in full agreement with the technicians, to exercise all control within and outside the factory.'[26] The technicians' strike thus brought about the ideal situation from the point of view of the reformist Union leaders, and made it seem possible for the Internal Commissions to fulfil the role assigned to them within the existing Union and industrial structure.

As the strike continued, however, opposition to the Union's interpretation of the Internal Commissions' role seems to have increased, even among the technicians. At a mass meeting on 19 April, it was proposed that the Internal Commissions of the technicians should take over the pay

[23] The motion passed at the Bologna meeting was printed in *Guerra di Classe* 28 June and 26 July 1919.
[24] *Avanti!* (Turin ed.) 1 April 1919.
[25] *Avanti!* (Turin ed.) 23 March 1919.
[26] Colombino's speech, in *Avanti!* (Turin ed.) 12 April 1919.

negotiations from the Union leaders;[27] and even though this proposal was
defeated, a few days later it was agreed that the individual Internal Commissions, because of the enormous variations in the way different factories
paid their technicians, should work out the pay increases, pending a
national agreement.[28] In fact, the strike was eventually resolved in this way,
by a series of meetings between employers and technicians' Internal
Commissions, with regular meetings also being held among the 56
Workers' Internal Commissions concerned, so as to achieve co-ordination
of activity. The strike had shown the importance of the new institution,
and had promoted solidarity at Turin between manual workers and their
superiors, along fashionable 'productivist' lines. As *Avanti!* wrote, at its
conclusion: 'The technicians' battle has taught all of us a great deal. From
it can be decided new norms for the struggle of labour, by both Union
leaders and ordinary Union members.'[29]

By May Day 1919 the industrial organisation of the Turin metal-
workers was changing rapidly, with the Trade Union's traditional
functions being increasingly taken over by the recently created Internal
Commissions. Within the factories, the new bodies had now assumed the
right to negotiate on central issues such as wages and hours; regional
agitations were sometimes entrusted to ad hoc Committees of Agitation,
which reported back to the Internal Commissions. It was increasingly true
that the 'real representatives of the workers' interests', entrusted with all
'the technical aspects of the Unions' work'[30] were the Internal Commissions; the Unions were in danger of being left as purely administrative
bodies.

There was clearly going to be a struggle. F.I.O.M. leaders were worried
men. Carlo Artesani, a member of the Committee of Agitation that had
negotiated the new national metal-workers' agreement between December
1918 and February 1919, wrote in May:

> There are comrades who maintain that the Internal Commissions
> should precede the Unions in all agitations, and especially in those

[27] Viberti's proposal, reported in *Avanti!* (Turin ed.) 20 April 1919.
[28] *Avanti!* (Turin ed.) 23 April 1919. The Technicians' Union achieved recognition,
and the technicians' Internal Commissions were recognised on the same basis as those
of the other workers.
[29] *Avanti!* (Turin ed.) 3 May 1919. A meeting of the Turin technicians later in the
month emphasised that the main lessons of the strike were the need for 'closer co-
operation with F.I.O.M. in all proletarian battles, and a search to see if there is any
possibility of setting up a single Union organisation. Watch must also be maintained
over the Internal Commissions, and their functioning must be disciplined in agreement with the other categories of workers.' (*Avanti!*, Turin ed., 28 May 1919).
[30] These phrases were used by 'Giantino', in his article entitled 'Per la Presa di
Possesso', in *Guerra di Classe* 31 May 1919.

which they think fit to initiate . . . some members of the *Fascio Sindacale d'Azione Rivoluzionaria* have declared that their programme includes the conquest of the Internal Commissions so as to impose a new policy on our branch . . . there is the danger that if the Internal Commissions are left free to act at their own pleasure, the directives imposed on the Federation and on the Branch by Congresses may be falsified, and there may result activity that is disjointed and contradictory, as between one factory and another, in the same industrial centre.[31]

The *F.I.O.M.* leaders emphasised that the Internal Commissions were a valid organ of workers' control within the factory, but they must observe, as well as enforce, the existing regulations; and there should be no question of them ever replacing the existing Unions.

The danger to the Unions was enhanced by political unrest directed against their reformist policies. The *U.S.I.* syndicalists had realised that the Internal Commissions made the seizure of the factories – which had always been among their main objectives – a practical possibility.[32] Furthermore, some Socialists also foresaw an even larger role for the Internal Commissions. In March 1919 a writer in the Young Socialists' journal, *Avanguardia,* called for the *immediate* transformation of the Internal Commissions and other similar bodies into local 'Soviets':

Our institutions will be transformed in the direction revealed by the spirit of the new age. The existing Trade Union institutions are too impregnated by the bourgeois bureaucratic systems. They have more of a corporative character, designed for immediate wage demands, than the real character of the institutions of a new State. There is no question of wanting to attack the Confederation of Labour, or any other Trade Union bodies. But these should be given a more modern, revolutionary nature by the institution of Workers' Councils.[33]

Thus the new institutions that had arisen during the war could have political, as well as economic functions. This situation was soon to find expression in the writings of a small group of young and comparatively unknown intellectuals and journalists.

[31] Artesani's article, entitled 'Tasks and Duties of the Internal Commissions', was printed in the propaganda hand-out of the local branch of *F.I.O.M., La Squilla,* on 15 May 1919.

[32] cf. 'Giantino', 'Per la Presa di Possesso' cit., in *Guerra di Classe* 31 May 1919.

[33] Alfonso Leonetti, 'All'Alba dell'Ordine Nuovo', in *Avanguardia* 9 March 1919. The title of the article is significant.

CHAPTER THREE

Gramsci and the *Ordine Nuovo*

THE previous chapter has described the spread and importance of 'Internal Commissions', especially in the metal-working industries of Turin. In the summer of 1919, a successful agitation was begun in Turin to turn these Internal Commissions into 'Factory Councils', designed to help bring about revolution. It is doubtful if this campaign would have been begun without the promptings and leadership of a small group of young intellectuals in Turin, who founded a weekly review, *Ordine Nuovo* (New Order),[1] there on 1 May 1919. Hence the 'workers' control' movement in Italy has a twin aspect, the 'structural' and the 'intellectual'. It cannot be understood without some reference to the background, early activity, and ideas of this group, and particularly of its outstanding member, a twenty-eight-year-old journalist from Sardinia, named Antonio Gramsci.[2]

Gramsci was born in January 1891, at Ales in Sardinia, where his father was in charge of the local Registry Office. He was born into a typical family of the Southern middle class. Gramsci's grandfather had been a colonel in the Carabinieri; and most members of the family occupied comfortable posts in the State bureaucracy (one of Gramsci's uncles was a Treasury official, another a Railway Inspector, another an Army officer

---

[1] Two collections of articles from the weekly review, the *Ordine Nuovo*, have been published. Gramsci's own writings in the periodical were published by Einaudi in 1955 (A. Gramsci, *Ordine Nuovo*, Einaudi, Turin 1955); whenever possible reference will be made to this volume. The other anthology contains writings by other contributors, as well as by Gramsci, and was edited by P. Spriano in 1963 (P. Spriano, *Ordine Nuovo*, Einaudi, Turin 1963). Reference to this volume will only be made when the article in question is not included in the earlier volume. When articles not included in either volume are quoted, reference will be made to the date of the issue concerned.

[2] The most sensitive and well written biography of Gramsci is by Giuseppe Fiori, *Vita di Antonio Gramsci* (Laterza, Bari 1966); English translation by Tom Nairn, *Antonio Gramsci: Life of a Revolutionary* (New Left Books, London 1970 and Dutton, New York 1971). Fiori's bibliography lists other biographies.

who had given military training to the future King Victor Emmanuel III).[3] However, the great characteristic of the Southern middle class was their bitter political in-fighting, especially over local government jobs, and Gramsci's father was one of the victims. In 1898, when Antonio was seven, his father was imprisoned for embezzlement – the accusation was almost certainly part of a political intrigue against Gramsci's father for having supported the losing candidate at a parliamentary election[4] – and the family circumstances changed dramatically. There were seven children, and no salary; his mother made clothes and took a lodger, but they remained desperately poor. In order to help pay the cost of his schooling, Gramsci had to work, from the age of eleven onwards, at shifting registers – $6\frac{1}{2}$ days a week, 10 hours a day, all for 9 *lire* a month, the price of a kilo of bread a day. As if all this were not bad enough, Gramsci was a hunchback, possibly the result of a fall downstairs;[5] and after he had finished primary school in 1903, there was no money to pay for him to go on to secondary school. Only after his father's return from prison could Gramsci resume his studies (aged nearly fifteen) – and this at a very poor *ginnasio* eleven miles from the family home at Ghilarza. Even so, he passed his exams from there and went on to the *Liceo* at Cagliari,[6] and while there began writing the occasional piece of journalism, in *L'Unione Sarda*.

In 1911, at the age of twenty, he left Sardinia and won a meagre scholarship to the University of Turin, where he studied linguistics and philology until 1915. His University years at Turin were scarcely more comfortable. He was poor, with a scholarship of only 70 *lire* a month, in a strange environment, and without friends or contacts; and his first few months at Turin was a period of poverty, hunger, cold, friendlessness, and absorption in study, a period of isolation from the outside world he did not yet feel able to face.[7]

As Gramsci emerged from his absorption in study, and from 'depro-

[3] G. Fiori, *Antonio Gramsci: Life of a Revolutionary* cit., pp. 10 and 42.

[4] *ibid.*, pp. 13–15.

[5] Gramsci always believed this himself. cf. his letter to Tatiana Schucht, 23 April 1933, in C. Casucci, 'Il Carteggio di Antonio Gramsci conservato nel Casellario Politico Centrale', in *Rassegna degli Archivi di Stato*, anno XXV, n. 3 (1965), pp. 5–7.

[6] G. Fiori, *Antonio Gramsci: Life of a Revolutionary* cit., pp. 51 ff.

[7] For information on Gramsci's student period, see D. Zucàro, 'Antonio Gramsci all' Università di Torino 1911–15', in *Società*, anno XIII, n. 6, (1957), pp. 1091–1111; and R. Martinelli, 'Gramsci e il Corriere Universitario di Torino', in *Studi Storici*, anno XIV, n. 4 (1973), pp. 906–20. For his poverty at this time, see G. Fiori, *Antonio Gramsci: Life of a Revolutionary* cit., pp. 71–3; and Gramsci's letter to his brother Carlo, 12 September 1927 (in A. Gramsci, *Lettere dal Carcere*, 2nd ed., edited by Sergio Caprioglio and Elsa Fubini, Einaudi, Turin 1965, pp. 124–7; English translation by Lynne Lawner available in A. Gramsci, *Letters from Prison*, published by Jonathan Cape, London 1975, pp. 100–3).

vincialising' his outlook, he became a Socialist. Previously he had been, if anything, a 'Sardinian nationalist', but his elder brother Gennaro had introduced him to Socialist ideas before he left the island, and in Turin he could see a powerful and militant labour movement in action.[8] Nevertheless, Gramsci's 'Sardism' never left him. His Sardinian background virtually ensured that Gramsci's Socialism would be less concerned with strengthening the central State apparatus, and rather more concerned with popular 'participation', than was customary. Giuseppe Fiori has summarised Gramsci's development admirably: 'Gramsci refused either to shelter within the Sardinian nationalism of his youth, or to let himself be converted passively to the ideology and political outlook of the Northern working class – an outlook corrupted at that time by corporative notions.'[9] Gramsci's Socialism was always *sui generis*.

Moreover, Gramsci was at University at one of the rare moments when the whole philosophical scheme of the past was under attack, i.e. when positivism was being challenged by the 'idealism' of Croce and his followers. There is little doubt that Crocian philosophy had an enormous influence on Gramsci, both at University and for a time afterwards; he wrote years later that in 1917 he was still 'somewhat Crocian in outlook'.[10] There was another reason why positivism seemed unattractive. It was associated in Italy with the criminological theories of Lombroso, Niceforo, Sighele, Ferrero and others – and the positivist school, concerned with 'innate criminality' and head measurements, paid much attention to the South.[11] It was natural for a Southerner like Gramsci to feel aggrieved by the positivists' pseudo-racial 'explanations' of Southern backwardness, and natural too for Gramsci to conclude that this positivist approach to social issues was ludicrous. It is, therefore, significant that Italian reformist Socialism had always been closely associated with the positivists, and hence a young Socialist's rejection of positivism could easily become associated with a rejection of reformism.

The first friends Gramsci made at University were Socialist Party members like Angelo Tasca, or at least sympathisers like Palmiro Togliatti. Indeed, the nucleus of what later came to be known as the '*Ordine Nuovo*

---

[8] cf. P. Spriano, *Socialismo e Classe Operaia a Torino, 1892–1913* (Einaudi, Turin 1958).

[9] G. Fiori, *Antonio Gramsci: Life of a Revolutionary* cit., p. 94.

[10] A. Gramsci, *Il Materialismo Storico e la Filosofia di Benedetto Croce* (Einaudi, Turin 1948), p. 199. For details of Turin University at this period, see P. Spriano, *Torino Operaia nella Grande Guerra 1914–18* (Einaudi, Turin 1960), pp. 22–31.

[11] cf. A. Niceforo, *L'Italia Barbara Contemporanea* (Sandron, Milan and Palermo 1898), which was on the South; and A. Renda (ed.) *La Questione Meridionale* (Sandron, Milan and Palermo 1900). One of Niceforo's best known works was entitled *La Delinquenza in Sardegna* (Sandron, Milan and Palermo 1897).

group' was formed in 1912–14. Reminiscing about these years in 1921, Gramsci wrote that 'Comrade Togliatti studied at University together with Comrades Gramsci and Tasca. All three were Socialists even then, and spent a great deal of time together [facevano vita comune]; they had even then decided to compile together a Socialist cultural periodical, which was to have been called the "Future City", but was in fact called the "New Order".'[12] Tasca, rather than Gramsci, was the most prominent figure at this time, and had extensive contacts with local Trade Union leaders, including the metal-workers' leader Bruno Buozzi. Tasca was convinced of the importance of 'culture', of 'education' for the working class, and spoke fervently on these lines to the Socialist Youth Congress at Bologna in 1912.[13] According to Giuseppe Berti, it was Tasca who brought Gramsci into the Socialist Youth movement in Turin (of which Tasca was a founder).[14] Another of Gramsci's friends, Umberto Terracini, was secretary of the Piedmontese Socialist Youth Federation in 1914. Thus by 1914 there existed at Turin a group of convinced young Socialists, all strongly influenced by the anti-positivist revolution in philosophy, and all convinced of the importance of cultural and ideological issues. I should add that the influence of 'Southern' critics of the labour movement was also very marked. Gaetano Salvemini's strictures on the selfish, protectionist, reformist Unions and Cooperatives of Northern Italy made a great appeal to youthful intellectual Socialists.[15]

This small group of Socialist students was broken up by the First World War. Gramsci and Togliatti were in favour of Italy's 'intervention' in the war, and left the Socialist Party for this reason. Indeed, Gramsci's first known political article defended Mussolini's view that war might bring revolution nearer, and that the Italian proletariat could not abandon itself to 'Buddhist contemplation'.[16] Giorgio Bocca's explanation is plausible: 'the profound influence of Salvemini on Gramsci and his friends, the

[12] A. Gramsci, 'Un Agente Provocatore', in *Falce e Martello* 4 June 1921.

[13] F. Trocchi, *Angelo Tasca e l'Ordine Nuovo* (Jaca, Milan 1973), esp. pp. 16–18 and pp. 23–4.

[14] G. Berti, 'Appunti e Ricordi 1919–26' in *Annali dell'Istituto Giangiacomo Feltrinelli*, anno VIII (1966), p. 173. cf. also P. Spriano, *Storia del Partito Comunista Italiano* (Einaudi, Turin 1967), vol. i, p. 14, quoting B. Santhià's testimony that Gramsci joined the *P.S.I.* towards the end of 1913.

[15] In 1914 Salvemini, who was not a member of the Socialist Party, was invited to stand as Socialist candidate at a by-election in Turin. He rejected the invitation.

[16] 'Neutralità Attiva e Operante', in *Il Grido del Popolo* 31 October 1914 (now in A. Gramsci, *Scritti Giovanili*, Einaudi, Turin 1958, pp. 3–7). J. M. Cammett, in his *Antonio Gramsci and the Origins of Italian Communism* (Stanford U.P., 1967), p. 38, is mistaken on two counts: Gramsci *was* 'interventionist', and he did not begin regular contributions to 'Grido del Popolo' in November 1914, but a year later (when the 'interventionist' crisis was over).

democratic-peasant ideology with its justification of 'people's wars', the war as promoting the interests of the proletariat.'[17] Both Gramsci and Togliatti were exempted from military service on health grounds, but Togliatti served with the Army Medical Corps, and in 1916 passed the medical examination and joined the Alpini;[18] he took no part in political activity until after the war. Gramsci came back into the Socialist fold in the second half of 1915, and rapidly became well-known in local left-wing journalism. Even so, he never managed to shake off a reputation for 'interventionism' – it was even hurled at him at the Congress of Leghorn (Livorno) in January 1921, when the Italian Communist Party was formed. Much of his real unpopularity in the *P.S.I.* after the war may be traced back to his article of October 1914; 'interventionism' was the unforgivable sin.

In 1921 Gramsci wrote a brief account of his own activity during the war:

> I joined the editorial staff of *Avanti!* on 10 December 1915. I was a journalist on *Avanti!* continuously from 10 December 1915 to 31 December 1920 – 5 years and 20 days. Of the hundreds and thousands of editorials, local articles, political commentary, and theatre criticism that I wrote for *Avanti!*, nothing was ever thrown into the waste-paper basket . . . I joined the staff of *Avanti!* at a time when the *P.S.I.* was reduced to the direst extremities, and everybody capable of writing was repudiating the Party and attempting to escape his obligations. I joined *Avanti!* of my own free will, out of conviction.[19]

Gramsci was a superb journalist, with a biting sarcastic wit. The life gave him what he had lacked – wide contacts in Turin, a sense of being at the centre of great events and able to influence them, above all self-confidence.

Moreover, in the Italian Socialist Party at this time journalism was the road to the top (one thinks of Mussolini, Serrati, and later Nenni). As a result of the bread riots of August 1917,[20] most of the local Socialist leaders were arrested, and this forced Gramsci into becoming both editor of the *Grido del Popolo* and, for a brief period, political secretary of the local branch of the Socialist Party.[21] He was even forced on to the national

[17] G. Bocca, *Palmiro Togliatti* (Laterza, Bari 1973), p. 20. cf. also G. Berti, 'Appunti e Ricordi 1919–26' cit., p. 14, pp. 43–5.

[18] G. Bocca, *Palmiro Togliatti* cit., p. 25.

[19] 'Un Agente Provocatore', in *Falce e Martello* 4 June 1921.

[20] See Chapter One, p. 23.

[21] By January 1918 Gramsci had lost this post. See the list of members of the executive committee of the Turin Socialist Section at that date, in which Gramsci's name is not included (Ufficio Centrale di Investigazione to Ministry of the Interior, 24 January 1918, and also Lt.-Gen. Sartirana, Comando del Corpo d'Armata Torino,

political scene for the first time, attending the secret meeting of the maximalist wing of the *P.S.I.* at Florence in November 1917 – where he was accused of 'Bergsonism' as a result of his attacks on the party's passive policy during the war.[22] Gramsci seems, however, to have had little taste for public speaking. Tasca later wrote that Gramsci 'had nothing of the orator about him, and hence was known and appreciated only within a narrow, restricted circle of intellectuals and workers.'[23] The Russian Vladimir Degot, who liked Gramsci, confirmed that he had 'no power of attraction for the masses, firstly because he is not much of a speaker, and secondly because he is too young, too short, and hunchbacked, which makes the audience uncomfortable.'[24] During the war it was Gramsci's journalism, rather than his practical political activities, that was to have the most lasting results.

The success of the Bolshevik revolution in Russia enabled Gramsci to develop his philosophical and political views further. In November 1917 he wrote one of his most famous articles, claiming that

> facts have overthrown the critical schema within which the history of Russia was supposed to be confined, according to the canons of historical materialism. The Bolsheviks deny Karl Marx, and affirm explicitly by their deeds that the canons of historical materialism are not so iron-like as might be thought, and as has been thought . . . [the Bolsheviks] are not Marxists, that's all. They live Marx's thought, the one that never dies, the continuation of Italian and German idealist thought, which was contaminated in Marx himself by positivist and naturalist incrustations.[25]

The influence of Croce is very marked in this passage, and it shows how the accusations of Bergsonism – like that of interventionism – could easily be levied at Gramsci by his opponents. But the passage also shows that Lenin's success proved the validity of what Gramsci had been thinking for years, that 'Marx's genuine doctrine' was that 'Man and reality, the instrument of labour and the will, are not disconnected, but become

---

to Ministry of War, 26 January 1918, both in *State Archives*, Ministero dell'Interno, Direzione Generale Pubblica Sicurezza, Divisione Affari Generali e Riservati, b. 31, 'Agitazione Contro la Guerra, Torino'). On Gramsci as editor of the *Grido del Popolo*, see P. Spriano, *Torino Operaia nella Grande Guerra* cit., pp. 315–38.

[22] For this episode, see P. Spriano, *Torino Operaia nella Grande Guerra* cit., pp. 281–7; and A. Gramsci, *Passato e Presente* (Einaudi, Turin 1954), p. 59.

[23] *Il Mondo* 25 August 1953; now in A. Tasca, *I Primi Dieci Anni del P.C.I.* (Laterza, Bari 1971), p. 97.

[24] V. Degot, *Pod Znamenem Bol'shevizma* (Moscow 1927), p. 146; quoted in B. Lazitch and M. Drachkovitch, *Lenin and the Comintern* (Hoover Institute, Stanford U.P. 1972), vol. i, p. 459.

[25] 'La Rivoluzione contro il "Capitale" ', in *Avanti!* (Milan ed.) 24 November 1917 (now in A. Gramsci, *Scritti Giovanili* cit., pp. 149–53).

identified in the historical act.'[26] Lenin and the example of Russia were
proof that he had not been wrong in struggling against positivist reformism within the Italian Socialist Party, against the 'philistines of Socialism'
among Union leaders and reformist deputies. Indeed, the Bolshevik
Revolution seems to have had a profound impact on Gramsci's thinking.
It led him to turn away from his quasi-Salveminian 'interventionist'
views, in favour of a more 'left-wing', 'revolutionary' position – but one
that was, of course, equally anti-reformist and equally contemptuous of
the traditions of the Italian labour movement.[27]

Another aspect of this struggle against reformism was the importance
Gramsci, like Tasca, attached to the 'cultural preparation' of the working
class for revolution. For Gramsci, Socialism always meant 'enormous
efforts to raise up the masses, to educate them, to civilise them, to free
them from vicious habits like alcoholism.'[28] It was in this field, clearly,
that the editor of a Socialist weekly could have the most influence, and
under Gramsci the *Grido del Popolo* became, in his own words, 'a little
review of Socialist culture'. For Gramsci, with his Crocian background,
the whole point of education was to produce a critical awareness of one's
own personality, historical role, and function in life; and this was, too, an
essential preliminary of successful revolution. 'Every revolution has been
preceded by intense critical activity, cultural penetration, and permeation
of ideas among groups of men at first unwilling to accept them.'[29] Hence
when in December 1917 the idea of founding an educational association
was put forward at Turin, Gramsci welcomed the idea enthusiastically;
political and economic activity, he wrote, should always be integrated
with cultural activity.[30] The Bolsheviks were specifically praised for working to create the *necessary conditions* – cultural and organisational conditions – for the Socialist programme;[31] it was sheer Utopianism to neglect

[26] 'La Critica Critica' in *Il Grido del Popolo* 12 January 1918 (now in A. Gramsci,
Scritti Giovanili cit., pp. 153–5). The whole article is a bitter attack on Italian reformism, which has 'converted the doctrine of Marx into the doctrine of the inertia
of the proletariat'.

[27] G. Berti, 'Appunti e Ricordi 1919–26' cit., p. 17.

[28] 'Mandarini', in *Ordine Nuovo* 23 June 1921 (now in A. Gramsci, *Socialismo e
Fascismo*, Einaudi, Turin 1966, p. 207).

[29] 'Socialismo e Cultura' in *Il Grido del Popolo* 29 January 1916 (now in A. Gramsci,
Scritti Giovanili cit., p. 24).

[30] 'Per Un'Associazione di Cultura' in *Avanti!* (Turin ed.) 18 December 1917 (now
in A. Gramsci, *Scritti Giovanili* cit., p. 144). The association was founded, and was
called a 'Club of Moral Life', but it only held three or four sessions – perhaps because
of Gramsci's insistence on the practice of public confessions. See P. Spriano, 'Il Club
di Vita Morale', in *Rinascita* 28 March 1964.

[31] 'Per Conoscere la Rivoluzione Russa' in *Il Grido del Popolo* 22 June 1918 (now in
A. Gramsci, *Scritti Giovanili* cit., p. 268).

the task of cultural preparation. Moreover, 'education, culture, the spreading organisation of knowledge and experience – this is the independence of the masses from the intellectuals . . . Socialism is organisation, and not only political and economic organisation, but also, especially, organisation of knowledge and of will, obtained through cultural activity.'[32]

It is impossible to over-emphasise this aspect of Gramsci's work. He did not despise 'bourgeois' culture; on the contrary, he sought to diffuse it. He did not romanticise existing workers (or existing labour institutions); on the contrary, he feared they might be inadequate for their future tasks. Workers had to be capable of running society, and this meant having not only technical ability and a perception of shared interests, but also a command of Italy's and the world's cultural heritage, a sense of self-confidence and of dominating the past. Gramsci, therefore, gave lectures to the Turin workers, but his journalism was more important; the experience he gained in this field during the war meant that he was appointed co-editor, with Ottavio Pastore, of the new separate Turin edition of the Socialist daily newspaper *Avanti!*. The first issue appeared on 5 December 1918. The existence of this daily was to prove important during the following two years.[33]

With the return to Turin after the war of Gramsci's friends and colleagues, the former group of young Socialists was rapidly reconstituted. They soon decided to found a weekly review to supplement the daily edition of *Avanti!* in the work of 'cultural penetration'. The review was initially financed by 6,000 *lire* provided by Angelo Tasca, the only member of the group to have good enough contacts with the local labour movement to raise some money.[34] The first issue of *Ordine Nuovo*, described as an 'organ of proletarian culture', came out on 1 May 1919. As Gramsci wrote over a year later, 'When, in April 1919, we decided, three, four or five of us, to begin publishing this review, the *Ordine Nuovo* . . . who were we? What did we represent? What message did we bring? Alas! The only thing that united us in our meetings was a vague passion for a vague proletarian culture.'[35] Nevertheless, as has been seen, the cultural theme was never totally separate from practical political aims in Gramsci's thinking, and even the first few issues of the review, vague

[32] 'Prima Liberi' in *Il Grido del Popolo* 31 August 1918 (now in A. Gramsci, *Scritti Giovanili* cit., pp. 301–2).

[33] Since December 1915 copies of *Avanti!* sold in Piedmont had contained one page of Turin news, but the paper had basically been the Milan edition.

[34] M. and M. Ferrara, *Conversando con Togliatti* (Rinascita, Rome 1951), p. 47. Costs remained low, since the leading contributors received their salaries from *Avanti!* (testimony of Pia Carena, quoted by G. Bocca, *Palmiro Togliatti* cit., p. 35).

[35] A. Gramsci, 'Il Programma dell' Ordine Nuovo' in *Ordine Nuovo* 14 August 1920 (now in A. Gramsci, *Ordine Nuovo*, Einaudi, Turin 1955, p. 146).

as they were, were aimed at formulating 'a maximum Socialist programme that will win and retain the support of the masses';[36] a programme, that is, opposed to the reformism of Union leaders and parliamentary deputies. Thus even in the early issues, before it adopted its
'Factory Council' programme, the *Ordine Nuovo* represented a potential
challenge to established Union practice and to political reformism.

Still, in one way Gramsci was right. The *Ordine Nuovo* could be
attacked – and was attacked – as a dilettante journal run by café intellectuals, young men with academic minds, good at journalism, but with
no experience whatever of industry or administration. Of them all, Tasca
was the one most in touch with the local labour organisations even in
1919; Togliatti's activity in the Socialist Party had barely begun, and both
he and Gramsci were known to have been 'interventionists'. Gramsci
himself, as a young man, had an unattractive Robespierrean side – self-
righteousness, contempt for lesser mortals and for the existing labour
movements, above all a Puritanical zeal in denouncing deviations,
ideological, financial or sexual. All this was a virtual guarantee of
unpopularity. But at least these café intellectuals were aware of their
weaknesses, and were very anxious to immerse themselves in industrial
reality.

Furthermore, they were aware of the weaknesses of the Italian State
and economy, and of the Italian bourgeoisie. Like many others, Gramsci
firmly believed that the old capitalism had collapsed. He insisted on this
theme again and again over the years. Far from regarding the expansion of industry during the war as evidence of vitality, he saw it as
having simply distorted and destroyed the pre-war economic system. He
admitted, for example, that Fiat's directors Giovanni Agnelli and Guido
Fornaca had been 'real captains of industry' pre-war, and very popular
with their workers; but the war had turned them into financial specu-
lators, obsessed with banking and political manoeuvres, heedless of
technical criteria, and incapable henceforth of organising industry.[37] The
bourgeois order, exhausted by war and speculation, was visibly decom-
posing in the factory. Similarly, in the State itself 'bourgeois legality' was
no longer respected, and Parliament and similar institutions were dis-

[36] 'Programma di Lavoro' in *Ordine Nuovo* 1 May 1919. One of the points in the
programme was discussion of 'the representative and administrative regime for direct
management by producers and consumers'.

[37] 'La Sconfitta della Fiat', in *Ordine Nuovo* 6 September 1921 (now in A. Gramsci,
Socialismo e Fascismo cit., pp. 322–4). Other examples of this argument, all dating
from 1921, are in 'Il Disco dell' Immaturità', in *Ordine Nuovo* 14 April, in 'Perché la
Borghesia non può Governare il Paese', in *Ordine Nuovo* 2 July, and in 'Gestione
Capitalistica e Gestione Operaia', in *Ordine Nuovo* 17 September (now in A. Gramsci,
Socialismo e Fascismo cit., pp. 138–40, pp. 222–4, and pp. 340–2).

credited. A 'New Order' was therefore essential, to be run by the workers themselves. But how would it be organised?

We have Gramsci's testimony that in April 1919, before the first issue appeared, the idea of studying the 'Internal Commissions', to see the uses to which this working-class institution could be put, had been discussed by the group drawing up the *Ordine Nuovo*'s policy.[38] As has been shown in Chapter Two, the Internal Commissions had become so important by then that it would have been surprising had they not been discussed; but there were additional reasons for doing so. The question was:

> Does there exist in Italy, as an institution of the working class, anything comparable to the Soviet, anything similar to it in character? Anything that will enable us to conclude that the Soviet is a universal institution, not merely a Russian one? To conclude that the Soviet is the institution in which, wherever there are workers struggling to achieve industrial autonomy, the working class embodies its desire for emancipation; that the Soviet is the institution of self-government for the working masses. Is there an aspiration towards, or intimation of, Soviet government in Italy, in Turin?[39]

The answer to this question was clearly that there was such an institution at Turin, in the form of the Internal Commission. It thus appears to have been Russian experience that first drew the attention of what must now be called the '*Ordine Nuovo* group' to the increasingly important workers' institution in the local factories.[40] On the other hand, it is perfectly possible that Gramsci used the success of the Russian Revolution to provide corroborative validity for ideas that he had already formulated on the basis of local experience. At all events, it was urged that the Internal Commissions were a possible means of 'revolutionary preparation': they would 'prepare' the workers both psychologically and technically for factory administration, and might prove useful in overcoming Union opposition to revolutionary political measures.

The discussions in April 1919, before the *Ordine Nuovo* was founded, had no immediate results because Tasca was reluctant to begin agitation immediately, before consultations with local Union leaders designed at achieving official action. However, by mid-June Gramsci and Togliatti

[38] See 'Il Programma dell' Ordine Nuovo' in *Ordine Nuovo* 14 August 1920 (now in A. Gramsci, *Ordine Nuovo* cit., pp. 146–7).

[39] 'Il Programma dell' Ordine Nuovo' in *Ordine Nuovo* 14 August 1920 (now in A. Gramsci, *Ordine Nuovo* cit., p. 147).

[40] This interpretation is strengthened by the fact that no emphasis had been laid on the Internal Commissions by Gramsci in the *Grido del Popolo* in 1918 (P. Spriano, *Torino Operaia nella Grande Guerra* cit., pp. 322–4).

had become convinced of the need to start unofficial agitation, and carried through an 'editorial coup d'état'[41] against Tasca, publishing, with Terracini's knowledge and consent, the first article to appear in *Ordine Nuovo* on the question of the Internal Commissions. This article, entitled 'Working-Class Democracy', appeared on 21 June, and urged that the workers should elect huge assemblies of factory delegates on the basis of the slogan 'All Power in the Workshop to the Workshop Committees', this to be a corollary of the more general aim of 'All Power in the State to the Workers' and Peasants' Councils'. There was as yet no mention of 'Factory Councils', and indeed the main emphasis was placed not on the Internal Commissions and workers' representative bodies *within* the factories, but on the election of delegates from the factories to sit on ward committees (*comitati rionali*), which would be representative of all types of worker living in a given ward, and which would form the basis for urban commissariats. The emphasis was clearly more on Workers' Councils on an urban basis – i.e. Soviets – than on Factory Councils as such. The purpose of these proposals was two-fold: to discipline and coordinate the masses, so that their revolutionary energies should not be dispersed; and to obtain 'a radical transformation of the workers' psychology, to make the masses better prepared and more able to exercise power'.[42]

Soon 'the problem of the development of the Internal Commissions became the central problem, the "idea" of the *Ordine Nuovo*; it was posed as the fundamental problem of the workers' revolution, it was the problem of "proletarian liberty"'.[43] The first essential, clearly, was to agree on methods of electing the 'Factory Committees'. There were two important principles here, both first laid down by Ottavio Pastore, the editor of the Turin edition of *Avanti!*, in mid-August 1919: firstly, henceforth the Internal Commission should be elected, not by Union members on the shop floor as hitherto, but by 'Workshop Commissars', or Shop Stewards (*Commissari di Reparto*), each of whom would represent the workers of a particular *reparto* (shop) in the factory; and secondly, all workers in the factory, whether Union members or not, should be

---

[41] The phrase used by Gramsci in his article 'Il Programma dell' Ordine Nuovo' in *Ordine Nuovo* 14 August 1920 (now in A. Gramsci, *Ordine Nuovo* cit., p. 148). Tasca wrote in 1953 that 'I did not notice any coup d'état happening.' He agreed, however, that the argument between Gramsci and himself was over the relations of Internal Commissions with official Union Organisations and Chambers of Labour (*Il Mondo* 25 August 1953, now in A. Tasca, *I Primi Dieci Anni del P.C.I.* cit., pp. 98–9).

[42] 'Democrazia Operaia' in *Ordine Nuovo* 21 June 1919 (now in A. Gramsci, *Ordine Nuovo* cit., pp. 10–13).

[43] 'Il Programma dell' Ordine Nuovo' in *Ordine Nuovo* 14 August 1920 (now in A. Gramsci, *Ordine Nuovo* cit., p. 149).

eligible to vote for a 'Commissar'.[44] Truly class institutions could only
be based on the process of production, 'in the factory, where the relations
are those of oppressor and oppressed, of exploiter and exploited';[45] and
since every factory was divided, for technical reasons, into workshops
and separate production units (*reparti, squadre di mestiere*), the electoral
system should be based on these 'natural' units, that were an inevitable
part of any industrial system. Hence the workers from each shop should
elect a 'Commissar' whose mandate could be revoked at any time. The
'Factory Council' would thus consist of the assembly of these delegates,
and it would in turn elect an executive committee from within its ranks,
to act as the Internal Commission.[46] Since the 'Commissars' represented
integral units of production, it followed that all the workers in the work-
unit should be entitled to vote for their own 'Commissar'.[47] The Factory
Council system was based on the organisation of industry, and each
worker was represented by virtue of his role as a worker in that industry;
this electoral system guaranteed the 'class nature' of the new institution.
'The workers' democracy is based not on mere numbers or on the
bourgeois concept of the "citizen", it is based on the function of labour,
on the order assumed naturally by the working class in the process of
industrial production within the factory.'[48]

The functions of the 'Workshop Commissars' were to be varied, and
included all those previously performed by the members of the old-style
Internal Commissions, i.e. complaints, application of wage agreements,
matters of hygiene etc, in all of which the Commissars were to act as
representatives of their own work-units on the Factory Council, and as
executive officers of the Factory Council within their own work-unit.
However, they also had far more important tasks. It was their job to
maintain discipline among their own workers, so as to ensure concerted
action in the event of a strike or demonstration. Above all, they were
supposed to study the technical methods of production in force within

[44] 'O.P.', 'Il Problema delle Commissioni Interne' in *Ordine Nuovo* 16 August 1919
(now in P. Spriano, *Ordine Nuovo* cit., pp. 244–8).
[45] 'Il Consiglio di Fabbrica' in *Ordine Nuovo* 5 June 1920 (now in A. Gramsci,
Ordine Nuovo cit., p. 124).
[46] 'Il Movimento Torinese dei Consigli di Fabbrica' in *Ordine Nuovo* 14 March 1921
(now in A. Gramsci, *Ordine Nuovo* cit., p. 183).
[47] Anticipating criticism of this proposal, Pastore explained, somewhat tactlessly,
that giving the vote to all would not mean any increased power in the hands of the
non-Union members: 'in practice the groups of Union members will always prevail,
and being more energetic, class-conscious and disciplined than the others, will easily
get their candidates elected' ('Il Problema delle Commissioni Interne' cit., in *Ordine
Nuovo* 16 August 1919, now in P. Spriano, *Ordine Nuovo* cit., p. 194).
[48] 'Il Programma dei Commissari di Reparto' in *Ordine Nuovo* 8 November 1919
(now in A. Gramsci, *Ordine Nuovo* cit., p. 194).

their own workshops, and in particular 'to find out precisely (1) the value
of the capital invested in the unit, (2) the return on this capital in relation
to all known expenses, and (3) what increased returns might be possible.'[49]
Great emphasis was laid by the *Ordine Nuovo* theorists on this aspect of
the Commissars' work, which, it should be noted, went far beyond the
generally accepted idea of 'workers' control'; it was felt to be an essential
preliminary of successful revolution, for only thus could the workers
replace the bourgeois technicians and administrative staff who might
otherwise betray them.[50]

In the *Ordine Nuovo*'s view, the proposals for Factory Council organisation outlined above would have several important effects. In the first
place, it would produce or strengthen a 'Communist consciousness'; and
Gramsci later wrote, in fact, that 'each worker, in order to set up a
Council, has had to become conscious of his position in the economic
field.'[51] According to this theory, the new habits acquired in the factory
would be the basis of future conquests, and indeed of future labour
organisation after the revolution.[52] Factory Councils were thus part of
the process of 'workers' education' whose importance for Gramsci has
been stressed. This aspect provided much of the moral fervour with which
the *Ordine Nuovo* movement was associated, and which was closely linked
with Gramsci's passionate rejection of positivism:

> Workers' solidarity . . . in the Councils is something positive, it is
> permanent, it is incarnate even in the most trivial aspects of industrial
> production, it is contained in the joyous consciousness of being an
> organic whole, a homogeneous compact system which, by performing
> useful labour and disinterestedly producing social wealth, affirms its
> sovereignty and actuates both its power and its own historical creative
> liberty.[53]

Secondly, the Factory Councils would bring about the *de jure* unity of
the working class. For Gramsci, *de facto* unity already existed, created by

[49] *ibid.*, p. 197.
[50] For the fullest outline of this view, see 'Che Cosa Sono i Consigli di Fabbrica?'
in *Bandiera Rossa* 15 January 1921. It was argued by some that such experience could
not possibly be obtained before the revolution (see 'R.X.', 'Il Problema delle Commissioni Interne' in *Ordine Nuovo* 23 August 1919, now in P. Spriano, *Ordine Nuovo* cit.,
pp. 249–51).
[51] 'Lo Strumento di Lavoro' in *Ordine Nuovo* 14 February 1920 (now in A. Gramsci,
Ordine Nuovo cit., p. 81).
[52] 'Ai Commissari di Reparto delle Officine Fiat-Centro e Brevetti' in *Ordine Nuovo*
13 September 1919 (now in A. Gramsci, *Ordine Nuovo* cit., p. 33).
[53] 'Sindacati e Consigli' in *Ordine Nuovo* 11 October 1919 (now in A. Gramsci,
Ordine Nuovo cit., p. 37).

economic progress and the relations of production within advanced industrial societies. However, the existence of different working-class parties and movements, founded at an earlier stage of economic development, prevented this unity from being clearly recognised and achieved *de jure*. Hence, once the workers became 'conscious' of their *de facto* unity, they would give it 'concrete expression' and themselves create true proletarian unity. This could be done effectively only by the workers themselves, and only through Factory Councils.[54] It is important to emphasise that this problem, too, was essentially one of 'consciousness'; the Councils would not create unity, but they would be the expression of it 'above the different categories brought about by the division of labour', which alone were expressed by existing working-class organisations.[55] This impatience with differences among workers is significant, and illustrates one of the main aims – and main weaknesses – of the Factory Council movement. The Turin working class may have been 'homogeneous' in the sense that a single industry was dominant – vehicle manufacture and engineering – but it was not 'homogeneous' in other senses.[56]

The main effect of the Councils, however, would be their contribution to successful Socialist revolution. Revolution, for Gramsci, was not a specific event, but a 'dialectical process of historical development':[57] 'the Communist method is the method of permanent revolution [rivoluzione in permanenza]'.[58] This revolutionary process had to be based on economic reality, on the productive process, for it was a basic tenet of historical materialism that all political power was merely the legal reflection of real economic power; just as the political power of the bourgeoisie was based ultimately on the factory, so must 'the revolutionary process . . . start from within production'.[59] Gramsci was very insistent on this point: a successful Socialist revolution did not merely mean power passing into the hands of Socialists, for such a revolution would be disastrous unless the relations of production had been transformed beforehand, and would

[54] The fullest discussion of this is in Gramsci's article 'L'Unità Proletaria', in *Ordine Nuovo* 28 February–6 March 1920 (now in A. Gramsci, *Ordine Nuovo* cit., pp. 96–101).
[55] 'Lo Sviluppo della Rivoluzione' in *Ordine Nuovo* 13 September 1919 (now in A. Gramsci, *Ordine Nuovo* cit., p. 29).
[56] See Chapter One, p. 27. Gramsci recognised both that Turin was a very 'original city', and that any city, and any working class, is strongly influenced by the prevailing local industry ('Il Programma dell' Ordine Nuovo' in *Ordine Nuovo* 28 August 1920, now in A. Gramsci, *Ordine Nuovo* cit., p. 151).
[57] 'Lo Sviluppo della Rivoluzione' in *Ordine Nuovo* 13 September 1919 (now in A. Gramsci, *Ordine Nuovo* cit., p. 30).
[58] 'Postilla' to R.X.'s 'Il Problema delle Commissioni Interne' in *Ordine Nuovo* 23 August 1919 (now in P. Spriano, *Ordine Nuovo* cit., p. 251).
[59] 'La Costituzione dei Soviet in Italia' in *Ordine Nuovo* 7 February 1920.

lead only to 'the setting up of a proletarian Communist regime unable to do anything except to make repeated and desperate attempts to produce, by its own authority, the economic pre-conditions of its survival.'[60] Hence the importance of the Factory Councils in the revolutionary process: the Councils could provide an organised, conscious mass basis for revolution, with the workers' industrial power guaranteeing their political power.

Gramsci therefore regarded successful revolution as being essentially an institutional question (and not, for example, a military one). The right institutions had to be set up, and made to generate the right kind of consensus. Factory Councils would enable workers to rid themselves of bourgeois assumptions, would train them in the problems of industrial management, and would enable them to retain control of a Socialist society – the ideological, technical and political aspects were in his mind inseparably linked. They would also incarnate an alternative kind of 'legitimacy', to replace discredited bourgeois institutions. This was a vital aspect of his theory, perhaps even the essence of it. Gramsci took for granted that industrial society was desirable, and that capitalism could not organise it except by repression; and he regarded Factory Councils as the main *legitimacy-creating* institutions of an industrial society. Only Factory Councils could legitimately exercise 'discipline' over workers; only Factory Councils could enable them to develop their own skills and their own ideas, to take initiative and responsibility, to become 'producers' instead of 'militants'. George Lukacs wrote despairingly in July 1920 that 'the proletariat is forced to seize power when it still inwardly accepts the bourgeois order of society as the truly legal one.'[61] Gramsci answered that this was not the case, the proletariat could not 'seize power' under those conditions, and it was vital that new institutions be set up to embody a new 'legal' authority.[62] It followed, therefore, that the Councils were useless except as conscious incarnations of an alternative order. There should never be any question of their being officially recognised, or of their limiting themselves to the exercise of any kind of 'workers' control'.[63]

Not only was the Factory Council an essential instrument for preparing

---

[60] 'Due Rivoluzioni' in *Ordine Nuovo* 3 July 1920 (now in A. Gramsci, *Ordine Nuovo* cit., p. 137).

[61] G. Lukacs, *Geschichte und Klassenbewusstsein* (Der Malik Verlag, Berlin 1923), p. 271.

[62] cf. Martin Clark, review of A. Gramsci, *Selections from the Prison Notebooks* (Lawrence and Wishart, London 1971), in *Political Studies*, vol. XX (1972), pp. 492–6.

[63] 'Controllo di Classe', editorial by Togliatti in *Ordine Nuovo* 3 January 1920 (now in P. Spriano, *Ordine Nuovo* cit., pp. 414–18).

revolution, it was also described in the *Ordine Nuovo* as the 'model of the Socialist State',[64] and as the incarnation of the dictatorship of the proletariat. The new State was to be a reflection of new industrial relations in the factory, and was to be based on factory organisation. Gramsci even wrote that 'all the problems inherent in the organisation of the proletarian State are inherent in the organisation of the Councils'.[65] Each Internal Commission (i.e. the 'executive committee' elected by the full Factory Council) was to elect a 'political secretary', who would sit on the Central Committee of the Councils together with the 'political secretaries' of other factories. This Central Committee was to be the nucleus of the local Soviet.[66] Thus Gramsci never formulated a theory of *purely* political Soviets. His Workers' Councils were to be based firmly on units of production, not on geographical areas – and, for him, the fact that successful political revolution was essentially a recognition of existing economic relations meant that Soviets could only arise after the establishment of a Factory Council system.[67] This theory of the Socialist State as being organised on industrial lines led him to important conclusions about the nature of the Factory Council. He considered it to be an institution of a 'public', not private, nature:

> The Factory Council . . . [is] a historic association which can be compared today only with the bourgeois State . . . the worker becomes a member of the Factory Council as a producer, i.e. as a result of his universal character, as a result of his position and function in society, in the same way that the citizen becomes a member of the democratic parliamentary State.[68]

The Factory Council, therefore, was an embryonic State, of which the worker was automatically a member; it was thus totally distinct from the Trade Unions or the Socialist Party, which were 'voluntary' bodies with functions within existing bourgeois society. It remained to work out the relationship between these two very different types of working-class organisations.

---

[64] 'Sindacati e Consigli' in *Ordine Nuovo* 11 October 1919 (now in A. Gramsci, *Ordine Nuovo* cit., p. 37).

[65] *ibid.*

[66] See 'Che Cosa Sono i Consigli di Fabbrica?' in *Bandiera Rossa* 15 January 1921.

[67] The main discussion of this is in the issue of 14 February 1920, especially Gramsci's 'Lo Strumento di Lavoro' (now in A. Gramsci, *Ordine Nuovo* cit., pp. 79–80), and Togliatti's 'La Costituzione dei Soviet in Italia' (now in P. Spriano, *Ordine Nuovo* cit., pp. 444–6). Gramsci was here clearly anticipating the 'Yugoslav model' of a Socialist society.

[68] 'Il Programma dell' Ordine Nuovo' in *Ordine Nuovo* 28 August 1920 (now in A. Gramsci, *Ordine Nuovo* cit., p. 150).

Gramsci's view of the desirable relationship between the Socialist Party and the Factory Councils was uncompromising. The main task of the Socialist Party, in the pre-revolutionary period, was to organise the proletariat into a position where it could become the dominant class in society; at a time of great social unrest, the essential task was to 'organise and incorporate the great masses in movement'.[69] The Factory Councils were seen as the means whereby the Party could fulfil its main function; hence the Party 'should promote the development of the proletarian factory institutions where they already exist, and make them arise [farle nascere] where they do not; and coordinate them locally and nationally.'[70] Without a flourishing system of Factory Councils, the Party would remain a 'mere academy of pure doctrinaires and politickers', deprived of any secure economic foundation for its political activity, and hence unable to carry out any coherent revolutionary policies.[71] But the Party should be careful not to *found* any Councils: Gramsci was very critical of the German Social Democrats for creating their own tame Councils 'from above', and he foresaw a lengthy struggle by Left Socialists and 'Communist Groups' before control of the Councils could be won.[72]

However, while emphasising the need for Councils, Gramsci never minimised the importance of the Party's role; he fully recognised the success of the Socialist Party in instilling class-consciousness among the workers in the past, and urged that the Councils could not hope to succeed unless they were strongly influenced by a militant Party. Indeed, he even wrote that 'the existence of a coherent, strongly disciplined Communist Party . . . to co-ordinate and centralise the proletariat's revolutionary activity, is a fundamental indispensable condition for trying any Soviet experiment.'[73] There was, therefore, a mutual dependence between Factory Councils and Party in Gramsci's thought: just as the Party could not fulfil its tasks without the Councils, the Councils would prove ineffective without the Party.

[69] 'Primo: Rinnovare il Partito' in *Ordine Nuovo* 24–31 January 1920 (now in A. Gramsci, *Ordine Nuovo* cit., p. 391).

[70] 'Per l'Internazionale Comunista' in *Ordine Nuovo* 26 July 1919 (now in A. Gramsci, *Ordine Nuovo* cit., p. 22).

[71] 'Due Rivoluzioni' in *Ordine Nuovo* 3 July 1920 (now in A. Gramsci, *Ordine Nuovo* cit., p. 138).

[72] 'Il Problema del Potere' in *Ordine Nuovo* 29 November 1919 (now in A. Gramsci, *Ordine Nuovo* cit., p. 60).

[73] 'Per Un Rinnovamento del Partito Socialista' in *Ordine Nuovo* 8 May 1920 (now in A. Gramsci, *Ordine Nuovo* cit., p. 122). The use of the term 'Communist Party' at this time implied the need for a revitalised Socialist Party; it should not be interpreted as a call for a new party in opposition to the *P.S.I.* See pp. 141–3.

The same close co-operation between Party and Councils would be necessary during 'post-revolutionary' reconstruction. The main necessity was to avoid the 'revolutionary myth' of a kind of 'dictatorship by local branches of the Party'. Communist society could only be conceived of as a 'natural' formation adhering closely to the processes of production and exchange. It followed that 'the Socialist Party is undoubtedly the main "agent" in this process of destruction and reconstruction, but it is not and cannot be understood as the "form" of this process.'[74] The 'form' had to be a system of Factory Councils, and the Party would win and retain control over the Councils by virtue of its 'prestige', which Gramsci defined as the 'conscious and spontaneous acceptance of authority recognised as indispensable for the success of a given enterprise.' In short, Gramsci rejected any 'sectarian' view of the Party's role. The revolutionary process could not be confined within the Party or its organisations, and any attempt to do so would turn the Party into an essentially conservative body unable to influence events. The Party undoubtedly did have a vital role in Gramsci's theory of the dictatorship of the proletariat, but its role was, inevitably, a political one, whereas the new State was to be based on industrial organisation.[75] Hence during and after the revolution, as well as before it, the relationship between Party and Councils remained one of mutual dependence.

Gramsci's view of this relationship cannot, however, be considered in the abstract; it was largely conditioned by his analysis of the Italian Socialist Party. For him, the Socialist Party was essentially a voluntary body, with an 'ideal democratic' structure (i.e. local sections, provincial federations, annual Congresses, elected Directorate) reminiscent of the political society envisaged by Rousseau, and based on the same contractual foundation.[76] Hence it was not surprising that the Party had regarded the democratic institutions of bourgeois society as eternal and sacrosanct: despite all the talk of revolution, it seemed to Gramsci to be a 'mere parliamentary party, confined within the narrow limits of bourgeois

[74] 'Il Partito e la Rivoluzione' in *Ordine Nuovo* 27 December 1919 (now in A. Gramsci, *Ordine Nuovo* cit., p. 68).
[75] There is a considerable literature on Gramsci's theory of the relationship between Councils and Party. See F. Ferri, 'Consigli di Fabbrica e Partito nel Pensiero di Gramsci', in *Rinascita* September 1957, pp. 461–7; A. Caracciolo, 'Serrati, Bordiga, e la Polemica Gramsciana contro il "Blanquismo"', in *La Città Futura* (Feltrinelli, Milan 1959), pp. 91–114; F. De Felice, *Serrati, Bordiga, Gramsci* (De Donato, Bari 1971), pp. 275–311; F. De Felice, *Relazione*, in Various Authors, *I Comunisti a Torino* (Riuniti, Rome 1974), pp. 3–23; and G. Bonomi, *Partito e Rivoluzione in Gramsci* (Feltrinelli, Milan 1973), pp. 144–50.
[76] 'Il Partito e la Rivoluzione' in *Ordine Nuovo* 27 December 1919 (now in A. Gramsci, *Ordine Nuovo* cit., p. 67).

democracy.'[77] It has been seen above how vital it was in Factory Council theory that there should exist a political party to 'concentrate and centralise proletarian activity ... bring about unity and simultaneous effort';[78] indeed, this was for Gramsci the only justification for a working-class political party. It was, therefore, a logical consequence of *Ordine Nuovo*'s views of the relationship between Councils and Party that when attempts to revitalise the *P.S.I.* failed, and the Party became patently incapable of fulfilling its role in Gramsci's schema, support should have been given to the idea of founding a new working-class party, the Communist Party of Italy.[79] It is significant again that for Gramsci the essential weaknesses of the *P.S.I.* were institutional ones, the existence of separate factions within the Party and the lack of Party discipline. The *Ordine Nuovo* agitation for Factory Councils therefore came to imply the creation of a centralised 'Communist' Party with tight internal discipline; as Gramsci wrote at the end of 1921, 'without it no other workers' body can make a real contribution to the revolutionary cause.'[80]

The two essential characteristics of such a Party were that it would be the Party of the 'proletarian vanguard', and that it would *not* be organised on the traditional basis of representative assemblies,[81] but on the same basis as the eventual workers' State, i.e. that of 'organic units of production', where Party members could most effectively help the working class in its task of preparing and carrying through the revolution. Gramsci, therefore, welcomed enthusiastically both the idea of setting up 'Communist groups' in the factories, and in later years the proposals for making the 'factory cell' the foundation of Party organisation.[82] The mutual dependence of Party and Factory Councils was part of a general scheme for linking political to industrial organisation; the Party, like the Councils, was to be organised on the basis of production, and it was this, rather than increased centralisation or tighter discipline, that would enable it to play its part as the 'Supreme Command of the working class'.

It remains to consider the relationship between Factory Councils and

[77] 'Per Un Rinnovamento del Partito Socialista' in *Ordine Nuovo* 8 May 1920 (now in A. Gramsci, *Ordine Nuovo* cit., p. 118). Gramsci even went so far as to compare the *P.S.I.* with the British Labour Party.

[78] *ibid.*, p. 119.

[79] For the attitude of the leading members of the 'Ordine Nuovo group' to the projected new party, see p. 203. The *Partito Comunista d'Italia* was founded on 21 January 1921, at Leghorn (Livorno), after almost a year of agitation by various Left-wing groups.

[80] 'Dopo Un Anno', in *Ordine Nuovo* 1 January 1922.

[81] See 'I Gruppi Comunisti' in *Ordine Nuovo* 17 July 1920 (now in A. Gramsci, *Ordine Nuovo* cit., pp. 140–3), for a detailed analysis of the weaknesses inherent in the need to win a majority at the Party's representative assemblies.

[82] See p. 222.

Trade Unions. For Gramsci, the 'Trade Union' was a fluid concept. It was an essential part of this aspect of his theory that 'the Trade Union cannot be defined; it *becomes* a particular definition, i.e. assumes a particular historical form, inasmuch as the working class forces and wills that constitute it impress upon it a particular nature and particular aims.'[83] This insistence helps to explain some apparent contradictions in Gramsci's view of the Unions. Gramsci simultaneously held that the Unions were 'objectively' organisations designed to regulate the labour-market within capitalist society, in a *legal* manner,[84] and also that 'the Trade Union is perhaps the most important proletarian body in the Communist Revolution.'[85] There was a big distinction between what the Unions were, and what they might be if suitably 'transformed'; and there was much debate in the columns of the *Ordine Nuovo* as to what contribution the Factory Councils could make to bringing about such a transformation.

Gramsci recognised that the existing Trade Unions had proved effective in defending the workers' interests within capitalist society, in limiting the employers' powers, and in imposing recognition of the workers' rights on such issues as wages and hours, as well as in helping to secure an extensive body of social legislation. The Unions' task was to defend 'the interests of the worker as a wage-earner'[86] in a competitive labour market; as such, Unions were the typical working-class organisations of a historical period dominated by capital, and 'their function is inherent in a regime based on private property.'[87] The Unions were fully integrated into capitalist society, and indeed were an essential element within the capitalist system. However, their achievements had depended on two factors: their ability to organise a large proportion of the workers in any given industry, in order to be able to dominate the labour market, and their ability to exercise effective discipline over their members, so as to give employers confidence in the Unions' ability to contract valid agreements. These two requirements could not be met without a permanent staff of specialist Union officials, in charge of organisation and wage negotiations. These

[83] 'Sindacati e Consigli', in *Ordine Nuovo* 12 June 1920 (now in A. Gramsci, *Ordine Nuovo* cit., pp. 131–2).

[84] These paragraphs refer, of course, to the Unions adhering to the *Confederazione Generale del Lavoro*, and led normally by reformist Socialists; the syndicalist Unions will be considered briefly below.

[85] 'I Sindacati e la Dittatura' in *Ordine Nuovo* 25 October 1919 (now in A. Gramsci, *Ordine Nuovo* cit., p. 40).

[86] As opposed to 'forming a consciousness of himself as a producer' (which was the Factory Councils' task). See 'La Relazione Tasca e il Congresso Camerale di Torino' in *Ordine Nuovo* 5 June 1920 (now in A. Gramsci, *Ordine Nuovo* cit., p. 129).

[87] 'Sindacati e Consigli' in *Ordine Nuovo* 11 October 1919 (now in A. Gramsci, *Ordine Nuovo* cit., p. 36).

officials rapidly formed a closed bureaucratic caste, out of touch with the workers whose interests they ostensibly represented.[88] Moreover, the Trade Union bureaucracy might be 'expert' in drawing up memoranda and in making speeches, but it was certainly not 'expert' in industrial or managerial problems, nor were such problems ever discussed at general meetings of all Trade Union members.[89] Hence the Unions could not be the cells of a future society of 'producers', nor could they embody 'industrial autonomy'. In any case the bureaucracy, confined to a routine of administration and negotiation, was unlikely to favour the overthrow of existing society, and in fact all the main Unions were controlled by reformists.[90]

However, although the Unions were incapable of leading the proletariat towards its emancipation, and although, under reformist leadership, 'Trade Union discipline can be nothing else than a service rendered to capital',[91] the Unions *were* capable of making a great contribution to the success of the revolution. This was because of their 'disciplinary energy and their systematic centralisation', their 'centralised absolute character',[92] which would enable them to 'coordinate the forces of production and impress a Communist structure on industry'.[93] The Unions would 'coordinate', would 'implement' decisions taken elsewhere by other workers' institutions. Their officials would be 'functionaries' (executive civil servants), but in a Socialist society would cease to be 'mandarins' (decision-takers).[94] Gramsci was insistent that it was the Unions which would be responsible for the socialisation of industry,[95] and he pointed to Russian and Hungarian experience in order to prove the importance of the Unions

[88] 'I Sindacati e la Dittatura' in *Ordine Nuovo* 25 October 1919 (now in A. Gramsci, *Ordine Nuovo* cit., p. 42).

[89] 'Le Masse e i Capi', in *Ordine Nuovo* 30 October 1921 (now in A. Gramsci, *Socialismo e Fascismo* cit., pp. 382–3). In 1921 Gramsci even compared the Trade Unions to eighteenth-century states, as being nothing but bureaucracies, destined to be replaced in the twentieth century by workers' councils, just as the absolutist state had been replaced in the nineteenth century by bourgeois parliamentary regimes ('Funzionarismo', in *Ordine Nuovo* 4 March 1921, now in A. Gramsci, *Socialismo e Fascismo* cit., pp. 89–91).

[90] cf. R. Michels, *Political Parties* (English translation published by Jarrold, London, n.d. [1915?]), pp. 314–21, for an analysis of this phenomenon. Gramsci was acquainted with Michels' work.

[91] 'Sindacati e Consigli', in *Ordine Nuovo* 12 June 1920 (now in A. Gramsci, *Ordine Nuovo* cit., p. 135).

[92] *ibid.*, p. 134.

[93] 'Il Partito e la Rivoluzione' in *Ordine Nuovo* 27 December 1919 (now in A. Gramsci, *Ordine Nuovo* cit., p. 71).

[94] 'Mandarini', in *Ordine Nuovo* 23 June 1921 (now in A. Gramsci, *Socialismo e Fascismo* cit., p. 208).

[95] 'I Sindacati e la Dittatura' in *Ordine Nuovo* 25 October 1919 (now in A. Gramsci, *Ordine Nuovo* cit., pp. 39–44; see especially pp. 40 and 43).

in determining the success or failure of the revolution. Whereas in
Hungary the Trade Union leaders had refused to play a constructive role,
because of their bureaucratic attitudes and their desire to perpetuate the
era of negotiated agreements and social legislation within bourgeois
society, in Russia

> the Unions have become the bodies in which the individual firms of a
> given industry are amalgamated and joined, so as to form large indus-
> trial units. Wasteful competition is eliminated, and the big admini-
> strative services, of supply, distribution, and accumulation, are unified
> in large-scale central headquarters. New work-systems, trade secrets,
> and new techniques become known immediately throughout the
> whole industry. The multiplicity of bureaucratic, disciplinary functions
> inherent in private ownership and in individual firms are reduced to the
> basic necessities of industry.[96]

Gramsci's views on the Unions thus have several interesting characteristics. The *existing* Trade Unions were likely to prove harmful to the cause
of revolution, because of their essential 'legality' – their leaders regarded
the present structure of society as eternal. However, Trade Union discipline and solidarity were vital for the success of the revolution. But the
Unions he envisaged as carrying out the essential task of 'coordination'
would clearly be Industrial, not Craft, Unions, i.e. would include clerical
staff and technicians as well as manual workers, and would be structurally
different from the existing Unions. He thus faced the task of gradually
'transforming' the Unions in two ways: (1) in order to set up Industrial
Unions,[97] and (2) to infuse the existing Trade Unions with revolutionary
discipline, 'a discipline that will appear to the masses as a necessity for the
triumph of the workers' revolution';[98] and this had to be done without
immediately overthrowing the 'industrial legality' on which so much of
the Unions' prestige, usefulness, and disciplinary powers were founded.

It must be emphasised that Gramsci's views on the Unions were
independent of his Factory Council proposals. The essential difference
between the two institutions was, once again, the question of legality.
Whereas the Factory Council was the negation of industrial legality, the

[96] 'Sindacati e Consigli' in *Ordine Nuovo* 11 October 1919 (now in A. Gramsci,
Ordine Nuovo cit., p. 38).

[97] It should be remembered, however, that the Italian Unions were in any case far
larger than most British Trade Unions; the metal-workers' Union, *F.I.O.M.*, for
example, had 200,000 members in 1920, including most manual trades in the engineering industries. Hence the problem of creating Industrial Unions was not so great as
might appear.

[98] 'Sindacati e Consigli', in *Ordine Nuovo* 12 June 1920 (now in A. Gramsci, *Ordine
Nuovo* cit., p. 134).

Trade Union was its incarnation;[99] whereas the Factory Council aimed at conquering industrial power, the Trade Union's task was to ensure that its members respected existing industrial arrangements. As the two institutions were so different in nature and functions, they must be kept strictly separate; the only possible link between them should be that 'the majority, or a conspicuous part, of the Council's electors are Trade Union members. Any attempt to link the two institutions by ties of hierarchical dependence can lead only to the destruction of both'.[100] If the Unions succeeded in controlling the Factory Councils, the latter would cease to express the revolutionary aspirations of the whole working class; if, on the other hand, the Unions became subordinated to the Factory Councils, they would be unable to maintain industrial legality and would thus 'lose their capacity to make commitments and their character as a disciplinary force regulating the impulsiveness of the working class.'[101] Hence the two institutions had to be kept separate; but Gramsci also insisted that the growing importance of the Factory Councils would have a big influence on the Trade Unions and would, by making the workers more 'conscious', make it possible for the reformist bureaucrats to be removed from the Union leadership and for the Unions to acquire the 'revolutionary discipline' he considered so desirable. 'The Factory Council . . . cannot be coordinated with or subordinated to the Union, but by its birth and development brings about radical changes in the structure and form of the Trade Union.'[102] It appears that Gramsci regarded this as an inevitable consequence of the Factory Council movement: 'the revolutionary character of the Council will have an influence on the Trade Union, and will dissolve Trade Union bureaucracy and officialdom'.[103] When this happened, the discipline enforced by the Unions would be accepted by the Councils, and there would then be no danger of revolutionary energies being wasted in impulsive, unorganised revolts.

Gramsci's insistence that the Factory Councils were totally distinct from the Trade Unions, and that there should be no organisational links between the two institutions, was not accepted by most of his colleagues

[99] Note Gramsci's use of the idea of 'legality' with reference to a 'private' (non-State) institution – perhaps a harbinger of his later views on 'hegemony'. On 'legality', see pp. 60–1.

[100] 'Sindacati e Consigli' in *Ordine Nuovo* 12 June 1920 (now in A. Gramsci, *Ordine Nuovo* cit., p. 133).

[101] *ibid.*, p. 134.

[102] 'La Relazione Tasca e il Congresso Camerale di Torino', in *Ordine Nuovo* 5 June 1920 (now in A. Gramsci, *Ordine Nuovo* cit., p. 130).

[103] 'Sindacati e Consigli', in *Ordine Nuovo* 12 June 1920 (now in A. Gramsci, *Ordine Nuovo* cit., p. 133).

on the *Ordine Nuovo*. In practice, it proved impossible to avoid linking the two problems of creating Factory Councils and of 'democratising' the Unions; and the *Ordine Nuovo* thus became associated with attempts to give the Workshop Commissars a decisive influence in Union decisions.[104] Proposals on these lines were first put forward as early as June 1919, by Enea Matta, who urged that the Internal Commissions should elect the members of the General Council of the local Chamber of Labour.[105] On 16 August 1919 Ottavio Pastore argued in the *Ordine Nuovo* that the Internal Commissions should be incorporated into the Unions, and made the basis of Union organisation. Gramsci never wrote a line in support of this policy, and it was clearly in contradiction with his view of the Factory Councils as purely revolutionary bodies. Nevertheless, much of the *Ordine Nuovo* movement's practical importance arose from the conflict with the Union officials that the policy brought about; and it remains true that even in Gramsci's own theory the Councils were regarded as the means whereby the Unions' reformism could be overthrown.

The *Ordine Nuovo* was often accused, by the reformist Trade Union leaders, of being a syndicalist movement; and there is no doubt that the revolutionary syndicalists of the *U.S.I.* were attracted by Gramsci's attacks on reformist Unionism, his wish to establish Industrial Unionism, and his evident desire for revolution.[106] Nevertheless, even if the syndicalists did often take the initiative in Factory Council agitation, especially outside Turin, this was hardly Gramsci's fault. Gramsci envisaged an essentially political movement, with a strong, centralised, political party; and Gramsci had nothing but contempt for the 'pseudo-revolutionary' syndicalists, who refused to 'prepare' for revolution, and whose greatest error was to 'regard as a permanent fact, as a perennial type of association, the Trade Union, in its present form and with its present functions'[107] – a form dictated by capitalist society, and therefore unable to supersede it.

The *Ordine Nuovo* has also been accused, more recently, of being a 'productivist' movement[108] – of being obsessed with the worker-as-producer (instead of the worker-as-exploited); of being devoted to the interests of skilled literate industrial workers in an advanced city of Northern Italy (instead of to the unskilled and peasants, still the bulk of the population); of being Puritanical and contemptuous of popular

---

[104] See pp. 84–6 and pp. 135–7.

[105] cf. E. Soave, 'Appunti sulle Origini Teoriche e Pratiche dei Consigli di Fabbrica a Torino' in the *Rivista Storica del Socialismo*, no. 21 (1964), p. 16.

[106] See Chapter Six, pp. 115 ff.

[107] 'La Conquista dello Stato', in *Ordine Nuovo* 12 July 1919 (now in A. Gramsci, *Ordine Nuovo* cit., p. 15).

[108] G. Maione, *Il Biennio Rosso* (Il Mulino, Bologna 1975), pp. 24, 79, 86–7.

traditions, especially insurrectionary traditions; above all, of advocating Taylorism, the 'scientific organisation of labour'. These charges are justified. Gramsci in 1919 was a serious revolutionary, not a popular demagogue. Factory Councils would 'educate' and 'discipline' the masses, and enable workers to *develop* their own 'authentic' consciousness through the hard lessons of political and industrial experience. They would advocate and incarnate hard work, skills, discipline – the traditional 'worker-aristocratic' virtues; and they were designed to overcome the useless insurrectionism, the mindless rioting and striking, which were in Gramsci's view characteristic of the Italian Left, and which would inevitably lead to defeat.

As for Taylorism, Gramsci's followers welcomed it in terms of an alliance between the 'productive forces' (workers and management) against the parasitic power of finance-capital.[109] Taylorism, like the Factory Council, was merely one aspect of a vast and necessary effort to 'make' an Italian working class, to produce a new type of worker, sober, disciplined, industrious and monogamous. Gramsci was concerned not only with the changes in men's consciousness that were necessary for 'revolution', but also with those necessary for any industrial system. Both Taylorism and the Factory Councils had their part to play. In his later Prison Notebooks, Gramsci wrote that the *Ordine Nuovo* had supported its own kind of 'Americanism' acceptable to the workers; and that the Italian workers had been, in these years, the bearers of new, more modern industrial requirements, and had never objected to innovations or to 'rationalisation' of labour.[110] No doubt he exaggerated. Even so, Gramsci's theories cannot be understood unless this aspect is stressed. Taylorism and the Factory Councils were linked. Rational factory organisation would promote a sense of participation in collective effort, and the Factory Councils themselves could be defined as an attempt to make 'subjective' what was given 'objectively', to make workers fully aware of the complexities of industrial production and factory organisation.[111] Gramsci always insisted on the need for discipline and sobriety – for example, he thought Prohibition in the U.S.A. an excellent idea[112] – and he regarded Taylorism – and perhaps even Marxism, at times – as a kind

[109] See C. Petri (Pietro Mossi), 'Il Sistema Taylor e i Consigli di Produttori', in *Ordine Nuovo* 25 October, 1, 8 and 15 November 1919. cf. also L. Paggi, *Gramsci e il Moderno Principe* (Riuniti, Rome 1970), vol. i, pp. 257–8; and P. Fiorentina, 'Ristrutturazione Capitalistica e Sfruttamento Operaio in Italia negli Anni Venti', in *Rivista Storica del Socialismo*, anno X, no. 30 (January–April 1967), pp. 134–54, esp. p. 135.

[110] A. Gramsci, *Note sul Machiavelli, sulla Politica e sullo Stato Moderno* (Einaudi, Turin 1955), pp. 317, 321–2.

[111] A. Gramsci, *Passato e Presente* (Einaudi, Turin 1954), pp. 78–9.

[112] A. Gramsci, *Note sul Machiavelli, sulla Politica e sullo Stato Moderno* cit., p. 311.

of late-industrial 'Methodism', with important ideological functions. They were both part of the education of the Italian working class; and through them, Italian workers would abandon their facile, spontaneous revolts and their traditional 'subversivism', and learn to take a broader, more 'modern' view.

These, then, were Gramsci's ideas on Factory Councils, as expressed during 1919–20. In many ways, they were a conceptual response to the particular political and social situation described in Chapters One and Two, and of course also to the Russian Revolution and other foreign experience;[113] but they also had (and have) improtant implications for future political and social activity. His concept of Factory Councils, designed to replace the parliamentary system and transform the whole nature of the Trade Unions, represented a full-scale attack on reformist right-wing Socialism; and his insistence that political action must be united with industrial action if it were to be effective, represented a full-scale attack on the domination of traditional left-wing Socialism by the rhetorical 'maximalists'.

I have outlined and analysed Gramsci's ideas at some length, because they are interesting ideas in themselves and because they have been influential. However, I am aware that to analyse them in this way may be misleading. I do not want to imply that Gramsci was always consistent. On the contrary, his views were painfully elaborated over an eighteen-month period, often in argument with others or because of the pressure of particular events. There were certainly shifts of emphasis in this period – 'Communist groups', for example, and the need for a 'Communist' Party (p. 174), became more frequent themes later in 1920. And it is worth remembering that many of Gramsci's ideas were not shared by his *Ordine Nuovo* colleagues. Tasca, in particular, was leading the local Trade Union opposition to his views by May 1920, and both Togliatti and Terracini had profound disagreements with Gramsci in the summer of 1920 (see Chapter Seven).

Gramsci's ideas were thus isolated within the *Ordine Nuovo*, and certainly the *Ordine Nuovo*'s ideas remained isolated within the Italian labour movement. The periodical was largely confined to Turin itself,[114]

---

[113] The *Ordine Nuovo* printed many articles on German and British experience of Workers' Councils and Shop Stewards, on the Hungarian Revolution and on the ideas of Daniel De Leon. On De Leon, see P. Spriano, *Ordine Nuovo* cit., pp. 55–8; and I. Silone, 'Influenze Americane nel Pensiero di Gramsci', in *Corrispondenza Socialista* 16 February 1958.

[114] But not entirely. According to Terracini, the fifth or sixth name on the list of regular postal subscribers was that of Gabriele D'Annunzio. (U. Terracini, 'Gramsci e i Consigli di Fabbrica', in *Il Calendario del Popolo* February 1955, p. 1931).

and never achieved a circulation above 6,000. Nevertheless, its influence in Turin was enormous. It rapidly became the most widely read political weekly in the city, and its method of distribution, 'almost exclusively through the 'direct action' of friends',[115] ensured that each copy was read by as many workers as possible. Of the total circulation of just over 3,000 reached by August 1919, only just over 150 were sold through news-agents; there were 400 postal subscribers, the remaining copies being sold through Socialist Party branches, youth organisations etc, and resold by their members in the factories.[116] This method of 'Communist distri-bution' ensured both a higher financial return per copy, and a means of overcoming normal commercial distribution difficulties while still reaching the public of intellectuals (via subscriptions, which eventually rose to 1,100) and workers (via factory distribution) for whom the review was intended.

Although attention has been concentrated in this chapter on Gramsci's *political* theories, it would be quite wrong to regard the *Ordine Nuovo* as *only* a vehicle for political ideas. Gramsci's emphasis on 'consciousness', and his conception of culture as a revolutionary force, gave the review an educational, even a moral, character. The range of contributions to the *Ordine Nuovo* was impressive. A typical week's issue (that of 13 August 1919, for example) contained an article by Gramsci on educational problems, an article by Tasca on 'professional culture', an anonymous article on Caporetto, a description of Jaurès by Anatole France, Lenin's 'Bourgeois Democracy and Proletarian Democracy', an article on Leonardo da Vinci, an article by Henri Barbusse on 'Religion and the Moral Law', Anatole France again on 'The Task of Teachers', a discussion of the Internal Commissions, and an article by Sylvia Pankhurst on inter-national affairs. Week after week, the workers of Turin were given an intense cultural 'preparation' that was an essential part of the *Ordine Nuovo*'s general revolutionary agitation.[117]

Indeed, at the height of the Factory Council campaign, in December 1919, when the movement was already a political reality at Turin, a 'school of propaganda' was set up to help the political education of the workers. All the main contributors to the *Ordine Nuovo* gave lectures on historical and theoretical topics.[118] These lecture-courses were designed to

[115] 'Cronache dell' Ordine Nuovo' in *Ordine Nuovo* 2 August 1919 (now in A Gramsci, *Ordine Nuovo* cit., p. 448).

[116] *ibid.* Circulation was reported as about 4,500 copies (plus 1,000–1,100 sub-scribers) in June 1920 ('Cronache dell' Ordine Nuovo', in *Ordine Nuovo* 26 June 1920).

[117] The best account of this aspect of the *Ordine Nuovo*'s activity is in L. Paggi, *Antonio Gramsci e il Moderno Principe* cit., vol. i, pp. 207–29. Paggi rightly stresses the influence of the pre-war Florentine review *La Voce*, and of the French *Clarté*.

[118] For the list of subjects, see *Ordine Nuovo* 29 November 1919.

complement the educational and revolutionary programme of the *Ordine Nuovo* itself. The 'school' did not last long enough for the original courses to be completed, being swamped by the success of the Factory Councils,[119] but it is arguable that this educational aspect of the *Ordine Nuovo*'s activity was as important to Gramsci as the Factory Council agitation itself. In the last resort, however deeply one may analyse Gramsci's Factory Council ideas or their political impact, Gobetti's judgement remains valid: 'Gramsci was more than a tactician or a militant: he was a prophet.'[120]

[119] 'La Scuola di Partito' in *Ordine Nuovo* 1 April 1925 (now in A. Gramsci, *La Costruzione del Partito Comunista*, Einaudi, Turin 1971, pp. 48–50).
[120] P. Gobetti, *Coscienza Liberale e Classe Operaia* (Einaudi, Turin 1951), p. 130.

CHAPTER FOUR

Factory Councils in Turin

THIS chapter will be mainly concerned with the impact of the Factory Council agitation on the industrial and political situation of Turin. However, it is important to remember that Gramsci regarded the campaign as an attempt to solve the problem facing the left wing of the Italian Socialist Party at *national* level – how to carry through a successful revolution despite the opposition of Trade Union leaders and reformist deputies, whose collaboration would be needed for any General Strike, and whose experience would prove invaluable after any seizure of power. I shall therefore start by discussing briefly developments in the *national* labour movement in the summer and autumn of 1919, and this will explain some of the reasons for the Factory Councils' eventual failure even in Turin.

In the summer of 1919 the dissension between reformists and maximalists was at its height, and one of the contentious issues was whether to co-operate with the *U.S.I.* syndicalists. On 17 April 1919, the syndicalists' leader, Armando Borghi, proposed a 'united revolutionary front'. His suggestion was that a 'National Committee of Revolutionary Action' should be set up, containing representatives of the *P.S.I.*, *C.G.L.*, *U.S.I.*, the anarchists, and the Railwaymen's Union; this proposal was enthusiastically welcomed at the May Day mass meeting in Turin and Milan.[1] If this 'united front' had been formed, perhaps the chances of successful revolution would have been greater. Some members of the *P.S.I.* Directorate, such as Bombacci, were in favour of accepting the proposal; but caution eventually prevailed, and it is worth investigating why. Fortunately, we have a police informer's report of the views of G. M. Serrati, the most influential member of the party Directorate and the editor of the party's newspaper *Avanti!* At this time Serrati, the leading 'maximalist' in the *P.S.I.*, was not ready to begin active preparations for revolt:

[1] *Guerra di Classe* 19 April and 24 May 1919. For information on the various labour organisations listed here, see p. 34.

[Serrati] believes that society is now ripe for a transformation, but this can only come about through a revolt, an organised revolt which is based on, and has roots among, the middle strata of the bourgeoisie, and especially in the barracks. According to him, revolutionary tendencies are fairly widespread in Italy, but they are not well organised, and hence the main task is to embark on this work of organisation so as to have a disciplined force at hand at the decisive moment. The recent workers' agitations can be regarded as a kind of training for the workers towards the goal of revolution, but Serrati has, however, had to admit that at the moment there is no cause for over-optimism, because with the exception of a few big centres in North Italy, some areas near Bologna, and to some extent the Marches, all the rest is incapable even of making any kind of collective gesture. Some of the demobilised soldiers have been recruited to our cause, he said, but this has only been because of their economic discontent; if they can manage to get along reasonably all right in the future in civilian life, it is certain that they will not respond to any revolutionary appeal.[2]

For Serrati, therefore, the vital necessity, before revolution could be begun, was to organise a disciplined striking force. It is easy to see why, holding views like these, he did not wish to cement a close alliance with the anarchists and syndicalists in April–May 1919.

The outlook of the party's maximalist Directorate was also revealed clearly by the food riots at the end of June 1919. These riots, which broke out only a week after the report on Serrati's attitude was sent from Paris, presented, to all appearances, the most serious threat to the established order that had yet occurred in post-war Italy. They were mainly caused by a sharp increase in food prices in May and June: the retail price index of foods at Milan rose from 287.5 in April to 344.9 in June (1912 = 100).[3] Rioting began in the syndicalist stronghold of La Spezia and in anarchist Forli, and spread throughout other anarchist and syndicalist areas in Liguria and Romagna before reaching the Socialist North and Emilia.[4] In some towns and villages, 'Soviets' were set up; almost everywhere, shops were sacked and local food committees were hastily improvised to deal with a

[2] R. Ambasciata d'Italia, Paris, to Ministry of the Interior 23 June 1919, in *State Archives*, Min. Int., Dir. Gen. P.S., Aff. Gen. e Ris., 1919, b. 58, 'Partito Socialista Ufficiale: Affari Generali'.

[3] Figures of the Ufficio Statistico Municipale of Milan, quoted by R. Bachi, *Italia Economica 1919* (Lapi, Città di Castello 1920), p. 161.

[4] For these riots, see A. Tasca, *Nascita e Avvento del Fascismo* (La Nuova Italia, Florence 1950), p. 25; P. Nenni, *Il Diciannovismo* (Ed. *Avanti!*, Milan 1962), pp. 40–4; and R. Vivarelli, *Il Dopoguerra in Italia e l'Avvento del Fascismo* (Istituto Italiano per gli Studi Storici, Naples 1967), vol. i, pp. 412–18.

situation that rapidly threatened to get out of the authorities' control. If ever it looked as if revolution was about to break out, had indeed already broken out, this was it; yet the *P.S.I.* Directorate could not take the lead in this agitation, for not only did it smack too much of a 'spontaneous' anarchist rising, but also the party lacked the organisation and discipline necessary to convert the agitation into a real attempt at revolution. Nor, of course, could the party Directorate afford to repudiate the agitation entirely, and certainly it could not allow its members to sit on the *official* food committees set up by local Prefects and sub-Prefects to deal with the situation. The Directorate therefore issued an order forbidding its members (and this applied particularly to local Trade Unionists) from participating in these committees, even where (as at Turin) the local Trade Union leaders had already accepted seats on them, and even where the local shopkeepers had taken their keys to the Chamber of Labour.[5] The food riots, therefore, far from being the beginning of the Italian revolution, merely served to accentuate the differences between party Directorate and Trade Union leaders, and to reveal the bankruptcy of the maximalists' policy.

This impression of maximalist bankruptcy was heightened by the failure of the 'international' strike on 20–21 July 1919, called to express solidarity with Russia and Hungary, to spark off the revolution expected in many quarters.[6] By the end of July 1919 there was, in fact, no coherent policy the Directorate of the party could pursue. It continued to make fitful attempts to organise an armed revolutionary militia, mainly by means of propaganda in the barracks, and this caused the government some anxiety,[7] but anti-militarist sentiment remained strong among both party leaders and supporters, and was accentuated by the use of troops against demonstrations and strikes.[8] The real centre of *P.S.I.* activity after the summer of 1919 lay elsewhere. As it was impossible to carry through any kind of revolutionary policy without a highly organised striking force – and in the face of opposition from most of the party's experienced organisers in the Trade Unions and local Councils – that strategy was

---

[5] *Avanti!* (Turin ed.) 7–9 July 1919. 500 shopkeepers did so at Turin.

[6] For this strike, see P. Nenni, *Il Diciannovismo* cit., pp. 42–6; R. Vivarelli, *Il Dopoguerra in Italia e l'Avvento del Fascismo* cit., vol. i, pp. 435–54.

[7] Prime Minister Nitti was still worried about this in May 1920 – see his telegram to all Prefects on 14 May 1920: 'From information I have received from a reliable source it is beyond doubt that the revolutionary parties are anxiously seeking weapons and arms. Every effort must be made to find where the weapons are stored and sequestrate them' (*State Archives*, Min. Int., Dir. Gen. P.S., Aff. Gen. e Ris., 1921, b. 66, C2 'Armi e Munizioni').

[8] For the *P.S.I.*'s military policy, see G. Rochat, *L'Esercito Italiano da Vittorio Veneto a Mussolini* (Laterza, Bari 1967), pp. 232–8.

gradually abandoned. By mid-August 1919 the *P.S.I.* was totally absorbed in preparations for the General Election, the first since before the war, to be held in mid-November; it was already reckoning that it would get between 1,800,000 and 2 million votes, and that at least 120 Socialist deputies would be elected. In these circumstances, 'Serrati is maintaining that it is necessary to attempt revolution by the ballot, and to postpone the further, violent revolution to a more suitable time.'[9] Throughout the late summer and autumn of 1919 this process of rethinking within the Italian Socialist Party continued. As has been argued, this rethinking was mainly the result of the abortive food riots and General Strike of June and July, which had demonstrated the futility of the maximalist position; but it was helped also by the growing strength of the syndicalists (who claimed over 300,000 members by September 1919).[10] The syndicalist threat persuaded many left-wing Socialists of the need to maintain the power and prestige of the Socialist-led Unions. Moreover, the onset of the General Election campaign in the autumn brought about a natural closing of ranks within the party and seemed to demonstrate the possibility of effective non-revolutionary activity.

All these factors, therefore, contributed greatly to the process of removing much of the overt dissension within the *P.S.I.*, and between it and the *C.G.L.* It was possible for the XVI Congress of the *P.S.I.*, held at Bologna on 5–8 October 1919, to reach agreement on a new party programme to replace the 'Genoa Programme' of 1892; and although the victorious maximalist motion at the Congress,[11] with its emphasis on violent revolution and the dictatorship of the proletariat, claimed that Parliament and local communes were bourgeois institutions that could not be transformed into 'organs for the liberation of the proletariat', nevertheless the party agreed by an overwhelming majority to take part in the elections to the bourgeois Parliament.[12] Once the party was committed to this, it clearly needed all the support it could muster, including that of the right wing and the Unions. Hence the attempt of Amadeo Bordiga's

[9] Head of Information section of the Navy to Ministry of the Interior, 13 August 1919, in *State Archives*, Min. Int., Dir. Gen. P.S., Aff. Gen. e Ris., 1919, b. 58 'Partito Socialista Ufficiale: Affari Generali'.

[10] *Guerra di Classe* 27 September 1919. This figure did not, of course, include the 200,000 members of the Railwaymen's Union, which worked closely with the syndicalist *U.S.I.* on most occasions. The Railwaymen usually took the lead in arranging the various conferences on proletarian unity that took place in 1919 and 1920.

[11] The motion was published in *Avanti!* (Milan ed.) 17 August 1919, and in *Comunismo* 1 October 1919.

[12] The abstentionist motion put by Bordiga secured only 3,413 votes, as compared with 48,411 for the maximalists and 14,880 votes for the 'centrist' motion presented by Lazzari, which was also supported by the reformists.

left-wing group to secure the expulsion of the reformists was bound to prove fruitless. With the party statutes revised, agreement reached on participation in elections, and the need for revolutionary violence and some form of dictatorship of the proletariat verbally accepted by all, the reconciliation between the various wings of the party was a real one, not a mere facade for electoral purposes. The fundamental choice had already been made by Serrati, when he recognised the need to be organised and 'ready' for the revolution – the party could only be this if all its organisations, both local and national, were intact. Given this recognition, there was only one possible answer to Treves, a leading reformist, when he asked 'Do you think it is wise for the Socialist Party to break off all contact with the economic organisations?'[13]

These tendencies in the party were naturally much strengthened by the results of the General Election, held on 16 November 1919: the party enjoyed an electoral triumph, winning 156 of the 508 seats in the Chamber of Deputies.[14] Henceforth, much of the party's energies – and the activity of most of its leading members – was to be concentrated in Parliament; and a party whose activity is centred on Parliament is unlikely to engage in serious revolutionary activity. By the autumn of 1919, therefore, the *P.S.I.* had very largely ceased its exceedingly lukewarm attempts to organise a revolution, was more united than it had been for years, and was fully committed to parliamentary activity and to support of the Trade Unions and other existing Socialist organisations, defending the Socialist voter within the existing order of society.

This new reconciliation within the Socialist Party was, needless to say, regarded with anxiety on its left-wing. Some of the maximalist leaders, such as Bombacci, remained committed, at least in public, to establishing the dictatorship of the proletariat immediately; and there were other groups within the party to the left of the maximalists. The most important was Bordiga's 'Abstentionist Faction', hostile to participation in elections and to parliamentary activity in general; its refusal to take part in

[13] *Il XVI Congresso Nazionale Socialista di Bologna* (Resoconto Stenografico), Ed. *Avanti!*, Milan 1920, p. 79.

[14] The *P.S.I.* secured 32.2 *per cent.* of the national vote, being particularly strong in Piedmont, Lombardy, Emilia and Tuscany (71 *per cent.* of the Socialist vote was in N. Italy and Emilia). It comprised two essential elements: the workers of the big Northern cities – Milan, Turin, Bologna, Florence; and the agricultural wage-earners of the Po valley. For more details, see P. Bignami, 'I Partiti Politici nelle Diverse Regioni d'Italia', in *Nuova Antologia* 16 February 1920; U. Giusti, 'I Partiti Politici nei Grandi Comuni Italiani alla Vigilia delle Elezioni Amministrative', in *Nuova Antologia* 16 May 1920; C. S. Maier, *Recasting Bourgeois Europe* (Princeton U.P. 1975), pp. 128–34; and G. Galli & A. Prandi, *Patterns of Political Participation in Italy* (Yale U.P. 1970), pp. 331–2.

parliamentary activity was a means to an end, the revolution. Bordiga advocated the creation of a unified, disciplined party on the Russian model, to 'prepare' for revolution. There would be no place in such a party for reformists like Turati or Treves, and the first issue of *Il Soviet*, Bordiga's weekly journal founded in Naples immediately after the war, called for their expulsion from the party.[15] Expulsion of the right wing was regarded as a logical corollary of abstentionism; if parliamentary activity and participation in local government were regarded as undesirable, there was no need to retain in the party those who were indispensable for these jobs. Bordiga argued, therefore, that the only vital task facing Italian Socialists was to set up a disciplined 'Communist' Party, purged of its reformist elements, and devoted solely to illegal activity and to the seizure of power; as early as February 1920 *Il Soviet* was talking about 'the revolution that failed', and calling for the creation of a single homogeneous 'revolutionary political body to assume and coordinate the tactical leadership of the revolutionary battle'.[16] This propaganda continued throughout the second half of 1919 and the whole of 1920, but Bordiga's followers, although highly disciplined and adequately organised, were too few in numbers to represent a serious threat to the leadership of the *P.S.I.*; his influence was restricted to small groups of dedicated revolutionaries scattered throughout Italy. Even so, the 'abstentionists' did have a national organisation,[17] they were influential in Turin itself (see below, pp. 91–2), and their uneasy relationship with the '*Ordine Nuovo* group' determined much of the future history of the Italian labour movement.

These national developments, and the fact that the maximalists appeared incapable of giving a lead, no doubt helped to ensure the rapid spread of Factory Council ideas in Turin. Two days after the publication of the first 'Factory Council' article in the *Ordine Nuovo*,[18] Gramsci began outlining his ideas more fully at a series of meetings of the Turin branch of the *P.S.I.* The final meeting passed by 'a very large majority' a resolution deploring the reformist activities of the Socialist parliamentary deputies, criticising the inactivity of the Party Directorate, and declaring that the local branch of the party would 'begin *on its own initiative* [my italics] the immediate

---

[15] *Il Soviet* 22 December 1918.

[16] 'Vecchia Storia', in *Il Soviet* 1 February 1920.

[17] *Il Soviet* 11 April 1920 and 6 June 1920 lists the main centres of abstentionist support. A list of the branches that voted for Bordiga's motion at the Congress of the Socialist Party in October 1919 was printed in *Il Soviet* 20 October 1919.

[18] The article 'Democrazia Operaia' in *Ordine Nuovo* 21 June 1919 (see p. 56). The article was probably written, in fact, for the party branch meetings. P. Spriano (*Ordine Nuovo*, Einaudi, Turin 1963, pp. 40–2) wrongly states that the article appeared on 27 June.

task of practical Communist education among the proletarian masses of
Turin and province.'[19] Gramsci thus won the immediate support of the
local Socialist party branch; he had already secured the backing of the
local 'Federation of Socialist Circles', which had agreed to allow their
rooms to be used for propaganda in favour of the 'Communist reorganisation of labour in each individual industry'. A few days later it was
suggested by the Turin edition of *Avanti!* that there should be a special
meeting of all the Internal Commissions in Turin 'to discuss the reorganisation of production and workshop organisation in a collective regime'.
This was clearly an attempt to give publicity to the *Ordine Nuovo*'s new
ideas,[20] but the appeal was unsuccessful. Such a meeting was actually held
on 16 July, but for a more limited purpose: it was called by the local
Chamber of Labour to discuss practical arrangements for the 'international' strike on 20–21 July, it being the task of the Internal Commissions to ensure the success of the strike in their own factories.[21]

However, during the late summer there was much discussion in Turin
of all the relevant issues. According to Terracini, 'the entire proletariat
in the city became enthusiastic, and heated discussions took place in
meetings, assemblies and groups.'[22] These discussions were usually held
at the rooms of the 'Socialist Circles' throughout the city, and the support
of the Federation of Socialist Circles was thus of considerable importance
in spreading *Ordine Nuovo*'s ideas. Indeed, when Councils were later set
up in factories, the normal meeting place initially was the nearest Circle
room to the factory.[23]

The most 'heated' discussions were of the proposal that non-Union
members should be allowed to vote for Workshop Commissars (see pp.
56–7). Eventually a compromise was agreed. All workers might vote for a
Commissar, but the Commissars themselves had to be Union members,
as of course did the members of the Internal Commission, which was
elected by the Commissars. Only about a quarter of the metal-workers
in Turin province were reckoned to be members of *F.I.O.M.* at this
time,[24] so obviously 'votes to the unorganised' was an important issue.

---

[19] *Avanti!* (Turin ed.) 30 June 1919.

[20] 'Per Un Convegno delle Commissioni Interne', in *Avanti!* (Turin ed.) 3 July
1919. Regular meetings of the various Internal Commissions at Turin were already
being held for more mundane purposes, such as the discussion of pay scales, etc.
(see p. 44).

[21] *Avanti!* (Turin ed.) 17 July 1919.

[22] U. Terracini, 'I Consigli di Fabbrica', in *Almanacco Socialista 1920*, pp. 94–120;
his article was written in February 1920.

[23] Unsigned article in *Falce e Martello* 4 September 1920.

[24] *F.I.O.M.* claimed 16,643 members in Turin province on 1 June 1919 ('Relazione
Morale' of A. Uberti, to *F.I.O.M.* branch November 1919, p. 23). There were

It seems probable that Gramsci, who rejected any narrow view of the Commissars' functions, accepted the compromise in the hope that it would make it easier to overcome reformist dominance of the Trade Unions. The other major issue in these early discussions was linked to the question of 'votes to the unorganised'. What was to be the relationship between the Workshop Commissars and Internal Commissions on the one hand, and the Trade Union on the other? What role would the 'new' Internal Commissions play in Union matters? Here no compromise was reached, and as will be seen the issue remained in dispute as long as the Factory Councils survived in Turin.[25]

All these discussions at Turin took place while the leaders of *F.I.O.M.* were engaged in leading a strike of 200,000 metal-workers in Lombardy, Liguria, and Emilia, to secure a guaranteed minimum pay-scale that had already been granted in Piedmont the previous June (see p. 42). Thus the Union leaders' absence during the strike (which lasted from 7 August to 26 September) contributed considerably to the rapid spread of the Factory Council agitation. It was perhaps only fitting that the Factory Councils – which after all aimed at providing an *alternative* to traditional forms of militancy – should have been formed in the only major metal-working area where there were no serious strikes in the autumn of 1919.[26] Moreover, unemployment was much lower in Piedmont than in other industrial regions.[27] Fiat was receiving plenty of orders – 20,000 vehicles were ordered in the first half of 1919[28] – and was still busy fulfilling government requirements left over from 1918.[29] In Turin, Giovanni Agnelli's strategy of 'Fordism' – high investment, high wages, a contented reliable labour force – stood some chance of success, *provided that* economic expansion continued, piece-rate grievances did not explode, and production could be maintained at high levels. Left-wing awareness of this

probably 50–60,000 metal-workers in the province at this time (G. Prato, *Il Piemonte e gli Effetti della Guerra sulla sua Vita Economica e Sociale*, Laterza, Bari 1925, p. 131, gives 60,000 in 1923).

[25] See p. 65 ff. for Gramsci's views.

[26] M. Abrate, *La Lotta Sindacale nella Industrializzazione in Italia* (Angeli, Milan 1967), pp. 213, 219, 234.

[27] It reached a peak of 21,716 at the end of April 1919, and was reduced to 12,794 by June, 6,955 by October; Lombardy at the same dates had 93,551, 61,551 and 43,068, and Emilia had 99,096, 104,591, and 66,485. In Liguria, the unemployment situation worsened as the year went on: 6,460 at the end of April, 10,516 by June, and 16,255 by the end of October (G. Prato, *Il Piemonte e gli Effetti della Guerra sulla sua Vita Economica e Sociale* cit., p. 112).

[28] V. Castronovo, *Giovanni Agnelli* (U.T.E.T., Turin 1971), p. 177. Fiat exported 2,440 vehicles in 1919 (300 more than in the last pre-war year), and 7,879 vehicles in 1920.

[29] V. Castronovo, *Giovanni Agnelli* cit., pp. 173-4, writes of 15,000 vehicles still on order by the State.

strategy – and of its vulnerability – gave the Factory Councils added impetus.

The first practical development occurred when the Internal Commission at the main Fiat works resigned, and was replaced by a temporary Commission with a mandate to organise the election of a 'Commissar' in each work-unit, or *reparto*.[30] However, this was not a simple case of a victory for *Ordine Nuovo*'s ideas. Several attempts had already been made to force the members of the former Internal Commission to resign, on the grounds of their 'old-fashioned ideas' and their close connection with F.I.O.M. – it was alleged that some of the members even held Union jobs.[31] The temporary Commission clearly hoped the election of workshop representatives would prevent interference by the local Union leaders; but the election of the Commissars, in which only Union members were allowed to vote,[32] failed to produce an anti-Union majority. The new Internal Commission chosen by the Commissars saw its task as merely that of 'assisting in all controversies that may arise in the workshops concerning agreements between the Industrial League and the Metal-Workers' Federation', in which it affirmed its confidence.[33] The Internal Commission at the main Fiat works was to prove the most 'conservative' – or 'militant' in the traditional manner – of the Internal Commissions in Turin during the next few months.

The *Ordine Nuovo* campaign had rather more success at the Brevetti Fiat works, where after a meeting on 31 August addressed by Gramsci, elections for Commissars were held in each work-unit.[34] All but three or four of the 2,000 workers in the factory voted, but only members of F.I.O.M. were eligible to be elected.[35] Throughout September and October the system was adopted by one metal-working factory after another; by the end of October nearly all the main factories in Turin had Workshop Commissars and an Internal Commission elected by them.[36] In

[30] *Avanti!* (Turin ed.) 21 August 1919. There were 42 *reparti*.

[31] *Avanti!* (Turin ed.) 10 September 1919.

[32] See Bordigari's speech to the Assembly of Commissars of the Workshop Councils on 27 November, reported in *Avanti!* (Turin ed.) 1 December 1919.

[33] *Avanti!* (Turin ed.) 16 September 1919.

[34] See reports in *Avanti!* (Turin ed.) 1 and 6 September 1919.

[35] cf. 'Cronache dell' Ordine Nuovo', in *Ordine Nuovo* 13 September 1919 (now in A. Gramsci, *Ordine Nuovo*, Einaudi, Turin 1955, pp. 455–7) for a description of the election and the names of the first Commissars. One elected Commissar, a member of the clerical Popular Party, was forced to resign when it was discovered he was not a member of F.I.O.M.

[36] At the Lancia works, the idea was approved on 17 September, and the first meeting of the Commissars was held on 12 October. By 16 October there was a new Internal Commission at the Fiat Lingotto Works; one had met on 22 September at Fiat Barriera di Nizza. The idea was approved at Ansaldo S. Giorgio by 17 October;

practice, however, the initial effect of the *Ordine Nuovo*'s propaganda was largely limited to establishing a new method for electing the Internal Commissions, whose actual functions were scarcely altered. Even this was not as novel as might appear: *F.I.O.M.* had always tried to maintain *fiduciari* in the workshops to act as dues-collectors, and the old Internal Commissions had always called in representatives from the individual work-units when specialised advice had been needed – indeed, the metal-workers' agreement of February 1919 had expressly allowed the Internal Commission to use the advice of three *fiduciari* from each workshop if necessary.[37] All this no doubt helped Factory Council ideas to be rapidly accepted; as the workers at the Spa factory put it in October:

> The workshop *fiduciari* used to carry out the tasks in the workshop that will now be carried out by the Commissars, but it is recognised that the introduction of the elective principle, and the organic organisation of the Commissars in accordance with the organisation of industry, in itself represents a step forward and is the basis of fertile social progress.[38]

The limits of the *Ordine Nuovo* campaign's success in its initial stages may be gauged from events at the Itala factory: after a favourable vote in a referendum held to decide whether Commissars should be elected, their election took place on 7 October, 'every worker being both elector and eligible';[39] yet when the Workshop Commissars met for the first time on 12 October, they elected all the members of the former Internal Commission on to the new one.[40]

Initially, therefore, the elements of continuity helped *Ordine Nuovo*'s ideas to be readily accepted, but it would be wrong to lay too much emphasis on the continuity of the old institutions with the new. Hostility soon arose between the Workshop Commissars and the reformist leaders of the local Chamber of Labour.[41] The first real clash occurred when the

elections of Commissars were held at Acciaierie Fiat on 23 October; and the workers at Ansaldo Pomilio had elected Commissars by 28 October (see *Avanti!*, Turin ed., 16 and 24 September, 16, 17, 24 and 29 October 1919).

[37] For the agreement, see p. 41; the full text of the agreement was printed in *Battaglie Sindacali* 8 March 1919.

[38] *Avanti!* (Turin ed.) 17 October 1919.

[39] *Avanti!* (Turin ed.) 7 October 1919. The result of the referendum was: 555 for Commissars, 19 against, and 162 undecided.

[40] *Avanti!* (Turin ed.) 13 October 1919.

[41] The Chamber of Labour was an organisation modelled on the French *Bourse du Travail*, and designed to unite all members of different Craft Unions, living in a given locality, for common action. It normally acted in conjunction with local Union leaders, and was usually controlled by them; there existed a few syndicalist Chambers, but most of them adhered to the reformist Socialist *C.G.L.*

Chamber of Labour accepted the local Prefect's ban on a mass meeting that was protesting against D'Annunzio's seizure of Fiume. On 17 October a special meeting of the newly elected Internal Commissions – i.e. the executive committees of the various Factory Councils – unanimously approved a motion describing the Chamber of Labour's order as proof of a 'retrograde spirit', and called for 'recognition by the Trade Union organisations of the new system of direct representation of the workers'.[42] Three days later, on 20 October, a further meeting appointed one member from each Internal Commission to sit on a provisional 'Committee of Study', designed not only to help coordinate the activity of the various Councils and draw up a policy-programme, but also to discuss the relations between the Councils and the Trade Unions, which by late October had come to be the main problem affecting the new organisations.[43]

This problem had to be faced urgently, in view of the forthcoming Annual General Meeting of the Turin branch of F.I.O.M., which had been called for 1 November. A further meeting of representatives of the Internal Commissions of seventeen factories was therefore held on 22 October, and those present pledged themselves to put forward a list of candidates, to be chosen by all the Commissars, for the new executive committee of the branch.[44] On 31 October, on the eve of the Annual General Meeting, a full meeting of Workshop Commissars met to discuss the 'programme' drawn up by the Committee of Study appointed on 20 October, as well as the more general problem of relations with the Union.

This 'programme', entitled 'Programme of the Workshop Commissars',[45] proclaimed that 'the Union members in the Councils accept without discussion that discipline in partial or general economic conflicts is laid down by the Unions, but only when the Unions' directives are themselves laid down by the Factory Commissars, as representatives of the working masses'. The Commissars of a given district or city were to elect the executive committee of the Union's local branch, and wage agreements had to be approved by the Commissars before becoming valid. The 'programme' was approved unanimously by the Workshop Commissars, and the meeting went on to express its conviction that 'the

[42] Avanti! (Turin ed.) 20 October 1919. 15 factories were represented at this special meeting.

[43] cf. Gramsci's discussion of the problem, in 'Cronache dell' Ordine Nuovo', in Ordine Nuovo 25 October 1919 (now in A. Gramsci, Ordine Nuovo cit., pp. 462–3). The members of the provisional Committee of Study were: Boero, Cerri, Matta, Bordigari, Montano, Tosi, and Brunero (Avanti!, Turin ed., 29 October 1919).

[44] Avanti! (Turin ed.) 25 October 1919.

[45] 'Programma dei Commissari di Reparto', in Ordine Nuovo 8 November 1919 (now in A. Gramsci, Ordine Nuovo cit., pp. 192–9).

Trade Union organisation should be the direct expression of the wishes of its members, and such wishes can only be expressed organically by institutions based on the workshop.' It was also decided to put forward a list of eleven names (with five given to the reformists) to form the provisional executive committee of the local branch of F.I.O.M.[46] It is clear, therefore, that the agitation at Turin was largely one of opposition to local Union reformists. Gramsci's ideas on the relations between the Factory Councils and the Unions were far more subtle than those of the provisional Committee of Study (see p. 65 ff.), and Ordine Nuovo printed repeated warnings that the two institutions should be kept separate,[47] but even so the Ordine Nuovo movement was henceforth stamped as an anti-Union campaign.

The meeting of the Turin branch of F.I.O.M. on 1 November was, therefore, largely concerned with the issue of theWorkshop Commissars and their part in Union organisation. Alessandro Uberti, the secretary of the branch, recognised that some reorganisation was necessary: at this time the branch had over 16,000 members,[48] and thus a general assembly of all the members had become a physical impossibility. He agreed, therefore, that Workshop Commissars should be elected, to replace the old assembly of members as the 'consultative organ' of the branch; but they should not be given any deliberative powers, nor should non-Union men be allowed to vote in their election.[49] He strongly opposed the suggestion that the Commissars should elect the branch executive committee, and urged that the executive committee should be appointed by a General Council, to consist of about 100–150 members, elected by all members of the Union. For Uberti, the very existence of the Union was at stake; the extension of the vote to non-Union men represented a negation of the Trade Union's raison d'être as a 'specialised organ of the class struggle and expression of the wishes of class-conscious workers',[50] and the proposal to allow non-Union members to have a say, however indirectly, in the election of the branch executive committee was anathema.

[46] These resolutions were printed in Avanti! (Turin ed.) 1 November 1919.

[47] Apart from Gramsci's own writings, discussed in Chapter Three (pp. 65–9), reference may be made to Togliatti's criticism of Gino Castagno, in Ordine Nuovo 1 November 1919, and his postscript to an article by Montagnana in Ordine Nuovo 15 November 1919 (for the postscript, see P. Spriano, Ordine Nuovo cit., pp. 366–70), where he insisted that the two problems of creating the Councils and of democratising the Unions should be kept separate.

[48] See note 24, p. 80.

[49] Reports of the meeting appeared in Avanti! (Turin ed.) 2 November 1919 and in La Squilla 2 December 1919.

[50] Avanti! (Turin ed.) 2 November 1919.

D

Uberti was opposed by Boero and Garino, speaking for the motion approved by the Workshop Commissars the previous day. There was also a third 'Centrist' motion, which called for the Commissars to have a deliberative – not merely consultative – voice in Union affairs, but insisted that non-Union men be excluded from the elections of Commissars;[51] otherwise the motion followed Uberti's proposals, and its supporters later joined him. The 'Centrist' motion was based on the 'Programme of the Workers at Fiat–Centro', which regarded the Internal Commission as nothing more than 'the representative of the Trade Union in the workshop';[52] this 'Programme' had been drawn up by the Internal Commission at the main Fiat works. The 'extremist' motion was carried by 'a large majority', and the provisional executive committee of eleven duly elected. When the results were announced, the *F.I.O.M.* spokesman Castagno shouted ironically '*Viva l'U.S.I.!*'.[53]

This debate was repeated on a national scale a week later, at the meeting of *F.I.O.M.* leaders in Florence on 9 and 10 November. The meeting was attended by four of the leading Factory Council supporters from Turin – Garino, Boero, Sanmartino, and Cerri – as well as by a representative of the Turin minority, Carmagnola.[54] The official Union view was expressed in a motion that was passed unanimously, with the four Turin representatives abstaining:

the Union organisation must have entire responsibility for the movement and activity of the class, both within and outside the factory, and it is the duty of Union members to fortify it and increase its authority both towards the industrialists and towards the non-Union masses; [we] draw the attention of all our members to the dangers and consequences within the Union that may arise from the creation of new institutions that may be regarded as superimposed on the Union, which would thus come to be placed under the predominant influence of the non-Union masses.

[We] decide to allow the experiment of Factory Councils, but only insofar as their functions are regarded as the continuation of the work of the Internal Commissions and are co-ordinated with those of the Union, on whose principles they must be based, insofar as they are restricted to centres containing the best Union elements, and insofar as they define their tasks so as to avoid the growth of facile illusions among the

[51] See Caretto's speech, in *La Squilla* 2 December 1919.
[52] This 'Programme' was printed in *Ordine Nuovo* 27 December 1919.
[53] *Avanti!* (Turin ed.) 2 November 1919.
[54] *Relazione Morale* of Turin branch of *F.I.O.M.*'s activity 1 November 1919 – 30 June 1920, p. 3.

masses, which would eventually cause great damage to the class Union itself.[55]

This motion, while not condemning the Councils outright, was the first official expression of *F.I.O.M.* disapproval of the movement; it dates from mid-November 1919.

Soon the Factory Council movement was no longer confined to the metal-workers. The Turin coach-builders and automobile body-workers approved the idea of Workshop Commissars on 29 November;[56] the local branch of the *P.S.I.* voted in favour of the scheme on 11 December;[57] the Turin branch of the Chemical and Tyre Workers' Union, after hearing a speech by Gramsci, voted unanimously on 12 December to set up Factory Councils;[58] and even the technicians in the metal-working factories voted on 6 December to support the creation of Factory Councils and to urge the Chamber of Labour to carry out a 'thorough systematic study of the question'.[59] In short, the reformist Union leaders in Turin were faced with a serious threat to their position; their attempts to absorb the Internal Commissions into the Union structure had proved unsuccessful.

The culmination of this initial phase was the debate on Factory Councils at the Congress of the Turin Chamber of Labour, on 14 and 15 December.[60] The debate was similar in most respects to the discussions at the local branch of *F.I.O.M.* a month earlier, but had more important repercussions locally and nationally, affecting as it did all local industries. It, too, centred on the question of relations between the Unions and the Factory Councils. Bianchi, of the *C.G.L.*, speaking in support of the Union leaders in the Chamber of Labour, saw the Turin proposals as a threat to existing Union institutions;[61] Terracini cheerfully agreed, saying that the Councils would have to take over some of the present functions of the Unions 'in order to prevent them dying of inactivity'.[62] On the other hand, Gramsci insisted that the Councils 'should be understood primarily as the basis of political power . . . thus removing any political reality from the present formal structure of parliamentary democracy';[63] but even he was forced to recognise that before the revolution actually occurred, the

[55] Report in *Battaglie Sindacali* 22 November 1919.
[56] *Avanti!* (Turin ed.) 3 December 1919.
[57] It also elected a new 'Committee of Study' on the subject. See p. 93.
[58] *Avanti!* (Turin ed.) 13 December 1919.
[59] *Avanti!* (Turin ed.) 7 December 1919.
[60] Reports of the debates appeared in *Avanti!* (Turin ed.) 15 and 16 December 1919.
[61] *Avanti!* (Turin ed.) 16 December 1919.
[62] Terracini was alleged to have used this phrase by Manlio Benetti, in *Avanti!* (Turin ed.) 22 December 1919. His speech was reported on December 15.
[63] *Avanti!* (Turin ed.) 16 December 1919.

Factory Councils 'could only function as an amplification of the [ordinary] Trade Union realm',[64] although their *disciplinary* functions would also prove important.

This somewhat academic discussion ended with the defeat of the Chamber of Labour leaders, who had proposed a motion denying non-Union men the right to vote, calling on the Party and the *C.G.L.* to organise the creation of Councils, and advocating the setting up of a committee to regulate the functions of the local Councils.[65] Such a committee was clearly the Union leaders' last hope of regaining control of the situation at Turin. Approval was given, instead, by 38,489 votes to 26,219, to a motion claiming that the Turin experiment had been a great success in 'organising the whole people in the system of Workers' Councils', and calling for more intense propaganda elsewhere in Italy so that a national system of Councils could be set up.[66] The motion passed at the Chamber of Labour did not link the Commissars with the Unions, as the earlier motion of the Turin metal-workers had done. Nevertheless, the Congress' vote was tantamount to a recognition of the metal-workers' experiment, and it therefore provided grounds for opposition to reformist Trade Union leaders in other industries, as they were bound by Chamber of Labour decisions – a fact that the Committee of Study on the Councils soon pointed out.[67]

In the new year the Factory Councils continued to spread throughout Turin industry. By mid-January 1920 fourteen of the city's chemical factories had Councils,[68] and they had been discussed by the textile workers and the local printers.[69] Even the Fabbrica Italiana di Pianoforti had a Factory Council by mid-February.[70] Yet the impetus was going out of the movement. Local expansion was becoming more difficult; and despite all the rhetoric and the Congress debates, it was difficult to find anything for the Councils to *do*. In practice, one of their main functions was to help organise demonstrations and strikes on general political issues.

[64] 'Ampliamento del dominio sindacale'. cf. Tasca's comments on this phrase in *Ordine Nuovo* 12 June 1920, and Gramsci's explanation of his meaning in *Ordine Nuovo* 5 June 1920 (now in A. Gramsci, *Ordine Nuovo* cit., pp. 129–30). Gramsci appears to have meant this 'amplification' as involving radical changes in the policy and role of the Unions.

[65] *Avanti!* (Turin ed.) 16 December 1919.

[66] Figures in *Avanti!* (Turin ed.) 16 December 1919. There were 5,047 abstentions.

[67] *Avanti!* (Turin ed.) 28 December 1919.

[68] *Avanti!* (Turin ed.) 17 January 1920.

[69] cf. *Avanti!* (Turin ed.) 7 January and 9 March 1920. The textile workers decided to take no local initiative, but to raise the matter at their next national Congress. The local printers approved of Councils, but only in conjunction with their existing Union structures.

[70] *Avanti!* (Turin ed.) 10 February 1920.

The Fiume demonstration of October 1919 has been mentioned, and there was another widespread agitation in mid-November, concerning a fine of one quarter of a day's pay imposed by the employers on workers who had marked the anniversary of the Russian Revolution by striking on 7 November. The Internal Commissions called a strike of all the metal-workers, which lasted a week; when agreement was eventually reached, work was resumed on 24 November, in all factories except the main Fiat works.[71] Interestingly, this indiscipline at Fiat was regarded by supporters of the Commissars as proof that the Councils alone could bring about workers' discipline – the Commissars at the main Fiat works had not been elected in the normal way, but by Union members alone (see p. 82). Parodi, a Commissar at Fiat, 'deplored the indiscipline of the workers at Fiat to the decisions of the Workshop Commissars'; and Garino, a leading anarchist supporter of Factory Councils, told the Fiat workers that they were 'endangering the proletarian organisation and the creation of Workshop Commissars'.[72] In early December came another 'demonstration' strike. When some Socialist deputies were beaten up and arrested in Rome, protest marches were held in Turin, there were street battles with the police, and a two-day general strike. All these 'public' agitations were, of course, depressingly 'traditional' in kind, and far removed from Gramsci's aims.

However, there was another side to Factory Council activity. The Commissars in the engineering factories did contribute to detailed piece-rate studies carried out by the local branch of *F.I.O.M.*, and won substantial pay-rises for certain groups of workers, after a series of short strikes and stoppages that exasperated the management.[73] But this other aspect of the Councils' work was very similar to 'normal' Trade Union agitation – perhaps more militant than usual, but undeniably 'corporative' and non-revolutionary, and equally disappointing from Gramsci's perspective. Furthermore, these agitations revealed a distressing tendency among many workers to reject 'productivist' criteria and technical innovations, especially when they might mean more work for less pay. It was important, from the point of view of both management and the *Ordine*

---

[71] *Avanti!* (Turin ed.) 25 November 1919; for details, see M. Abrate, *La Lotta Sindacale nella Industrializzazione in Italia* cit., pp. 220–4.

[72] Both speeches reported in Prefect of Turin's telegram to Ministry of the Interior 25 November 1919, in *State Archives*, Min. Int., Dir. Gen. P.S., Aff. Gen. e Ris., 1919, b. 54, 2° Fascicolo. See also G. Maione, *Il Biennio Rosso* (Il Mulino, Bologna 1975), p. 61.

[73] See the report of the Consiglio d'Amministrazione of Fiat to the Annual Share-holders' Meeting in March 1921 (summarised in *Ordine Nuovo* 27 March 1921); and 'Un Anno di Lotte Formidabili contro la Schiavitù Capitalistica', in *Avanti!* (Turin ed.) 30 October 1920.

Nuovo, that these piece-rate issues should be settled quickly so that plant could be 'reconverted' to peace-time uses, but there is no evidence that the new Workshop Commissars were any more successful at 'disciplining' workers than the old Internal Commissions and Trade Unions had been,[74] and the number of agitations and stoppages strongly suggests otherwise. The Internal Commission at the main Fiat works claimed that there were 800 disputes (mainly on piece-rates and discipline) between October 1919 and 20 March 1920; and Giuseppe Prato reported 54 working days lost there in 1919, out of 306 (75 were lost in 1920, not including the Occupation of the Factories in September).[75]

Moreover, in practice it was impossible for the Workshop Commissars to acquire any very complete information about their factories. Finances, order books, new models, production plans and the like remained secret, except perhaps in some of the smaller firms like Lancia.[76] Thus both the 'disciplinary' and the 'preparatory' aspects of the Factory Councils' work proved unsatisfactory.

And the Councils were still restricted to Turin. Clearly the *Ordine Nuovo* had to become a national movement if it were to succeed in its national aims. Yet the rapprochement within the *P.S.I.*, between the maximalist Directorate and the reformist trade union leaders, ensured that Gramsci's proposals did not in fact secure the support of the maximalist party leadership.[77] The maximalist opposition to the *Ordine Nuovo* movement was based on the simple truth that the Factory Councils, as constituted at Turin, would undermine the authority and functions of the Trade Unions. By February 1920 Serrati was convinced that the *C.G.L.* was 'the only body in our country that does not live off bluff and beating the big drum.'[78] It has been seen that Gramsci's ideas were accepted at Turin because they were regarded as a practical means of overthrowing the power of the existing Union leadership. It is ironic that they were rejected at national level for precisely the same reason.

These disappointments account for Gramsci's increasing emphasis,

[74] V. Castronovo, *Giovanni Agnelli* cit., p. 219; G. Maione, *Il Biennio Rosso* cit., p. 50.

[75] 'Relazione del Comitato Esecutivo dei Commissari di Reparto alla Fiat-Centro', in *Ordine Nuovo* 27 March 1920; G. Prato, *Il Piemonte e gli Effetti della Guerra sulla sua Vita Economica e Sociale* cit., p. 148. Admittedly the Internal Commission at the main Fiat works had not been 'properly' elected, so perhaps disputes there should not be taken as evidence for the Councils' failure.

[76] Vincenzo Lancia, a splendid engineer and character, who often went drinking with his workers in the evenings, was not opposed to the Councils' activities. See M. Abrate, *La Lotta Sindacale nella Industrializzazione in Italia* cit., pp. 254–5, 260.

[77] For the maximalists' attitude to the *Ordine Nuovo* movement in general, see Chapter Six, pp. 124–9.

[78] 'Unione o Scissura?' in *Comunismo* 15–29 February 1920.

early in 1920, on the need to transform the Socialist Party,[79] and for his approaches to Bordiga's left-wing 'abstentionist' faction within the party. At Turin, the local abstentionists backed the Factory Council campaign enthusiastically. Their leader, Boero, even advocated Workers' Councils at the *P.S.I.* Congress in Bologna, but his speech was greeted with 'noise, conversation in the hall, and signs of weariness'.[80] In February 1920 an alliance between abstentionists and Gramsci's supporters on the *Ordine Nuovo* won a majority on the executive committee of the local Socialist party branch. These elections were important, for they revealed a serious conflict among the members of the original '*Ordine Nuovo* group':

A general assembly of members of the branch gave a mandate to an Electoral Committee, of which Tasca was a member, to draw up an electoral list ratifying the alliance between the Left and the abstentionists. But three days before the elections, Tasca broke with the abstentionists, and produced a list including some well-known reformists, even Garnerone. This list was luckily defeated by a list drawn up in a great hurry, consisting of eight abstentionists and three from the *Ordine Nuovo*, Gramsci, Togliatti, and Matta.[81]

The effect of this episode was to transform the working alliance between local abstentionists and the *Ordine Nuovo* into an alliance *against* the rest of the local party, with a programme ranging far beyond the original Factory Council one, and largely incompatible with the aims of the *P.S.I.* The printed programme of the successful candidates, after a general introduction condemning the domination of the *P.S.I.* by parliamentary reformists, and calling for Workers' Councils throughout Italy, went on to demand the expulsion of the reformists, an emergency Congress of the

[79] 'Primo: Rinnovare il Partito', in *Ordine Nuovo* 24–31 January 1920 (now in A. Gramsci, *Ordine Nuovo* cit., p. 389).

[80] Boero's speech was printed in *Il XVI Congresso Nazionale Socialista di Bologna* (Ed. *Avanti!*, Milan 1920, pp. 150–9). Sylvia Pankhurst, who attended the Bologna Congress as an observer, wrote that Boero was the only manual worker among the delegates (*Comunismo* 1–15 December 1919).

[81] 'Postilla', by Gramsci, to Tasca's 'Opportunismo di Destra e Tattica Sindacale', in *Lo Stato Operaio* 5 June 1924 (dated wrongly 5 May 1924; now in A. Gramsci, *La Costruzione del Partito Comunista*, Einaudi, Turin 1971, p. 188). Details of the episode remain obscure. The Electoral Committee's names, for example, given in *Avanti!* (Turin ed.) 7 January 1920, do not include Tasca's. Matta's name was included on both lists, despite his protests, and Terracini was included on the 'official' list, opposing Gramsci and Togliatti. Garnerone was one of the leaders of the local branch of the Printers' Union. The members of the new executive committee were: Matta, Furno, Togliatti, Gramsci, De Marta, Gilodi, Parodi, Pianezza, Boccalatte, Boero, and Roccati; their votes ranged from 239 to 234 (excluding Matta, who was on both lists and secured 434 votes), as compared with 215 for Terracini, who headed the 'official' list (*Avanti!*, Turin ed., 17 February 1920).

P.S.I., and the creation of a 'Central Commission of Workers' Control'. The question of abstentionism was left vague, the programme merely stating the candidates' intention to 'promote a full discussion on the best means of participation in local elections'.[82] It is noteworthy, too, that from this time the *Ordine Nuovo* began urging the formation of 'Communist groups', to be set up in every factory and Trade Union, in order to 'make the Party's point of view triumph';[83] the 'groups' were being strongly advocated by Bordiga at this time, but the first mention of them in the *Ordine Nuovo* was in the 'Programme of Action of the Turin Socialist Branch', drawn up in alliance with the local abstentionists.[84] Thus a split had taken place in the Turin branch of the *P.S.I.* by February 1920 that was similar to the national split at Leghorn eleven months later (see p. 197 ff.). Because of maximalist hostility to Factory Council ideas, the *Ordine Nuovo* was henceforth committed to alliance with the abstentionists, based on the above programme, if it wished to exert any political influence, even locally.[85]

Gramsci was later to regret this dependence. In 1924 he wrote:

> In 1919–20 we committed some very grave mistakes that we are still fundamentally paying for. Out of fear of being called 'arrivistes' or of being accused of career-mindedness, we failed to set up a proper faction and did not seek to organise one throughout Italy. We were not willing to make the Factory Councils at Turin into an independent centre of leadership, which might have exercised immense influence throughout the country, because we were afraid of splitting the Trade Unions and of being expelled from the Socialist Party too soon.[86]

However, this is a misleading account. In fact, Gramsci had very little choice but to try and ally with the abstentionists. In early 1920 he was becoming more concerned with questions of party organisation, and with 'Communist groups'; and the '*Ordine Nuovo* group' was badly split, and

[82] The programmes of both sides were printed in *Avanti!* (Turin ed.) 14 February 1920.

[83] *Avanti!* (Turin ed.) 16 March 1920.

[84] Published in *Ordine Nuovo* 24–31 January 1920.

[85] Bordiga was at Turin during the week-end when the hasty alliance between the *Ordine Nuovo* and the local abstentionists was formed. On 13 February he addressed a meeting at the Chamber of Labour, proclaiming the necessity of creating Workers' Councils and transforming the Trade Unions into effective weapons in the class struggle (Prefect of Turin to Ministry of the Interior 21 February 1920, in *State Archives*, Min. Int., Dir. Gen. P.S., Aff. Gen. e Ris., 1920, b. 67). This politic speech may be compared with Bordiga's views on the Factory Council movement – see p. 119 ff.

[86] Letter of Gramsci to Leonetti 28 January 1924, now in P. Togliatti, *La Forma-zione del Gruppo Dirigente del P.C.I.* (Ed. Riuniti, Rome 1962), p. 183.

thus could not control what was happening to the Councils even in Turin. In December 1919 the Socialist party branch had elected a new 'Committee of Study on Factory Councils', to 'define and regulate the relationships that should exist between the Trade Unions and Factory Councils, in order to avoid conflicts of competence and *prevent the existing organisations from being weakened, and to ensure that they acquire greater prestige in the eyes of the masses*'[87] [my italics]. The new Committee contained most shades of opinion, including several local reformists as well as Tasca and Togliatti, but Gramsci was not a member. By this time, therefore, Gramsci was almost isolated on the Factory Council question, with many of his colleagues on the *Ordine Nuovo* anxious to preserve the strength of the Unions.

Inasmuch as the activities of the various Factory Councils were coordinated by anybody, the Committee of Study did it; and the Committee *did* try to 'exercise influence throughout the country'. Its most interesting proposal was that a national Congress of Workshop Commissars should be held in Turin, with representatives from every big factory in Italy.[88] At the end of March a Manifesto was issued calling on all workers in Italy to form Councils, and proclaiming the value of Factory Councils in 'destroying the oppressive bureaucracy of the Trade Unions'.[89] This national Congress never met, because of the Piedmontese General Strike in April (see Chapter Five). If it had met, it might well have ratified some kind of workshop organisation acceptable to Union leaders and to Tasca, rather than have provided a platform for Gramsci's views.

This impression of diversity, of Factory Councils far removed from Gramsci's purposes, is strengthened by looking at the activities of the syndicalists of the *U.S.I.* (see p. 34). Factory Councils seemed to the syndicalists an excellent method of implementing one of their traditional aims – seizure of the factories. On 17 February 1920, the predominantly syndicalist workers in the main metal-working and shipbuilding plants in Sestri Ponente, Cornigliano, and Campi, in Liguria, occupied their factories as a result of a break-down in negotiations over a pay-claim. They were soon removed and agreement was eventually reached on the pay issue, but the episode focused attention on the Factory Councils,

[87] *Avanti!* (Turin ed.) 12 December 1919. The motion quoted here was signed by Tasca and Togliatti. cf. G. Berti, 'Appunti e Ricordi 1919–26', in *Annali dell' Istituto Giangiacomo Feltrinelli*, anno VIII (1966), pp. 58–9. The new Committee replaced the former provisional Committee of Study appointed on 20 October (see p. 84 and note 43). The 15 members of the new one were: Togliatti, Tasca, Boero, Matta, Montagnana, Vabente, Racca, Aprà, Zangheri, Sanmartino, Chignoli, Gino Guarnieri, Garnerone, Bertolini and Luigi Borghi.

[88] *Ordine Nuovo* 21 February 1920.

[89] The Manifesto was printed in *Ordine Nuovo* 27 March 1920 (now in P. Spriano, *Ordine Nuovo* cit., pp. 471–4).

which had played a leading part in running the factories for the time they were occupied (two to four days), and which thus came to be even more closely associated with syndicalist agitation.[90] All this was particularly important because by March 1920 the syndicalists were virtually the only spokesmen left for popular discontent, which remained at a high pitch. On 5 March the Prefect of Milan reported he was expecting an occupation of the engineering factories there, as a result of 'the sullen discontent that prevails among the metal-workers of Piedmont, Liguria and Lombardy.'[91] Discontent was heightened by the continuous rapid inflation – the general price index rose from 634.7 in January to 855.7 in April 1920;[92] and the result of the *P.S.I.*'s having effectively abandoned a revolutionary perspective was that, as Anna Kuliscioff wrote about the situation in Milan, 'anarchism dominates the piazza, and Malatesta and Borghi are the bosses' (of the workers' movement).[93] Thus in the spring of 1920, as the syndicalists provided temporarily the most influential leadership for many sections of the Italian working class, the idea of Factory Councils as a means to actual factory occupation became successfully established in the minds of thousands of *U.S.I.* members in Lombardy and Liguria. The *Ordine Nuovo* regarded this as a disaster, realising that occupation of individual factories could never overthrow the State; according to Togliatti and Viglongo, the Ligurian episodes showed that there could be a 'new type of opportunism – the opportunism of revolt.'[94]

Events at the Mazzonis cotton mills in Pont Canavese and Torre Pellice, near Turin, revealed an even more disturbing aspect of Factory Councils. After a strike lasting over a month, over the dismissal of a female employee and the employers' refusal to appear before, or accept the findings of, a 'Commission of Conciliation',[95] the factories were occupied by their workers on 28 February; the occupation was encouraged by Textile

[90] For these occupations, see *Il Lavoro* 19–21 February 1920; *Comunismo* 15–29 February 1920; and G. Perillo, 'I Consigli di Fabbrica a Sestri', in *Movimento Operaio e Contadino in Liguria*, anno III (1957), pp. 55–9. The role of the Councils in the occupations was emphasised by the Prefect of Genoa in his report to the Ministry of the Interior on 26 February 1920 (in *State Archives*, Min. Int., Dir. Gen. P.S., Aff. Gen. e Ris., 1920, b. 74, 'Affari Metallurgici: Genova').

[91] Prefect of Milan to Ministry of the Interior 5 March 1920 (in *State Archives*, Min. Int., Dir. Gen. P.S., Aff. Gen. e Ris., 1920, b. 81).

[92] R. Bachi, *Italia Economica 1920* (Lapi, Città di Castello 1921), p. 143.

[93] Letter of 2 March 1920, in *Carteggio Filippo Turati – Anna Kuliscioff* (Einaudi, Turin 1953), vol. v, p. 258.

[94] 'Rapporto sui Fatti di Sestri', in *Ordine Nuovo* 13 March 1920. There had been occasional factory occupations earlier, the best known being that of the Franchi–Gregorini steelworks at Dalmine in February 1919; Mussolini had welcomed it as a 'creative strike that does not interrupt production' (*Popolo d'Italia* 21 March 1919).

[95] The judgement of the Commission was given in *Avanti!* (Turin ed.) 19 February 1920. The strike had begun on 19 January, and a 24-hour strike of all Turin textile

Union leaders, as the only means to secure the State intervention they were demanding.[96] Provisional Factory Councils were elected, an 'emanation of the Textile-Workers' Union'.[97] On 2 March the Prefect of Turin issued a decree requisitioning the factories and placing them under the control of a local Industrial Inspector, on the grounds that the management's persistent refusal to obey the findings of the arbitration commission would lead to 'grave disturbances of public order'.[98] The Inspector agreed that there should be, in future, Internal Commissions in the factories, but they would have merely 'the powers normally allowed them in the other cotton mills of the province'[99] – i.e. they would remain under Union control. The occupation of the Mazzonis works was not a result of *Ordine Nuovo* agitation; it was decided on and led by the Unions as a 'legal' means of bringing pressure to bear on the employers. Nevertheless, it is clear that this episode, and the events at Sestri, meant that the Factory Councils were in future associated with a policy of seizing the factories; even in Turin itself, a meeting of sixty Workshop Commissars on 3 March decided that 'the factories should be seized, and this is what the task of the Workshop Commissars consists of.'[100]

This decision, reached after six months of *Ordine Nuovo* agitation and debate, is perhaps the best measure of how far the movement had failed to put its ideas across. Moreover, the factory occupations, and especially the government support given to the Mazzonis occupation, naturally aroused grave alarm among the local industrialists. They soon went on the offensive against the Workshop Commissars. The next chapter will demonstrate their success.

workers was held in sympathy on 6 February. For the Mazzonis' occupations generally, see *Battaglie Sindacali* 17 April 1920; L. Einaudi, 'Il Caso Mazzonis', in *Corriere della Sera* 3 March 1920; L. Einaudi, *La Condotta Economica e gli Effetti Sociali della Guerra Italiana* (Yale U.P. and Laterza, Bari 1933), pp. 319–22; G. Prato, *Il Piemonte e gli Effetti della Guerra sulla sua Vita Economica e Sociale* cit., pp. 145–6; M. Abrate, *La Lotta Sindacale nella Industrializzazione in Italia* cit., pp. 249–53; G. Maione, *Il Biennio Rosso* cit., pp. 97–102.

[96] It seems highly probable that the Union leaders did request State intervention. The State Archives contain a telegram (no date) to D'Aragona: 'Prefect informs attempt persuade Mazzonis accept judgment conciliation commission failed completely urge government action against firm stop otherwise inevitable proclamation general strike Cravello Chignoli Bertola' (in *State Archives*, Min. Int., Dir. Gen. P.S., Aff. Gen. e Ris., 1920, b. 60, 'Ordine Pubblico: Torino'). Chignoli was secretary of the Turin Chamber of Labour; Bertola was secretary of the Textile-Workers' Union; and Cravello a leader of the National Textile Federation.

[97] *Avanti!* (Turin ed.) 3 March 1920.

[98] Published in *Battaglie Sindacali* 17 April 1920.

[99] *Avanti!* (Turin ed.) 9 March 1920.

[100] Prefect of Turin to Ministry of the Interior 17 March 1920 (in *State Archives*, Min. Int., Dir. Gen. P.S., Aff. Gen. e Ris., 1920, b. 75).

CHAPTER FIVE

The Piedmontese General Strike, April 1920

THE Turin industrialists were fortunate in having well organised and sophisticated employers' associations available to counter workers' militancy. These associations were no novelty in Piedmont. The *Società Promotrice dell' Industria Nazionale* had been founded in Turin in 1868, and by 1906 a more overtly political organisation, the Industrial League, included 75 employers from various industries and was involved in collective bargaining.[1] Its secretary was Gino Olivetti,[2] a brilliant lawyer who gradually extended the scope of the League, and who also ran the regional employers' associations in the engineering and vehicle-making industry. The growth and concentration of industry in the war made employers realise the need for a national organisation, and the Italian General Confederation of Industry (*C.G.I.I.*) was founded in March 1919; its Secretary-General was Gino Olivetti, who retained his post with the Industrial League at Turin until mid-1920 and also became a deputy in November 1919.[3] Olivetti normally worked closely with Giovanni Agnelli, the founder of Fiat and President of the local engineering employers' association. Olivetti was energetic, able and ambitious; moreover, he was convinced that 'rogue' employers like Baron Mazzonis (see pp. 94–5), who refused to join employers' associations or accept discipline, were a menace to their class. In the face of Trade Union solidarity, employers must be united too, if capitalism were to survive.

The Turin employers were naturally hostile to the election of Workshop Commissars in the autumn of 1919.[4] Early in 1920 they decided to act, as they realised that the local Trade Union leadership could no longer

[1] M. Abrate, *La Lotta Sindacale nella Industrializzazione in Italia* (Angeli, Milan 1967), pp. 37–9.
[2] Gino Olivetti was not related to Camillo Olivetti, the founder of the famous typewriter firm at Ivrea.
[3] M. Abrate, *La Lotta Sindacale nella Industrializzazione in Italia* cit., p. 207.
[4] *ibid.*, p. 220, pp. 226–7.

exert discipline, and as a series of wild-cat stoppages over piece-rates hit production (see p. 90).[5] In mid-February a meeting of the Industrial League was held to discuss the problem of the Factory Councils. It was addressed by Gino Olivetti, and approved a motion expressing solidarity in the fight against the Factory Councils, pledging each member to 'communicate immediately to the League headquarters any attempt to set up Factory Councils or Workshop Commissars', and expressly forbidding members to 'perform any act that may compromise the issue'.[6] The meeting also approved changes in the League's constitution, to guarantee discipline in the event of a dispute.[7]

There were other signs of the employers' determination to act against the Councils. On 20 February the director of the main Fiat works, Agnelli, suddenly refused to recognise the Commissars or to discuss complaints submitted by them; thereupon the Factory Council ordered work to stop immediately throughout the factory, and, as *Avanti!* remarked, 'the Director had to give way, but the episode should make all workers take note: perhaps the time is coming to enter battle, to defend the new conquests'.[8]

Clearly it was. The industrialists' alarm was increased by the workers' occupation of the Mazzonis mills and the events at Sestri Ponente. On 3 March the Industrial League passed a motion of protest against the 'grave violation of the law that took place when industrial enterprises were invaded, and against the failure of the authorities to ensure observance of the laws.'[9] On 7 March Gino Olivetti made another speech, this time to the nationwide General Confederation of Industry. He called for the suppression of the Factory Councils, on the grounds that there could not be 'two authorities in the factory', and while expressing the hope that the government would intervene, he declared that the industrialists must be prepared to take resolute action alone if government support were not forthcoming.[10] Olivetti's speech was a realistic summary of Factory Council ideas, which he fully understood. He obviously had little faith in the ability of government authorities to help the employers suppress the

---

[5] The industrialists' initial attempt to appeal to the local Trade Union leaders failed, as the latter were bound by the decisions of the Chamber of Labour Congress in December 1919. See *Informazione Industriale* 26 February 1920.

[6] The motion was published in full in *Informazione Industriale* 19 February 1920.

[7] G. Maione, *Il Biennio Rosso* (Il Mulino, Bologna 1975), p. 117.

[8] *Avanti!* (Turin ed.) 21 February 1920.

[9] Prefect of Turin to Ministry of the Interior 4 March 1920 (in *State Archives*, Min. Int., Dir. Gen. P.S., Aff. Gen. e Ris., 1920, b. 60).

[10] *Corriere della Sera* 9 March 1920; Olivetti's speech was also summarised in *Ordine Nuovo* 15 May 1920. cf. A. Gramsci, 'Superstizione e Realtà', in *Ordine Nuovo* 8 May 1920 (now in A. Gramsci, *Ordine Nuovo*, Einaudi, Turin 1955, pp. 108–14).

Councils – in April he was to send a confidential circular to members of the Confederation, giving instructions on the attitude to be adopted to Factory Councils. His opinion of the government's attitude may be gauged from the following passage: 'if pressure is brought to bear by local political authorities to make concessions in this field, it is the duty of member organisations to refuse co-operation and to warn the Confederation immediately so that it can take any measures it thinks suitable'.[11]

On 20 March Taddei, the Prefect of Turin, sent the following report to the Ministry of the Interior:

> This morning I was visited by the Hon. Olivetti, Commendatore De Benedetti, the President of the local Industrial League, and Commendatore Agnelli, who informed me that indiscipline and the workers' continual exorbitant demands in the industrial factories have reached such a point that the industrialists have decided to have recourse, within a very brief period, to a general lock-out.[12]

Taddei protested against this plan, as a danger to public order; but he pledged the support of the public authorities to the industrialists if they wished to apply existing factory regulations rigorously, and he declared his readiness 'on all occasions to intervene in order to repress any violence that might occur, or any criminal attacks on their rights.'[13] The industrialists therefore agreed to give up their plans for a lock-out, but they warned that they would 'apply the proper disciplinary sanctions in every case of non-observance of the regulations or agreements.'[14] As no agreements mentioned Factory Councils, the industrialists had in effect secured State backing for their aims, with the knowledge that the government would intervene to prevent any occupation of their factories by the workers.

The conflict began over a banal issue – the introduction of summer-time on 21 March. 'Legal time' was a characteristic feature of war-time Industrial Mobilisation, and its introduction was thought to indicate the bourgeois government's desire to maintain war-time industrial conditions. The executive committee of the Chamber of Labour said summer-time

[11] The circular fell into the hands of the Prefect of Genoa, who sent it to the Ministry of the Interior 28 April 1920 (*State Archives*, Min. Int., Dir. Gen. P.S., Aff. Gen. e Ris., 1920, b. 78).

[12] Prefect of Turin to Ministry of the Interior 20 March 1920 (*State Archives* cit., 1920, b. 75); cited in P. Spriano, *Storia del Partito Comunista Italiano*, vol. i (Einaudi, Turin 1967), p. 52.

[13] *ibid.*

[14] Prefect of Turin to Ministry of the Interior 24 March 1920 (*State Archives* cit., 1920, b. 75).

was 'intolerable to proletarian sentiments, mindful of the dictatorial decrees of the war period',[15] and on 20 March it issued a manifesto calling on workers to ignore the new arrangements. There was considerable confusion in Turin for a few days, as industry continued to use solar time, while schools and all State institutions adopted 'legal time'. On 22 March the Internal Commission of the Fiat-owned Industrie Metallurgiche works asked the management to put back the hands of the factory clock, which had been altered even though inside the factory work was proceeding according to solar time; when the Director refused, the Internal Commission asked a clock-maker to do it. The following day the members of the Internal Commission were dismissed for insubordination, whereupon the workers decided on an 'internal strike' – i.e. they stopped work, but remained inside the factory.[16]

At the same time, another conflict arose in Turin over the rights of Internal Commissions, at the Acciaierie Fiat works. There the workers came out on strike on 23 March when their demand that members of the Internal Commission should be paid for the time they spent on their duties was refused; the workers failed to use the stipulated bargaining machinery whereby the local branch of *F.I.O.M.* negotiated on their behalf, and in that sense their action was a clear breach of the national metal-workers' agreement.[17] Both these disputes were regarded by workers and employers alike as matters of principle; in both of them, the employers' authority within the workshop was the issue at stake; and they both demonstrated the industrialists' new-found determination to insist on the rigorous application of national agreements, in accordance with the understanding reached between them and the Prefect of Turin.

The Prefect's support for the employers was, in fact, a crucial factor in the situation. On 24 March he promised the industrialists that he would expel the workers from the Industrie Metallurgiche works,[18] and he was fully backed by the Minister of the Interior, who on the same day urged him to forbid public meetings, expel all suspicious foreigners, arrest known trouble-makers, and generally 'inspire the conviction that the Government intends to guarantee order and calm, and take bold measures

---

[15] *Avanti!* (Turin ed.) 24 March 1920. The agitation against summer-time was confined to Turin, although the Chamber of Labour made strenuous efforts to have it extended nationally.

[16] *Avanti!* (Turin ed.) 25 March 1920, and M. Guarnieri, 'Cronaca', in *Battaglie Sindacali* 24 April 1920.

[17] *Battaglie Sindacali* 24 April 1920.

[18] Prefect of Turin to Ministry of the Interior, 24 March 1920 (in *State Archives*, Min. Int., Dir. Gen. P.S., Aff. Gen. e Ris., 1920, b. 75, 'Torino: Agitazioni Metallurgiche').

against all trouble-makers.'[19] Nevertheless, neither the Prefect nor the central governmental authorities had any awareness of the nature of the Factory Council movement; they regarded the unrest at Turin as being purely a matter of public order, which it was their duty to preserve.

The workers at the Industrie Metallurgiche were expelled by police and troops during the evening of 24 March. The fact that the employers realised, and were prepared to face, the possible consequences is shown in this dispatch from the Prefect:

> Commendatore Agnelli, as managing director of Fiat, requested me to clear the factory, which had been illegally occupied by the workers, who were holding meetings there but not working. As a result, I gave instructions for clearing it by force, and this is beginning at this moment. I renew my urgent request for ten officers trained in street fighting methods, because it is probable that tomorrow work will be abandoned in all factories and there will be a general strike . . .
>
> Prefect Taddei[20]

Later negotiations failed to settle the question of principle. The management eventually agreed to rescind the dismissals, but insisted that the members of the former Internal Commission should not hold office again for a year, and this was regarded by the factory's Workshop Commissars as an attack on the principle that 'the Internal Commission emanates from the workers alone, without interference from the industrialists.'[21] Moreover, the employers demanded that in future the Internal Commission's functions should be restricted to the limited ones laid down in the national agreement.[22]

The local branch of *F.I.O.M.*'s executive committee therefore called a meeting of Workshop Commissars from all the metal-working factories on 26 March, to discuss the situation at Industrie Metallurgiche. They decided – perhaps following the Ligurian example – to go on 'internal strike' throughout Turin, and this began on 27 March in 44 of the city's engineering factories.[23] Although called off the next day by the Workshop

[19] Minister of the Interior to Prefect of Turin, 24 March 1920 (*State Archives* cit., 1920, b. 75).

[20] Prefect of Turin to Ministry of the Interior, 21.00 hrs., 24 March 1920 (*State Archives* cit., 1920, b. 75).

[21] *Avanti!* (Turin ed.) 26 March 1920. Gramsci wrote that this proposal would deprive the Commission members of their 'proletarian civil rights' ('Superstizione e Realtà', in *Ordine Nuovo* 8 May 1920, now in A. Gramsci, *Ordine Nuovo* cit., p. 110).

[22] 'Cronaca', in *Battaglie Sindacali* 24 April 1920.

[23] *Avanti!* (Turin ed.) 28 March 1920.

Commissars,[24] the 'internal strike' in fact continued unofficially. On 29 March the industrialists retaliated with a lock-out, again effected by troops.[25] Although not all the local employers joined the lock-out, its success was assured by State support. At the Diatto Frejus works, troops put up two rows of barbed wire to keep the workers out, and *Avanti!* wrote that there were enough troops in Turin to 'quell an entire region in revolt'.[26] The dispute was patently a very peculiar one: in addition to the State intervention, the workers' main aim was to defend an 'unofficial' institution that had been bitterly attacked by the Unions. Yet the negotiations, both then and later, were formally always about the powers and role of the *Internal Commissions,* the only bodies recognised in factory regulations. 'Factory Councils' and 'Workshop Commissars' were never mentioned, which obviously made a negotiated settlement on this issue impossible.[27] Moreover, the workers were being led not by Trade Union representatives but by a Committee of Agitation, hastily elected by the Workshop Commissars of all the metal-working factories on 26 March.[28]

Negotiations continued during the lock-out, on the original disputes at the Industrie Metallurgiche and Acciaierie Fiat works. On 2 April the workers' representatives outlined the concessions they were prepared to make. In the case of the Industrie Metallurgiche, they agreed that the Internal Commission had no business to alter the clock hands, that its members should resign, that the clock should show legal time, that the workers should not be paid for the hours of stoppage, and that the workers there should have consulted the local branch of *F.I.O.M.* before striking.[29] In the case of the Acciaierie Fiat, they said that the Internal Commission there had only requested the same facilities as existed in other Fiat works, and these should be granted. On the more general issue of the functions of Internal Commissions, the workers were willing to agree that

[24] M. Abrate, *La Lotta Sindacale nella Industrializzazione in Italia* cit., p. 263; G. Maione, *Il Biennio Rosso* cit., p. 128.

[25] The Prefect of Turin expected work to be resumed on March 29, as local Union leaders had promised him (Prefect to Ministry of the Interior, 11.25 a.m., 29 March 1920, in *State Archives*, Min. Int., Dir. Gen. P.S., Aff. Gen. e Ris., 1920, b. 75). When it was not, he agreed to send troops into all factories in the evening, so that when the workers turned up to continue their internal strike on 30 March they found the factories closed. The industrialists' letter to the local branch of *F.I.O.M.*, informing them of the lock-out, was published in *Avanti!* (Turin ed.) 30 March 1920.

[26] *Avanti!* (Turin ed.) 31 March 1920.

[27] G. Maione, *Il Biennio Rosso* cit., p. 141. It was a constant theme of the Industrial League's propaganda that negotiations were *not* about Factory Councils.

[28] According to *Avanti!* (Turin ed.) 2 April 1920, this Committee consisted of: Carmagnola, Scaravelli, Boero, Garino, Berra, Alenti, and Roncarolo. It was replaced on 3 April.

[29] The memorandum is given in *Avanti!* (Turin ed.) 4 April 1920.

the local branch of *F.I.O.M.* should pledge itself to 'recall the Internal
Commissions to their specific functions of safeguarding the workers'
interests in matters concerning wage agreements and factory regulations' –
provided that the concessions made in certain factories to the Commissions, but not recognised in official regulations, were maintained.[30] The
employers accepted, with a few minor modifications, the proposals made
for Industrie Metallurgiche, but proposed that the Acciaierie Fiat workers
should be fined for striking without going through the usual Union
machinery, and on the Internal Commissions they concluded:

> As a result of this conflict it has clearly become necessary for *F.I.O.M.*
> to pledge itself to recall the Internal Commissions to their specific
> functions, which consist exclusively in safeguarding the workers'
> interests with regard to labour contracts and agreements, and for it to
> ask the Commissions to function within the limits of the existing
> regulations.
>   And while it is noted that *F.I.O.M.* is ready to make such a pledge,
> we feel that with regard to the clarifications needed in certain cases,
> where concessions have been made in certain factories based on a wider
> interpretation of regulations, it is absolutely essential that such impor-
> tant details should be cleared up before work is resumed, and we
> therefore invite you . . . to come to an agreement containing such
> clarifications.[31]

The employers' insistence on this issue faced the Turin strike leaders
with the choice, of either ending the agitation or of trying to extend it
locally and nationally. They therefore called in the Turin Chamber of
Labour and, more importantly, the national committee of *F.I.O.M.* itself,
in the hope of securing a national extension of the dispute.[32] By 6 April
the negotiations on the workers' side were being led by the national
secretary of *F.I.O.M.*, Bruno Buozzi, by Garino, an anarchist supporter of
Ordine Nuovo, and by Carmagnola, the secretary of the local branch of
F.I.O.M.; assistance was also given by the leaders of the Turin Chamber
of Labour, Chignoli, Cattaneo and Gino Guarnieri.[33] The issues in the

[30] *Avanti!* (Turin ed.) 4 April 1920.

[31] *Avanti!* (Turin ed.) 4 April 1920. By *F.I.O.M.* is meant the local branch.

[32] The local *F.I.O.M.* branch sent a letter to the central committee of *F.I.O.M.* on
3 April appealing for assistance. This letter was printed in 'La Cronaca del Movimento', in *Battaglie Sindacali* 1 May 1920. This was the first time that the national
Union leaders had played any part in the dispute, for the new constitution of the
Turin branch of *F.I.O.M.*, agreed in November 1919, had ensured that until then all
policy decisions had been taken by the executive committee and the Committee of
Agitation, both elected by the Workshop Commissars.

[33] 'Cronaca del Movimento', in *Battaglie Sindacali* 1 May 1920.

Industrie Metallurgiche dispute were soon settled, and the industrialists dropped their claim that all the city's metal-workers should be fined for their internal sympathy strike. On 8 April agreement was reached at last on the Acciaierie Fiat dispute. The workers were to be fined a nominal one hour's pay for going on strike without calling in the local branch of F.I.O.M., as regulations required; the money was to go to their Unemployment Fund. The management promised to pay the members of the Internal Commission in future for the time they spent on their duties. It was also agreed to hold discussions about changes in factory regulations at a later date; the joint communique expressed the belief that agreement would soon be reached 'given the conciliatory spirit of both parties'.[34] The Prefect described the agreed terms as a 'notable victory for the industrialists';[35] it is evident that Buozzi's intervention had aroused the hope that the Internal Commissions' 'abuses' could be eliminated with the help of the national F.I.O.M. organisation.

However, when the terms were referred back to the local branch of F.I.O.M. for approval, they were rejected by eight votes to five, and this rejection was repeated at an assembly of Workshop Commissars, after long debate.[36] It was therefore decided to hold a referendum of all Turin metal-workers to decide whether or not to fight on. This referendum, which took place in the afternoon of 9 April, gave a majority of 794 in favour of a resumption of work on the terms reached; however, only 11,588 votes were cast, out of a total 50,000 metal-workers in the city.[37] The Workshop Commissars decided to accept the results of the referendum, and to resume work on Monday, 12 April. This decision was only reached, however, after two stormy meetings, and it is probable that the attempts by some of the Commissars to annul the referendum increased the industrialists' suspicions of the Factory Councils and of the need to discipline them.[38]

Thus when the two sides met at the Prefecture on 11 April to sign the agreement, the original disputes at the Acciaierie Fiat and at Industrie Metallurgiche had been settled. It was at this meeting, however, that the real issues of the dispute were fully revealed. The industrialists suddenly put forward a scheme to deprive the Internal Commissions of most of their functions. All urgent complaints would have to be made in the first instance to foremen, and the workers would be allowed to contact the

---

[34] Communique printed in *Battaglie Sindacali* 1 May 1920.
[35] Prefect of Turin to Ministry of the Interior 9 April 1920 (in *State Archives*, Min. Int., Dir. Gen. P.S., Aff. Gen. e Ris., 1920, b. 75).
[36] *Avanti!* (Turin ed.) 9 April 1920.
[37] *Avanti!* (Turin ed.) 11 April 1920.
[38] 'Cronaca del Movimento', in *Battaglie Sindacali* 1 May 1920.

Internal Commission only outside working hours.[39] The industrialists' change of tactics was perhaps due to a realisation that they had a fine opportunity to discipline the Internal Commissions and crush the Factory Council movement; it is possible that the results of the referendum suggested to them that the Turin workers were less militant than they had supposed. Nevertheless, their new proposals were no different in spirit from their declared policy throughout the dispute and indeed before-hand.[40] The industrialists' new proposals came as a shock, at a time when the whole dispute seemed to be settled. The Prefect of Turin wired on 11 April, at 9.45 p.m., that 'some difficulties have arisen at the last minute', and on 13 April he confirmed that the difficulties had arisen 'only at the moment of signing the agreement. The point of disagreement consists mainly in the industrialists' firm intention to introduce norms into the agreement to regulate and discipline the Internal Commissions . . . this would represent a withdrawal of recognition from the present state of affairs agreed on, or at least tolerated, in the factories.'[41] By 13 April the dispute was unequivocally about the new factory institutions. The Work-shop Commissars rejected the employers' proposals, despite Buozzi's pleas that they were a big advance on the existing official regulations, and the local branch of *F.I.O.M.* began appealing for wider support.

These appeals were successful. On 13 April the Chamber of Labour proclaimed a General Strike in Turin, to defend the Factory Councils in the metal-working factories. Its action can be explained in terms of

[39] The detailed proposals were outlined by the Prefect on 14 April:

(a) direct contacts between workers and members of the Internal Commission should take place only outside working hours;

(b) during working hours members of the Internal Commission must stay at their jobs;

(c) all requests made by the Internal Commission to the management should be written, in a special book; any verbal discussion will be between the management and individual members of the Commission, appointed in turn. There would be meetings with the full Commission only if no agreement could be reached;

(d) in urgent cases workers should address complaints first to their foreman (Capo Reparto or Capo Officina), and later, in the event of not receiving satisfaction, may request the management to permit the intervention of two members of the Internal Commission or of the whole Commission if necessary.

(Prefect of Turin to Ministry of the Interior 14 April 1920, in *State Archives*, Min. Int., Dir. Gen. P.S., Aff. Gen. e Ris., 1920, b. 75).

[40] 'From the earliest negotiations we have always demanded that the regulations concerning the functioning of the Internal Commissions should in future be observed' (*Informazione Industriale* 16 April 1920).

[41] Prefect of Turin to Ministry of the Interior 11 & 13 April 1920 (in *State Archives* cit., 1920, b. 75).

pressure by the local branches of the *P.S.I.* and of *F.I.O.M.*, the disgust felt at the industrialists' last-minute intransigence, the fact that many other categories of workers, totalling 80,000, were on strike in any case (e.g. all State employees, tailors, paper-makers, etc.), the imminence of an annual Congress of the Chamber of Labour – which would certainly have condemned its leaders had they shown reluctance to support the metalworkers – and the Chamber of Labour's desire to control the strike and lead the negotiations at its conclusion.

In fact, as both the Chamber of Labour and the local branch of the *P.S.I.* wanted to lead the strike,[42] a compromise Committee of Agitation was formed on 14 April, appointed by the *P.S.I.* branch, the Chamber of Labour and the *P.S.I.*'s Provincial Federation.[43] This Committee led the strike, and issued regular strike bulletins, which were printed in special editions of *Avanti!*, entitled *Lavoratori Avanti!*.[44] The Committee's main task was to try to maintain morale, and it also tried to extend the Internal Commission agitation to all local industries, so as to give other groups of workers a positive goal in the General Strike.

The question of whether to attempt to extend the dispute nationally proved more complex. The Committee of Agitation's first Bulletin, dated 14 April, appealed to the *C.G.L.* and to the *P.S.I.* Directorate to 'intervene in this struggle, which is not of a local nature, but of national interest, since it concerns questions of principle, and since it can be the start of a vast national movement.'[45] Two days later, however, the dangers of this course had been realised, and the industrialists' proposals for the negotiations to be conducted in Milan by the *C.G.L.* and the *C.G.I.I.* (the Employers' Confederation), were rejected on the grounds that the issues involved were not of sufficient national importance to warrant the intervention of the main national organisations.[46] This shift of attitude illus-

---

[42] Speech of Gino Guarnieri at the Turin Chamber of Labour Congress 25 May 1920, in *Avanti!* (Turin ed.) 27 May 1920.

[43] *Avanti!* (Turin ed.) 15 April 1920. It is unfortunate that the names of the Committee's members were not given. G. Maione (*Il Biennio Rosso* cit., pp. 136–7) writes that the *Ordine Nuovo* supporters had a majority on it, but gives no evidence. Gramsci wrote four years later that the strike of April 1920 was led by the executive committee of the local branch of the *P.S.I.* ('Postilla', to Tasca's article 'Opportunismo di Destra e Tattica Sindacale', in *Lo Stato Operaio* 5 June, dated 5 May, 1924; now in A. Gramsci, *La Costruzione del Partito Comunista*, Einaudi, Turin 1971, p. 188).

[44] *Lavoratori Avanti!* appeared from 16 to 24 April 1920 inclusive.

[45] *Avanti!* (Turin ed.) 15 April 1920.

[46] *Lavoratori Avanti!* 17 April 1920. The Workers' Commission made the point that such national negotiations would logically imply the extension of the strike throughout Italy. They also claimed that Article 34 of the metal-workers' regulations stated that modifications might be made to it in order to conform with prevailing local conditions, and that this clause ought to be applied in Turin, where the workers were merely requesting a legal recognition of what had already been granted them *de facto*.

trates the dilemma of the Turin movement. It could not hope to succeed unless national support were obtained, yet its leaders were aware that the C.G.L. and the P.S.I. would not negotiate in order to secure the recognition and establishment of the Factory Council system – a factor of which the industrialists were also aware.

The P.S.I.'s attitude was expressed in a motion passed at a meeting of the Party Directorate on 17 April, which spoke of the Italian people's sympathy for the Turin strike 'showing itself in energetic action *if* the Government seeks to smash the unity of the Turin workers by force.'[47] The Government had far more sense, especially since the strike coincided with the international conference at San Remo. As Prime Minister Nitti put it:

> I regard the situation as extremely serious as I believe it is a pre-arranged political movement. I have made all arrangements to avoid being taken unawares. The situation at Turin is acute because it is only political and the new requests are exclusively political, put forward while I am here. This worsens the foreign exchange rate and general conditions . . . Faced with the spread of madness there is only proud resistance and repression. But I would not want serious events to take place now, during the Conference. I urge you to follow the situation carefully and consult Commendatore Quaranta.[48]

The attitude of the government and of the Socialist leaders was in fact rather similar. Both hoped the Turin General Strike would fade away, but both knew that they might have to act if a real insurrection broke out.[49]

The Turin Committee of Agitation, aware of this, tried to extend the General Strike as widely as possible. On 17 April it called for a General Strike throughout Piedmont.[50] The Committee was encouraged by the outbreak of a peasants' strike at Vercelli, Novara and Pavia – called not out of solidarity with Turin, but in order to defend the peasants' own Employment Offices, which the Turin Strike Committee optimistically

[47] The motion is printed in *Lavoratori Avanti!* 18 April 1920.

[48] Nitti's telegram from San Remo to Commendatore Magno at the Ministry of the Interior, 10.35 a.m., 17 April 1920 (in *State Archives*, Min. Int., Dir. Gen. P.S., Aff. Gen. e Ris., 1920, b. 79: 'Anarchici: Affari Generali').

[49] The Union leaders also shared this attitude. The Prefect of Milan reported that 'at the present moment the C.G.L. does not intend to adhere to the Turin General Strike and would adhere to it only if provoked by conflicts that might occur in Turin or by the anarchists, who want to begin a revolution immediately' (Prefect of Milan to Ministry of the Interior 19 April 1920, in *State Archives* cit., 1920, b. 79).

[50] *Lavoratori Avanti!* 18 April 1920.

called 'parallel institutions to the Internal Commissions.'[51] By 19 April the
General Strike was fairly complete in the provinces of Turin, Novara,
Alessandria, and Pavia; the dockers at Genoa and Leghorn, and the
railwaymen at Florence and Pisa, had refused to help transport troops to
Turin; and the whole of Liguria was said to be ready to fight. The
Committee of Agitation therefore concluded that the Party Directorate
could no longer refuse to intervene, and proclaimed that:

> there is an atmosphere throughout Italy of vibrant sympathy for the
> Turin movement, and this attitude is anxious to assume a more concrete
> and resolute form. The Committee, in the belief that a decisive phase of
> the movement has now been reached, has decided to request the inter-
> vention of the Directorate of the *P.S.I.* and that of the *C.G.L.*, so as to
> examine the situation together and take the necessary decisions.[52]

However, the spread of the agitation failed to alter the party's attitude.
On 20 April a leading member of the maximalist Directorate, Gennari,
expressed his views in forthright terms:

> We must avoid localism, which can lead to the gravest dangers. We
> cannot allow comrades who are members of our own party to commit
> acts, or prepare for action, that may lead to a grave situation, whether or
> not they are suffering from an illusion or are impelled by the purest
> revolutionary idealism – and all this without the party's central organi-
> sation even being informed! The central organisation has the right to
> know what is happening, not least so that it can make preparations.
> I realise that one may always be surprised by events that occur accident-
> ally – but to be surprised by events that have been prepared by comrades
> who are members of our own party – this is an impossible situation![53]

The party's National Council in Milan passed by a majority of 61,562 to
26,351 a resolution calling on all party organisations to 'maintain close
links with the Directorate and to uphold discipline, avoiding at all costs,
in the interests of the Party and of the Revolution, any localist initiatives

---

[51] *Lavoratori Avanti!* 19 April 1920. Viglongo, in *Ordine Nuovo* 8 May 1920, later
called the Employment Offices 'real bodies to study the physical resources and conditions of employment and production in each area'. Actually they were designed to
enforce a closed shop.

[52] 'Bollettino n. 6', in *Lavoratori Avanti!* 20 April 1920.

[53] Gennari's speech was printed in pamphlet form, as *I Compiti Attuali del Partito
Socialista* (Ed. *Avanti!*, Milan 1920). In the same speech, Gennari used the concept of
'localism' to rule out any prospect of immediate revolution: 'We intend to subordinate our revolutionary activity to the international situation, according as it is
more or less favourable to the development of our revolution' (*Lavoratori Avanti!*
22 April 1920).

or any manifestations of tendencies which are in opposition to the activity of the Party.'[54]

The Turin Chamber of Labour leaders realised that since the *P.S.I.* and *C.G.L.* had refused to intervene to secure a 'political solution', a negotiated 'economic' settlement was inevitable. Such a settlement was also becoming essential for many of the city's workers, especially the metalworkers, who had been without pay for over three weeks; some of the city's pawnshops had to be closed 'because of the large amount of stuff that kept arriving'.[55] The local Union leaders even promised the Prefect that they, like the industrialists, would be opposed to the Workshop Commissars having any part in the negotiations, and that they had every intention of 'regularising the functions of the Internal Commissions'.[56] By 21 April the negotiations were once more restricted to the metalworking factories, and were being conducted between D'Aragona, the secretary-general of the *C.G.L.*, and the secretary of the *C.G.I.I.*, Olivetti. Even nominally the negotiations had been transferred to the Chamber of Labour and the Turin Industrial League, so that the Committee of Agitation was left with no function other than to proclaim the necessity of the workers' remaining united until negotiations were concluded.[57] The final agreement, signed on 23 April, when the strike was called off, established that:

> While the existing regulations, and the rules for the functioning of the Internal Commissions contained in them, or added to the regulations of the Automobile Factories, remain in force, and the parties pledge themselves to respect and to ensure that their representatives respect such regulations and rules,
>
> (a) reciprocal contacts between Internal Commissions and workers shall take place outside the normal working hours, on all days of the week;
>
> (b) reciprocal contacts between Internal Commissions and the managements of the factories may take place during working hours;
>
> (c) the members of the Internal Commissions, during normal

---

[54] Cazzamalli motion, printed in *Lavoratori Avanti!* 22 April 1920.

[55] Engineer Herenfreund (Turin Railways), intercepted telephone conversation with Engineer Crova (Rome Railways), 8.00 a.m. 19 April 1920 (*State Archives* cit., 1920, b. 74, 'Metallurgici: Genova').

[56] Prefect of Turin to His Excellency Ferraris, Ministry of the Interior, 18 April 1920 (in *State Archives*, Min. Int., Dir. Gen. P.S., Aff. Gen. e Ris., 1920, b. 74).

[57] *Lavoratori Avanti!* 23 April 1920.

working hours when they are engaged in negotiations with the
management, shall be summoned by the management, on their
own request; and they shall receive, when on piece rates, their
hourly pay plus a sum equal to the average earned by them during
their previous work period; otherwise they shall receive their
hourly pay, plus a supplement.[58]

These new rules represented a considerable victory for the industrialists,
and especially for their leaders, Agnelli and Gino Olivetti. The Internal
Commissions lost, at least temporarily, many of their powers within the
factories. There were also more important consequences. The Industrial
League had set up twelve 'Commissions of Civil Defence' on 15 April, to
maintain public services throughout the province.[59] About 300 volunteers
were recruited, to run postal services, distribute food, etc. They also
maintained 'order' and carried out propaganda; a special journal, entitled
Lavoratori Attenti! was produced, and dropped from aeroplanes over the
city.[60] Mario Abrate has argued that this was 'the true novelty of the
April General Strike'.[61] It was the industrialists, not the State, that organised essential public services, and after the strike the twelve Commissions
became a semi-permanent 'Committee for Civil Organisation', financed
with 100,000 *lire* from the Industrial League, and run by Col. Setti.[62] The
Industrial League had proved a disciplined and skilful body. Its members
saw themselves as having preserved the State and society against revolution, and they had no intention of allowing their position to be undermined in future.

On the workers' side, the Workshop Commissars' call on 27 March for
a *general* 'internal strike' in the Turin metal-working factories was
recognised to have been a mistake. Even Gramsci admitted that 'in the
metal-workers' strike that preceded the gigantic movement of last April,
in a few factories the 'Communist group', as soon as it was set up, had to
assume leadership over the masses, as a result of the ineptitude of the
Workshop Commissars.'[63] Hence the failure of the April strike discredited the Factory Council movement even in Turin.

---

[58] The agreement was published in *Informazione Industriale* 29 April 1920. There
were additional clauses settling the original two disputes.

[59] M. Abrate, *La Lotta Sindacale nella Industrializzazione in Italia* cit., pp. 268, 317–8;
V. Castronovo, *Giovanni Agnelli* (U.T.E.T., Turin 1971), p. 227.

[60] M. Abrate, *op. cit.*, p. 318; R. Ghezzi, *Comunisti, Industriali e Fascisti a Torino
1920–23* (Ed. Eredi Botta, Turin 1923), p. 27.

[61] M. Abrate, *op. cit.*, p. 268.

[62] *ibid.*, p. 325.

[63] 'I Gruppi Comunisti', in *Ordine Nuovo* 17 July 1920 (now in A. Gramsci, *Ordine
Nuovo* cit., pp. 142–3).

Moreover, it discredited the *Ordine Nuovo* writers. The failure of leadership had not been only by the Workshop Commissars. Despite all Gramsci's criticisms of the empty maximalist rhetoric of the *P.S.I.*, there had been precious few signs of effective action by him or the Turin Socialist party branch during April. There was much bitterness afterwards on this score. Tasca wrote – even in the 1950s – that 'the movement which was supposed to 'develop production', improve it, amounted to the unleashing and final victory of chaos, which they (i.e. the *Ordine Nuovo* writers) had hoped to dominate and channel. They didn't dominate anything, they were *débordés*.'[64] The same point was put even more graphically in early May 1920 by a Socialist deputy, Frola: 'You are not revolutionaries, you are mere windbags [chiacchieroni]. My dog is more revolutionary than you are, because at least it once pissed on the shoes of a Carabiniere captain.'[65] These picturesque words illustrate the strength of feeling against the *Ordine Nuovo* movement in much of the Italian labour movement; what happened later is incomprehensible unless this bitterness is borne in mind. In any case, it was obvious by the end of April 1920 that the *Ordine Nuovo*'s attempt to make Factory Councils the means of overcoming the reformists' domination of Italian Labour had completely failed. The political significance of the Factory Council movement appeared to be over.

[64] Quoted by G. Berti, in 'Appunti e Ricordi 1919–26', in *Annali dell' Istituto Giangiacomo Feltrinelli*, anno VIII (1966), p. 48.

[65] Anonymous report 'reserved personally for His Excellency Nitti' 15 May 1920 (in *State Archives*, Min. Int., Dir. Gen. P.S., Aff. Gen. e Ris., Atti Speciali (1898–1940), b. 3, f. 26).

CHAPTER SIX

Factory Councils outside Turin: the National Debate

THE Factory Council movement in Turin naturally attracted a great deal of attention from all sections of left-wing opinion throughout Italy. Emilio Colombino, one of the most prominent of the *F.I.O.M.* leaders, wrote in March 1920 that 'the Factory Council question now occupies three quarters of the space in our political and Trade Union journals.'[1] However isolated the *Ordine Nuovo* remained in its approach to the problems of revolution, it did succeed in forcing all the various elements in the Italian Labour movement to examine the theoretical and practical issues involved. This chapter will be concerned with the attitudes of the different groups of the Italian Left – anarchists, syndicalists, maximalists, abstentionists and reformists – to the *Ordine Nuovo* and to the Factory Council movement. This examination should make clearer the nature and limits of Gramsci's achievements and of his isolation, and reveal more clearly the problems which confronted him in the summer of 1920, after his realisation of the inadequacies of the existing Socialist party.

1. The Trade Union Leadership and the *C.G.L.*

In November 1918, as has been seen (p. 33), the *C.G.L.*'s Directive Council appealed for a 'Constituent Assembly', elected by trade groups, and also for the 'right of control by workers' representatives in the management of the factory.'[2] Such control could most usefully be exercised by strengthening Internal Commissions under Union domination. There could be no question, therefore, of the Union leaders making a whole-hearted attack on *all* the proposals put forward by the *Ordine*

---

[1] Emilio Colombino, 'I Consigli di Fabbrica nel Movimento Sindacale', in *Battaglie Sindacali* 27 March 1920.
[2] *Battaglie Sindacali* 8 March 1919; see also the issue of 17 May 1919.

Nuovo. Moreover, Gramsci's views on the desirable relationship between Councils and Unions were not shared by most of his supporters in Turin, who aimed at making the Workshop Commissars the basis of Union organisation (see p. 69).

The local Union leaders in Turin were naturally the first to express their mistrust of the new movement. In October 1919 Gino Castagno, of the Turin Cooperative Alliance, warned of the dangers of 'particularism' inherent in the Factory Councils – it might mean the loss of any central leadership in economic disputes. Although this later became an important argument, used by many Union leaders, Castagno was at this stage mainly concerned to show that the Internal Commissions, if they had been left alone, would have achieved full 'control' of discipline, wages, hours, sackings, fines, and even, eventually, the distribution of labour; for him, as for other Trade Unionists, the Factory Councils were ruining a 'natural' and very hopeful historical development, the achievement of 'workers' control' by bodies representing the Unions.[3] A week later Castagno argued that it was the employers who would derive most benefit from *direct* negotiations with the workers. The collective contract was an essential safeguard for the workers' interests, and it was being undermined by the proposed new Union structure. Moreover, the proposed new method of electing branch leaders would destroy the close links between the *P.S.I.* and the Unions, for the *C.G.L.* was recognised by the party as the sole legitimate representative of the working class' economic interests.[4] In short, the Union leaders emphasised their interest in workers' control, and appealed to the maximalists in the *P.S.I.* to support them; this appeal was strengthened by the Turin attempt to make the local branches of the Unions dependent on the Commissars, for in these circumstances it was possible for the Union leaders to portray the *Ordine Nuovo* as an essentially anarchist group, whose activities were indistinguishable from those of the syndicalists.[5]

Moreover, the Trade Unionists were realistic enough to see that Socialist Party support would be more likely if they were to draw up their own proposals for making the Unions more democratic. Castagno was prepared to admit that the Unions' structure was outdated, and called

[3] G. Castagno, 'Commissioni Interne d'Officina o Commissari di Reparto?', in *Battaglie Sindacali* 25 October 1919. He also argued that the giving of the vote to 'unorganised' workers would make people less willing to join the Unions, and justify the attitude of blacklegs; the Union would have no further function, except as a friendly society paying out benefits.

[4] G. Castagno, 'Commissari di Reparto', in *Battaglie Sindacali* 1 November 1919.

[5] 'Postilla', by 'g.c.' (Castagno), in *Battaglie Sindacali* 8 November 1919. The accusation was frequently repeated in the following months.

for greater powers to be given to the Internal Commissions (elected by Union members only), who would 'control' production under the general guidance of the Unions' central organisations; he was even prepared to allow the local branch executives to be elected by the Commissions, and for them to be the 'deliberative organ of the Trade Union in the given area'.[6] This amounted to a complete reorganisation of Trade Union structure, and it is an indication of how worried Union leaders were by the success of the Factory Council agitation in Turin.

Soon the Union leaders were mounting a campaign to set up Factory Councils themselves. At Milan, the Provincial Socialist Congress in January 1920 approved a resolution put forward by Bianchi, one of the C.G.L.'s secretaries; in the words of Castagno, this motion claimed that 'Factory Councils are organs of Trade Union activity for the control of the factories, and for preparation for the direct management of the factories . . . [the Unions must therefore] assume responsibility for the setting up of Councils in the factories and for maintaining them as their own direct organs under Trade Union discipline.'[7] An attempt to do this in practice was made as early as October 1919 by Violante, the secretary of the Chemical Workers' Union, who advocated the adoption of the existing system of workers' 'Centurions', hitherto peculiar to the Pirelli works at Milan, throughout the industry.[8] Violante was supported by Bianchi, of the C.G.L., in urging the Chemical workers to form Internal Commissions under Union and local Chamber of Labour control, with no non-Union men being allowed the vote.[9] A similar decision was reached by the Rome Gas Workers at the end of November 1919. The Gas Workers were strongly influenced by events at Turin and accepted that non-Union men should be allowed to vote for the Workshop Commissars, but they looked to their Union to set up the new institutions, and urged that 'any conflict between the Trade Union and the factory organisation must be avoided.'[10]

The culmination of the Union leaders' efforts to absorb the Factory

[6] G. Castagno, 'Il Problema della Rappresentanza Operaia', in *Battaglie Sindacali* 8 November 1919.

[7] G. Castagno, 'I Sindacati ed il Controllo Operaio', in *Battaglie Sindacali* 7 February 1920.

[8] The 'centurion' system combined the virtues of a 'democratic' representational system – one delegate being elected by every 100 workers – and Union control. For a report of the Chemical Workers' Congress (26–8 October 1919, in Milan), see A. Viglongo, 'I Consigli nell' Industria Chimica' in *Ordine Nuovo* 8 November 1919.

[9] *ibid.* This was the first time that Factory Councils were discussed in a National Congress of any Italian Trade Union; the leadership's motion was carried by 15,361 votes to 6,530, most of the majority votes coming from the Union's Milan branch.

[10] *Avanguardia* 30 November 1919.

Councils into the existing Union structure was the 'Baldesi Project', drawn up by Gino Baldesi, a prominent member of the C.G.L.; it was discussed by the C.G.L.'s Directive Council on 13 May 1920, but a decision was postponed until a study group had reported on Russian organisational innovations.[11] Baldesi refused to grant that the Factory Council might be a revolutionary body, or that it might ever 'control' production, but he allowed it 'some contingent functions in defence of the workers within the factory, and in technical preparation for control over the means of production.' Given these limited functions, Baldesi was prepared to concede the vote to non-Union men, but the Unions and Chambers of Labour were to co-ordinate all local activity, and the Factory Councils were required to accept Union discipline in all national agitations. Even this project was opposed by D'Aragona, the General Secretary of the C.G.L., and by Bianchi; but Buozzi, of F.I.O.M., supported it,[12] and it was embodied in the compromise between the Unions and the Turin movement carried at the Turin Chamber of Labour meeting in late May 1920 (see pp. 135–6).

All this discussion helps to explain the united attitude of the C.G.L. and of the P.S.I. Directorate when they were faced with the Piedmont General Strike in April 1920. Trade Unionists succeeded in portraying the strike as a 'localistic illusion',[13] in the syndicalist rather than the Socialist tradition. Moreover, the F.I.O.M. leaders were successful in retaining the support of their own members throughout most of Italy: at the National Meeting of the Union in Genoa in May, the conduct of F.I.O.M.'s Central Committee during the strike was approved by 84,819 votes to 26,196.[14] The Genoa meeting decided to leave the Factory Council question to the next Congress of the C.G.L., but even at this late stage the meeting was divided not on whether Councils should be set up, but on whether they were to be controlled by the Union.[15]

Much of the national discussion about the Factory Council movement centred on the vexed question of 'votes to the unorganised'. Yet it is clear that the real issues at stake were rather different. Colombino of F.I.O.M.

[11] A report of the meeting appeared in *Avanti!* (Turin ed.) 15 May 1920.

[12] *Avanti!* (Turin ed.) 15 May 1920. The Baldesi project was published in *Battaglie Sindacali* 8 May 1920.

[13] The phrase was used by 'm.g.' (Mario Guarnieri), in 'Il Congresso della Federazione Metallurgica', in *Battaglie Sindacali* 29 May 1920.

[14] A report of the Congress appeared in *Il Lavoro* 25 May 1920. The defeated motion was presented by the Savona branch, but most of its support came from Turin itself – 20,780 votes. A minority of 5,191 Turin votes went to the Central Committee's motion. Apart from Savona, Busto Arsizio, Biella, Andorno, Mongrando, and Fornaci di Barga also supported Turin.

[15] *Battaglie Sindacali* 29 May 1920.

was, like Baldesi, prepared to accept that non-Union men might vote for Factory Councils that would look after 'control' in the factories, provided that these Councils had no say in the existing Union structure,[16] and this position later became part of official *C.G.L.* policy on Factory Councils.[17] It was, in fact, remarkably similar to that of Gramsci himself; and the fact that Colombino could use the argument that any seizure of power, and any administration of national resources, would have to be centrally directed by the Unions as an argument *against* the *Ordine Nuovo* is an indication of how remote the actual Factory Council movement soon became from Gramsci's own ideas.

In practice, the Union leaders were helpless to deal with the situation in Turin, at least until April 1920. Any attempt to crush the Councils would have laid them open to the charge of collaborating with the employers. The most they could hope to achieve was to secure the support of the *P.S.I.*; and their arguments, by showing willingness to adopt the idea of workers' control, and by showing the necessity for the central direction of economic activity, were admirably suited to this aim. The Baldesi project of May 1920 provided final proof that the issue at stake in the Trade Unionists' attacks on the Councils was not 'votes to the unorganised', but the central direction of economic affairs – an issue on which they easily secured the support of a centralising Socialist party.

2. The Anarchists, Syndicalists, and the *U.S.I.*

It has been seen that the Italian Syndicalist Union (*U.S.I.*) enjoyed considerable support, especially in Liguria, Romagna and the Marches (see p. 34); and that the metal-workers' Union affiliated to the *U.S.I.* had protested strongly against the national metal-workers' agreement of February 1919, on the grounds that it curtailed the powers of the Internal Commissions (see pp. 42–3). It has also been noted that the *U.S.I.* was all in favour of 'proletarian unity' in the cause of revolution, and had in April 1919 proposed that 'Committees of Revolutionary Action' should be set up (see p. 74). The syndicalists' traditional support for direct action at the economic rather than the political level, their opposition to reformist Unionism in general and to *F.I.O.M.* in particular, their concern with the

---

[16] 'I Consigli di Fabbrica nel Movimento Sindacale', in *Battaglie Sindacali* 27 March 1920; Colombino had expressed his views on this previously, in the Turin edition of *Avanti!* 18 December 1919.

[17] See M. Guarnieri's *Relazione sui Consigli di Fabbrica*, to the *C.G.L.* Congress at Leghorn, February 1921 (printed as pamphlet by La Tipografica, Milan 1921).

role of the Internal Commissions, and their emphasis on the need for proletarian unity, converged to make the leaders of the *U.S.I.* welcome any movement that seemed to guarantee a struggle against Union reformism. It will be seen that the most important short-term result of the Turin movement was its effects on the *U.S.I.*

The first prominent syndicalist to notice what was happening in Turin was the secretary of the *U.S.I.* metal-workers' Union, Giovannetti. He wrote in December 1919 that the Factory Councils deserved support because they implied Unions on an Industrial, not Craft, basis, because their members were revokable – and hence their structure was anti-bureaucratic – and, most important of all, because they aimed at taking direct possession of the factories, and at managing them directly.[18] It was this idea that fired syndicalist enthusiasm; and succeeding articles and speeches by the *U.S.I.* leaders were to hammer home the thesis that the real function of the Councils was to make workers grasp the need for direct action.[19] The syndicalists were, naturally, always opposed to the idea that the Factory Councils might become the basis of *F.I.O.M.* organisation at local level, and it was also difficult for them to accept the idea of Factory Councils replacing the (syndicalist) Trade Union as the main instrument of revolution; but they did give the movement their unqualified support, and they were the first to link the idea of Factory Councils to the normal syndicalist idea of seizing factories.

Thus at the *U.S.I.*'s National Congress, held in Parma at the end of December 1919, the *C.G.L.*'s opposition to the Factory Councils was the subject of particular criticism; and the Workshop Commissars at Turin were invited to send a delegate to give fuller details. The delegate chosen was Enea Matta, a frequent contributor to the *Ordine Nuovo*: his speech tactfully emphasised that the Factory Councils had made real progress only while the *F.I.O.M.* leaders were busy with the metal-workers' strike outside Piedmont (see p. 81), and that they had vetoed the movement immediately they found out how far events had moved in Turin during their absence.[20] Despite Matta's insistence that the *Ordine Nuovo* did not regard the Trade Union as a potentially revolutionary instrument, and some speeches from the floor that showed disquiet at any lessening of the (syndicalist) Trade Union's role, the Congress' final motion approved highly of the Councils. The *U.S.I.* leaders were willing to ignore some of

[18] Giovannetti's 'Relazione' to the Parma Congress, printed in advance in *Guerra di Classe* 6 December 1919.

[19] See, for example, an article by Italo Garinei, of Turin, 'Ancora dei Consigli di Fabbrica', in *Guerra di Classe* 12 December 1919.

[20] A report of Matta's speech, and of the Parma Congress, appeared in *Guerra di Classe* 7 January 1920.

the more disturbing features of the Factory Council movement – such as the dangers of reformist collaboration, the emphasis on immediate workers' control (before the revolution), and the question of the relative revolutionary capacity of Trade Unions and Factory Councils – and recognised the Councils' claim to be achieving working-class unity and to be the instruments of direct action.

The support of the 'political' anarchists in the Italian Anarchist Union (*U.A.I.*) for the Factory Council movement was based on similar grounds to that of the syndicalists, with whom their movement was closely associated. The *U.A.I.* was by no means as strong as the syndicalists,[21] but the anarchist leader, Errico Malatesta, enjoyed great personal popularity throughout Italy. It was, therefore, important that Malatesta warmly endorsed the Turin experiment as helpful to proletarian unity and as likely to bring revolution nearer. On 9 March 1920 he said at La Spezia that the setting up of Factory Councils and the seizure of factories would 'certainly provoke the bourgeoisie to reaction, which is essential if revolution is to be achieved.'[22] The 'political' anarchists were less embarrassed than the syndicalists at the possibility of the Factory Councils taking over many of the revolutionary functions of the Trade Union, and their daily newspaper, *Umanità Nova*, rapidly became very committed in its support for the Councils. The newspaper was particularly influential in Milan, where it was produced and where there was soon a great deal of anarchist and syndicalist activity in favour of Factory Councils and of factory occupation.[23]

This agitation in Milan became more important after the factory occupations at Sestri Ponente in February 1920, which confirmed the anarchist and syndicalist view of the Factory Councils' functions (see pp. 93–4). On 13 March Togliatti visited Milan and lectured on the Factory

[21] The Prefects were asked in December 1919 to report on the number of anarchists in each province (their reports are in *State Archives*, Min. Int., Dir. Gen. P.S., Aff. Gen. e Ris., 1920, b. 79: 'Anarchici: Affari Generali'). There were estimated to be 500 in Pisa, and 1,000 in Piombino; 760 in Ravenna, and 300 in Piacenza; 200 in Parma, Genoa and Rimini. The largest number was reported from Massa – 3,000. Milan was said to have 150, and Turin 300 – 'very few of them can be considered truly dangerous'. Except for Rimini, these figures refer to the numbers in each *province*. The headquarters of the *U.A.I.* was at Ancona, where 250 anarchists were reported.

[22] Prefect of Genoa to Ministry of the Interior 10 March 1920 (in *State Archives* cit., 1920, b. 80).

[23] In addition, the syndicalist journal *Guerra di Classe* was transferred from Florence to Milan in March 1920 – the first issue printed in Milan appeared on 6 March. For details of anarchist and syndicalist agitation for Factory Councils, see *Umanità Nova* 13 March, and *Guerra di Classe* 13 March 1920. For the anarchists' importance at Milan by March, see Anna Kuliscioff's remarks quoted on p. 94.

E

Council movement to an audience of 'a few Socialists and a large number of us [i.e. syndicalists]';[24] and the local secretary of the U.S.I., Mariani, went round the Milanese factories discussing the issue.[25] The Milanese anarchists and syndicalists gave full support to the Turin strike of April 1920; according to the Prefect of Milan, there was an agreement between the local anarchists, syndicalists, and some of the extreme Socialists to occupy the factories immediately after the P.S.I. National Council meeting.[26] They also strongly opposed the Schiavello project for Factory Councils (see below, p. 129 ff.), and put forward their own alternative proposals based on Turin practice.[27] The anarcho-syndicalist agitation for Factory Councils continued long after the failure of the Piedmontese General Strike. On 30 May a special Congress of anarchists from all over Lombardy met to discuss them, and called for a big propaganda campaign in favour of Factory Councils as a means towards factory occupation and the 'united front of the masses'.[28] The national Congress of the U.A.I., held at Bologna in early July, also gave formal approval to the idea of setting up Factory Councils. Borghi, of the U.S.I., even claimed that the Turin comrades had been the only Socialists to oppose C.G.L. reformism effectively.[29]

The anarchists and syndicalists did not merely give national support to the Factory Council movement; they were also prominent locally at Turin itself, where many of the local anarchists played an important part in the Councils. This was particularly true of those metal-workers who, like Maurizio Garino or Nonio De Bartolomeis, had worked in the C.G.L. rather than in the U.S.I. during the war;[30] but anarchist support for the Councils was widespread, and Umanità Nova noted with pleasure that 'in every workshop where there are some of our comrades, they have been chosen by their work comrades to be Commissars.'[31] However, it remained true, as the Prefect remarked, that 'in this city the adherents of the Anarcho-Syndicalist Union are very few in comparison with the

[24] Reports appeared in Guerra di Classe 20 March 1920, and Umanità Nova 17 March 1920.

[25] Guerra di Classe 20 March 1920.

[26] Prefect of Milan to Ministry of the Interior, 5 April 1920 (State Archives cit., 1920, b. 66).

[27] The 'Melli plan', printed in Umanità Nova 14 May 1920.

[28] A report of this meeting was printed in Umanità Nova 2 June 1920.

[29] Borghi's speech was printed in the report on the Congress given in Umanità Nova 6 July 1920.

[30] See P. C. Masini, Antonio Gramsci e l'Ordine Nuovo Visti da un Libertario (Ed. Impulso, Leghorn 1956), and his Anarchici e Comunisti nel Movimento dei Consigli di Fabbrica (Ed. Gruppo Barriera di Milano, Turin 1951), especially p. 12.

[31] 'Commissari di Fabbrica a Torino', in Umanità Nova 1 March 1920.

organisations of other subversive associations.'[32] As late as January 1920 there was no branch of the *U.S.I.* in Turin, and according to Pietro Ferrero, a leading local anarchist, the Turin syndicalists had ceased their attempts to set one up, or to engage in 'proselytising or propaganda activities', once the Council movement had begun.[33] The anarchists preferred to work within the Council movement; and some anarchists, especially Ferrero and Garino, displayed much enthusiasm for Council propaganda and activity. The anarchists' importance in Turin was shown after the April strike, when they provided virtually the only opposition to the Tasca compromise between the Factory Councils and the Trade Unions (see pp. 135–8).[34]

The significance of anarchist and syndicalist support for the Factory Council movement was that the idea of Factory Councils as a means of overcoming the reformism of the *C.G.L.*, and as a means to actual factory occupation, was successfully established in the minds of thousands of *U.S.I.* members in Lombardy and Liguria. In Milan, in particular, the Council idea had become a kind of rallying-cry for all the forces of the extreme Left by May 1920, and was the recognised instrument for working-class unity. After the failure of the Piedmont General Strike in April 1920, the main supporters of the Council movement were, in fact, the syndicalists. It was due to them that the Factory Council movement became firmly linked to the idea of seizing factories, at a time when the *Ordine Nuovo* leaders themselves were concentrating on political activity. The syndicalists were perhaps selective in their choice of aspects of the Factory Councils of which to approve; but they were to prove more successful than the *Ordine Nuovo* itself in applying the theories.

3. Amadeo Bordiga and the 'Abstentionist Faction of the *P.S.I.*'

As has been seen (pp. 78–9), the only nationally organised 'faction' in the *P.S.I.* was that of the 'abstentionists', based on Naples and led by

[32] Prefect of Turin to Ministry of the Interior 26 July 1920 (*State Archives* cit., 1920, b. 79). According to *Umanità Nova* 14 August 1920, there were only four *U.S.I.* members employed in the Lancia works at Turin.

[33] *Avanti!* (Turin ed.) 1 December 1919. Borghi admitted there was no *U.S.I.* branch at Turin in *Guerra di Classe* 18 January 1920. By July one had been set up – see *Guerra di Classe* 17 July 1920.

[34] Ferrero and Garino put forward an alternative motion to the Chamber of Labour Congress, but it was defeated. See *Umanità Nova* 18 June 1920.

Amadeo Bordiga.[35] The abstentionists called for the expulsion of reformists from the party, and their other bugbear was the Trade Unions, which they regarded as anti-revolutionary bodies controlled by reformists. Thus the abstentionists' two main targets – the Unions and the parliamentary right wing – were the same as those of the *Ordine Nuovo*. More generally, both groups passionately rejected many of the traditions of Italian Socialism – a major point of agreement, and one that explains much of how the Italian Communist Party came to be founded. Yet Bordiga himself was a very different personality from Gramsci – far less subtle, far more energetic, far more authoritarian.[36] For him, revolution was something carried out by disciplined revolutionaries. It came from above, not below, and the essential was to organise the right kind of political party. Bordiga, in short, had all the qualities needed to lead a sect. He was doctrinaire, insensitive, self-assured – yet also committed and respected by all. His personality matters, because he dominated the Abstentionist Faction (and later the Communist Party) far more than Gramsci ever dominated the *Ordine Nuovo* group; and his basic attitudes were incompatible with the *Ordine Nuovo*'s proposals.

In February 1919 the abstentionists' journal, *Il Soviet*, attacked the C.G.L.'s proposal for a Constituent Assembly, elected by 'professional categories' (see p. 33), on the grounds that the proletariat could only be represented on a political basis, not on the basis of any kind of trade organisation. In Russia, the article claimed,

> the Soviet is a political institution of the working class, whose delegates do not represent given categories, but given local and regional groups of worker-electors ... It is true that local Soviets are composed of workers' delegates elected factory by factory. But this was merely a practical method of setting up an elective system of workers' representation. If it had been desired to preserve the trade criterion, the delegates to the central Soviet would have been elected directly by the various categories of workers, whereas in fact – we repeat – they are elected by territorial groupings.[37]

[35] On Bordiga, see A. De Clementi, *Amadeo Bordiga* (Einaudi, Turin 1971). For his activities in Naples during and after the war, see also R. Colapietra, *Napoli fra Dopoguerra e Fascismo* (Feltrinelli, Milan 1962), esp. p. 36 and pp. 54–6.

[36] There is a brilliant pen-picture of Bordiga by G. Berti, 'Appunti e Ricordi 1919–26', in *Annali dell' Istituto Giangiacomo Feltrinelli*, anno VIII (1966), esp. pp. 19–20 and p. 127. Berti emphasises that Bordiga 'was likeable – he was always understanding, affectionate and, in political activity, open and loyal'. cf. also P. Spriano, *Storia del Partito Comunista Italiano*, vol. i (Einaudi, Turin 1967), pp. 264–5, for Ruggero Grieco's description of Bordiga.

[37] 'La Parodia del Soviet', by 'D.L.', in *Il Soviet* 16 February 1919.

Thus three months before the foundation of the *Ordine Nuovo*, the abstentionists were arguing against any attempt to base workers' representation on a craft system; their argument was directed against the reformist Unions, but it could serve equally well against the Turin movement. Bordiga's ideal was the 'Soviet', a purely political organ set up by a purged political party.

Bordiga was simply not interested in 'economism', or in Trade Union activity. He regarded such activity as necessarily anti-revolutionary and as diametrically opposed to real, revolutionary action.[38] In elaborating this argument, *Il Soviet* revealed an almost Marcusian conception of the meaning of 'proletariat'. In June 1919 it attacked the idea of the 'workers as producers': 'the class should be considered not as a mere aggregate of productive categories, but as a homogeneous complex of men whose living conditions show fundamental analogies'.[39] The article pointed to the example of a worker who owned a small-holding, and urged that such a worker – although he might very well be a 'producer' and a member of a Trade Union – was not a 'proletarian' at all, for his living conditions were totally different. The Trade Unions were, therefore, unfitted to represent the working class, as they contained non-proletarians; the 'Programme of the Communist Faction' urged that 'elections to local Workers' Councils shall be held separately from the professional categories to which they belong, and shall be divided into urban and rural constituencies.'[40] It is clear that the *Ordine Nuovo* and *Il Soviet* approached the problem of how to counter right-wing reformist Trade Unionism from entirely different angles. In Turin, with its large-scale industry, it was natural to regard the working class as a class of 'producers', with the factory as its focal point; in Naples, there was little industry and a mass of unemployed or semi-employed. Skilled engineering workers were bound to appear as 'worker-aristocrats' there, and their families might well own land in the surrounding province. In Naples, the 'proletariat' included many *non*-workers, the undifferentiated body of 'the poor'.

The specific argument between the abstentionists and the *Ordine Nuovo* began in September 1919. Viglongo had queried the phrase in the 'Programme of the Communist Faction', that elections to local Councils 'shall be held separately from the professional categories to which they belong.' Viglongo maintained that the power of the Soviet must derive from the

---

[38] See, for example, *Il Soviet* 2 February 1919, 30 March 1919, 18 June 1919, 20 July 1919, etc.

[39] 'L'Errore dell' Unità Proletaria', in *Il Soviet* 1 June 1919. The article was unsigned, but almost certainly by Bordiga himself.

[40] The Programme, which was drawn up as the basis for Bordiga's 'faction', was published in *Il Soviet* 13 July 1919.

masses voting in their places of work; Bordiga repeated that the Soviet was the *political* representative of the working class, defined not as the workers in a trade, but as the 'disinherited, with an interest in the rapid realisation of Communism.' He maintained that there must be a clear distinction between 'Soviets', elected more or less on the existing constituency boundaries, and Factory Councils, which he was willing to accept but which would be limited to 'technical and disciplinary functions during and after the socialisation of the factory.'[41] Thus the positions previously assumed in argument against reformist Trade Unions were turned against the Factory Councils, from the very beginning of the *Ordine Nuovo*'s campaign. Bordiga insisted that all illusions about the 'intrinsic revolutionary value' of Factory Councils be abandoned. The emphasis should be laid on the Party, whose local sections would become the nuclei of the future Soviets.[42] Finally, Bordiga was uncertain whether there was any point in trying to set up even 'Soviets' in Italy *before* the seizure of power, for they might be controlled by the reformists.[43]

With his hatred of 'economism', Bordiga does not seem to have fully grasped that the *Ordine Nuovo* movement *was* directed against the Trade Unions. On 11 January 1920 he wrote that it was a reformist movement, which might at best lead to a few modifications in Trade Union structure or perhaps to a bourgeois law for workers' control.[44] For Bordiga, Factory Councils could never overcome the particular, 'corporate' interests of individual groups of workers, nor could they represent the general interests of the proletariat (unemployed as well as employed). Hence it was unimportant whether the Directive Council of the Turin branch of *F.I.O.M.* was elected by Workshop Commissars or not – it would still be in conflict with the 'general interests' of the whole 'proletariat' unless it were subordinated to the party.[45] Moreover, as from January 1920 Bordiga strongly advocated 'Communist groups' within the Unions to capture them for the Communist Left, and this idea, also, could

[41] A.B., 'Il Sistema di Rappresentanza Comunista', in *Il Soviet* 14 September 1919.
[42] A.B., 'Formiamo i Soviet?', in *Il Soviet* 21 September 1919.
[43] The 'Programme of the Communist Faction' (July 1919) had called for the creation of provisional Workers' Councils 'to prepare and organise action to overthrow bourgeois domination', and Bordiga wrote to the Third International on 11 January 1920 reasserting that 'it is our intention to take the initiative in setting up municipal and rural Soviets'. On the other hand, in November 1919 he had also asked the International for guidance 'on the practical problem of setting up Soviets in a bourgeois regime and on the limits of such action', and his article 'La Costituzione dei Consigli Operai', in *Il Soviet* 1 February 1920, was much more doubtful about them. The letters to the International were published by Roberto Gabriele in *Rivista Storica del Socialismo* no. 27, anno IX (January–April 1966), pp. 183–8.
[44] 'Per la Costituzione dei Consigli Operai', in *Il Soviet* 11 January 1920.
[45] 'La Costituzione dei Consigli Operai', in *Il Soviet* 1 February 1920.

replace the Factory Councils as a weapon to be used against the reform-ists.[46] Although Bordiga allowed his local followers to participate in the Factory Council movement, and clearly did not oppose the working alliance between the abstentionists and the *Ordine Nuovo* in Turin, he certainly was never persuaded by Gramsci's arguments that the Factory Councils might liberate the Italian Trade Unions from reformist control.

Bordiga's whole position on the Factory Councils was finally summar-ised in the 'Theses on the Constitution of Workers' Councils Proposed by the Central Committee of the Communist Abstentionist Faction of the *P.S.I.*' This document placed most emphasis, not on the creation of Workers' Councils, but on the problem of ensuring that political power did in fact pass into their hands after the revolution. This could be achieved only by a purified party. Article 8 proclaimed that:

> The present necessities of Italian revolutionary activity do not consist in any artificial bureaucratic creation of Workers' Councils, nor – even less – in activity devoted to working in the Trade Unions or Factory Councils as ends in themselves, but in the setting up of a Communist Party which is free of opportunist reformist elements; a party of this nature will always be ready to act and intervene in the Soviets, when the hour comes for their vital transformation, which is not now far distant.[47]

The failure of the Piedmontese General Strike in April 1920 confirmed all Bordiga's views: he regarded it as proof that workers' control before the seizure of power was inconceivable – even if it were granted, it could only be a reformist concession bestowed by the bourgeois State.[48]

The failure of the strike also brought Gramsci to grips with the need to 'renew' the Socialist Party, which meant an alliance with Bordiga. In May 1920 he attended the National Conference of the Abstentionist Faction at Florence, and urged that if a new party were to be formed, it could not be 'on the narrow basis of abstentionism, but that a wide contact with the masses was necessary: this could only be achieved by means of new types of economic organisation'.[49] His words fell on deaf

---

[46] The idea was adopted in *Il Soviet* 11 January 1920.

[47] The Theses were printed in *Il Soviet* 11 April 1920. The whole emphasis was on the party's role in bringing about revolution; Soviets were said to arise 'at the moment of insurrection, but they can arise beforehand, during the crisis of the bourgeoisie.' This was clearly a compromise.

[48] A.B., 'Lo Sciopero di Torino', in *Il Soviet* 2 May 1920. Even after the revolution, wrote Bordiga, workers' control would have to be subordinated to the general interests of the proletariat, as expressed through the party.

[49] A report of the meeting appeared in *Il Soviet* 16 May 1920. Gramsci emphasised that in Turin the local abstentionists 'almost always' agreed with the *Ordine Nuovo's* policies.

ears. The failure to win over Bordiga and his supporters, or even to achieve a working compromise with them at national level, was perhaps the biggest political failure of the *Ordine Nuovo* movement. It settled which ideas on mass action, on Trade Unions and political parties, and on 'proletarian unity' were to dominate among the only section of the Italian Socialist Party that remained pledged to revolution, and which ideas were later to dominate the Italian Communist Party.

4. The Maximalists and the Directorate of the *P.S.I.*

Gramsci's proposals, designed as they were to solve the main problems of successful revolution, might have been expected to appeal to the maximalist left wing of the *P.S.I.* However, it has been seen (p. 77) that from the summer of 1919 onwards the maximalist Directorate of the Socialist Party had in effect allied with the reformist Trade Union leaders and parliamentarians. The first influential maximalist to comment on the events at Turin was Serrati, the editor of the main edition of *Avanti!* at Milan. His article, written in early November, poured sarcastic scorn on the Turin metal-workers' movement and on the idea of workers' unity being forged by the 'unorganised'; and he also denied that the Trade Unions' role was over – for as yet the Turin experiment was limited to a few factories, and the new institutions 'were more a mental sketch than a concrete fact'.[50] Serrati was confident of the eventual revolutionary outcome, but was determined to do nothing meantime that might undermine existing Socialist institutions. As he told Lenin at the end of December 1919:

> I am of the opinion that we should proceed in such a way that the revolution breaks out in its own time. Neither coups de main, nor excessive delays – that, it seems to me, should be our tactics. We should await events calmly yet actively, for they are maturing in our favour. During this waiting period – which should be as active as is possible for us – we should make ready those institutions which you have had to set up and improvise, amid great difficulties. There is a discussion going on here about setting up Factory Councils, with which some syndicalists, and even some Socialists, want to replace the existing labour organisations and Party. Some people claim that the New Order should arise from them and only from them. We think that we should be ready to set up all the bodies needed for the dictatorship of the

[50] 'Perché non si Equivochi', by g.m.s., in *Avanti!* (Milan ed.) 4 November 1919.

proletariat, but we should not now devalue the institutions that have
served us well hitherto and that may prove a great help in the near
future – the Cooperatives, the Trade Unions and the local authorities
that are in our hands.[51]

Serrati thought that *all* existing working-class institutions had to be
preserved and strengthened, for otherwise Socialists would not be able
to control the revolution once it had started, or administer society after it
had occurred. He therefore opposed both Gramsci's attacks on the
reformist Union leaders, and Bordiga's call for the expulsion of the right
wing from the Socialist Party. Here again, it is curious to see how the
Turin movement's reorganisation of Trade Union structure enabled
Serrati to use the argument that the Unions were essential for building
the Socialist economy as an argument *against* the Factory Councils,
although it was a view that Gramsci himself fully shared (see pp. 66–7).

The maximalists were also, of course, able to appeal to Russian experience in asserting the need for centralised Trade Unions. Serrati's views
were repeated by 'Carlo Niccolini',[52] who argued that in Russia 'the
controversy between the Factory Committees and the Trade Unions has
been resolved by the victory of the Trade Unions, which represent the
interests of the workers of the whole industry against local egoism, and in
favour of the collective principle ... in the end the Russian Factory
Committees have become fused into the Trade Union organisation.'[53]
This was the first suggestion that the Turin Factory Council experiment
was opposed to Russian practice. The argument was obviously both valid
and effective, and it gave added weight to the party Directorate's warnings
of the danger of 'localism'.

Nevertheless, the arguments of Serrati and Niccolini did not immediately convince all sections of maximalist opinion. The official maximalist
motion that had been put forward to the Bologna *P.S.I.* Congress in
October 1919 had pledged the party to 'organise Councils of Workers in

[51] Letter of Serrati to 'Carissimo', 28 December 1919 (in *State Archives*, Mostra della
Rivoluzione Fascista, Carteggio Serrati, b. 139, cartella 9, n. 59). The letter has been
published by Paolo Spriano (in *Rinascita* 3 February 1967), who gives convincing
reasons for thinking it was addressed to Lenin. Serrati used much the same arguments
in his article 'Unione o Scissura?', in *Comunismo* 15–29 February 1920, and very
frequently in his polemics against the Third International towards the end of 1920
(e.g. 'Il Dovere dell' Ora Presente', in *Comunismo* 1–15 October 1920).

[52] 'Niccolini' was Nikolai Markovich Liubarski, a Russian sent to Italy in 1919 by
the Third International. He was a personal friend of Serrati at this time, and stayed in
Serrati's house (G. Berti, 'Appunti e Ricordi 1919–26' cit., p. 81).

[53] C. Niccolini, 'I Comitati di Fabbrica', in *Comunismo* 15–31 December 1919.
cf. Paul Avrich, 'The Bolshevik Revolution and Workers' Control in Russian
Industry', in *Slavic Review*, a. XXII (1963), no. 1, pp. 47–63.

all branches of industry, among workers and peasants; preparing them to be, today, instruments of propaganda, persuasion and struggle (and also giving them some immediate contingent tasks), and tomorrow, organs of proletarian government.'[54] Although this wording was changed, it remained true that the final motion approved by the Congress had committed the party to the creation of Workers' Councils.[55] Moreover, the events in Turin soon aroused interest elsewhere. In Milan, some maximalists supported the Turin experiment and urged its adoption;[56] and in some other centres, such as Alessandria and Savona, the local maximalists supported Factory Council ideas and invited guest speakers from Turin to expound them.[57] The Italian Young Socialist Movement, in particular, initially welcomed the news from Turin as being the 'first concrete manifestation of a real revolution in Italy'; its journal printed the Turin 'Programme of the Workshop Commissars', and its central committee appealed to all members to join in the work of founding Factory Councils, which it called 'the most maximalist work that we can perform today.'[58] Hence the party Directorate's opposition to the Factory Councils in Turin could not be total; the Socialist leaders found it necessary to bring forward alternative schemes to those proposed at Turin.

They began doing so at the meeting of the Party's National Council at Florence in January 1920. Bombacci, generally regarded as the most extreme of the prominent maximalists, presented a plan for the 'Constitution of Soviets in Italy';[59] and his proposal that a further National Council meeting should be held within two months to draw up a definite constitution for Workers' Councils, was carried by 64,304 votes to 11,106.[60] The Bombacci project represents the first attempt by the maximalists to provide an alternative system of Workers' Councils to those being advocated at Turin. This was, indeed, admitted in its preamble, which pointed out that 'Workers' Councils are totally distinct and different from Factory Councils . . . the latter are organs for managing and controlling industry, whereas the Soviets are the basis of the Socialist State.'[61] The scheme itself was incoherent and hastily conceived. 'Soviets'

[54] 'Il Programma Massimalista', in *Comunismo* 1 October 1919.
[55] 'Impressioni del Congresso Socialista', in *Ordine Nuovo* 18 October 1919.
[56] See, especially, the columns of the weekly Milan Socialist paper *Compagni!* in the first half of 1920.
[57] cf. *Bandiera Rossa* of Savona, 13 March 1920; and *Idea Nuova* of Alessandria, 6 March 1920.
[58] *Avanguardia* 23 November 1919.
[59] Printed in full in *Avanti!* (Turin ed.) 28 January 1920.
[60] *Avanti!* (Turin ed.) 14 January 1920.
[61] *Avanti!* (Turin ed.) 28 January 1920.

were to be formed immediately, for they alone could 'channel the present period towards the final revolutionary struggle'. The party should set up a 'Provisional Central Executive Committee' of ten members (four from the *P.S.I.*, three from the *C.G.L.*, one from the League of Cooperatives, and two from the *U.S.I.*) charged with the task of organising them throughout Italy. The Central Committee was to appoint local and regional committees with the same task. There were to be two types of 'Soviet' – individual Soviets formed by workers, peasants, or State employees, and 'general' Soviets with representatives from all these categories. Some concessions to Factory Council principles were apparent in Bombacci's proposals for the specifically Workers' Soviets – all workers would be allowed to vote, and it was laid down that

> where internal Factory Councils, consisting of Commissars elected by individual workshops, have already been formed, the appointment of representatives to the Soviets may be carried out by the Commissars themselves, who will inform the masses of the names of the elected delegates and will, in general, act as liaison bodies between the delegates and the mass of the workers.[62]

Bombacci emphasised that the Soviets were to be fully controlled by the party until the revolution had occurred, and he also stressed that it was no part of the Soviets' task to help organise an insurrection, although they might prove useful if one broke out as a result of the bourgeoisie's 'violent resistance to a change of regime'.

Further radical thinking was provided by another member of the maximalist Directorate, Egidio Gennari. Gennari suggested that the Communes and local governments with Socialist majorities should set up new Soviet bodies and should then 'yield up to them – de facto, even if not de jure, as long as bourgeois law forbids it – the administrative authority won by our party ... the new Town Councils will be merely the executive organs of the decisions made by the Workers' Councils. They will give legal authority to the decisions of the Soviets.'[63]

A few weeks later Gennari produced a full-scale plan for a system of urban Soviets,[64] designed to amplify Bombacci's scheme. Like Bombacci, Gennari agreed that some form of factory representation could easily be incorporated in the new system – elections to the urban Soviets could take place in the factories. He was even prepared to allow elections of delegates in the larger factories to take place workshop by workshop, as at Turin,

---

[62] *Avanti!* (Turin ed.) 28 January 1920.
[63] 'Prepariamoci Dunque', in *Avanti!* (Turin ed.) 9 January 1920.
[64] 'Per Un Soviet Urbano', in *Avanti!* (Milan ed.) 21, 22 and 24 February 1920.

and to concede that the Workshop Commissar might also be the delegate to the Soviet, but he specifically warned against this ever becoming the normal situation, and he urged that the distinction between the nature and role of the Factory Councils and of the Soviets should be maintained at all times. The 'urban Soviet' was also to contain delegates elected by the unemployed, small artisans, shopworkers, domestic servants and nearby farm workers; it was to be divided into 'sections' based on districts in the town. Each section would elect its own executive committee, on which would also sit non-elected members appointed by the *P.S.I.* and the local Chamber of Labour; the executive committee of the urban Soviet itself would be formed from the executive committees of each of the various 'sections' and would also contain non-elected members. Gennari allowed all 'who live from their own labour' to vote for delegates to the Soviets, provided that 'such labour is a socially useful one' – he clearly envisaged only those engaged in industry, commerce or agriculture having the vote, and he also excluded all blacklegs, as being the 'venal instruments of capitalism'. The delegates themselves, however, had to be members of a political or economic working-class organisation.

These futile schemes were described by Serrati himself in March as 'idealistic Utopia-building'. Yet, as Gennari pointed out at the next meeting of the *P.S.I.*'s National Council at the end of February, 'it is essential to answer the demands of the masses somehow';[65] and the various projects, hastily drawn up as they were, did prove useful in enabling the party Directorate to appear to its followers to be pursuing a truly revolutionary policy. The National Council even decided, on Serrati's suggestion, that an experimental Soviet should be set up in one city, and that the scheme could gradually be extended to other areas as need arose.[66]

At the next meeting of the party's National Council, held at Milan in mid-April 1920 during the concluding stages of the Piedmontese General Strike, the party finally decided to set up a system of Soviets immediately. The various party branches were to begin the task, 'bearing in mind the norms laid down by the Directorate, which maintain the harmony between the party and the economic organisations';[67] the plan was supported by Baldesi for the *C.G.L.*, on the grounds that the setting up of Soviets would not harm the Trade Unions in any way. The Turin section of the party strongly criticised this policy for its reformist bias, and called for the creation of a strong 'Communist' party without which any Soviet

[65] *Avanti!* (Milan ed.) 2 March 1920.
[66] *Avanti!* (Turin ed.) 16 March 1920.
[67] *Lavoratori Avanti!* 23 April 1920. The motion was passed by 94,935 votes to 21,950.

experiment would be doomed to failure.[68] The real purpose of the maximalists' motion on Soviets was soon made clear. Immediately after the 'Soviet' project had been approved, the party went on to discuss Factory Councils, and approved a motion urging that:

> the Workshop Commissars must be coordinated, disciplined and regulated so as to avoid there being any confusion of powers or functions; (the National Council) charges the Secretariat of the party with the task of making agreements with the *C.G.L.* to define the relations that should exist between the Soviets now being set up and the Factory Councils, and to lay down the precise limits within which the two new bodies have to act'.[69]

In practice, the National Council meeting in April marked the end of the maximalists' need to put forward proposals for a Soviet type of organisation: with the end of the Turin strike in defeat, nothing more was heard of Bombacci's or Gennari's projects. The Piedmontese strike showed the dangers of 'localism' too clearly for the party leaders to want to instigate a similar experiment in another centre. Yet their proposals had performed some useful functions: in addition to satisfying their own supporters, the maximalists had distracted attention from what was going on in Turin, and had prevented the Turin movement from having too great an influence on the Italian labour movement in general. They had also succeeded in showing that the Factory Councils were totally distinct from 'Soviets', and had prevented the Turin movement from securing the prestige that accrued from the success of the Russian Revolution.

5. The Factory Councils in Milan: the Schiavello Project

The most likely place outside Turin for the *Ordine Nuovo*'s ideas to be accepted was Italy's only other highly industrialised centre, Milan. Gramsci fully realised the importance of winning converts there, and in January 1920 wrote that 'the immense factory of capitalist profit that is the

[68] cf. pp. 62–4, for Gramsci's view that Factory Councils necessarily required a strong party. It was at this meeting that the famous document 'For A Renewal of the P.S.I.' (now in A. Gramsci, *Ordine Nuovo*, Einaudi, Turin 1955, pp. 116–23) was first put to the party by the Turin section. Nevertheless, the Turin representative at the meeting, Tasca, voted for Gennari's Soviet project (cf. I. Fridman, 'La Fondazione del P.C.I.' in *Studi Storici* no. 3, 1964, pp. 550–64).

[69] *Lavoratori Avanti!* 23 April 1920.

bourgeois State has its vital centre in Milan . . . a Communist revolution in Milan means a Communist revolution in Italy, because Milan is the real capital of the bourgeois dictatorship.'[70] Milan was the centre of Italian maximalism, and the main edition of *Avanti!* was edited there by Serrati; it was also the home of the reformist leader Turati and, especially from early 1920, an important centre of anarchist and syndicalist agitation.[71] Some of the local maximalists, such as Cesare Seassaro, were in close contact with the *Ordine Nuovo*; and in January 1920 Alfonso Leonetti, hitherto a frequent contributor, moved from Turin to Milan and began an unceasing agitation on behalf of the Turin movement. Although the local syndicalists soon took the lead in the agitation for Factory Councils, some local Socialists also played an important part in it and, apart from Turin, Milan represented the biggest threat to the party Directorate's policy on Workers' Councils; conversely, the Turin movement's failure to secure a hold in Milan was one of the most important factors in its isolation.

The Milan Socialist Federation first discussed Factory Councils on 25 January 1920.[72] It decided that 'the question of setting up Factory Councils is an argument that concerns our *central* political and Trade Union organisations,'[73] and 'invited all comrades not to prejudice the issue of principle by attempts to set up Councils in haste.'[74] The discussion was thus postponed for a time, and it was not until 2 April, after much agitation by Leonetti and Seassaro,[75] that the local Socialist Party met again to discuss the issue. Schiavello, a leading local maximalist, put forward a first draft of his plan for Factory Councils.[76]

The Schiavello project was the most interesting of all the maximalist attempts to provide an alternative to the *Ordine Nuovo*. In the first place, it was 'drawn up in full agreement between the [Milan] Socialist section,

---

[70] 'La Funzione Storica delle Città', in *Ordine Nuovo* 17 January 1920 (now in A. Gramsci, *Ordine Nuovo* cit., p. 321). Gramsci returned to this theme in 1924, in his first article in the new party daily *L'Unità*: 'Il Problema di Milano', in *L'Unità* 21 February 1924 (now in A. Gramsci, *La Costruzione del Partito Comunista*, Einaudi, Turin 1971, pp. 7–10).

[71] From March 1920 both *Guerra di Classe* (weekly) and the anarchist daily *Umanità Nova* were being published in Milan.

[72] A report of this meeting appeared in *Avanti!* (Milan ed.) 27 January 1920. See also p. 113 for Bianchi's motion which was approved by the meeting.

[73] The Bianchi motion is given in *Battaglia Socialista* 31 January 1920. cf. p. 113, for Gino Castagno's comments on it.

[74] Schiavello motion, also in *Battaglia Socialista* 31 January 1920.

[75] See, in particular, *Compagni!* 16 February, 1 March and 16 March, *Battaglia Socialista* 27 March, and *Avanti!* (Milan ed.) 1 April 1920.

[76] The meeting was reported in *Avanti!* (Milan ed.) 4 April, and in *Battaglia Socialista* 10 April 1920.

the *C.G.L.*, and the executive committee of the Chamber of Labour';[77] and secondly, it was undeniably true that 'our project overthrows the entire present structure of our economic organisations',[78] and that it called for a transformation of the Trade Unions, on a factory and Industrial Union basis, and of the traditional structure of the Chambers of Labour. Schiavello followed Turin practice in advocating the election of Commissars from each workshop, and in laying down their tasks, although he would not allow non-Union members to vote. The General Council of the Union should henceforth consist of one or more members from each factory, elected by the Commissars, and all wage agreements, etc, should be invalid until ratified by an assembly of Factory Councils. The General Council of the local Chamber of Labour would also be elected by the Workshop Commissars, although full-time Trade Union officials would be entitled to sit on it. Both in the case of the Chamber of Labour and of the Trade Unions, the executive committees would be appointed by the General Councils, and thus ultimately depend on the Workshop Commissars. Provision was also made for the Workshop Commissars of every district in the city to form 'Ward Councils' (*Consigli di Rione*), which would clearly fulfil many of the functions of Gennari's 'Urban Soviets'.[79] Thus in Milan with its concentration of industry, the maximalists were forced into adopting a factory basis for their alternative proposals to the *Ordine Nuovo*; the scheme shows the influence of Factory Council ideas outside Turin.

The project was not discussed by the Milan Socialist Party until after the failure of the Piedmontese strike in April, and the discussion of it was therefore of little practical value. Serrati approved the scheme on 20 May, because it recognised that the Factory Council was not the equivalent of the Soviet, and was concerned purely with the running of production; but he urged that no immediate decision be taken, since the *C.G.L.* had decided to discuss the matter at their next National Congress.[80] Nevertheless, the local party approved the Schiavello project 'provisionally', reserving its right to modify it later when the 'central political and

[77] Bianchi's words to the General Council of the Milan Chamber of Labour on 24 April 1920, reported by the Prefect of Milan (Prefect of Milan to Ministry of the Interior 26 April 1920, in *State Archives*, Min. Int., Dir. Gen. P.S., Aff. Gen. e Ris., 1920, b. 66).

[78] 'Proposta di Costituzione dei Consigli di Fabbrica e Riordinamento delle Organizzazioni Economiche' (the Schiavello project), copy sent by Prefect of Milan to Ministry of the Interior 26 April 1920 (in *State Archives* cit., 1920, b. 66).

[79] *ibid.*

[80] *Avanti!* (Milan ed.) 23 May 1920. *Il Soviet* reported that Serrati 'left the impression of wanting the matter to blow over without a decision' (*Il Soviet* 6 June 1920).

economic organisations' laid down alternative proposals.[81] There was opposition to the plan both from Seassaro, who followed the *Ordine Nuovo* in demanding the vote for non-Union men, and from the abstentionists, who regarded the scheme as replacing the local party by the Chamber of Labour.[82] The Schiavello project was also approved by the Milan Chamber of Labour, which on 5 June called on its member Unions to arrange the election in each factory of delegates to a new General Council;[83] this appeal was ignored, as was a similar one made at the end of July.[84]

In the end, Serrati's policy of letting the issue die down prevailed. The scheme had only been produced to meet the challenge from Turin, and could therefore be allowed to expire when, after April 1920, the Factory Council movement appeared to be a challenge no longer. However, this 'success' was bought at the cost of considerable unrest among Milanese Socialists, of a crisis in the Milan Chamber of Labour in July 1920,[85] and above all of leaving the whole issue to the local syndicalists. The cost was a high one, as events in the late summer were to show.

[81] *Avanti!* (Milan ed.) 28 May 1920.

[82] See Repossi's speech, reported in *Avanti!* (Milan ed.) 2 June 1920. cf. *Il Soviet*'s view of the scheme as a *vero minestrone*: 'the workers think very differently and want to set up Factory Councils so that both organised and non-organised can be represented' (*Il Soviet* 6 June 1920).

[83] *Avanti!* (Milan ed.) 6 June 1920.

[84] *Avanti!* (Milan ed.) 31 July 1920.

[85] The Prefect of Milan, Flores, telegraphed news of the crisis on 17 July: the Secretary General and three secretaries resigned after a dispute with the executive committee (Flores to Ministry of the Interior 17 July 1920, in *State Archives* cit., 1920, b. 66). This news was confirmed in *Avanti!* (Milan ed.) 29 July 1920; the executive committee issued a statement to the effect that the Schiavello project had not been abandoned and that Factory Councils would soon be set up.

CHAPTER SEVEN

Isolation in Turin

It has been seen (pp. 109–10) that the Factory Council movement in Turin was discredited by the failure of the Piedmontese General Strike in April 1920. The impact of this failure was considerable. Different people drew different conclusions from it, but Gramsci found his ideas rejected by almost all sections of Turin Socialist opinion, as well as by most of his colleagues on the *Ordine Nuovo*.

The significance of the strike for Gramsci was that:

> For the first time in history there occurred the case of a proletariat that waged a struggle for control over production, without being driven to action by hunger or by unemployment. Moreover, it was not merely a minority, a working-class avant-garde that undertook this struggle, but the entire mass of workers in Turin who went into battle without a thought for sacrifice or privations, and waged the struggle to the end.[1]

This was obviously a rhetorical attempt to cheer people up, but it was not *only* rhetoric – the April General Strike *was* the longest and most complete strike that had ever taken place in Piedmont,[2] and in any case Gramsci's conclusions were important. This great mass movement had been 'betrayed' by the Socialist leaders, or at the very least its defeat had been largely caused by their failure to 'prepare' the Italian masses adequately for a national revolution, by the fact that 'in Italy organised revolutionary energies capable of centralising a vast profound movement, capable of creating a State and giving it a revolutionary dynamism . . . do not exist.'[3]

---

[1] 'Il Movimento Torinese dei Consigli di Fabbrica', in *Ordine Nuovo* 14 March 1921 (but written for the 2nd Congress of the Third International in the summer of 1920; now in A. Gramsci, *Ordine Nuovo*, Einaudi, Turin 1955, p. 176).

[2] G. Prato, *Il Piemonte e gli Effetti della Guerra sulla sua Vita Economica e Sociale* (Yale U.P. and Laterza, Bari 1925), p. 149.

[3] 'Superstizione e Realtà', in *Ordine Nuovo* 8 May 1920 (now in A. Gramsci, *Ordine Nuovo* cit., p. 111).

Gramsci had held this view of the *P.S.I.*'s weakness at least since January (see p. 91), but the April strike increased his contempt for the maximalists, and convinced him that a strong disciplined party, committed to revolutionary policies, and not dominated by the Unions, was urgently necessary.[4] All this meant that Gramsci had to seek allies who also rejected the *P.S.I.*'s structure and traditions; and so, as has been seen, he attended the National Conference of the Abstentionist Faction at Florence in May.

The general feeling at Turin after the strike was rather different from Gramsci's. Both reformists and revolutionaries agreed that it had been a mistake to wage the struggle in apparent defence of the Internal Commissions' right to 'commit abuses in the factories'.[5] The struggle should have been extended nationally, not by any appeal to the *P.S.I.* to proclaim a revolution, but by an appeal for a national agitation in favour of 'workers' control over production'.[6] Even Gramsci shared the view that such an appeal would have won greater support,[7] although he characteristically saw workers' control as a 'means of giving the Italian Revolution a concrete programme'. Thus most criticism at Turin centred on the lack of action, or even 'betrayal', by the *C.G.L.* rather than by the *P.S.I.*, and the tendency to regard Factory Councils purely as a means of reforming the Trade Unions – a tendency to which Gramsci had been opposed since the beginning of the movement – was strengthened.

All this became evident almost immediately, at the Congress of the Turin Chamber of Labour held on 23–6 May. Much of the Congress' time was taken up with angry recriminations over the strike, and over the lack of support shown by the Chamber of Labour's executive committee for the whole Factory Council movement;[8] and the conduct of the former executive committee was only approved eventually by a majority of 53,722 votes to 47,709.[9] The Congress then went on to discuss the Factory Council issue. The discussion was opened by Tasca, who made a three-hour speech outlining his new proposals for a reconciliation between the

[4] cf. the Turin manifesto 'Per un Rinnovamento del Partito Socialista', in *Ordine Nuovo* 8 May 1920 (now in A. Gramsci, *Ordine Nuovo* cit., pp. 116–23), sent to the party's National Council in Milan while the April strike was on, calling for a new Party Congress and a purge of the reformists. Gramsci's complex views on the party at this time are further discussed below (pp. 141–2).

[5] Prefect of Turin to Ministry of the Interior 25 April 1920 (*State Archives*, Min. Int., Dir. Gen. P.S., Aff. Gen. e Ris., 1920, b. 75).

[6] O. Pastore, 'Dopo la Battaglia', in *Avanti!* (Turin ed.) 25 April 1920.

[7] cf. 'I Risultati Ottenuti', in *Avanti!* (Turin ed.) 1 May 1920.

[8] *Avanti!* (Turin ed.) 26 and 27 May 1920.

[9] *Avanti!* (Turin ed.) 28 May 1920. The opposition included all the local metalworkers and indeed a majority of the workers in the city of Turin; the executive committee was saved by the workers from the outlying province.

various opposed views on the Councils.[10] After Tasca's breach with the other original members of the *Ordine Nuovo* in January, he had worked closely with the leaders of the local Chamber of Labour. Nevertheless, what he said apparently came as a surprise to most local Union leaders present, as indeed to all other sections of Turin opinion.[11]

Tasca's proposals were very similar to those put forward by Schiavello at Milan. He concentrated on the relationship between Factory Councils and Trade Unions, and on the need to 'democratise' the latter. For Tasca, Factory Councils and Trade Unions could not be separate bodies with different functions, for internal factory issues were inseparable from national ones – hence '[we are concerned with] a single body, for the "Council" is merely the expression of Trade Union activity in the place of work, and the Trade Union is the general body that groups the Councils according to their branch of production, co-ordinating and disciplining their activity.'[12] He therefore proposed that the Trade Unions and the Factory Councils should be fused into a single organisation. 'Control' of production in the factory would be shared by the Factory Council and the Union, 'because such control must be exercised from without, by the Union, which will therefore be entrusted with control of the branch of industry concerned.'[13] The Factory Councils were also to be the 'vital element' in the task of transforming the craft Unions into Industrial Unions, of which each Factory Council would be the local cell; in future 'the metal-workers' Union will reckon its strength from the number of factories, instead of from the number of individual subscriptions.'[14] Representatives of the technicians and clerical staff, as well as those of the manual workers, were to be included within the single Factory Councils of his scheme.

More importantly, Tasca's proposals effectively re-established the Union leaders' position locally. Workshop Commissars would continue to exist, and would continue to elect the Internal Commissions; but in future there would be no question of their taking policy decisions. Henceforth, the executive council of the local branch of *F.I.O.M.* was to be elected, not by the Workshop Commissars as previously, but by all the local members of the Union (although the list of candidates was to be

---

[10] Tasca's speech was reported in *Avanti!* (Turin ed.) 28 May 1920 and in *Ordine Nuovo* 29 May 1920; the complete text was printed in pamphlet form as *Il Problema Politico e Sindacale dei Consigli di Fabbrica* (Tipografia Alleanza, Turin 1920).

[11] See, especially, the speeches of Gino Guarnieri and of Maurizio Garino in *Avanti!* (Turin ed.) 28 May 1920.

[12] *Il Problema Politico e Sindacale dei Consigli di Fabbrica* cit., p. 39.

[13] *ibid.*, p. 36.

[14] *ibid.*, p. 29.

drawn up by the Workshop Commissars). Policy decisions could only be taken if there were agreement between the executive committee of the local branch and the majority of Commissars; but otherwise a new body was to be convened, the 'General Council' of the branch, which was to become the highest local deliberative body. The composition of this body is significant. It was to consist of all the members of the Internal Commissions, from those factories where Union members were more than 75 *per cent.* of the total labour force; where they were not, the factory was to be represented on the General Council by 'federal committees' elected by Union members alone. Tasca concluded optimistically that since it was one of the tasks of the Workshop Commissars to encourage workers to join the Union, all factories would eventually achieve 75 *per cent.* membership and thus the General Council would come to consist entirely of Internal Commissions from the local factories.

Tasca's proposals proved so acceptable to the local Union leaders that they withdrew their opposition motion at the Congress and supported Tasca's. Boccignoni, the leader of the local bakers, said that he had previously opposed all suggestions for Councils, but would now work enthusiastically for them in his own Union.[15] Buozzi, the General Secretary of *F.I.O.M.*, even asked Guarnieri and Tasca to draft a joint scheme for Factory Councils throughout Italy.[16] The only opposition to Tasca came from the anarchists and syndicalists. Tasca's proposals surprised and confused them, but they drew up an alternative motion in great haste,[17] proclaiming that Factory Councils were 'bodies absolutely opposed to the State'; it secured a mere seven votes, and otherwise the entire Congress supported the Tasca plan for Factory Councils under Union control. The Congress also elected a new executive committee, including Luigi Borghi of the Technicians' Union and also Tasca, who became 'political secretary' of the Chamber of Labour. Although a motion praising the work of the *Ordine Nuovo* was passed – unanimously – the result of the Chamber of Labour Congress demonstrated that the April strike had ended the possibility of an autonomous Factory Council campaign in Turin. Gramsci's own views were not represented by a single speaker at the Congress, and the *Ordine Nuovo*'s main purpose — revolutionary 'preparation' — was ignored.[18]

Tasca's proposals seemed particularly acceptable to the delegates at

---

[15] *Avanti!* (Turin ed.) 28 May 1920.

[16] *ibid*; Buozzi asked that the draft scheme 'should not be either too theoretical or too practical'.

[17] The motion was published in *Avanti!* (Turin ed.) 29 May 1920.

[18] Viglongo, one of the few supporters of *Ordine Nuovo* to oppose Tasca's scheme, pointed this out in *Avanti!* (Turin ed.) 31 May 1920.

the Chamber of Labour Congress because Tasca was still generally thought to be a leading member of the *Ordine Nuovo* group. Gramsci therefore had to dissociate the journal from Tasca's plans, even though this could only be done at the cost of revealing his own isolation in Turin. The next few issues of the *Ordine Nuovo* were accordingly devoted to a detailed refutation of Tasca's proposals and a more complete exposition of Gramsci's views on the relationship that should exist between Factory Councils and Trade Unions.[19] Gramsci accused Tasca of coming 'to the aid of the opportunists and reformists who have always tried to distort the Factory Councils . . . by appealing to bureaucratic "discipline".'[20] Three years later Gramsci wrote of this quarrel between the two original founders of the *Ordine Nuovo*:

> Tasca was attacked on two grounds: (1) because he intervened at the Congress of the Chamber of Labour and supported a policy there that was opposed to the policy of the local branch of the party, taking us completely by surprise, and following an individualist tradition that has to be fought against; and (2) because we had to show all the dangers inherent in his proposals, which would have led to the subordination of the Factory Councils to the Trade Unions, at a time when the Trade Unions were still dominated by reformists.[21]

Tasca's main argument in reply was that the State, not the Factory Council, must control production, so as to ensure rational economic planning and capital investment.[22] He also accused Gramsci of anarcho-syndicalism, which was by this time rapidly replacing 'interventionism' as the arch-crime. The fact that so much of the *Ordine Nuovo*'s space in the summer of 1920 was devoted to acrimonious disputes, and to bitter criticism of proposals that had already been almost unanimously approved locally, is an indication of the journal's loss of influence after the April strike.

Tasca, as the new 'political secretary', was able to present his ideas as the Chamber of Labour's official policy. He was strongly supported by Enea Matta, another former contributor to the *Ordine Nuovo*, who had

[19] See, especially, Gramsci's 'La Relazione Tasca e il Congresso della Camera di Lavoro di Torino', in *Ordine Nuovo* 5 June 1920; and his 'Il Programma dell' Ordine Nuovo', in *Ordine Nuovo* 14 and 28 August 1920 (both are now in A. Gramsci, *Ordine Nuovo* cit., pp. 127–31 and 146–54).

[20] 'La Relazione Tasca e il Congresso della Camera di Lavoro di Torino' cit., in *Ordine Nuovo* 5 June 1920 (now in A. Gramsci, *Ordine Nuovo* cit., p. 131).

[21] 'Postilla', in *Lo Stato Operaio* 5 June (dated 5 May) 1924 (now in A. Gramsci, *La Costruzione del Partito Comunista*, Einaudi, Turin 1971, p. 189).

[22] Tasca's replies were published in *Ordine Nuovo* 12 and 19 June, and 3 July 1920 (now in P. Spriano, *Ordine Nuovo*, Einaudi, Turin 1963, pp. 518–30 and 534–41).

become the secretary of the Chamber of Labour's new 'Commission for Political Propaganda and for the Organisation of Workshop Commissars', on which many local reformist leaders also sat.[23] On 20 June Tasca spoke to the Shoemakers' Union, proclaiming that 'the Trade Union organisation will be the main organ of the new society; the task of the Councils is to study and get to know all aspects of production and thus enable the Trade Union to control industrial and commercial operations.'[24] However, no serious attempt to implement Tasca's proposals for re-organising the structure of the local Unions was ever made, despite the overwhelming support given them at the Congress. They remained part of the local reformists' programme for the rest of the summer, but in practice they were soon dropped.[25]

It is difficult, therefore, to know how seriously to take Tasca's plan — and the Schiavello plan in Milan, which it much resembled (see p. 129 ff.). Gramsci supposed it was merely a reformist manoeuvre to counter the Factory Council campaign, or even a personal manoeuvre by Tasca to secure a Union job.[26] Tasca's scheme was undeniably welcome to the reformist Union leaders, but there was more in it than that. Tasca was opposed to 'class collaborationism', and after all he did join the new Communist Party a few months later. He regarded his plan as a means of preserving the best of Italian Socialist institutions and traditions (especially the Chambers of Labour), while giving them a more 'revolutionary' content and indeed strengthening the central direction necessary for revolution — and of course he was impressed by Russian experience. In assessing his proposals, it is worth recalling that the *P.S.I.*'s reformists and maximalists were by this time working in fairly close harmony; and that the institutions of the grand old party *were* under strong attack from the syndicalists (see below). Thus Tasca's scheme seemed acceptable to Socialists of most persuasions,[27] and it was important that both in

[23] The Commission's names were given in *Avanti!* (Turin ed.) 17 June 1920.

[24] *Avanti!* (Turin ed.) 21 June 1920.

[25] The only sign of any intention to implement them came in early July, when Matta, as Secretary of the Commission, wrote to all the local Trade Unions asking them what measures they were taking to 'transform your craft organisation into an industrial one, including workers, technicians and clerical staff.' His letter was published in *Avanti!* (Turin ed.) 12 July 1920.

[26] 'Postilla', in *Lo Stato Operaio* 5 June (dated 5 May) 1924 (now in A. Gramsci, *La Costruzione del Partito Comunista* cit., p. 188).

[27] Tasca later claimed that Togliatti and Terracini had supported his scheme (*Il Mondo* 25 August 1953, now in A. Tasca, *I Primi Dieci Anni del P.C.I.*, Laterza, Bari 1971, pp. 106–8). This is possible, although there is not enough evidence to be sure. Togliatti had certainly supported him on the Factory Council issue in December 1919 (see p. 93), and both Togliatti and Terracini were to split with Gramsci during the local party branch elections two months later (see below).

Milan and Turin the Chambers of Labour were committed by the summer of 1920 to a radical reorganisation of Union structure, and to pressing for a kind of 'workers' control'.

Moreover, the new government formed by Giovanni Giolitti in June 1920 was likely to favour some kind of national project along these lines. A new Ministry, the Ministry of Labour and National Insurance, had been set up, and Giolitti had appointed a former syndicalist, Arturo Labriola, to the post.[28] Labriola's views were well known. Six months earlier he had told the Chamber of Deputies that it was

> absolutely necessary to move towards a democratic organisation of the enterprise, by means of Workers' Councils in firms . . . to control production and to share profits. The federation of enterprise councils, sector by sector, unifies all production under the control of workers and peasants . . . the complete realisation of Socialism is in the factory, managed directly by the workers under the collective control of the State and of the Union.[29]

On 6 July 1920, as Minister, he returned to this theme. Factory Councils with limited functions were excellent means of improving factory discipline; and he went on:

> Certainly, if we were to go further, if the Factory Councils were to become a means of supervising (*vigilare*) firms and giving producers an interest in the products and profits, we would be entering new territory, and we should look at these problems without prejudice or preconceived ideas. I, for my part, regard these solutions with the greatest sympathy.[30]

It seems at least possible, therefore, that the Giolitti government might have made serious efforts in the autumn of 1920 to encourage reorganisation along Tasca or Schiavello lines, and to pass a law for some kind of 'Trade Union control' of industry. But the 'Occupation of the Factories' intervened in September, and transformed the Italian political situation; although the government did bring forward a proposal for 'Trade Union control' in the middle of the Occupation (see p. 171), it was by this time regarded as simply a manoeuvre to restore normal working. If the

---

[28] cf. D. Marucco, *Arturo Labriola e il Sindacalismo Rivoluzionario in Italia* (Fondazione Luigi Einaudi, Turin 1970), pp. 267–77. The Ministry was set up in the last few days of the previous Nitti government, by Decree-Law 3 June 1920 n. 700.

[29] Speech of 11 December 1919, in Atti Parlamentari, Camera dei Deputati, Legislatura XXV, Sessione I (1919–20), Discussioni, Tornata 11 Dicembre 1919.

[30] Speech of 6 July 1920, quoted in D. Marucco, *Arturo Labriola e il Sindacalismo Rivoluzionario in Italia* cit., p. 270.

'Occupation of the Factories' had not happened, perhaps Tasca's scheme would have had a considerable influence on the whole history of the Italian labour movement. This is, of course, speculation; but it is indisputable that it was Tasca, not Gramsci, who was at the head of the local labour organisation in Turin, and who had secured mass support there for a 'Factory Council' scheme.

Gramsci's isolation was fully revealed during the crisis of the local Socialist party branch later in the summer. The local party had been controlled since February 1920 by an alliance between the abstentionists and the *Ordine Nuovo*. This alliance broke up in the summer of 1920, mainly over the important issue of whether Socialists should collaborate with anarchists and syndicalists. Tasca and Terracini were opposed to any collaboration with them; the branch secretary Boero, an abstentionist, was not, and on 7 July he took part in a major syndicalist demonstration in support of the insurrection at Ancona (see below, p. 144).[31] Moreover, on 16 July the Turin branch invited 'all branches in Italy to give the Party Directorate a mandate to take part in the meeting at Genoa of revolutionary and Trade Union organisations, with the sincere aim of achieving a unity of action that will correspond to the existing unity of spirit among the masses.'[32] This resolution, allied to disagreements over the question of whether to take part in the forthcoming municipal election campaign, provoked a split in the executive committee. In late July it resigned. The subsequent branch elections gave the most complete indication of how the original *Ordine Nuovo* group had split up. Gramsci summarised the situation in a letter four years later:

> Palmi [Togliatti] should remember how in August 1920 I broke away both from him and from Umberto [Terracini]. At that time it was I who wished to maintain relations with the Left rather than with the Right, whereas Palmi and Umberto had reached some kind of agreement with Tasca, who had separated from us as early as January.[33]

In fact, this split in the *Ordine Nuovo* group dates from before August[34] — Gramsci had, in fact, 'maintained relations with' the Left throughout the

---

[31] *Avanti!* (Turin ed.) 8 July 1920.

[32] *Avanti!* (Turin ed.) 18 July 1920. For this meeting, see below, p. 146 and note 55. The issue was particularly important at this time, because of inter-Union rivalry during the metal-workers' dispute – see pp. 149–50.

[33] Letter of Gramsci to Scoccimarro 5 January 1924, printed in P. Togliatti, *La Formazione del Gruppo Dirigente del Partito Comunista Italiano* (Ed. Riuniti, Rome 1962), pp. 151–2.

[34] Gramsci wrote in another letter dating from 1924 of an 'April split' (Gramsci to Leonetti 28 January 1924, *ibid.*, p. 183).

summer, as his visit to the national conference of Bordiga's 'Abstentionist Faction' at Florence in May showed.

Gramsci's position in the summer of 1920 was, indeed, somewhat peculiar. He supported the abstentionists, and this implied commitment to the idea of forming a new political party, as did his bitter criticism of the 'bureaucratic' nature of the *P.S.I.*[35] He warned that a new party would have to be founded, unless the new 'Communist groups' could manage to revitalise the old one; and, like Bordiga — but unlike practically all other left-wing Socialists — he was quite prepared to jettison old Socialist traditions and institutions *en bloc*. But even so, he did not yet make any specific call for a new party, perhaps because he realised that he was not going to secure the kind of new party, based on Councils and mass action, that he wanted.[36] The most coherent account of his views dates from 3 July:

> We have always thought that the duty of the Communist groups within the Party should not be to fall into particularist illusions (e.g. the problem of electoral abstentionism, the problem of setting up a 'truly' Communist Party, etc.), but to work to create the mass conditions in which it is possible to resolve all individual problems within the framework of the problem of the organic development of the Communist revolution. Can there be, in fact, a Communist Party (a party that will be a party of action and not merely an 'academy' of pure doctrine and of politicians who think 'correctly' and express the 'correct' line on Communism) unless there exists among the masses a spirit of historical initiative and an aspiration for industrial autonomy? . . . And since the formation of parties and the rise of real historical forces of which parties are the reflection does not come about overnight, out of nothing, but happens according to a dialectical process, is it not the main task of the forces of Communism to strengthen the consciousness and the organisation of the forces of production, which

[35] See, especially, Gramsci's article 'Dove va il Partito Socialista?' in *Ordine Nuovo* 10 July 1920 (now in A. Gramsci, *Ordine Nuovo* cit., pp. 401–4).

[36] Gramsci's most detailed and famous criticism of the *P.S.I.* was the document sent to the Milan National Council meeting of the party in April 1920 (published in *Ordine Nuovo* 8 May 1920, and now in A. Gramsci, *Ordine Nuovo* cit., pp. 116–23), which did not call for the formation of a new party and was, in fact, entitled 'For a Renewal of the P.S.I.'. This criticism was praised by Lenin, who also did not yet envisage a 'separatist' Communist Party (see p. 198). For Lenin's views, see K. Shirinya, 'Lenin e la Formazione del P.C.I.: Nuovi Documenti Sovietici', in *Critica Marxista*, anno VIII, n. 6 (Nov.–Dec. 1970), pp. 107–29, esp. p. 110; and *Leninski Sbornik*, XXXVII, p. 219. Gramsci's first specific call for a new party was in October 1920, in his article 'Il Partito Comunista', in *Ordine Nuovo* 9 October 1920 (now in A. Gramsci, *Ordine Nuovo* cit., pp. 158–63).

are essentially Communist, so that they may develop and by expanding create the secure economic permanent basis of political power in the hands of the proletariat?[37]

With these preoccupations, Gramsci and his few supporters[38] were unable to support either the abstentionists or his former colleagues on the *Ordine Nuovo* in the elections to the new executive committee of the party branch. They were both arguing about an unreal and secondary problem, and he therefore contented himself with issuing a 'simple declaration' on behalf of his newly formed – and exiguous – 'Communist Education Group'. The 'declaration' remarked despairingly that the very fact that the elections were being fought partly over the 'fictional' issue of whether or not to take part in bourgeois elections, showed 'how the level of political education is still very mediocre even among Party members', and why the masses were turning from the *P.S.I.* to 'the empty demagogic phraseology of the syndicalists'. Gramsci's group declared that they would ask their supporters to leave their ballot-papers blank, although there was not a sufficiently high degree of political discipline in the local party for this to be effective. Despite his evident pessimism, Gramsci still regarded the question of founding a new party as less important than that of mass action, and had not yet become convinced that a Communist Party would be a more effective instrument of mass action than the existing Socialist party.

Meanwhile almost all Gramsci's colleagues on the *Ordine Nuovo* – including Togliatti, Terracini, Montagnana and Matta – had joined the 'Electionist Communist' group. This group was, like the abstentionists, officially committed to an eventual purge of the *P.S.I.*'s reformist right wing and to the formation of 'Communist groups'; the purge, however, was not to take place immediately, and so the local reformists could and did support the programme and candidates of the 'electionists'. The 'electionists' support for taking part in elections was not on grounds of 'propaganda', as was Gramsci's; local elections could enable a 'position of power' to be seized from the bourgeoisie, and so had to be contested with all possible vigour. The 'electionists' also declared their support for Factory Councils throughout Italy 'in conformity with the programme already approved by the majority of Turin Socialists', and deplored the

---

[37] 'Due Rivoluzioni', in *Ordine Nuovo* 3 July 1920 (now in A. Gramsci, *Ordine Nuovo* cit., p. 138).
[38] The extent of Gramsci's support in the local party branch was shown in the voting for a new Electoral Committee to organise the executive committee election. Gramsci's group secured a mere 17 votes, compared with 141 for the electionists and 54 for the abstentionists (*Avanti!*, Turin ed., 27 July 1920).

strength of the anarchists and syndicalists. This was perhaps the key issue. At a time of 'anarchist contagion', all good men should come to the aid of the Party. The abstentionists, for their part, adopted the national policy-programme of Bordiga's 'faction'. They too advocated 'Communist groups' in the factories, and called for an *immediate* purge of the reformists, so that an Italian Communist Party, adhering to the Third International, could be formed as soon as possible. They also, more interestingly, called for active propaganda for Factory Councils, and advocated 'meetings of representatives of the various organisations, and among the workers of city and country, to create unity of thought and action' – a clear reference to the syndicalists.[39]

The results of the elections showed a clear majority for the 'electionists'. Togliatti headed the list of successful candidates and became secretary of the local party in place of the abstentionist leader Boero.[40] Once again, a leading *Ordinovista* had secured a top post in the Turin labour movement, without Gramsci's backing.[41] And once again it is interesting to speculate how events might have gone if there had been no 'Occupation of the Factories'. Bordiga would no doubt have founded a new Communist Party anyway, on the basis of the Twenty-one Conditions (see p. 198); but would Togliatti, Tasca and Terracini have been members? Perhaps not, judging by their alignment in these branch elections in August; and one cannot be absolutely certain even of Gramsci himself. Even as it was, there was no question of the *Ordine Nuovo* forming a homogeneous group, able to assert its views within the new party. The Communist Party of Italy was to be founded and dominated by Bordiga, and the dissensions within the former *Ordine Nuovo* group were at least partly responsible.

Thus the failure of the April strike did not result in an agitation for the foundation of a Communist Party. Most of Gramsci's former supporters remained committed to the existing party, and Gramsci himself, despite his 'relations with' the Left, remained unconvinced that a new party would solve the problems of revolution, and never abandoned the quest

[39] The various manifestoes of the three groups were printed in *Avanti!* (Turin ed.) 12 August 1920. They were reprinted as an appendix to F. Ferri's article 'La Situazione Interna della Sezione Socialista Torinese nell' Estate 1920', in *Rinascita* April 1958, pp. 259–65.

[40] With 466 votes, as compared with 186 for the leading abstentionist candidate, Boero (*Avanti!*, Turin ed., 16 August 1920).

[41] However, there seem to have been no bitter polemics later between Gramsci and Togliatti, as there were between Gramsci and Tasca. On the whole episode, see also G. Bocca, *Palmiro Togliatti* (Laterza, Bari 1973), p. 44; E. Ragionieri, Introduction to vol. i of P. Togliatti, *Opere* (1917–26) (Riuniti, Rome 1967), pp. lxvi–lxviii; P. Spriano, Introduction to *Ordine Nuovo* (anthology) (Einaudi, Turin 1963), pp. 88–96; L. Paggi, *Gramsci e il Moderno Principe* (Riuniti, Rome 1970), pp. 309–16; A. Lepre and S. Levrero, *La Formazione del Partito Comunista d'Italia* (Riuniti, Rome 1971), p. 247.

for a new type of mass organisation based on industrial units. At the time of the crisis in the local party, in July and August 1920, he was far more concerned with trying to revive some kind of practical Factory Council organisation than with either local or national political affairs.

The 'revival of Trade Union bureaucracy and of opportunist elements within the local branch of the Socialist Party'[42] after the April strike meant that the local syndicalists became more prominent as the only remaining spokesmen for popular discontent. At a time when the cost of living was still rising very sharply,[43] and when it seemed as if the local employers were taking advantage of their victory in April in order to wage an all-out offensive against their workers,[44] there was a great deal of discontent in Turin; and it came to a head in early July over the government's plans to send troops to Albania. The Albanian venture provoked protests through-out Italy, and caused a mutiny of the troops concerned and a popular rising in the port from which the troops were to leave, Ancona.[45] Ancona was a major anarchist centre, with a long tradition of revolt. In these circumstances, the syndicalists in Turin proclaimed that they were the only real opponents of a Libyan-type colonial adventure. The mass meeting called in Turin to express solidarity with the Ancona insurgents was called by the local syndicalists.[46]

The Ancona issue soon merged into a related question, whether work on war materials and munitions – clearly designed to be sent to Albania or to aid the Allied intervention in the Soviet Union – should be boycotted. In early July there was a lock-out at the Romeo works in Milan, as a result of the workers' refusal to work on war materials;[47] and at Terni, an arms

[42] 'Cronache dell' Ordine Nuovo', in *Ordine Nuovo* 31 July 1920.

[43] The average weekly expenditure of a working-class family of five persons, according to the figures of the Ufficio Statistico Municipale in Milan, rose from 124.67 *lire* in January 1920 to 153.9 *lire* in June (and reached 167.9 *lire* in September). The increase over the whole year 1920 was 60.6 *per cent.*, compared with an increase of 10.58 *per cent.* in 1919 over 1918. (P. Bachi, *Italia Economica 1920*, Lapi, Città di Castello 1921, p. 195).

[44] *Avanti!* (Turin ed.) 11 July 1920 commented on 'the host of little incidents' that had taken place in the local factories during the previous few weeks. On 10 July 200 workers at the main Fiat works were sacked, ostensibly because of a lack of raw materials; they included many well-known Socialists and some of the Workshop Commissars (*ibid*). See also M. Abrate, *La Lotta Sindacale nella Industrializzazione in Italia* (Angeli, Milan 1967), pp. 326–7; and G. Maione, *Il Biennio Rosso* (Il Mulino, Bologna 1975), pp. 180–2.

[45] For the Ancona revolt, see P. Nenni, *Il Diciannovismo* (Ed. *Avanti!*, Milan 1962), pp. 104–6; and A. Tasca, *Nascita e Avvento del Fascismo* (La Nuova Italia, Florence 1950), p. 111. The Prefect's reports of the uprising are in *State Archives*, Min. Int., Dir. Gen. P.S., Aff. Gen. e Ris., 1920, b. 65.

[46] A report of the demonstration appeared in *Avanti!* (Turin ed.) 8 July 1920.

[47] *Avanti!* (Turin ed.) 8 July 1920.

factory was seized by its workers as a protest.[48] These incidents had considerable repercussions at Turin, given the city's importance in the munitions industry. *F.I.O.M.*'s official attitude that local Union leaders should treat each case of war materials manufacture on its merits[49] was condemned even by the Chamber of Labour as 'absurd, anti-class and defeatist'.[50] On 15 July a mass meeting of dues collectors, Internal Commissions and Workshop Commissars from the metal-working factories condemned *F.I.O.M.*'s line and urged that the local workers should 'follow a line of conduct more responsive to the revolutionary spirit of the class'.[51]

Thus by mid-July the Turin metal-workers were once more in opposition to their official Union leadership about a 'revolutionary' issue; it was, however, the syndicalists, and not the *Ordine Nuovo*, who were at the head of the movement. The growth of syndicalist strength at Turin in the early summer of 1920 had been testified by *Avanti!* even before the main agitation over war materials and the Ancona risings:

> For some time now little groups of anarchists and syndicalists have been carrying on intense activity within our Trade Union organisations, with obvious secessionist intentions. A large number of manifestoes have been distributed among the metal-workers inviting them to set up their own branch of the *U.S.I.*[52]

By the end of the first week in July a branch of the *U.S.I.* metal-workers' Union had, in fact, been set up in Turin, and meetings were being held of the Workshop Commissars that supported the *U.S.I.*

The increasing importance of the syndicalists was not confined to Turin: it was a national phenomenon. In Milan, particularly, the summer saw a great increase in syndicalist strength, and Anna Kuliscioff wrote that:

> The working class is going through a mauvais quart d'heure of anarchist contagion. Nowadays *Avanti!* is almost boycotted here, and the workers read only *Umanità Nova*, which I am told has a circulation of more than 100,000 copies. This is said by people who go regularly to the

---

[48] *Avanti!* (Turin ed.) 11 July 1920.
[49] This decision had been taken at the Genoa Congress of *F.I.O.M.* in May, which had spent some time discussing the issue of war materials. For a report of the Congress see *Battaglie Sindacali* 29 May 1920.
[50] 'La Questione del Materiale Bellico', in *Avanti!* (Turin ed.) 17 July 1920. The executive committee of the Chamber of Labour adopted unanimously a resolution containing the phrase quoted.
[51] *Avanti!* (Turin ed.) 17 July 1920.
[52] 'Tentativi Sindacalisti di Secessione', in *Avanti!* (Turin ed.) 3 July 1920.

Chamber of Labour, and by people who travel by tram in the morning, where there is not a single worker without a copy of *Umanità Nova* in his hand.[53]

The importance of the syndicalists was even briefly recognised by the P.S.I.[54] In June 1920 the Socialist Party agreed to hold discussions with the U.S.I. at Genoa on matters of common interest. The party soon reversed its decision,[55] but its change of heart was unpopular, and indeed triggered off the crisis in the Turin branch discussed above (see p. 140).

Popular grievances, and syndicalist strength, helped bring about a revival of the Factory Councils in Turin. Factory Councils had continued to exist after the April strike, at least in the sense that Workshop Commissars had met together occasionally, but little more had happened. On 8 July a meeting of syndicalist Workshop Commissars, called to express solidarity with the Ancona revolt, also decided to intensify propaganda for Factory Councils.[56] A new 'Committee of Study' on the Factory Councils was elected at the end of July;[57] its task was defined by the *Ordine Nuovo* as 'defence of the Factory Councils against open or hidden aggression by Trade Union bureaucracy',[58] and many of its members were prominent local syndicalists. This Committee of Study, as Tasca sarcastically remarked some years later, 'did little and studied less'.[59] However, it did issue a manifesto on 11 August calling on all Italian workers to organise Councils, and on 12 August a normal meeting of representatives of Turin Factory Councils was well attended, for the first time since April. *Avanti!* remarked that this was 'another symptom of the reawakening of the working-class masses, after the despondency that followed the General Strike'.[60] The meeting decided, appropriately enough, to send the secretary of the Committee of Study, Viglongo, to a meeting

[53] Anna Kuliscioff to Filippo Turati 16 August 1920 (A. Schiavi, ed., *Carteggio F Turati – Anna Kuliscioff*, vol. v, 1919–22, Einaudi, Turin 1953, p. 386).

[54] A police informer told Prime Minister Nitti in May that the Socialist deputies 'would not be averse even to a little reaction, to induce the masses to return to the orders of their leaders who have lost influence through the fault of anarchist propagandists' (*State Archives*, Min. Int., Dir. Gen. P.S., Atti Speciali, b. 3, f. 26, unsigned report 15 May 1920 'reserved personally for His Excellency Nitti').

[55] The conference was first postponed for a week, from 26 June to 2 July, and then postponed *sine die*. cf. *Guerra di Classe* 17 July 1920.

[56] *Avanti!* (Turin ed.) 9 and 10 July 1920.

[57] Its first meeting was held on 20 July. The names of the members were given in *Avanti!* (Turin ed.) 28 July 1920.

[58] *Ordine Nuovo* 31 July 1920.

[59] 'Opportunismo di Destra e Tattica Sindacale' by A. Tasca, in *Lo Stato Operaio* 5 June (dated 5 May) 1924 (now in A. Gramsci, *La Costruzione del Partito Comunista* cit., p. 186).

[60] *Avanti!* (Turin ed.) 12 August 1920.

at Florence called by the Anarchist Union on behalf of 'political victims'.[61]

Thus, by August 1920 a classic clash between rival concepts of 'workers' control' was shaping up. On the Right, the government, the Milan and Turin Chambers of Labour, and the reformists of the *C.G.L.*, were willing to countenance 'participation' at all levels and a reorganisation of Union structure; on the Left, popular discontent was being expressed mainly by the syndicalists, who were impatient and mistrustful, and actively opposed to the capitalist system on principle. The situation was resolved in September by the 'Occupation of the Factories', a typically syndicalist act.

[61] The meeting was held at Florence on 16 August. Viglongo was at this time virtually the only prominent *Ordine Nuovo* supporter to share Gramsci's political position.

CHAPTER EIGHT

The Origins of the Occupation

THE famous 'Occupation of the Factories' in September 1920 was not, of course, brought about by syndicalist agitation alone. It was also the culmination of a 'normal' campaign by the Italian metal-workers for higher wages, led by the reformist Socialist Metal-workers' Union, *F.I.O.M.* The campaign began in May when the *F.I.O.M.* Congress at Genoa called for considerable pay increases, adequate cost of living allowances, and an agreed system of minimum pay scales throughout the country.[1] These last two issues had been left to regional negotiations after the national metal-workers' settlement of February 1919, but agreement had been reached in two regions only, Piedmont and Tuscany; the lack of agreement had caused the two-month strike in Emilia, Liguria and Lombardy in August–September 1919 (see p. 81), but even this strike had been inconclusive and the settlement unsatisfactory. Indeed, in 1921 the Union leaders declared roundly that 'the national metal-workers' agitation that took place between July and September 1920 was a direct consequence of the strike in August–September 1919 in three regions – Lombardy, Liguria, and Emilia – to obtain a settlement on a minimum pay scale.'[2] At Genoa, the Union's Central Committee received a mandate to draw up formal proposals, and these were submitted on 18 June. It also proclaimed that the agitation was likely to 'be far more important than any fought previously by any class organisation.'[3]

Even so, *F.I.O.M.*'s proposals for minimum pay scales and adequate cost of living adjustments were a purely routine pay claim, in no way different from the campaign that the Union had led the previous autumn.

[1] *Relazione del Comitato Centrale della F.I.O.M. sull' Agitazione dei Metallurgici Italiani (Luglio, Agosto e Settembre 1920)*, typewritten copy supplied to the author by *F.I.O.M.*, of a document originally published in 1921 by Tipografia Alleanza, Turin; the reference is to p. 2 of the copy.

[2] *ibid.*, p. 1.

[3] *ibid.*

Factory Councils, Internal Commissions and workshop discipline were not mentioned.[4] The claim was for an increase in the average basic wage of 0.90 *lire* an hour, or 7.20 *lire* daily,[5] plus a cost of living allowance of 0.15 *lire* an hour, to be adjusted automatically on the basis of statistics issued by the Milan Statistical Office. This increase, it was argued, would do no more than compensate the metal-workers for the increase in the cost of living since the previous agreements (see p. 144). It was vitally important for *F.I.O.M.* that there should be no separate agitations by its own members during the negotiations, and the Union therefore arranged that a 'broad representative group of workers from the various regions and most important industrial centres should take part in the negotiations.'[6]

The *U.S.I.* (syndicalist) Metal-workers' Union also drew up a pay claim, which was officially approved at their National Council meeting in Florence on 18–19 May 1920.[7] It was very similar to *F.I.O.M.*'s claim, but the syndicalists also denounced the existing factory regulations – which they had strongly opposed when introduced, and had never formally recognised – and called for 'the abolition of the existing Internal Commissions and the nomination of Workshop Commissars.'[8] The two other Metal-workers' Unions, the (Catholic) National Mechanical Workers' Union and the Union affiliated to the *U.I.L.*, put forward substantially similar wage claims.

F.I.O.M. therefore had to decide whether to agree to negotiate at the same table as the representatives of the *U.S.I.* and the other smaller Unions. The first meeting of *F.I.O.M.*'s National Committee of Agitation[9] laid down that the agitation should be restricted to factories where *F.I.O.M.* members were a majority of the labour force, and that the *F.I.O.M.* representatives would therefore refuse to negotiate on the same footing as the other labour organisations. This decision was expected. *F.I.O.M.* had had constant disputes with the *U.S.I.* Metal-workers' Union throughout 1919 and 1920 (see p. 115), and the *C.G.L.* had recently

[4] V. Castronovo, *Giovanni Agnelli* (U.T.E.T., Turin 1971) p. 230.

[5] The average basic wage was 18 *lire* daily, so the increase claimed was 40 *per cent.* See *Memoriale presentato il 18 giugno 1920 alla Federazione Nazionale Sindacale dell' Industria Metallurgica e Meccanica (F.I.O.M.* 1920), pp. 6–7.

[6] *Relazione* cit., p. 2.

[7] For the meeting, see *Guerra di Classe* 22 May 1920. The Union's memorandum (pay-claim) was published in *Lotta Operaia* 30 May 1920.

[8] *ibid.* See also the report by the Prefect of Genoa to Ministry of the Interior 6 June 1920 (in *State Archives*, Min. Int., Dir. Gen. P.S., Aff. Gen. e Ris., 1920, b. 74, 'Affari Metallurgici: Sampierdarena') of a speech by the *U.S.I.* leader Faggi explaining the *U.S.I.* claim to Ligurian workers.

[9] The Committee consisted of representatives of the largest branches, the federal and regional secretaries, and members of the central committee (*Relazione* cit., p. 5).

F

repeated its refusal to consider joint action with the *U.S.I.* (see p. 146). The popular insurrection over Albania at the end of June may also have influenced the *F.I.O.M.* committee's decision, for *F.I.O.M.* could not have restricted the agitation to a purely routine wage claim if it had accepted *U.S.I.* support at such a time. The decision also meant that the Union leaders could avoid discussing the existing 'factory regulations' and the whole Factory Council issue at a time when there was considerable agitation, especially in Milan, about the lack of Factory Councils in the metal-working factories (see p. 119).

The *U.S.I.* Metal-workers' Union itself tried hard to come to some agreement with *F.I.O.M.* in fighting the common battle.[10] *F.I.O.M.*'s refusal to recognise the *U.S.I.*'s right to share in the negotiations was made 'despite the conciliatory votes of our organisations and despite the insistence of our comrades in Turin, who are members of the *F.I.O.M.*, that *F.I.O.M.* should come to an agreement with the *U.S.I.* on this issue.'[11] It was all very embarrassing for the *F.I.O.M.* leaders. In addition to Turin, meetings of their members in Milan and Leghorn also called on them to co-operate with the *U.S.I.*[12] The slogan of 'working-class unity' had a powerful appeal, especially since the anti-war agitation going on at the time over Albania was reminiscent of earlier anti-war campaigns. The *U.S.I.*, with its commitment to joint negotiation, to factory seizures and to united action for revolution, was ideally placed to benefit from workers' feelings of 'solidarity'.

The employers, too, were well placed to exploit *F.I.O.M.*'s embarrassment. They insisted at the first meeting of the negotiating body that negotiations should take place simultaneously with all four Unions.[13] *F.I.O.M.* was thus forced to break off the initial talks.[14] The manoeuvre was a success for the employers, who were not anxious to negotiate. Many of them could not afford to. On 13 July the Prefect of Turin warned that Fiat needed to cut down on labour because of a declining demand for vehicles, so 'the present agitation might, in these circumstances, lead to a lock-out'.[15] Numerous sackings took place at the Ansaldo works in

[10] See *Guerra di Classe* 7 August 1920, which also reports a resolution of syndicalist members of Milanese Internal Commissions in favour of agreement.

[11] *Guerra di Classe* 10 July 1920.

[12] *Guerra di Classe* 7 August 1920. The motions passed at meetings of Internal Commission members in Milan and Turin were printed in *Lotta Operaia* 24 July 1920.

[13] *Relazione* cit., p. 6.

[14] *Avanti!* (Turin ed.) 17 July 1920. *F.I.O.M.*'s letter of protest is also given in *Relazione* cit., pp. 6–8. Buozzi appears to have been surprised by the employers' attitude.

[15] Prefect of Turin to Ministry of the Interior 13 July 1920 (*State Archives* cit., 1920, b. 75).

Sestri Ponente in July; the Prefect of Genoa thought the reason was 'the industrialists' difficulty in making immediate payments in cash, given the banks' credit restrictions, for the banks are very mistrustful of the industry'.[16] By 23 July 5,000 workers were locked out at the Ansaldo works at Cornigliano Ligure, and the workers were demanding the immediate arrest of the Perrone brothers, the owners of Ansaldo, whom they regarded as being responsible for the 'artificial crisis'.[17] There was another lock-out during most of July at one of the workshops of the Ansaldo S. Giorgio factory in Turin. The Ansaldo works were peculiarly susceptible to the economic recession, but there is no need to doubt that most employers were genuinely suffering, as they claimed, from foreign competition, the lack of essential raw materials such as coal and pig iron, and the credit squeeze in Italy. All these factors made any concession to F.I.O.M. pointless.[18]

Matters were further complicated by the fact that the employers were not merely in conflict with F.I.O.M., but also with the government. Giolitti's proposed Commission of Enquiry into military expenditure, his 'confiscation' of excess profits made on war contracts, and his decree of 24 July 1920 laying down that share-ownership should be publicly registered (nominatività dei titoli) – these measures thoroughly alarmed the leading engineering and steel-making firms. The steel industry was particularly affected by the proposals, and in any case it was an 'artificial' sector, kept alive by protective tariffs and government contracts, as liberal economists constantly pointed out. Hence the industrialists' refusal to negotiate with F.I.O.M. could be seen as a means of putting pressure on the Giolitti government, even as a 'bosses' strike' against government fiscal policy.[19] Prefects and police informers soon began to report that the industrialists were planning a lock-out. Under these circumstances, the government was obviously unwilling to support the employers, and adopted a policy of strict non-intervention.

F.I.O.M. managed to put pressure on the employers eventually by issuing a ban on overtime, which came into effect on 26 July. The ban seems to have been effective, and the employers resumed talks on the

[16] Prefect of Genoa to Ministry of the Interior 17 July 1920 (in State Archives cit. 1920, b. 74, 'Metallurgici: Genova').
[17] Prefect of Genoa to Ministry of the Interior 23 July 1920 (in State Archives cit., 1920, b. 74). The lock-out lasted three and a half days.
[18] cf. M. Abrate, La Lotta Sindacale nella Industrializzazione in Italia (Angeli, Milan 1967), p. 330; R. Romeo, Breve Storia della Grande Industria in Italia (Cappelli, Bologna 1961), pp. 127–8. The recession was international.
[19] M. Abrate, La Lotta Sindacale nella Industrializzazione in Italia cit., pp. 282–3; V. Castronovo, Giovanni Agnelli cit., p. 245.

29th.[20] Nevertheless, no negotiations took place at this meeting. The industrialists merely outlined the economic difficulties facing them, which made any concessions impossible. The *F.I.O.M.* leaders were forced to content themselves with asking the industrialists to meet them two weeks later with 'all the elements needed to *prove* the truth of the mere statements contained in the note handed to the workers' organisations on 29 July.'[21] *F.I.O.M.* was by this time in a helpless position. It was unwilling to accept *U.S.I.* support in the negotiations, but it was nevertheless unable to settle the pay claim in a normal Trade Union manner.

The chances of a 'Trade Union' settlement worsened in the next two weeks, before negotiations were resumed. At Turin, the metal-workers found that they were liable to pay increased accident and old-age insurance contributions; the employers' offer of unpaid summer holidays was regarded as a manoeuvre to achieve a lock-out; and the ban on overtime caused some economic hardship, especially among the unskilled workers and labourers.[22] Meetings of metal-workers were held every day to protest about these grievances and about the lack of results from the national negotiations in Milan; and at some of these meetings the essentially syndicalist idea of factory seizure was revived. On 23 July the Prefect of Turin reported:

> I am informed in confidence that the members of the local branch of *F.I.O.M.*, after an animated discussion of how to oppose the industrialists' possible refusal to negotiate on the proposals put to them in the well-known memorandum now being discussed in Milan, have decided to propose to the central committee that the management and administrative offices of the individual firms should be occupied suddenly, so that direct management can be carried out. This occupation should be carried out by the workers of the factory concerned, who will then have to adopt every available means of defence in order to maintain their position.[23]

On 10 August a further meeting between employers and Union leaders took place in Milan. Once more negotiations were not even begun, both sides limiting themselves to a recital of the 'conditions of the industry'.[24] *F.I.O.M.*'s request that the memorandum should at least be discussed was finally rejected on 13 August, on the usual economic grounds. The Union

[20] *Relazione* cit., p. 10.
[21] *ibid.*, p. 14.
[22] *Avanti!* (Turin ed.) 4 August 1920.
[23] Prefect of Turin to Ministry of the Interior 23 July 1920 (in *State Archives* cit., 1920, b. 75).
[24] *Relazione* cit., pp. 14–15.

leaders therefore called a meeting of the National Council of Agitation,[25] to decide what to do next. A strike was ruled out, both for financial reasons[26] and because it would have been ineffective at a time of reduced demand; the National Council decided on a go-slow ('obstructionism') instead, as the only possible alternative to seizure of the factories.[27] 'Obstructionism' began on 21 August, specific instructions being circularised among F.I.O.M. members giving details of how it was to be carried out. These instructions contained a concession to the more extreme members of the Union: Article 8 read 'if the firm proclaims a lock-out, the workers will have to enter the factory at all costs, even to the extent of storming the gates, and will then set to work in the normal way.'[28] However, F.I.O.M. clearly hoped that 'obstructionism' would be enough by itself to force the employers to negotiate.

The syndicalist Metal-workers' Union also held a Congress after the break-off of negotiations. The syndicalists in Liguria had denounced 'obstructionism' as early as 30 July, before the policy had been adopted by F.I.O.M.[29] On 17 August the U.S.I. Metal-workers' Union as a whole clarified its opposition to 'obstructionism':

> The Congress, after examining the situation brought about in the metal-working industry as a result of the industrialists' refusal to negotiate with the proletarian organisations on the basis of economic and other improvements, and considering that a struggle against the employers is inevitable, in order to sustain the requests forwarded by the metal-workers of Italy; considering that a 'passive strike' is not practicable in present circumstances, confronted as we are by the industrialists' attitude and interest in exhausting the proletariat's energies; that obstructionism would meet with severe practical difficulties; considering that in order to oppose the employers' resistance energetically and effectively, recourse must be had to any measure, and especially to a simultaneous

[25] As opposed to the 'National Committee of Agitation' (see p. 149). The 'National Council' was equivalent to a full Union Congress.

[26] F.I.O.M. was not in a position to afford a major strike, as it had had to pay out 15 million *lire* in strike maintenance money during the two month strike in Lombardy, Emilia and Liguria in August–September 1919. (*Relazione*, p. 21).

[27] The Vice-Prefect of Milan reported that there were some delegates in favour of factory seizure, but that Buozzi's more moderate line prevailed (P. Spriano, *L'Occupazione delle Fabbriche*, Einaudi, Turin 1964, p. 43).

[28] Copy of 'Norme per l'Applicazione dell' Ostruzionismo', sent by Prefect of Turin to Ministry of the Interior n.d. (in *State Archives* cit., 1920, b. 75). They are summarised in P. Spriano, *L'Occupazione delle Fabbriche* cit., p. 42, and in International Labour Office, *Studies and Reports*, Series A, no. 2, pp. 9–10. cf. also M. Abrate, *La Lotta Sindacale nella Industrializzazione in Italia* cit., pp. 330–1.

[29] *Guerra di Classe* 7 August 1920.

general invasion of the factories by workers belonging to both national Unions; believing therefore that unity of action by the metal-working proletariat, over and above Trade Union divisions, is likely to prove useful; declares that it gives a mandate to the Committee of Agitation to inform its line of conduct according to the criteria expressed above, but without the preceding considerations being allowed to prevent any possible agreement being made with *F.I.O.M.*; and declares that if such an understanding is not achieved, it nevertheless commits its own organisations to follow the course of action laid down by *F.I.O.M.*, but reserves to itself the right to advocate among the masses of metal-workers the adoption of those methods of struggle that this Congress considers to be most suitable in fighting the employers' arrogance effectively.[30]

Thus although the syndicalists were prepared, in the overriding interests of workers' unity, to accept 'obstructionism' and to carry it out themselves in the factories where they were a majority, they also continued their agitation for factory seizure.

The policy of 'obstructionism' was observed in most industrial centres, and at Turin the local edition of *Avanti!* claimed on 25 August that production in the metal-working factories had been halved.[31] However, the industrialists still refused, despite the government's pleas, to resume negotiations.[32] By the last week of August 1920 the 'go-slow' had developed into something approaching an 'internal strike' in most centres. By this time the workers in Turin were collecting weapons. A police informer reported on 19 August that at the slightest sign of a lock-out, the workers would take guns into the factories and then refuse to leave, having already made arrangements with the Turin Cooperative Alliance to be supplied with essential foodstuffs.[33] Many employers did in fact want a lock-out, especially in the larger firms where production had been worst hit by the 'excesses of obstructionism'.[34] A special meeting of the Turin

[30] *Guerra di Classe* 28 August 1920. The Congress was also reported in *Avanti!* (Turin ed.) 19 August 1920.

[31] The I.L.O. report (*Studies and Reports*, Series A, no. 2), p. 10, gives figures for the period of 'obstruction' at the main Fiat works: $25\frac{3}{4}$ vehicles were produced daily, instead of the normal $67\frac{1}{2}$.

[32] For the Minister of Labour's role, see P. Spriano, *L'Occupazione delle Fabbriche* cit., p. 48. *F.I.O.M.*'s chief negotiator, Buozzi, agreed to suspend obstructionism if the industrialists would only open negotiations.

[33] Police informer Castagnetto to Ministry of the Interior 19 August 1920 (in *State Archives* cit., 1920, b. 75).

[34] These included the Romeo works at Milan, where the first lock-out in fact occurred. See M. Abrate, *La Lotta Sindacale nella Industrializzazione in Italia* cit., p. 293.

Engineering Employers' Association (*A.M.M.A.*) on 26 August authorised the association's executive to decide on the closure of any factory where serious and demonstrable damage had been done by the go-slow, or where production was virtually halted.[35] On 27 August the Prefect of Milan reported that the industrialists there were 'resolute for a lock-out'.[36] Conversely, the *U.S.I.* Metal-workers' Union had already decided that 'obstructionism' would not, after all, force the employers to negotiate against their will and that therefore 'the seizure of factories by the metal-workers of all Italy should be carried out simultaneously and immediately, before the workers can be forestalled by a lock-out . . . the workers' united front must exist in reality.'[37]

Thus by 30 August an impossible situation had been reached throughout the Italian metal-working industry. The employers were adamant in their refusal to negotiate, regarded the 'go-slow' as akin to industrial sabotage, and were anxious to forestall the real possibility of their factories being seized. Meanwhile *F.I.O.M.* was being forced to ratify a violent solution to what it had always tried to maintain as a normal Trade Union dispute. The situation was resolved on 30 August by the action of the Romeo works in Milan, which locked its gates, despite the representations of the Prefect of Milan.[38] The 2,000 workers at the Romeo works were known to be among the most militant in Milan; they had gone on strike in early July over the 'war materials' question, and had also stopped work briefly on 24 August.[39] The capital of the Romeo works was allegedly 'in the hands of the Banca di Sconto, controlled by the Perrone brothers who also own the Ansaldo works in Liguria,'[40] and it was this group of industrialists who were the most anxious for a lock-out.

After the Romeo lock-out, the Milan branch of *F.I.O.M.* ordered the seizure of all the other metal-working factories in the city, to forestall further lock-outs.[41] Perhaps this was an exaggerated response, but the atmosphere was very tense by this time. Even so, the central committee of *F.I.O.M.*, which held a meeting the same day at Turin, did *not* call for a nation-wide factory occupation. It expressed its approval of the Milanese metal-workers' action in seizing over 300 factories, but saw the incident primarily as proof of the workers' 'unity and solidarity', called for the

[35] M. Abrate, *La Lotta Sindacale nella Industrializzazione in Italia* cit., pp. 289–90.
[36] P. Spriano, *L'Occupazione delle Fabbriche* cit., p. 50.
[37] *Umanità Nova* 25 August 1920.
[38] For the Prefect's opposition to the Romeo management's move, see P. Spriano, *L'Occupazione delle Fabbriche* cit., p. 51.
[39] *ibid.*, p. 49.
[40] Anonymous circular dated 1 September 1920 (in *State Archives* cit., 1920, b. 74).
[41] P. Spriano, *L'Occupazione delle Fabbriche* cit., pp. 51–2.

policy of 'obstructionism' to be continued in other areas, and expressed the hope that no further attempts at a lock-out would be made.[42] The position of the *F.I.O.M.* leaders was obviously very difficult. Although they had to assume responsibility for the Milan occupations, they clearly hoped to avoid further seizure of factories if possible, by appealing to the workers' sense of discipline and by emphasising that 'obstructionism' must continue.[43]

The occupation of the Italian metal-working factories in September 1920 was, therefore, forced on *F.I.O.M.* by the employers' refusal, or inability, to negotiate. On 31 August the industrialists' Confederation ordered a national lock-out (to be organised by each regional body). The next day, when lock-outs were attempted in Rome, Turin and Genoa, the workers occupied the factories there as a result. The Under-Secretary of the Interior telegraphed the news to the Prime Minister: 'The workers are occupying the factories as a reaction to the lock-out. Declarations made to me personally by the industrialists reveal their desire to go to extremes. I confirm that the Government does not intend to interfere in the conflict, responsibility for which is almost exclusively theirs.'[44] The occupation, then, was no impulsive movement of a passionate revolutionary crowd. On the other hand, neither was it simply a 'rational', 'tactical' move in pursuit of well-defined and limited demands – collective bargaining by other means – although *F.I.O.M.* liked to portray it as such. It was a normal Trade Union dispute, forced into 'revolutionary' channels by the refusal of employers to grant concessions, by Union reluctance to face a strike, by rational fears of a lock-out, by the failure of the 'official' reformist labour movement to retain adequate support from its members, and by the strength of syndicalist ideas.

In Turin, too, the local branch of *F.I.O.M.*, obviously influenced by the action of its Milanese counterpart two days previously, regarded seizure of the factories as the only possible response to the employers' lock-out. The Turin occupation was a consequence of the national agitation. Neither the *Ordine Nuovo*'s Factory Council campaign, nor Gramsci's tentative efforts at 'Communist Education', can be regarded as directly responsible.

[42] *Avanti!* (Turin ed.) 31 August 1920. The text is also given in the *Relazione* cit., pp. 22–3.

[43] On 31 August – the day after the Milan occupations – *F.I.O.M.* issued an appeal to its members: 'your leaders have foreseen all the consequences of 'obstructionism', including the seizure of the factories. Be ready to carry out, therefore, the orders of your Union' (*Relazione* cit., p. 24).

[44] G. De Rosa, *Storia del Movimento Cattolico in Italia*, vol. ii, *Il Partito Popolare Italiano* (Laterza, Bari 1966), p. 124. The government's attitude remained one of strict non-intervention.

CHAPTER NINE

The Occupation of the Factories

THE 'Occupation of the Factories' in September 1920 was certainly the most spectacular episode of the whole post-war period. Like the General Strike in Britain, or the 'Events of May' 1968 in France, the Occupation of the Factories aroused strong emotions – first euphoria, then disillusion and bitterness, among militant workers; fear and resentment among industrialists; political excitement and intensity among spectators. At local level, it was a colourful 'psychodrama', full of red flags and rhetoric, the stuff of which later myths are made. At national level, the picture was very different – one of sober, sceptical men, manoeuvring for advantage, worrying that things might be getting out of hand, absorbing and deflecting trouble, seeking and finding compromises. Both pictures are valid; neither is complete without the other. This chapter will therefore try to combine the two aspects, and consider both the national movement and its local impact on Turin – and how the whole performance looked to that brilliant theatre critic, Antonio Gramsci.

Nationally, the movement was certainly extensive. Engineering factories, steelworks, foundries, shipbuilding plants and small workshops were taken over in the first few days of September. Over 400,000 workers were directly involved, and millions more indirectly. Nearly all parts of Italy were affected, not merely the most 'organised' factories of the North.[1] In some areas the red flag flew over the factories; in others the anarcho-syndicalists took the initiative. The occupation took place nearly everywhere without violence, and neither police nor troops made any attempt to defend the factories. There was one death in Liguria, and elsewhere a few cases of managers being 'kidnapped' for a few hours, but they were soon released. Of course, the discipline and order of the initial factory occupations could not be maintained for ever. In the next three or four weeks, as tension grew, many factories began to make guns or bombs

---

[1] P. Spriano, *L'Occupazione delle Fabbriche* (Einaudi, Turin 1964), pp. 60–1.

for defence, and there were some political vendettas and shooting-matches. Even so, the incidence of political murder during the occupation was lower than either before or after it,[2] and the most frequent crime was looting of factory stocks.

The occupation obviously stimulated 'Factory Council' activity everywhere. Although 'obstructionism' was maintained initially, productive work *was* continued; and in the absence of many of the technical and managerial staff, some kind of workers' organisation in the factory was needed to organise it. In most centres the old Internal Commissions ruled the factories virtually unchanged, with the help of the local *F.I.O.M.* leaders and the local Chamber of Labour. However, in Liguria, where the syndicalists were particularly strong, Factory Councils on the Turin model were elected in most workshops, and the Workshop Commissars were made responsible for safeguarding and issuing all stores.[3] But there was no coordination of the various workshops: 'even after two weeks of occupation, the local committee of agitation in Genoa was still urging the workers to let it have a list of members of the Factory Councils.'[4]

In Turin, as elsewhere, the occupation immediately revived the Factory Councils. On the first morning, the Internal Commission and the Workshop Commissars at the main Fiat works took over responsibility for registering attendance, for carrying out an inventory of the raw materials available and the finished work completed, and for discipline.[5] The workers' Internal Commission was in permanent session, as was that of the technicians, and work proceeded fairly normally: on 3 September the factory produced 35 vehicles, compared with an average 25¾ during the period of 'obstructionism'.[6] The Fiat Factory Council appointed special Commissars to organise defence, to maintain transport and to guarantee supplies of raw materials.[7] As the occupation continued, the

---

[2] *ibid.*, p. 147. This refers to the whole of Italy. But in Turin, according to Spriano, there were nine deaths during the occupation: five policemen, one nationalist and three workers. Robert Michels reported the head of the Turin forensic medicine department, a personal acquaintance of his, as estimating the total deaths at sixteen (R. Michels, 'Uber die Versuche einer Besetzung der Betriebe durch die Arbeiter in Italien', in *Archiv für Sozialwissenschaft und Sozialpolitik*, April 1921, pp. 469–503, at p. 481).

[3] P. Spriano, *L'Occupazione delle Fabbriche* cit., p. 71.

[4] *ibid.*, p. 141; *Il Lavoro* 15 September 1920.

[5] *Avanti!* (Turin ed.) 2 September 1920.

[6] *Avanti!* (Turin ed.) 4 September 1920.

[7] *Avanti!* (Turin ed.) 4 September 1920. The Factory Council at Fiat issued regular communiqués, which were printed in *Avanti!*, and were reprinted by G. Parodi in his article 'La Fiat–Centro in Mano agli Operai', in *Lo Stato Operaio*, anno IV (1930), n. 10, pp. 635–55.

Factory Council assumed more and more functions – organising defence, exchanging information with other plants,[8] and replacing absentee clerical staff (the employers had ordered technical staff to stay in the factories, to make sure machinery was not damaged, but most clerical workers stayed away).[9] One of the Councils' main tasks was maintaining discipline. Alcohol was strictly forbidden, and theft rigorously punished. Two workers caught stealing spare parts at Fiat were given six days 'imprisonment' on bread and water, and 'committed to the contempt of the working masses, who wanted to exact summary justice on them.'[10] At the Ferriere Piemontesi (a Fiat-owned foundry) the Factory Council complained that 'the orders we have issued are treated with excessive frivolity, and the discipline that distinguishes the other factories seems, at the Ferriere, to be regarded as a new oppression, even worse than the bourgeois one.'[11] Even so, the Councils tried their best, and *Avanti!* was justified in writing at the end of the first week that 'the old management, which fled in haste on the very day of the lock-out, has been replaced by the Factory Council, to which not only the workers but also the technicians and the clerical staff show obedience and discipline. The Factory Council directs the whole general work of the vast firm and is in permanent session.'[12]

However, Factory Councils were not the only workers' organisations to become important during the occupation. 'Red Guards' were set up to defend the factories from possible assault, and much of the production in the early days of the occupation was of weapons for their use. At Spa, the workers began making bombs on 2 September, and were soon selling them to other factories;[13] and at the main Fiat works, one workshop (*reparto*) was turned over to making arms and barbed wire.[14] The 'Red Guards' were entirely defensive, and their main task was to defend the

---

[8] The main Fiat works and the Lancia factory sent each other committees of technicians to investigate work methods and 'industrial secrets'. Parodi reported that this was very useful for both firms ('La Fiat–Centro in Mano agli Operai' cit., p. 646).

[9] At Fiat, 90 *per cent.* of the technical staff and 60 *per cent.* of the clerical workers were reporting for work at the end of the second week, according to Parodi (*op. cit.*, p. 647). At Spa, Battista Santhià claimed only five technicians were absent, but only four clerical workers (out of seventy) were *present* (B. Santhià, 'La Lotta contro i Riformisti in una Fabbrica Occupata', in *Lo Stato Operaio*, anno IV (1930), nos. 11–12, pp. 717–33, at p. 722).

[10] G. Parodi, 'La Fiat–Centro in Mano agli Operai' cit., p. 649.

[11] U. Camuri, 'L'Occupazione delle Fabbriche', in *Nuova Antologia* 16 March 1934, p. 264.

[12] *Avanti!* (Turin ed.) 10 September 1920.

[13] B. Santhià, 'La Lotta contro i Riformisti in una Fabbrica Occupata' cit., pp. 724–8.

[14] G. Parodi, 'La Fiat–Centro in Mano agli Operai' cit., p. 647.

factories on Sundays and at night, when most workers went home.[15] The other workers' bodies to have an important role during the occupation were the 'Communist groups', which had been formed in March and had revived in the summer. There were some fierce quarrels between them and 'reformist' workers.[16] Nevertheless, these other institutions were in a sense escondary. The 'Red Guards' were appointed by the Factory Councils, and the 'Communist groups' worked through them. The very nature of the factory occupations, which created isolated 'proletarian republics' in danger of being cut off from contact with outside organisations, made some kind of semi-autonomous Factory Council organisation inevitable.

By 3 September, *Avanti!* claimed that 185 metal-working factories had been occupied in Turin. They included all the main vehicle-producing factories, as well as the main coachbuilding works and foundries.[17] It was an urgent task to co-ordinate their efforts and to provide for exchange of products and for supplies of raw materials. A 'Directive Committee', containing several technicians, was therefore set up by the local branch of F.I.O.M. to attend to these problems.[18] This Committee became responsible for all exchanges of materials or products between the different firms. The Factory Councils themselves were expressly forbidden to sell the products of their factories on their own initiative, although exchanges between different branches of the same firm did not require permission from the Committee.[19] The Committee's first task was to request the various Factory Councils to send it a list of all stocks of raw materials, work in progress, etc., so that the city's economic life could continue on a 'Communist basis'.[20]

[15] V. Bianco, 'La Organizzazione Militare Rivoluzionaria durante la Occupazione', in *Lo Stato Operaio*, anno IV (1930), nos. 11–12, pp. 733–8. Parodi ('La Fiat–Centro in Mano agli Operai' cit., p. 649) says there were 1,000 men involved in 'Red Guard' work at the main Fiat works, mainly in defending the factory at night; B. Santhià reports 160 Guards at Spa ('La Lotta contro i Riformisti in una Fabbrica Occupata' cit., p. 723). The situation in Milan seems to have been very similar, although there was also a 'Directing Committee of Red Guards' at the Chamber of Labour, organised by Vittorio Ambrosini (Quaestor of Milan to Director General of Public Security 19 November 1920, in *State Archives*, Ministry of the Interior, Direzione Generale Pubblica Sicurezza, Affari Generali e Riservati, 1920, b. 66: 'Guardie Rosse').

[16] For details in the Spa factory, see B. Santhià, 'La Lotta contro i Riformisti in una Fabbrica Occupata' cit., pp. 724, 727.

[17] For a list of the 106 metal-working firms in Turin that were occupied, see M. Abrate, *La Lotta Sindacale nella Industrializzazione in Italia* (Angeli, Milan 1967), pp. 483–4. Various other firms were also occupied (e.g. six tyre works), and these are also listed by Abrate. Some of these firms had several plants.

[18] *Avanti!* (Turin ed.) 5 September 1920.

[19] *ibid.* For more details on how the F.I.O.M. Committee proposed to organise the sale and exchange of products, see *Avanti!* (Turin ed.) 12 September 1920.

[20] *Avanti!* (Turin ed.) 7 September 1920. Four copies were requested, for the Factory Council, the Turin Committee, the Regional Committee, and the national

As the occupation continued, the organisation of the Turin engineering industry became necessarily more complex. The lack of raw materials and the need for supplies from ancillary industries soon led to the occupation of other factories, such as the works of the Italian Oxygen Company on 4 September, or the Michelin Tyre works on 10 September.[21] Some textile and chemical works were also occupied, the largest being the Cotonificio Hoffman. These other occupations, of factories that contained few, if any, members of F.I.O.M., provided the Turin Chamber of Labour with its opportunity. On 13 September it issued a communiqué proclaiming that it was taking over the movement, with the agreement and help of the local branch of the Socialist Party; no more occupations should take place without its permission.[22] The F.I.O.M. 'Directive Committee' was replaced by a new 'Directive Committee', consisting of the executive committee of the Chamber of Labour, plus one representative of F.I.O.M.;[23] four sub-committees were also set up – legal, technical, supply, and propaganda – to provide specialised services.[24] At the same time, the Chamber of Labour set up a special 'Exchange and Production Committee', with membership drawn from F.I.O.M. and from the Technicians' Union, but with a Chamber of Labour leader as chairman; all Factory Councils were required to supply the new Committee with a list of products ready for sale.[25] The problem of paying the wages of the occupying workers was met in various ways. 'Communist kitchens' were set up in the factories, with provisions supplied by the Turin Co-operative Alliance. Any money found in the coffers of the factory offices was seized and distributed to the workers' families – 250,000 *lire* at the main Fiat works, and 60,000 at Fiat Brevetti.[26] In addition, 200,000 vouchers with a face value of 5 *lire* each were issued by the Chamber of Labour; they were exchangeable for goods at all retail outlets of the Co-operative Alliance and, it was hoped, at any retail store.[27]

Technical Committee in Milan. It was reported on 10 September that the main Fiat works had enough stocks to continue production for two months.

[21] *Avanti!* (Turin ed.) 5 and 11 September 1920.

[22] *Avanti!* (Turin ed.) 14 September 1920.

[23] *Avanti!* (Turin ed.) 15 September 1920.

[24] For a discussion of the functions of the various committees, see P. Spriano, *L'Occupazione delle Fabbriche* cit., p. 138.

[25] *Avanti!* (Turin ed.) 14 September 1920. See also E. Alessio, 'Rilievi Pratici', in *Ordine Nuovo* 16–23 October 1920; and P. Borghi, 'Gli Insegnamenti di Settembre', in *Ordine Nuovo* 24 December 1920.

[26] *Avanti!* (Turin ed.) 12 and 15 September 1920.

[27] *Avanti!* (Turin ed.) 18 September 1920. G. Parodi says that the Turin Union of Small Shop-Keepers agreed to accept them ('La Fiat–Centro in Mano agli Operai' cit., p. 646); and Gramsci later wrote that shopkeepers were sympathetic to the

Thus by mid-September the factory occupations at Turin had widened into a complex, if improvised, local economic system. Although there are no reliable estimates of the amount or value of the work done,[28] production in the factories certainly continued. The Factory Councils fulfilled complicated functions of discipline, distribution and exchange, and their activity was coordinated at city level by specialised committees of the Chamber of Labour. Only in Turin was all this achieved. The Turin situation was markedly different from that of the rest of Italy, both as regards the role of the Factory Councils and as regards coordination between factories. No doubt the previous months of *Ordine Nuovo* agitation contributed to this result, as did the key positions of Tasca and Togliatti (secretaries of the Chamber of Labour and the local Socialist Party branch respectively).

What was Gramsci's reaction to these events? It has been seen (p. 156) that the *Ordine Nuovo* played no part in the events leading directly to the occupation in Turin, and that it was opposed in principle to factory seizure as a method of class struggle. After the occupation, Gramsci insisted that it was *not* 'an experiment in Communist society', since all the powers of the State remained in the hands of the bourgeoisie: 'the proletariat has no coercive means to overcome the sabotage of technicians and the clerical staff, it cannot provision the factories with raw materials, and cannot sell the goods produced.'[29] It was vital that workers should *not* think the revolution was as easy as occupying undefended factories.

If the workers became convinced that the occupation of the factories was an attempt at direct Communist management, they would rapidly become disillusioned, and this would have a tremendous effect: the revolutionary organisation of the working class would break up, convinced Communists would become a minority; and the demoralised

workers' cause and 'accepted the workers' vouchers as sound currency' ('Ancora delle Capacità Organiche della Classe Operaia', in *L'Unità* 1 October 1926, now in A. Gramsci, *La Costruzione del Partito Comunista*, Einaudi, Turin 1971, p. 347).

[28] cf. P. Spriano, *L'Occupazione delle Fabbriche* cit., pp. 93 and 138; on p. 138 he quotes U. Camuri, 'L'Occupazione delle Fabbriche' cit., as reporting steel production at Ferriere Piemontesi at 3,978 tons in July, 3,093 in August, and 1,895 in September. However, the bare figures are misleading. Camuri also argued that consumption of fuel and raw materials was excessive in September, that most of September's production was in the first few days, and that the previous months' output had been lowered by the overtime ban and 'obstructionism'. After the occupation, workers at the foundry agreed to accept 146 *lire* each as the value of their work, compared with a previous monthly average of 485 *lire*: 'and this was more eloquent than any speech in persuading the workers of the futility of their fleeting illusions'. Of course, he was writing in the full Fascist period.

[29] 'L'Occupazione', unsigned article in *Avanti!* (Turin ed.) 2 September 1920. The article is attributed to Gramsci by Sergio Caprioglio, and published in A. Gramsci, *Scritti 1915–21* (Quaderni de 'Il Corpo', Milan 1968), pp. 130–2.

and dejected majority . . . would bow their heads under the capitalist yoke.[30]

This was prescient; and it was attitudes like these that led Piero Gobetti, in a letter to his fiancée on 7 September, to write: 'Here we are in the middle of a real revolution . . . a tiny minority (basically the *Ordine Nuovo*, not Gramsci and Togliatti, but the workers who support them) has assumed authority, with a complete disregard for personal sacrifices.'[31]

Nevertheless, Gramsci did not oppose the occupation as such. In the prevailing atmosphere of euphoria, he too thought it showed the weakness of the bourgeois regime, and the fragility of existing social hierarchies. He hoped it would make all workers realise that the day of normal Trade Union agitations was over, that in the new circumstances the Union leaders were incapable of providing the masses with effective leadership, and that 'the masses must solve the problems of the factory with their own methods, with their own men.' The revival of Factory Council activity was naturally also welcome. Above all, the very hopelessness of the position of isolated factories meant that workers would have to go on to further revolutionary acts: 'the problem of setting up an urban Soviet now faces the working class in a concrete way.' Gramsci visited several factories during the occupation, to talk to the inhabitants of the 'proletarian republics constituted by the occupied factories'.[32] There seems little doubt that his initial hesitation was soon overcome by the revival of Factory Council activity and by the central coordination of economic activity which the occupation in Turin brought about, and which made the occupation seem to him less like anarcho-syndicalism, and more like real revolutionary preparation.[33]

Needless to say, the government did not share this view of events. Giolitti's initial policy was one of benign neglect. He told the industrialists that troops would not be used to expel the workers from the

---

[30] *ibid.*

[31] The letter is in the Gobetti Centre at Turin; it is quoted by S. F. Romano, *Gramsci* (U.T.E.T., Turin 1965), p. 434. In 1924 Gramsci himself referred to the 'pessimism that dominated me in 1920, especially during the occupation of the factories' (in a letter to Zino Zini 2 April 1924, quoted in *Rinascita* 25 April 1964). cf. also A. Gramsci, *Scritti 1915–21* cit., p. 187; P. Spriano, *Storia del Partito Comunista Italiano*, vol. i (Einaudi, Turin 1967), p. 81; and L. Paggi, *Gramsci e il Moderno Principe*, vol. i (Riuniti, Rome 1970), pp. 320 ff.

[32] The quotations come from Gramsci's article 'Domenica Rossa', in *Avanti!* (Turin ed.) 5 September 1920 (now in A. Gramsci, *Ordine Nuovo*, Einaudi, Turin 1955, pp. 163–7).

[33] 'Cronache dell' Ordine Nuovo', in *Ordine Nuovo* 2 October 1920 (now in A. Gramsci, *Ordine Nuovo* cit., pp. 486–8).

factories. It was much better to leave them inside, where they were quite harmless ('the workers occupying the factories have no interest in wrecking the machinery, as they know that this would cause very lengthy unemployment').[34] Expelling them by force would be senseless – for even if it could be done without a bloodbath, it would leave the workers in control of the city streets, and the army beleaguered in the factories.[35] Giolitti even thought it was unwise to offer to mediate between the employers and Unions, for fear of antagonising one side or the other; and he disavowed Labriola, the Minister of Labour, when the latter tried to mediate. The best policy was to do nothing, and wait for the movement to fade away – as it was bound to do when raw materials ran short, credit was stopped, and orders cancelled. As he wrote in his Memoirs: 'I was firmly convinced that the government should . . . allow the experiment to carry on for a time, so that the workers could become convinced that their plans were unrealisable, and so that the ringleaders could not throw the blame for their failure on to other people.'[36]

However, as time went on this lofty indifference became less tenable. Railwaymen were helping to shift supplies to the occupied factories, arms were being manufactured inside them, and foreign bankers were alarmed. The government began to put the pressure on, especially on the intransigent Milanese industrialists. On 11 September Giolitti told Corradini, the Under-Secretary at the Ministry of the Interior, that the industrialists 'will yield if they receive instructions from the banks, on whom their existence depends. You must act energetically, especially on Pogliani.'[37] Thus, by the second or third week of the occupation, the government was no longer 'neutral': it was using the banks to persuade the Milanese employers to settle. This overt partisanship was much resented, and had important consequences, as will be seen.

The Government's views were very similar to those of the national Trade Union leadership. The leaders of *F.I.O.M.* and of the *C.G.L.* were

[34] Giolitti to Corradini 2 September 1920, quoted in G. De Rosa, *Storia del Movimento Cattolico in Italia*, vol. ii, *Il Partito Popolare Italiano* (Laterza, Bari 1966), p. 125. The full text is given in P. Spriano, *L'Occupazione delle Fabbriche* cit., pp. 172–3.

[35] Giolitti's speech to the Senate 26 September 1920, quoted in N. Valeri, *Giovanni Giolitti* (U.T.E.T., Turin 1972), pp. 293–4. P. Spriano, in *L'Occupazione delle Fabbriche* cit., p. 88, points out that the government could not rely on the troops in any case, after the mutiny at Ancona in July. The 60,000 Carabinieri and 25,000 Royal Guards were more reliable, but not numerous enough to hold 600 factories and maintain public order as well.

[36] G. Giolitti, *Memorie della Mia Vita* (Garzanti, Milan 1922, reprinted 1967), p. 364.

[37] G. De Rosa, *Storia del Movimento Cattolico in Italia* cit., vol. ii, p. 128. Pogliani was a Director of the Banca di Sconto, and the government suspected this bank of supporting the most intransigent industrialists.

very concerned to restrict the agitation to economic issues, and were anxious to reach an agreement as quickly as possible, before the movement became difficult to control.[38] The same was often true of local Trade Union leaders. Even in Turin, the *F.I.O.M.* Committee of Agitation issued a proclamation immediately after the occupation denying that the workers were undermining the existing order:

> In order to prove that no revolutionary intentions are among the plans of this Union, let the industrialists make a fair and just offer, and only if it is rejected will they be justified in claiming that *F.I.O.M.* is using underhand methods to reach a hidden goal . . . the factories are in the hands of the workers only in order to prevent a lengthy struggle; this dispute must be resolved within a few days, thus saving the country any more agitations and the workers any more useless sacrifices.[39]

However, once several non-engineering factories had been occupied,[40] it became impossible to limit the aims of the agitation to the metal-workers' original wage claim. Any solution had to embrace all branches of industry. On 4 September the *C.G.L.* leaders called a meeting in Milan of representatives from all the major industrial centres to discuss the situation. The meeting came up with the ideal slogan – 'Trade Union control of industry'. This was an ingenious solution, for the new goal was sufficiently broad to be applicable to all industries, and at the same time it had the requisite revolutionary ring. The Union leaders later claimed that they realised 'Trade Union control' was necessary when workers in Turin discovered various documents in the offices of Fiat, proving that the industrialists operated a spy-system in the factories, and that there was a black-list of trouble-makers whom all members of the employers' association had agreed not to employ.[41] In these circumstances 'control' seemed necessary, if the Unions were to safeguard their members against discrimination. The discovery of a black-list perhaps contributed, but the Union leaders' proposal was in line with their arguments since the war, and was especially in line with their arguments against the Factory Council movement in Turin (see p. 111 ff.). The meeting at Milan therefore passed a

---

[38] Buozzi was reported by the Prefect of Milan as being anxious for a settlement to the dispute to be reached before it spread to other industries (Prefect of Milan to Ministry of the Interior 4 September 1920, quoted by P. Spriano, *L'Occupazione delle Fabbriche* cit., p. 75). The Prefect also reported on 5 September that *F.I.O.M.* was willing to accept a pay increase of 5 *lire* a day instead of the previously demanded 7 *lire* (*ibid.*).

[39] *Avanti!* (Turin ed.) 3 September 1920.

[40] cf. M. Abrate, *La Lotta Sindacale nella Industrializzazione in Italia* cit., p. 484; P. Spriano, *L'Occupazione delle Fabbriche* cit., pp. 90–1.

[41] *Avanti!* (Turin ed.) 6 and 9 September 1920.

resolution calling on the *C.G.L.* and the *P.S.I.* to take over the leadership of the movement (from *F.I.O.M.*), and for them to hold a joint conference on 10 September to decide further action; and meanwhile the aim of the agitation was said to be 'control of firms so as to lead to collective management and to the socialisation of all forms of production'.[42] It was perhaps a good way out of a difficult situation, rather than a serious attempt to secure major industrial reform.

Although the newly declared aim of 'control over industry' was generally welcomed,[43] the position of *F.I.O.M.* and of the *C.G.L.* leaders soon became increasingly difficult. There was still no sign that the industrialists might be willing to negotiate. More factories were occupied every day, especially in Milan and Turin; and the syndicalists were still very active and still calling for a United Revolutionary Front. On 6 September the *U.S.I.* called a meeting at Genoa, attended by various independent but powerful Unions – the Railwaymen, the Postal Workers, Seamen and so forth.[44] The meeting decided to await the outcome of the *C.G.L.*–*P.S.I.* conference on 10 September before acting, but it was becoming obvious that the workers could not remain in the factories and continue production unless they achieved political power.[45] It was in this situation that a preliminary meeting of representatives of the *P.S.I.* Directorate and of the *C.G.L.*'s Directive Council took place in Milan, on 9 September.

At this meeting the representatives from Turin made their views known to the national leaders. The tone of militant opinion in the Turin factories may be judged by the telegram sent by the Fiat Factory Council to the *F.I.O.M.* Committee of Agitation in Milan the following day, 10 September, announcing that 'the workers of Fiat–Centro Turin intend to open negotiations only if the dominant and exploiting class is abolished; otherwise immediate war until a complete victory.'[46] But the official representatives of Turin Socialism, Togliatti from the city party branch and Benso from the Provincial Federation, were far more cautious. When asked by the *C.G.L.* leaders whether a successful insurrection at Turin

[42] *Relazione del Comitato Centrale della F.I.O.M. sull' Agitazione dei Metallurgici Italiani* (*Luglio – Agosto – Settembre 1920*), typewritten copy supplied to the author by *F.I.O.M.* of a document originally published by Tipografia Alleanza, Turin 1921, p. 28; L. D'Aragona, *La C.G.L. nel Sessennio 1914–20* (Relazione del Consiglio Direttivo della C.G.L. al V Congresso della C.G.L., Livorno 1921, published Milan 1921), p. 84. For a transcript of this whole meeting, see G. Bosio, *La Grande Paura* (Samonà and Savelli, Rome 1970), pp. 73–94.

[43] Even the Turin edition of *Avanti!* welcomed the proposal on 6 September 1920.

[44] G. Maione, *Il Biennio Rosso* (Il Mulino, Bologna 1975), pp. 256–8.

[45] As the *F.I.O.M.* leaders themselves admitted (*Relazione* cit., p. 29).

[46] *Avanti!* (Turin ed.) 11 September 1920.

were possible,[47] Togliatti replied that the workers in Turin were adequately armed to defend their factories against any conceivable attack, but they could not contemplate leaving their factory-bastions in order to undertake an offensive campaign in the streets:

> The city is surrounded by a non-Socialist zone,[48] and to find working-class forces that would help the city you would have to go as far as Vercelli and Saluzzo . . . You should not count on an action undertaken in Turin alone. We shall not attack alone; in order to attack we need a simultaneous action in the countryside, and particularly the action would need to be nation-wide. We want assurances on this point because otherwise we do not want to commit our proletariat.[49]

Despite his preoccupation with the danger of being isolated, Togliatti went on to explain that he personally was in favour of a nation-wide insurrection, and the *C.G.L.* and Party Directorate, 'being fully aware of the national situation', should issue instructions for one if at all possible. The other representative from Turin, Benso, took a different line. In his opinion the countryside was not ready to help an insurrection, so a normal Trade Union solution to the conflict had to be found.[50] In Turin memories of the General Strike of the previous April, in which the national political

[47] The motives for this question were immediately suspect at Turin, where it was thought that the *C.G.L.* leaders were seeking to manoeuvre the Turin representatives into an isolated position, as during the Piedmontese General Strike of April 1920 or the riots of August 1917. D'Aragona later said that the question was asked because Turin was regarded as the most revolutionary city in Italy, and if no revolution were possible there the agitation could not conceivably be allowed to have a 'political outcome' (D'Aragona to the V Congress of the *C.G.L.* at Leghorn 1921, in *Resoconto Stenografico del V Congresso della C.G.L.*, Milan 1921, p. 253). This explanation is plausible – the Union leaders had every interest in calling the bluff of the 'revolutionaries' in Turin and elsewhere.

[48] According to Gramsci a year later, the countryside around Turin, which had supported the city in April, was no longer willing to do so in September; as a result of 'the rascally campaign that Trade Union officials and Serratian opportunists carried out against the Turin Communists, the whole organisation created for the region from Turin had completely collapsed.' ('I Più Grandi Responsabili', in *Ordine Nuovo* 20 September 1921, now in A. Gramsci, *Socialismo e Fascismo*, Einaudi, Turin 1966, p. 343).

[49] *Ordine Nuovo* 1 March 1921; see also *La C.G.L. nel Sessennio 1914–20* cit., p. 87; P. Spriano, *L'Occupazione delle Fabbriche* cit., p. 97; G. Bosio, *La Grande Paura* cit., p. 101. V. Bianco (in 'L'Organizzazione Militare Rivoluzionaria durante la Occupazione' cit.) wrote that the Turin workers could easily have taken over the city, given the arms they had and the sympathy of local troops. They failed to do so, because the abstentionists and the *Ordine Nuovo* group were jealous of each other and would not collaborate, and because the local Socialist party branch made no attempt to coordinate military work. The implied criticism of Togliatti, who was secretary of the local party branch, is remarkable in an article published in 1930.

[50] G. Bosio, *La Grande Paura* cit., pp. 102–4; *Ordine Nuovo* 1 March 1921.

and Union leaders had failed to support the local Socialists, were clearly still fresh.

On the morning of 10 September, the *P.S.I.* Directorate proclaimed it would 'assume the responsibility and leadership of the movement, extending it to the whole country and to all the proletarian masses'[51] – all factories and all the land were to be occupied, as a first step towards the seizure of political power. It is worth noting that some prominent members of the party Directorate, including Serrati, were not present, as they were still returning from their visit to Soviet Russia for the Second Congress of the International. On the same day, the National Council of the *C.G.L.* proclaimed that 'the leadership of the movement shall be assumed by the *C.G.L.*, with the help of the *P.S.I.*' The *C.G.L.* National Council defined the objective again as being 'recognition on the part of the employers of the principle of Trade Union control over industrial firms, aiming in this way to open the path to collective management and to socialisation, thus resolving the problem of production in an organic way.'[52]

The positions of the *C.G.L.* and of the *P.S.I.* were, therefore, completely different. The *C.G.L.* was seeking to limit the conflict as much as possible, and find a 'normal' solution; the *P.S.I.* Directorate was, at least verbally, trying to extend the agitation into a real revolution. In fact, the maximalists on the party Directorate had no wish to lead a revolution. They were merely trying to reassure their supporters, who thought the hour of revolution had arrived. On 11 September the leaders of the *C.G.L.* called their bluff. D'Aragona and his colleagues on the *C.G.L.* Directive Council offered to resign, on the grounds they did not want to lead the proletariat to suicide: if the party wanted to find a 'political' solution, it would have to do so alone.[53] The party leaders hastily backtracked. Far from insisting that the occupation movement was political, and that under the terms of the Pact of Alliance (see p. 33) they had the right to lead it, they agreed to allow a vote to be held by the *C.G.L.*'s National Council on the nature of the situation, and on the proper solution to be sought. And so the decision on whether a revolution should be proclaimed was put to the vote of the *C.G.L.* National Council. The maximalists must have calculated that this body would reject revolution, that the odium for 'betrayal' would then fall on the *C.G.L.*, and that the party would retain the support of its followers. The vote, not surprisingly,

[51] P. Spriano, *L'Occupazione delle Fabbriche* cit., p. 99; *La C.G.L. nel Sessennio 1914–20* cit., p. 84.

[52] *Avanti!* (Turin ed.) 12 September 1920. Thus the *C.G.L.* formally took over the agitation from *F.I.O.M.*

[53] *La C.G.L. nel Sessennio* cit., p. 92; G. Bosio, *La Grande Paura* cit., pp. 158–62.

was a victory for the 'moderate' motion calling for Trade Union control of industry.[54] On the declaration of the result, Gennari, the most prominent maximalist present, proclaimed solemnly that the Party Directorate would respect the wishes of the C.G.L., but would 'reserve the right to assume the leadership in the course of time, in a changed political situation.'[55] Once again, the dilemma of the maximalists was clearly revealed: unwilling to act without Union support, they were forced to pose as 'revolutionaries' while pursuing a policy designed to avoid revolution.

The voting at the National Council of the C.G.L. on 11 September ensured that a political outcome of the conflict was henceforth impossible, and that therefore an 'economic' solution had to be found. The C.G.L. immediately set up a central Committee of Agitation,[56] and this in turn called for a Joint Commission of Unions and employers to work out details of the projected 'control of industry'.[57] Such 'control', it was claimed, was necessary to enable the Union leaders to learn 'the true state of industry', and thus acquire knowledge relevant for wage bargaining. It would also mean that the Unions would 'be able, through their factory representatives — who are an emanation of the Trade Union — to contribute to the observance of regulations, have a say in the hiring and dismissal of labour, and encourage normal activity within the factory.'[58] Obviously the C.G.L. was going to make sure that 'control' at factory level remained under Union auspices.

These proposals for 'Trade Union control' sounded alarming, even to some Government Ministers. Corradini, Undersecretary at the Interior, thought they were unacceptable, for the employers would insist on retaining discipline and management prerogatives. The leading reformist deputy, Turati, had to reassure him. 'Trade Union control' would mean class collaboration and increased production:

we must go beyond the factory council or enterprise council, which was founded with extremist, subversive and, I would add, anti-

[54] The voting was 591,243 to 409,369, with 93,623 abstentions. The F.I.O.M. leaders abstained, although favouring the solution of 'Trade Union control'. The Turin representatives voted with the minority, calling for the party Directorate to lead a 'political' movement.

[55] Avanti! (Turin ed.) 12 September 1920.

[56] Its members were: D'Aragona, Giuseppe Bianchi, Gino Baldesi, Buozzi, Colombino, Marchiaro, Missiroli, Raineri, Dugoni and Cravello (Avanti!, Turin ed., 14 September 1920). But the F.I.O.M. Committee of Agitation remained in being, 'so as to guarantee the continued resistance of the workers in the factories' (Relazione cit., p. 32).

[57] The C.G.L. Committee of Agitation's manifesto was printed in Avanti! (Turin ed.) 14 September 1920.

[58] Relazione cit., p. 33.

Socialist aims, and limit its role to minor disciplinary and technical questions. For everything else we should support and strengthen the Trade Unions, and start them acting and thinking on a more comprehensive scale, in the national interest.[59]

This view was, of course, characteristic of the reformists and of Union leaders (see p. 111 ff.), although Turati was perhaps over-enthusiastic about the reformist 'victory' — 'if we manoeuvre successfully, we might achieve a universally useful result.'[60] In any case, the government needed little convincing. Giolitti himself told Corradini on 12 September that:

definitive solution of the industrial problem would be to give workers interest in industry, with a share in profits, even in the form of share-distribution, and especially participation by workers' representatives on the Boards of Directors, so that they get to know the true state of industry and the amount of profits. I believe that the more intelligent industrialists in Turin would accept.[61]

During the next few days the government imposed the wage settlement and 'Trade Union control' on the reluctant industrialists, using the possibility of credit restrictions as a threat to convince the waverers (see above, p. 164). On 15 September Giolitti met five of the C.G.L. leaders and several representatives of the employers in Turin. He told them he intended to set up a Commission, containing employers' and Union representatives, to draft a Bill on worker participation and 'Trade Union control'.[62] Some employers panicked, as did the editor of the *Corriere della Sera*, Luigi Albertini.[63] The pill was sweetened by tariff concessions, hastily announced on 14 September — Gino Luzzatto estimated Fiat would benefit by 120 million *lire p.a.*, compared with 40 million 'lost' through extra wages.[64]

Of course, not all industrialists were intransigent. Some, like Gino Olivetti and Ettore Conti, thought it best to play along with Giolitti for

[59] Turati to Corradini 19 September 1920, in G. De Rosa, *Il Movimento Cattolico in Italia*, vol. ii, *Il Partito Popolare Italiano* cit., p. 133.

[60] *ibid.*, p. 132.

[61] *ibid.*, p. 130.

[62] This proposal came from Ettore Conti, a leading industrialist. See M. Abrate, *La Lotta Sindacale nella Industrializzazione in Italia* cit., p. 297; V. Castronovo, *Giovanni Agnelli* (U.T.E.T., Turin 1971), p. 253.

[63] A hysterical telephone conversation between Albertini and Giovanni Amendola on 15 September was intercepted by the police, and is given in P. Spriano, *L'Occupazione delle Fabbriche* cit., pp. 187–91. The *Corriere della Sera* thundered (21 September) that even a Socialist government would be preferable to one 'formed by these accomplices of our perdition'.

[64] The estimate is quoted in V. Castronovo, *Giovanni Agnelli* cit., p. 252.

the time being. Conti thought — or claimed later to have thought — that the employers-Union Commission would never be able to agree on a Bill, and that the whole scheme would collapse when the forthcoming recession became severe a few months later.[65] These arguments prevailed. On 17 September the National Council of the Industrialists' Federation accepted the principle of 'Trade Union control', by a majority of 21 to 14. The opposition was led by the iron and steel interests, especially Ansaldo and Ilva, but included many smaller employers and even some leading Turin industrialists like Emilio De Benedetti, the President of the Turin Industrial League. The employers emphasised that their acceptance of the idea of 'Trade Union control' was a result of government insistence, not of their own free will.[66]

On 19 September, therefore, Giolitti issued a decree setting up a Commission of six members from the Unions' side, and six from the employers', to draft proposals for a law on 'Trade Union control'.[67] The more mundane issue of the metal-workers' original pay claim was also settled at tripartite talks in Rome, on the basis of a four *lire* per day wage rise. However, the question of payment for work done during the occupation was left to be resolved by the individual firms, on the basis of their assessment of its value.[68] The leaders of *F.I.O.M.* insisted that the whole agreement should be submitted to a referendum of all metal-workers before being valid.

In the meantime an extraordinary National Congress of *F.I.O.M.* had been taking place in Milan, to discuss the progress of negotiations. At the opening session on 17 September, the Union secretary Buozzi carefully emphasised that 'we have requested two types of control: that over industry in general, which will have to be exercised by the Trade Union organisations, and that over the individual workshops, which will have to be carried out by the workers themselves, and which will be concerned with dismissals, suspensions, etc.'[69] Obviously Buozzi was trying to show that 'Trade Union control' was not designed as an alternative to the system of Factory Councils that had arisen during the occupation, particularly in Turin. The Congress called on the industrialists to accept 'Trade Union control', and Buozzi warned that if the employers did not

---

[65] E. Conti, *Dal Taccuino di un Borghese* (Garzanti, Milan 1946), p. 239; cf. also P. Spriano, *L'Occupazione delle Fabbriche* cit., pp. 122–3.

[66] P. Spriano, *L'Occupazione delle Fabbriche* cit., pp. 121–3.

[67] The text of the decree is given in Italian in *C.G.I.I., I Consigli di Gestione* (Milan 1947), vol. ii, p. 27; and in English in International Labour Office, *Studies and Reports*, Series A, no. 11, pp. 4–5.

[68] The agreement is given in *Relazione* cit., pp. 37–40.

[69] *Avanti!* (Turin ed.) 18 September 1920.

give in, *F.I.O.M.* would press for a general occupation, in all industries.[70] The Congress continued on 21 September, after adjourning briefly during the final negotiations at Rome. Colombino reminded the delegates that the occupation had been originally ordered 'not as a definitive measure, but as a means of preventing a lock-out';[71] that such a reminder was necessary is an indication of how quickly the fact of occupation had changed the political and industrial situation. Eventually the delegates decided, by 117 votes to 18, to go ahead with the referendum on whether the Rome agreement should be accepted.[72]

Throughout this Congress, the opposition to the *F.I.O.M.* leaders' policy was led by the Turin branch of the Union. Partly this was because only at Turin had any considerable production been achieved during the period of occupation, and so Buozzi's inability to secure payment for the work done was most keenly resented there. It is also true that the Turin opposition at the *F.I.O.M.* Congress was led by anarcho-syndicalists like Ferrero and Garino, who in other cities would have been members of the *U.S.I.* (the *U.S.I.* was strongly opposed to 'Trade Union control' and to the referendum, which it urged its members to boycott).[73] Above all, it was in Turin that the impact of the occupation had been greatest, because of the city's industrial structure; and in Turin the decisions of the National Council of the *C.G.L.* on 10–11 September had been bitterly resented. A golden opportunity for revolution had been thrown away. Giovanni Parodi, of the main Fiat works, later wrote: 'only some-one who was in the factories at that time can imagine the complete despondency felt by the workers. It was like a body-blow to the confidence that the workers had had up until then in our organisations'.[74] On 14 September the 'Communist groups' of three leading Turin factories, Officine Rapid, Carrozzeria Fiat, and Fiat Barriera di Nizza, met and called for the Turin branch of the *P.S.I.* to assume sole leadership of the movement, as it was now solely 'political'.[75] Boero, the abstentionist former secretary of the Turin party, criticised his successor Togliatti for being lukewarm in urging a revolutionary extension of the movement during the *C.G.L.* National Council (see above, p. 167).[76] On 16 September a meeting of

(see above, p. 167)

---

[70] *Avanti!* (Turin ed.) 19 September 1920.

[71] *Avanti!* (Turin ed.) 22 September 1920.

[72] *Avanti!* (Turin ed.) 23 September 1920. The opposition motion was put by Ferrero of Turin; it deplored the economic outcome of the dispute and condemned the agreement.

[73] *Umanità Nova* 19 September 1920.

[74] G. Parodi, 'La Fiat–Centro in Mano agli Operai' cit., p. 650.

[75] *Avanti!* (Turin ed.) 17 September 1920.

[76] *Avanti!* (Turin ed.) 16 September 1920. Boero's criticism was echoed by Ferrero and Garino at a General Council of the Turin Chamber of Labour (*ibid.*).

Workshop Commissars from all the metal-working factories in Turin approved almost unanimously a motion calling for an extension of the movement and the seizure of all public and private industries.[77]

The *Ordine Nuovo* group was, as usual, split on these issues. Tasca and Pastore (the editor of the Turin edition of *Avanti!*) regarded the Giolitti decree on 'Trade Union control' as a great victory.[78] Togliatti was more cautious: workers' control was only valuable as a means to revolution, but even so 'class control' — not 'State control' — might be a first step towards conquest of the means of production and exchange.[79] Gramsci claimed in delight that the emergent workers' control proposals justified the whole *Ordine Nuovo* campaign — 'workers' control no longer seems a madcap scheme thought up by fanatics — nobody thinks this now, not even the industrialists. The workers of Turin were right in April 1920 . . . today it is acknowledged that there *can* be *two* authorities in the factory.'[80] But, of course, 'control' should not mean worker involvement in the bourgeois regime, nor sinecures for Union officials. It must mean independent factory bodies, elected by the workers alone, and the establishment of committees to co-ordinate and organise production and exchange; and it must mean 'the complete expulsion from the field of production of the class of owners as such'.[81] By this time Gramsci had come to see the occupation as essentially a 'political' movement, and perhaps this view was a natural continuation of the *Ordine Nuovo's* attempts during the previous year to make the Factory Councils the basis of a new political order.

Yet did Gramsci really believe that a 'revolutionary' outcome was possible? It seems unlikely. I have discussed his initial pessimism; and Togliatti, after all, had refused to take the initiative when challenged to do so in Milan. It is not surprising that both Trade Union leaders and maximalist Socialists later accused the *Ordine Nuovo* group of hypocrisy, or that more recently it has been argued that the *Ordinovisti* were very good at theorising about revolution, but quite inept at leading one.[82] Perhaps

---

[77] There were only four votes against the motion (*Avanti!*, Turin ed., 17 September 1920).

[78] cf. Tasca's speech to the General Council of the Chamber of Labour (in *Avanti!*, Turin ed., 16 September 1920) and Pastore's 'La Vittoria È' (in *Avanti!*, Turin ed., 22 September 1920).

[79] P. Togliatti, 'Controllo di Classe', in *Avanti!* (Turin ed.) 17 September 1920.

[80] 'Cinque Mesi Dopo', in *Avanti!* (Turin ed.) 14 September 1920 (now in A. Gramsci, *Scritti 1915–21* cit., p. 137).

[81] *ibid.* cf. also Gramsci's similar views at the end of the occupation, in 'Cronache dell' Ordine Nuovo', in *Ordine Nuovo* 2 October 1920 (now in A. Gramsci, *Ordine Nuovo* cit., pp. 486–8).

[82] R. Del Carria, *Proletari senza Rivoluzione* (Oriente, Milan 1966), vol. ii, p. 123.

it is fairer to say that Gramsci, yet again, was taking a longer-term, more detached view. The occupation proved he had been right about the importance of Factory Councils, and showed that workers were capable of industrial and political self-government. But it also provided some less gratifying lessons, among them that Revolution was like War: it had to be 'planned in minute detail by a working-class General Staff.'[83] No war would ever break out if the people were asked their views first, or if parliamentary approval were required, and the same was true of revolutions. The Socialist Party had shown itself too 'parliamentary', too 'democratic', too burdened with the machinery of representative assemblies and preliminary consultations, and quite incapable of planning strategically or seizing the military initiative. This was unfortunate language, for it was reminiscent of 'interventionism', and it provided more ammunition for Gramsci's critics.

Gramsci went on to draw the conclusion that it was essential to set up a new party immediately, one that could act as a genuine working-class avant-garde. It was impossible to have any confidence in the P.S.I. after the events of 10–11 September in Milan. Gramsci claimed that Turin could have risen if the Socialist organisation of the surrounding countryside had not been deliberately destroyed after the April strike, and he suspected that the C.G.L. leaders had tried to provoke an insurrection in Turin so as to be able to abandon the movement to its fate. A year later Gramsci explicitly admitted that the occupation had convinced him of the need for a new party: 'in those days we acquired, perhaps somewhat tardily, a precise and firm conviction of the need for a split',[84] and his first explicit call for the founding of a new party appeared immediately after the occupation period.[85]

Many people in Turin shared these views. Insistence on a 'political' outcome to the dispute necessarily meant rejecting the policy of the P.S.I.'s Directorate, and this led on to rejecting the P.S.I. itself. On 18 September the executive committee of the Turin branch of the party – elected in August on a platform which implied opposition to plans for a separate Communist Party – issued a manifesto saying that the P.S.I.'s failure to carry out revolution had shown the necessity for a Communist Party, and added:

[83] 'Capacità Politica', in *Avanti!* (Turin ed.) 24 September 1920 (now in A. Gramsci, *Ordine Nuovo* cit., p. 171).

[84] 'I Più Grandi Responsabili', in *Ordine Nuovo* 20 September 1921 (now in A. Gramsci, *Socialismo e Fascismo* cit., p. 344).

[85] 'Il Partito Comunista', in *Ordine Nuovo* 9 October 1920 (now in A. Gramsci, *Ordine Nuovo* cit., pp. 158–63).

At all events the executive committee of the Socialist branch invites comrades to confront the problem of the formation of a Communist Party now; if this problem is not resolved today, it will prejudice the success of any future revolutionary action. If the conviction of the need for a new party arises out of the present uncertainty and confusion, this will be a great gain.[86]

The local abstentionists were even more disillusioned with the *P.S.I.* On 20 September the abstentionist group at the main Fiat works demanded the formation of a Communist Party immediately, on the grounds that it was impossible to remain in the same party as the reformist elements that had prevented revolution.[87] The following day the members of the official 'Abstentionist Faction' in Turin approved the Fiat workers' resolution and called on the 'Faction's' national central committee to 'begin work towards the immediate creation of the Communist Party, the Italian section of the Third International, and to convene a national Congress of the Faction to set up the necessary executive organs'.[88] Bordiga refused to do anything of the kind: the new party would have to be given as broad a base as possible, and he would wait for the next *P.S.I.* party Congress.[89] The situation was so serious that the International's representative in the Latin countries sent a warning to the Turin abstentionists:

Dear Comrades of the Abstentionist Faction in Turin

I have heard news that as a result of recent events you have decided to leave the Party. I recommend and entreat you, in the name of the executive committee of the Communist International, not to take any hasty steps, even if you are impelled by revolutionary motives. This is not the tactics that we must adopt; these divisive manoeuvres may help our opponents. We must, instead, remain for the time being in the party, and devote all our energies to winning control of it, so that it may become a truly Communist party, and respect all the decisions of the Communist International, the guide of the proletariat all over the world. It will be the reformists, the opportunists, and the pink Communists who will have to abandon the party, leaving it in the hands of strong and resolute Communists.[90]

[86] *Avanti!* (Turin ed.) 18 September 1920.

[87] The motion is given in P. Spriano, *L'Occupazione delle Fabbriche* cit., pp. 139–40, and in G. Parodi, 'La Fiat–Centro in Mano agli Operai' cit., p. 652.

[88] The motion was reprinted, with critical comments, in *Il Soviet* 3 October 1920.

[89] *Il Soviet* 3 October 1920. Bordiga wrote of 'this very serious and unexpected motion passed by our comrades in Turin'.

[90] Copy sent by the Prefect of Turin to the Ministry of the Interior 3 October 1920

The referendum among the metal-workers to decide whether the Rome agreement should be accepted caused more heated debates in Turin. Mass meetings were held on 20 September, and the results were almost uniformly unfavourable to the agreement. At the main Fiat works, a motion was passed that was laconically summarised in *Avanti!* as 'censure of the decisions taken without consulting the masses, invitation to the representatives to make no final agreement without knowing the wishes of the masses, no confidence in "control", struggle to the end.'[91] Similar motions were passed at the other factories.[92] In the evening a meeting of liaison secretaries from fifty-eight factories, held at the Chamber of Labour, also called for rejection of the Rome terms, and gave a mandate to the Turin representatives at the *F.I.O.M.* Congress to vote against them.[93]

However, the referendum, which was held throughout Italy on 24 September, gave a majority in favour of returning to work on the terms agreed at Rome: 127,904 votes to 44,531, with 3,006 blank papers. Even in Turin there was a majority – albeit much smaller than elsewhere – in favour of acceptance. The final results for the city were 18,740 in favour, 16,909 against, with 1,024 blank ballot-papers. These figures may be compared with those at Milan, where there were 23,570 in favour, 6,668 against, and 1,155 blank papers.[94] In both centres, and indeed nationally, the number of abstentions was high; the *U.S.I.* boycotted the referendum.[95] By this time, of course, the engineering workers had

(in *State Archives*, Min. Int., Dir. Gen. P.S., Aff. Gen. e Ris., 1920, b. 67). The writer was almost certainly either the Bulgarian Christo Kabakchev or the Hungarian Matthias Rakosi, who both represented the International at the Leghorn Congress in January 1921.

[91] *Avanti!* (Turin ed.) 21 September 1920; also in G. Parodi, 'La Fiat–Centro in Mano agli Operai' cit., p. 651.

[92] The Lancia works demanded pay for the period of occupation, and full recognition of the powers of the Internal Commissions. Scat considered the agreement 'absolutely unacceptable'. Brevetti Fiat demanded guarantees against reprisals. Fiat Lingotto were in favour of workers' management. Acciaierie Fiat demanded payment for the period of occupation, and for the Internal Commission to have the right to dismiss workers. Only the workers at the Spa factory were in favour of acceptance (*Avanti!*, Turin ed., 21 September 1920).

[93] *Avanti!* (Turin ed.) 21 September 1920.

[94] *Avanti!* (Turin ed.) 25 and 26 September 1920. The figures for the main Fiat works in Turin were not given exactly, but were estimated at 6,000 for, and 4,000 against the agreement; at Diatto Fiat, they were 286 for, and 581 against; at Brevetti Fiat, 636 for, and 925 against; at Scat, 137 for, and 344 against; at Acciaierie Fiat, 303 for, and 620 against; at Lancia, 486 for, and 273 against; at Itala, 539 for, and 128 against; at Fiat Lingotto, 606 for, and 334 against; and at Industrie Metallurgiche, 203 for, 575 against.

[95] The anarchist paper *Umanità Nova* carried the headline 'A Proletarian Caporetto' on 1 October 1920. The International Labour Office (*Studies and Reports*, Series A,

received no 'normal' pay for over three weeks. It was understandable that, once the possibility of a 'political' outcome no longer existed, they should be willing to evacuate the factories. The vote also shows how disillusioned many workers had become by this time. At the main Fiat works in Turin the day-workers also voted no confidence in the Factory Council, although it remained in office for the time being.[96]

The referendum ensured that the pay increases and the decree on Trade Union control would be accepted by the workers, but the question of payment for work done during the occupation still had to be settled with the individual factories. In Turin, this was a job for the Factory Councils, which had to work out how much pay was due to each worker.[97] The occupation in Turin ended, therefore, with detailed negotiations between the factory managements and the Factory Councils. Giovanni Agnelli of Fiat was quite willing to pay up, realising that the workers had to be given some material benefits in their hour of defeat; but the majority of Turin employers greatly resented it (paying the 'Red Guards' for their 'work' was particularly obnoxious), and there were some angry scenes later in the industrialists' organisations.[98] It was not until agreements were reached that the factories were formally evacuated, although by this time there was much absenteeism and apathy – Parodi later wrote that only about fifty workers (out of 13,000) stayed inside the main Fiat works on the last night of the occupation.[99]

The Factory Councils naturally tried not only to secure payment, but also to safeguard their future positions. The main Fiat works was evacuated on 30 September, in return for payment of work done and the recognition of new 'norms' for the Internal Commission. These 'norms' essentially re-established the position that had existed before the General Strike the previous April. Three of the six members of the Internal Commission were authorised to remain in the Commission's office, or circulate round the factory, during working hours; the other three, although required to work in the normal way, were allowed to go to the office in case of emergency. Workshop Commissars were not only recognised, they were allowed in urgent cases to bring complaints to the

no. 11, p. 8) reported (without quoting a source) that opposition was strongest in the smaller firms, employing less than 75 workers. These workers were given a pay rise of 3.20 *lire* per day, instead of the 4 *lire* in the larger factories: 'There was, therefore, no question of a maximalist manifestation, but rather of the expression of discontent from the economic point of view'.

[96] G. Parodi, 'La Fiat–Centro in Mano agli Operai' cit., p. 653.

[97] *Avanti!* (Turin ed.) 30 September 1920.

[98] V. Castronovo, *Giovanni Agnelli* cit., pp. 257–8; M. Abrate, *La Lotta Sindacale nella Industrializzazione in Italia* cit., pp. 333–4.

[99] G. Parodi, 'La Fiat–Centro in Mano agli Operai' cit., p. 654.

notice of the Internal Commission during working hours. This wide-ranging agreement was made by the Fiat Factory Council, without any support from the national or local *F.I.O.M.* organisation, or even by the absentee Fiat workers.[100] The local metal-workers' journal wrote a few months later: 'In October the powers of the Internal Commission at Fiat–Centro were unlimited, despite the verbal reservations made by the management of Fiat, and made known to the Union concerned only six months later.'[101] Similar agreements were reached in the other main factories; and the local branch of *F.I.O.M.* had to appeal to the Factory Councils to send a copy of the agreements reached to the local Union headquarters.[102]

Thus the Factory Councils' revival, brought about by the occupation, was formally ratified at the end of the agitation in the main metal-working factories of Turin. For the local edition of *Avanti!*, this was extremely important:

> One fact above all others is worthy of notice, and is characteristic of this resumption of work, after the battle. This fact is the regained liberty of action of the Internal Commissions. It has been ratified by the Fiat works and in some other big factories in agreements specially signed, and it may be said to be recognised de facto by all the metal-working industrialists. In this way there stands revealed the truth of one of the fundamental theses in the programme of the supporters of the Factory Councils, i.e. that their development is correlative to the development of the whole activity of the class, that their fate is one with the fate of every struggle fought by the proletariat . . . Examples of this liberty, episodes which show how the work of spontaneous organisation of the whole class in the place of work is reviving at Turin, are occurring in every factory and it is pointless to quote them: every worker knows them, every worker knows their value, indeed every worker feels that the conquest of control, at a time when the Trade Union and political organisations are still discussing its value and its practicability and its methods, is beginning to be a reality in the new breath of life that is now reviving the workers' factory organisations in Turin.[103]

---

[100] The agreement was published in *Avanti!* (Turin ed.) 30 September 1920. According to Parodi, the new regulations were a victory for 'a handful of men who remained at their post to the end' ('La Fiat–Centro in Mano agli Operai' cit., p. 654).

[101] 'Il Problema della Crisi e della Disciplina Operaia e Sindacale nella Vertenza Fiat', anonymous article in *Il Metallurgico* June 1921.

[102] For the other agreements, see *Avanti!* (Turin ed.) 1 and 2 October 1920.

[103] Unsigned article in *Avanti!* (Turin ed.) 8 October 1920.

Even so, the 'Occupation of the Factories' ended amid general disillusionment and bitterness. Soon came the reprisals. At Fiat, the 'Communist' Internal Commission insisted that 954 workers and 40 technicians, who had opposed the occupation, should be sacked as blacklegs.[104] Elsewhere it was the syndicalist or 'Communist' workers who were purged by frightened managements, sometimes encouraged by Union leaders anxious to restore their authority and impose Union 'control'. In general, the future pattern of the Italian labour movement became set. Small groups of left-wing militants tried to maintain morale, but most workers were clearly disillusioned, and as the recession bit deeper there were far fewer strikes and labour agitations in Italy.[105] Similarly, the syndicalists lost much of their influence once their favourite weapon – factory seizure – had been shown up as ineffective.

Giolitti congratulated himself. It had all worked out according to plan. He told the Senate he had always trusted the C.G.L. leaders, and they had not betrayed his confidence.[106] However, his was a Pyrrhic victory. Many employers strongly resented the government solution to the Occupation of the Factories, and were alarmed by the Giolitti proposals for a law on 'Trade Union control'. They simply refused to allow it to happen. The Commission entrusted with the task of drafting the law ended its labours a month later, in almost total disagreement.[107] The C.G.L. then put forward its own proposals for 'Trade Union control': all industries, including the mines, were to be 'controlled', with Trade Union representatives attending all directors' meetings, and the term 'control' was to include all matters of administration and management, financial operations, and technical processes. There was also to be a

[104] M. Abrate, *La Lotta Sindacale nella Industrializzazione in Italia* cit., p. 344; G. Prato, *Il Piemonte e gli Effetti della Guerra sulla sua Vita Economica e Sociale* (Yale U.P. and Laterza, Bari 1925), p. 154.

[105] G. Prato (*ibid.*, p. 144) gives the following official figures for strikes and days lost in Italy (excluding the occupation of the factories):

1920, 1,881 strikes, 16,398,227 days lost;
1921, 1,045 strikes, 7,772,870 days lost.

The figures for Piedmont are:

1920, 196 strikes, 2,727,006 days lost;
1921, 104 strikes, 672,976 days lost.

[106] Speech to the Senate 26 September 1920, quoted by P. Spriano, *L'Occupazione delle Fabbriche* cit., p. 21.

[107] The one thing they agreed on was the need for tariff protection. The liberal economist Giuseppe Prato commented acidly that this was 'the finest proof of what would inevitably have been the logic of the system' (G. Prato, *Il Piemonte e gli Effetti della Guerra sulla sua Vita Economica e Sociale* cit., p. 159). The text of the Commission's final communiqué is in *C.G.I.I., I Consigli di Gestione* cit., vol. ii, p. 27. cf. also *Battaglie Sindacali* 13 November 1920.

Higher Commission of Control for each industry.[108] The industrialists suggested a scheme as well, and Giolitti eventually put a Bill to Parliament in February 1921;[109] but nothing came of it. By this time the growth of unemployment, and Fascist attacks on workers' organisations, had ended the Unions' power to impose terms on unwilling employers. The project for 'workers' control' thus served its purpose in persuading the workers to abandon the occupied factories, but it also alienated some of the most powerful interests in the country,[110] and drove them into even stronger opposition.

In the longer run, therefore, Giolitti's strategy proved disastrous. The Occupation of the Factories was too dramatic, too much of a real psychological shock, perhaps too 'Russian', for it to be easily forgotten or forgiven. It thoroughly discredited Giolitti's (and the Trade Unions') policy of compromise and collaboration. Militant workers raged against 'betrayal' by Union bosses; industrialists feared that the government of the day was in league with the Unions and harming their legitimate interests. The Giolittian system had antagonised too many people, and was visibly breaking down.

[108] G. Bosio, La Grande Paura cit., pp. 193–8; C.G.I.I., I Consigli di Gestione cit., vol. ii, pp. 28–32; R. Rigola, Storia del Movimento Operaio Italiano (Domus, Milan 1946), pp. 450–2. The text is given in English in International Labour Office, Studies and Reports, Series B, no. 7, pp. 3–10.

[109] International Labour Office, Studies and Reports, Series B, no. 7, pp. 17–31; C.G.I.I., I Consigli di Gestione cit., vol. ii, pp. 33–46; and F. Magri, La Crisi Industriale ed il Controllo Operaio (Unitas, Milan 1922), pp. 281–327.

[110] M. Abrate, La Lotta Sindacale nella Industrializzazione in Italia cit., p. 340, pp. 361–2, reports a highly critical motion passed unanimously by the Turin Industrial League on 14 February 1921, on government fiscal policy and 'Trade Union control'.

CHAPTER TEN

The End of the Factory Council Movement

THE 'Occupation of the Factories' confirmed two of Gramsci's central beliefs. Firstly, a disciplined 'Communist' party was urgently necessary, and secondly, 'the Factory Councils have shown themselves to be the revolutionary institution that is historically most vital and necessary to the Italian working class.'[1] The foundation of the Communist party will be discussed in the next chapter; this chapter will concentrate on the Councils, which had run the factories for a month, and in Turin had retained much of their power at the end of the occupation. Gramsci's two beliefs were, as always, linked – the strength of the Councils would enable the new party to be formed with mass working-class support.

But Gramsci was not the only one to note the Turin Factory Councils' strength. Even during the occupation Giovanni Agnelli, the founder of Fiat, had declared he could not continue working in Italy, because of the appalling state of industrial relations in his factories. On 18 September he suddenly offered to turn Fiat into a workers' co-operative; the former shareholders would receive debentures guaranteed by the National Co-operative Institute.[2] Was this a genuine offer, evidence of the despair and disillusionment of the Turin industrialists as they saw their life-work being destroyed? Or was it a clever manoeuvre, designed to call the bluff of militant workers and demonstrate that the firm's managers and directors were indispensable?[3] Probably it was both at once – a manoeuvre

[1] 'Cronache dell' Ordine Nuovo', in *Ordine Nuovo* 2 October 1920 (now in A. Gramsci, *Ordine Nuovo*, Einaudi, Turin 1955, p. 487). A year later Gramsci repeated this view: during the occupation 'workers' control and the power of the Factory Councils reached the maximum of efficiency' ('Gestione Capitalistica e Gestione Operaia', in *Ordine Nuovo* 17 September 1921, now in A. Gramsci, *Socialismo e Fascismo*, Einaudi, Turin 1966, p. 341).

[2] 'La Fiat Diventerà una Co-operativa?', in *Avanti!* (Turin ed.) 1 October 1920 (now in A. Gramsci, *Ordine Nuovo* cit., pp. 172–6).

[3] cf. V. Castronovo, *Giovanni Agnelli* (U.T.E.T., Turin 1971), pp. 255 and 262 (he regards it as an attempt to create a more conciliatory atmosphere); M. Abrate,

which, if it didn't work, would at least enable shareholders to recoup some of their investment (Fiat shares stood at 182 *lire* in October 1920, compared with 376 *lire* in January).[4] If it *was* a manoeuvre, it succeeded brilliantly. Togliatti, pessimistic as ever, was 'convinced that after a few months the workers' co-operative would have only two alternatives: either declare bankruptcy and bring back the bosses, or invoke the help of the State.'[5] And Gramsci warned that invoking the help of the State would 'create dangerous relationships, in which the workers' revolutionary impulses would be lost.'[6] The Turin workers should keep to the stern path of revolutionary duty, and refuse to become involved in political intrigues for more State funds or more State orders. Eventually the plan was rejected by the (reformist) National League of Co-operatives, who realised it was impractical, especially since a recession was imminent.

But it was an important and revealing episode. In the next year there were several other such schemes. In February 1921 came a proposal for an engineering co-operative at Reggio Emilia, which Togliatti helped to get rejected on the grounds that the workers would become 'a falsely privileged minority, a tiny spurious workers' aristocracy, living off the backs of the enormous majority of exploited workers in Italy.'[7] In May 1921 the Metal-workers' Consortium at Genoa applied to be allowed to run five State-owned arsenals and shipyards. Gramsci was furious, and regarded the plan as a dangerous attempt to emasculate a combative group of workers.[8] Gramsci was perhaps right to be suspicious of possible deals between Northern reformists and the Giolitti government, and he was certainly right in thinking that the Italian Co-operative movement was dependent on State support via concessions of public works, tariff protection and the like. Much of his opposition to these schemes came from his 'Southern', Salveminian background. In 1926, when he returned to this theme again, he did so in his famous essay on the Southern Question. The 'Fiat Co-operative' scheme had all been part of a 'Giolittian'

La Lotta Sindacale nella Industrializzazione in Italia (Angeli, Milan 1967), p. 301; and R. Rigola, Storia del Movimento Operaio Italiano (Domus, Milan 1946), pp. 464–5. Agnelli may also have been influenced by the imminent slump in the car industry.

[4] R. Bachi, *Italia Economica 1920* (Lapi, Città di Castello 1921), p. 131.

[5] 'Co-operative o Schiavitù?', in *Avanti!* (Turin ed.) 7 October 1920 (now in P. Togliatti, *Opere*, vol. i, Riuniti, Rome 1967, p. 184). cf. also *Avanti!* (Turin ed.) 9 October 1920, for the workers' reasons for rejecting the offer.

[6] 'La Fiat Diventerà una Co-operativa?', in *Avanti!* (Turin ed.) 1 October 1920 (now in A. Gramsci, *Ordine Nuovo* cit., p. 175).

[7] 'I Metallurgici di Reggio Contrari al Co-operativismo dei Riformisti', in *Ordine Nuovo* 3 February 1921 (now in P. Togliatti, *Opere* cit., vol. i, p. 210).

[8] 'Questione Pregiudiziale', in *Ordine Nuovo* 3 June 1921 (now in A. Gramsci, *Socialismo e Fascismo* cit., pp. 175–8). cf. also 'Il Piano di Amsterdam', in *Ordine Nuovo* 8 June 1921 (now in A. Gramsci, *Socialismo e Fascismo* cit., pp. 182–4).

plot to absorb the Turin working-class into the bourgeois State: 'the Turin proletariat will no longer exist as an independent class, but only as an appendage to the bourgeois State. Class corporativism will have triumphed, but the proletariat will have lost its position and function as leader and guide; it will look to the masses of poorer workers like a privileged caste.'[9]

However, Gramsci's unease about the scheme went deeper still. Clearly it undermined the 'productivist' foundations of *Ordine Nuovo* theories. If managers and technicians *were* indispensable, or if workers could not go it alone without becoming 'absorbed' as parasites upon the Giolittian 'system', perhaps the *Ordine Nuovo* had been based on myths all the time. No wonder that Gramsci was infuriated by these proposals, or that he returned to the theme again and again in later years. He recognised that 'there is no counter-revolutionary programme more astute than this', for the reformists were using many of the same arguments – for workers' autonomy, for disciplined production instead of 'militancy' – that he had used himself in the previous two years. In attempting to refute them, Gramsci came perilously close to rejecting his own *Ordine Nuovo* ideas. In June 1921, for example, he drew a sharp distinction between what was possible 'before' and 'after' the revolution:

> some people [i.e. the revolutionaries] say that effort should be directed above all towards the seizure of power, and only later, when all power has passed into the hands of the workers, only then should the workers and peasants consider the problem of production as the essential problem of their life and the focus of action of their institutions; other people [i.e. the reformists] say that workers' energies should be directed even now to the rebuilding of the economy, which the capitalists have destroyed, and which cannot be rebuilt without the co-operation of the workers.[10]

It was all very worrying. Gramsci was probably right in thinking that the 'Fiat Co-operative' would have had a short and subordinate life;[11] but the fact remained that the workers at Fiat had had the opportunity for

[9] 'Alcuni Temi della Questione Meridionale' (now in A. Gramsci, *La Costruzione del Partito Comunista*, Einaudi, Turin 1971, pp. 137–58, at p. 148). Gramsci is here reporting his words of the time.

[10] 'Il Piano di Amsterdam' in *Ordine Nuovo* 8 June 1921 (now in A. Gramsci, *Socialismo e Fascismo* cit., p. 183).

[11] cf. the collapse of the building workers' 'Guilds' in the recession of 1921 in Britain. On the whole episode of 'Fiat–Co-operative', see D. Tornquist, 'Workers' Management – the Intrinsic Issues', in G. Hunnius, G. D. Carson & J. Case (eds), *Workers' Control* (Random House, New York 1973), pp. 374–95, esp. p. 392.

self-management, and that they (and Gramsci) had rejected the challenge.

The episode had a curious sequel. On 3 October Agnelli and his managing director Fornaca 'resigned' from the Fiat Board, again on the grounds that discipline within the factory was essential. As with the 'Fiat Co-operative' offer, his move was probably meant to prove managerial indispensability, this time to shareholders and to Agnelli's fellow-industrialists in Turin (who were very critical of his 'conciliatory' behaviour during the Occupation of the Factories). Fornaca was even 'caught' asking for the latest vehicle designs to take home for further study, and this well-publicised request was also no doubt designed to convince people that the management was about to take its skills abroad.[12] At Fiat's Annual General Meeting on 28 October, the shareholders refused to accept Agnelli's 'resignation'. Two days later came the funeral of Agnelli's mother, and the *Corriere della Sera* reported 3,000 Fiat workers present, with cries of 'Come Back to us'.[13] All this support was welcome. By late November Agnelli was back, and he soon set about destroying the Factory Councils' powers and achieving undisputed charge of the factory. It took him five months.

His task was easier in that the revival of Factory Council activity during the occupation was confined to the metal-workers. Gramsci and his supporters could not extend the system to other industries, even though syndicalists and other isolated groups of workers tried to do so occasionally. In mid-October Togliatti, as secretary of the local party, made a speech to the national Congress in Turin of the Textile Workers' Union. In a debate specifically on Factory Councils, Togliatti made no reference to them at all, and emphasised 'Communist groups' as the main Communist method of acting in factories and Trade Unions.[14]

The metal-workers' Factory Councils themselves gradually became less effective after the occupation. One of their prime aims and pre-suppositions, 'working-class unity', was being shattered by the formation of the Communist Party (see Chapter Eleven), and the post-occupation disillusionment was worsened by the onset of economic recession leading to unemployment. As early as mid-October, the Central Committee of F.I.O.M. was forced to issue a communiqué to all Italian metal-workers

---

[12] V. Castronovo, *Giovanni Agnelli* cit., p. 270; M. Abrate, *La Lotta Sindacale nella Industrializzazione in Italia* cit., pp. 334–5.

[13] V. Castronovo, *Giovanni Agnelli* cit., p. 276.

[14] *Avanti!* (Turin ed.) 13 October 1920. The Congress re-affirmed the Tasca motion on Factory Councils passed at the Turin Chamber of Labour Congress the previous May (see pp. 135–6), with the sole difference that non-Union members were not to be allowed to vote for Workshop Commissars.

advising them not to seek work in Turin, for 'that industrial labour market is in the middle of a serious crisis and does not offer any opportunities of employment; the unemployed are numerous already.'[15] Many workers in Turin regarded the recession as a politically-inspired manoeuvre, designed to weaken their movement. This was not true, for the recession was international; but it was true that militant Communist workers were likely to be dismissed earlier than others.[16]

Thus when the Annual General Meeting of the Turin branch of *F.I.O.M.* was held at the end of October, unemployment was increasing daily. At this meeting the by now traditional discussion of Factory Councils was held. Carmagnola, of the local branch of *F.I.O.M.*, and Buozzi of *F.I.O.M.*'s Central Committee, reiterated their acceptance of Factory Councils, provided they were subordinated to and controlled by the Unions;[17] but the meeting unanimously confirmed its confidence in the previous executive committee of the branch, and in the Factory Council policy it had pursued. It also decided that the new executive committee should be elected by all the metal-workers in the city, and this decision was taken for carefully specified reasons. It was argued that the annual meeting had inevitably been bound to support the Factory Council policy, because such meetings were only attended by the really active, politically conscious workers who were all in favour of Factory Councils and had been active in them for the previous year. A referendum, on the other hand, would involve the votes of all members of the Union, including those who never went to meetings. The results would therefore enable the local leaders to assess 'a point of special importance, i.e. how profoundly the tactics of the Councils are felt and followed by the masses as a whole, to see how far the active minority that fights for them is succeeding in attracting the others, and all those whose political consciousness is not yet fully developed.'[18]

By this test the results of the referendum, held on 21 November, were very disappointing. Only 3,133 votes were given to the most successful candidate, Pignata, and the most prominent names on the list, those of Garino, Parodi and Ferrero, secured very considerably less – Garino 2,153;

---

[15] *Avanti!* (Turin ed.) 19 October 1920.

[16] For an analysis of the causes and intensity of this depression, see P. Bachi, *Italia Economica 1920* cit., pp. 101–9; G. Salvemini, *Under the Axe of Fascism* (Gollancz, London 1936), pp. 167–81; and Salvemini's article 'Economic Conditions in Italy, 1919–22' in the *Journal of Modern History*, vol. xxiii, no. 1 (March 1951), pp. 29–37. Official unemployment figures, which ranged between 88,000 and 107,000 in 1920, rose to a height of 602,000 by February 1922 (*Under the Axe of Fascism* cit., p. 178).

[17] *Avanti!* (Turin ed.) 1 November 1920.

[18] *Avanti!* (Turin ed.) 19 November 1920. The same issue gives the names of the Communist or syndicalist candidates.

Parodi 2,150; and Ferrero 2,147.[19] The new executive committee was unwilling to assume office with such a low level of support among the masses, so new elections were called. This time the city was divided into ten zones, and the voting took place in the ten local ward offices of the Socialist Party – industrial conditions made it impossible to hold the elections in the factories.[20] The 'Communist' candidates triumphed once more over their reformist opponents, 'by a two-thirds majority', but *Avanti!* failed to publish the voting figures.[21] It seems reasonable to conclude that the results were, once again, a disappointing indication of how disillusioned and apathetic a large number of Turin workers had become, after the successive failures of the General Strike in April and the Occupation in September, and at a time of Fascist aggression.[22]

Nevertheless, the elections were fought mainly over the issue of Factory Councils, and the result was a confirmation of Factory Council policy for the future. The opposition group's manifesto had called for greater centralism in *F.I.O.M.*, and for unity round the Union; and it had been denounced by the 'Communist' candidates as 'a manoeuvre with the aim of undermining the revolutionary institution of the Factory Councils and of the Workshop Commissars'.[23] And at the same time as the elections to the local branch executive were taking place, so were new elections to the Factory Councils in all the main factories. The provisions for the elections were similar to those of the previous year, except that for the first time it was laid down that the technicians' and clerical staff's Commissars should join those of the manual workers, to form a single Factory Council. The Factory Council members would then elect their executive committee, or Internal Commission, but their choice would have to be ratified by an assembly of *all* workers before it became valid.[24] This was a new departure, for throughout the Factory Council movement in Turin most of the Councils had been elected by the manual workers alone (the clerical and technical staff had continued to elect their own Internal Commissions directly, without having Workshop Commissars). The new type of 'mixed' Factory Council, electing a 'mixed' Internal Commission,

[19] *Avanti!* (Turin ed.) 22 November 1920. The Turin branch of *F.I.O.M.* had claimed 22,000 members in March 1920, in its report to the annual Congress of the Turin Chamber of Labour May 1920, pp. 9–10.

[20] *Avanti!* (Turin ed.) 11 December 1920. The candidates were slightly different at these new elections: see *Avanti!* (Turin ed.) 16 December 1920.

[21] *Avanti!* (Turin ed.) 22 December 1920.

[22] The results of the Turin municipal elections on 7 November pointed the same way. The 'Bloc of Order' (Liberals, Conservatives, and clerical Popolari) won, with 48,742 votes, against the Socialists' 48,499.

[23] *Avanti!* (Turin ed.) 11 December 1920.

[24] This too was a new departure. *Avanti!* (Turin ed.) 4 December 1920.

was symbolic of the 'proletarian unity' achieved during the Occupation of the Factories, and needed more than ever in the fight against unemployment. Some factories failed to hold elections, but they took place in most of the city's factories throughout the first fortnight in December. At the main Fiat works, of the 310 Workshop Commissars elected, 240 were 'Communists', as were all the members of the new Internal Commission.[25] The new Workshop Commissars elected in December 1920 were normally those who had distinguished themselves during the occupation. Nevertheless, their powers were drastically reduced during the months ahead.

By the end of 1920 the industrial situation in Turin had become so serious that the Chamber of Labour decided to press for a 6-hour day for all workers, in an attempt to prevent too high a level of unemployment in the city.[26] There was even talk of another factory occupation, in protest against unemployment.[27] The main function of the new Factory Councils elected in December was, therefore, to try to prevent dismissals, or at least to 'control' them, i.e. to make sure there was no discrimination on political grounds. Indeed, it could be argued that the Factory Council revival in late 1920 contained the seeds of its own destruction, for it depended on the extent of the economic depression and on the threat of unemployment.

In early February 1921 Fiat suddenly threatened to sack 1,300 workers, a tenth of their labour force.[28] Although this threat did not materialise, 500 workers were dismissed, and the working week was reduced, first to 44 hours, then to 40. At the Michelin tyre works, a 32-hour week was introduced, and 900 sackings were announced, to take effect from 7 February.[29] At the Acciaierie Fiat works, 40 men a week were laid off; the firm's aim was to dismiss 450 eventually, out of a total labour force of 1,100 men.[30] The management at the main Fiat works presented the Internal Commission with a choice: a 24-hour week, or agreement to work on munitions and war materials, which the Internal Commission

[25] *Avanti!* (Turin ed.) 20 December 1920.

[26] There were 3,968 unemployed metal-workers in Piedmont on 31 December, according to the official Employment Office (*Ordine Nuovo* 12 February 1921).

[27] This was discussed at a meeting of about 1,000 Workshop Commissars from all factories, reported in *Avanti!* (Turin ed.) 31 December 1920, and in the Prefect of Turin's dispatch to Ministry of the Interior 1 January 1921 (in *State Archives*, Ministero dell' Interno, Direzione Generale Pubblica Sicurezza, Affari Generali e Riservati, 1921, b. 71, 'Metallurgici: Torino').

[28] *Ordine Nuovo* 12 February 1921.

[29] *Ordine Nuovo* 5 February 1921.

[30] Prefect of Turin to Ministry of the Interior 5 February 1921 (in *State Archives* cit., 1921, b. 71: 'Vertenze Metallurgiche: Torino').

considered might be used against the Soviet Union.[31] A mass meeting of Workshop Commissars, Internal Commissions, and 'Communist groups' from all Turin factories rejected the idea of working on munitions, and claimed that the crisis was artificial and was designed to isolate the Turin workers' movement, as during the General Strike of April 1920.[32] Because of this fear of isolation negotiations were left to Buozzi and the members of F.I.O.M.'s Central Committee, who were distrusted by many of the Turin workers. The Union leaders negotiated a 36-hour week, and an assurance that there would be no more dismissals in the immediate future.[33] Despite the intervention of F.I.O.M., the Workshop Commissars were the people who were forwarding the complaints of dismissed workers, and agitating for shorter hours as an alternative to dismissals.

By this time the Fascist squads were attacking Unions and Peasant Leagues, the rivalries within the labour movement were acute, and 'Trade Union control' (see pp. 179–80) was being buried. Gramsci insisted again that only Factory Councils could really achieve 'control', and called for a national form of 'control', exercised by a 'national council of the working class', elected in all its grades by the Factory Councils.[34] In mid-February 1921 the Ordine Nuovo was once more summoning a national Congress of Factory Councils and Internal Commissions.[35] Gramsci and his supporters still hoped that the Factory Councils could unite the working-class – against Fascism and against the capitalist regime, but also against the reformists in the C.G.L.[36]

The long-awaited Congress of the C.G.L., held at Leghorn in February 1921,[37] sparked off more discussion in Turin. The Tasca motion

---

[31] Ordine Nuovo 16 February 1921. The work shifts were to be divided between two sets of workers, each working three days a week. The 'war materials' would be 10,000 machine guns, 50,000 pistols and 3,000 trucks. According to the Prefect, this offer had already been made to (and refused by) the full Factory Council of Fiat in January (Prefect of Turin to Ministry of the Interior 29 January 1921, in State Archives cit., 1921, b. 71).

[32] A report of the meeting appeared in Ordine Nuovo 17 and 19 February 1921. 1,200 workers attended, according to the Prefect of Turin (Prefect of Turin to Ministry of the Interior 18 February 1921, in State Archives cit., 1921, b. 71).

[33] Ordine Nuovo 18 February 1921. The agreement was confirmed by a mass meeting at the main Fiat works on 19 February (Prefect of Turin to Ministry of the Interior 20 February 1921, in State Archives cit., 1921, b. 71).

[34] 'Come Funzionerà il Controllo', in Ordine Nuovo 10 February 1921 (now in A. Gramsci, Socialismo e Fascismo cit., pp. 67–9; the article's title is there given as 'Controllo Operaio').

[35] As in March 1920; see p. 93.

[36] m.s. (Scoccimarro), 'Per un Convegno dei Consigli di Fabbrica', in Ordine Nuovo 27 February 1921.

[37] For this Congress, see C.G.L., Resoconto Stenografico del X Congresso della Resistenza, V della C.G.L. (Milan 1921); summary in L. Marchetti (ed.), La Confedera-

approved by the Turin Chamber of Labour in May 1920 (see pp. 135–6) had deferred decisions regarding a national organisation of Factory Councils to this next *C.G.L.* Congress. Gramsci made a final appeal for a national Congress of Factory Councils, and proclaimed that:

> the struggle for the formation and development of Factory Councils and Workshop Councils is, we believe, the specific struggle of the Communist Party. It must put the party in a position to graft itself directly on to a centralised working-class organisation, an organisation that must be superior to all existing ones and that must be recognised by the masses as the only competent one, authorised to issue orders for general action. By means of the struggle for Councils it will be possible to win over the majority of the *C.G.L.* in a stable and permanent way, and thus come, if not during the revolutionary period, at least during the post-revolutionary period, to win executive posts in it as well.[38]

Factory Councils, although on the agenda at Leghorn, were not discussed. The issue was postponed to the next National Council meeting of the *C.G.L.*, held in Milan 22–5 April 1921, which also postponed a decision – although it did condemn local 'initiators of Factory Councils with political objectives, aiming to transform the structure of Trade Unions and the functions of workers' representatives in the factories'.[39] After the *C.G.L.* Congress, in fact, this type of propaganda died down. Although the call for a Congress of Factory Councils was occasionally repeated by Communist spokesmen, none was ever held. Bordiga's lack of enthusiasm, and the strict enforcement of party discipline, crushed any national agitation for Factory Councils, just as the events of March–April 1921 crushed their short-lived practical revival in Turin.

By mid-March 1921, the industrial situation at Turin had grown very serious. It was claimed that 1,200 workers in the tyre industry had been dismissed, out of a total labour force of 5,000.[40] The local chemical works had dismissed 12 *per cent.* of the labour force by mid-March; and 10,000

---

zione Generale del Lavoro 1906–26 (Ed. *Avanti!*, Milan 1962), pp. 313–22. The reformist motion at this Congress secured 1,435,873 votes, and the Communist-syndicalists 432,558.

[38] 'La Confederazione Generale del Lavoro', in *Ordine Nuovo* 25 February 1921 (now in A. Gramsci, *Socialismo e Fascismo* cit., p. 83). cf. G. Berti, 'Appunti e Ricordi 1919–26', in *Annali dell' Istituto Giangiacomo Feltrinelli*, anno VIII (1966), p. 54. Gramsci repeated the same view, of the need for the *C.G.L.* to be won over by Factory Councils, in an editorial 'Il Funzionarismo', in *Ordine Nuovo* 4 March 1921 (now in A. Gramsci, *Socialismo e Fascismo* cit., pp. 89–91).

[39] L. Marchetti (ed.), *La Confederazione Generale del Lavoro 1906–26* cit., p. 329; *Battaglie Sindacali* 30 April 1921.

[40] *Ordine Nuovo* 3, 4, and 13 March 1921.

workers were registered as unemployed. Vehicle production was worst hit. 2,000 workers had already been dismissed by Fiat, 1,000 by Dubosc, and 2,500 by the small workshops. To the local workers, this situation seemed blatantly 'political', and there is no doubt that, as the *Ordine Nuovo* commented, employers did see it as an excuse to 'strike a particular blow at the leading members of the Factory Councils'.[41] The Ministry of the Interior was told that many of the workers, especially the 'Communist groups', convinced that 'the crisis is provoked artificially by the industrialists in order to crush the political organisations and throw the workers into poverty', were planning an occupation of the factories, and possibly an armed rising.[42]

At the Michelin works the large number of dismissals caused an 'internal strike', and this 'act of sabotage' provoked a lock-out by the management. As this, in turn, might well have roused the workers to occupy the factory, the Prefect sent in troops to occupy it and forestall them.[43] The Michelin conflict rapidly turned into a struggle between the Socialist-controlled *F.I.O.C.* (Chemical-workers' Union), which agreed to accept the 800 dismissals, and the local tyre-workers, many of whom were Communists; according to the *Ordine Nuovo*, those dismissed included *all* the Workshop Commissars and most of the 'good Communists'.[44] This 'betrayal' by the official Union meant that the dismissed workers were forced to ask their former colleagues to resume work, which they did on 4 April.[45] The episode is important, for it shows that the Communist workers in Turin were particularly liable to be isolated from their Socialist-controlled national Unions, and that the Giolitti government – anxious to conciliate right-wing opinion for the forthcoming General Election – was by this time prepared to take much stronger measures to deal with industrial unrest.

The threat of unemployment was also real among the metal-workers, particularly those employed by the largest firm in Turin, Fiat. Fiat's car section employed 13,700 workers at the end of 1920.[46] By mid-March the management was aiming to introduce a 36-hour week and sack 1,500 workers immediately, with the possibility of more dismissals later; 16 *per cent.* of the year's production (1,500 vehicles) remained on their

[41] 'La Crisi nelle Industrie Torinesi', in *Ordine Nuovo* 13 March 1921.

[42] Col. Vigevano, Stato Maggiore del R. Esercito, to Ministry of the Interior 22 March 1921 (in *State Archives* cit., 1921, b. 64, 'Ordine Pubblico: Torino').

[43] Prefect of Turin to Ministry of the Interior 14 March 1921 (in *State Archives* cit., 1921, b. 64). See also *Ordine Nuovo* 15 March 1921.

[44] *Ordine Nuovo* 27 March 1921.

[45] *Ordine Nuovo* 29 March 1921.

[46] 'La Crisi nelle Industrie del Metallo – la nostra Intervista coi Dirigenti la Fiat', in *Ordine Nuovo* 20 March 1921.

hands.[47] The Fiat workers refused to accept the dismissals, which were therefore suspended.[48] No negotiations took place until 2 April, but by this time the management had firmly decided on a lock-out. On 30 March the Prefect of Turin reported that Fiat was preparing a lock-out, which would throw 13,000 workers out of work, as well as affecting 10,000 workers in other factories; and he appealed for an extra 300 carabinieri to be sent to the city, as an occupation by troops and police would probably be necessary.[49]

The Government's new policy of intervention in favour of the employers, first shown at the Michelin works the previous month, was thus to be continued. Knowing this, Agnelli insisted on the 1,500 dismissals already announced – although the names of the dismissed workers had not been given – and also, more importantly, affirmed Fiat's decision to apply the national metal-workers' agreement on factory discipline and organisation – i.e. to revoke the concessions to the Factory Councils that he had been forced to grant at the end of the occupation.[50] Having secured the government's backing, the Fiat management hoped to use the industrial crisis to destroy the Factory Councils at Fiat, in the knowledge that the national workers' organisation, F.I.O.M., would be unlikely to support its Turin members on this issue. The final negotiations on 5 April[51] proved fruitless because of Fiat's insistence on the Factory Council and Workshop Commissar system coming to an end. Even payment of compensation for dismissal was made dependent on the workers' accepting the industrialists' proposals on Internal Commissions, which were:

In order to guarantee the regular functioning of the industry, which is an essential condition for its survival, especially at the present time of world crisis, the management regards it as indispensable that the organisation of labour should be better disciplined, and therefore intends that discipline and authority within the factory should be carried out by its own organisations alone, without any arbitrary interference

[47] *ibid.* The Fiat Internal Commission claimed, on the other hand, that the unsold stocks were old vehicles, and that the firm had urged an increase of production, to 80 vehicles a day, as late as January (*Ordine Nuovo* 22 March 1921). cf. also C.G.I.I., *L'Occupazione delle Fabbriche nel Settembre 1920 e le sue Ripercussioni nei Rapporti Economici coll' Estero* (Ed. Soc. Poligrafico Nazionale, Rome 1921).

[48] *Ordine Nuovo* 24 March 1921.

[49] Prefect of Turin to Ministry of the Interior 30 March 1921 (in *State Archives* cit., 1921, b. 64).

[50] *Ordine Nuovo* 5 April 1921.

[51] Negotiations were carried out, on the workers' side, by the secretary of the local branch of *F.I.O.M.*, Ferrero, together with the Internal Commission of the main Fiat works and one representative from the Internal Commissions of other Fiat plants (*Ordine Nuovo* 3 April 1921).

by any individuals, nevertheless recognising the right of the workers' Internal Commission to safeguard the collective interests of the staff; since, moreover, the interpretation given to the provisional regulations agreed last October has proved to be too broad, the [national] metal-workers' regulations, generally in force throughout the engineering industry, must apply and be recognised as the only valid ones by both parties.[52]

The break-down of negotiations was immediately followed by the occupation of all the main Fiat factories by troops.

The Prefect's report of this event is significant. He admitted that one of the main causes of the whole dispute was the Factory Council issue: 'with the nomination of Workshop Commissars, according to the management, an attempt was being made to create an organisation above and outside the Internal Commissions, and the industrialists never had any intention of recognising them'; and he went on to say that he had ordered the troops in, as requested by the management, as their fears of another factory occupation seemed to him to be reasonable.[53] The real issue, of course, was whether the Communist Factory Council was to 'control' the dismissals; neither side would give way. In addition to the main Fiat works, troops occupied the subsidiary plants of Fiat Lingotto, Fiat Barriera di Nizza, Carrozzeria Fiat, Brevetti Fiat, Fiat Aviazione, and Fonderia Cilindri.[54] These occupations prevented any counter-occupations by the workers. Once again the Turin workers found themselves isolated against government, employers, and their own Trade Unions on the issue of Factory Councils.

The lock-out enabled Fiat to notify individually the 1,500 workers who were to be dismissed, while they were at home, thus preventing any 'control' of the dismissals. Those who received dismissal notices were instructed to inform the local branch of F.I.O.M.; of the first 250 who did so, 40 were Workshop Commissars, some of them very prominent in the Factory Council movement – they included Parodi, Bordigari and Tornielli from the main Fiat works.[55]

[52] *Memoriale* of the Management, dated 5 April 1921, sent by the Prefect of Turin to the Ministry of the Interior 6 April 1921 (in *State Archives* cit., 1921, b. 64).
[53] Prefect of Turin to Ministry of the Interior 6 April 1921 (in *State Archives* cit., 1921, b. 64).
[54] *ibid.*; and *Ordine Nuovo* 6 April 1921.
[55] For a full list, see *Ordine Nuovo* 10 April 1921. cf. the report of the Prefect of Turin to Ministry of the Interior 6 April 1921 (in *State Archives* cit., 1921, b.64): 'the management of Fiat will issue notification of dismissal to the 1,500 workers, among whom, there is reason to believe, will be many of the workers whose behaviour in their judgment is a hindrance to the regular disciplined functioning of the workshops.'

Despite daily meetings of the locked-out workers, there was little that either the local branch of *F.I.O.M.* or the Internal Commissions could do. On 13 April Fiat issued a communiqué to those workers who had not been dismissed. They would be taken back if they would sign an undertaking to accept the national agreement on factory discipline, and declare their willingness to carry out any work that might be given them – i.e. work on military equipment, which the Internal Commissions had always opposed.[56] The local leaders were indignant at this attempt to appeal to the factory workers over their heads, but the Prefect reported the following day that 'very many' requests for re-employment had been received by Fiat;[57] four days later he reported 6,000 such requests.[58]

The industrialists' strategy succeeded because of the divisions among the workers. Factory Councils, both in theory and in practice, depended on a considerable degree of 'working-class unity', but the antagonism and mutual distrust between Socialist and Communist workers, and between the Communists controlling the local branch of *F.I.O.M.* and the Socialists on its Central Committee, made it easier for the industrialists to appeal to the workers individually and to ignore the Union organisations. *F.I.O.M.*'s national organisation was not called in until 19 April, and even then refused to discuss changes in factory regulations unless members of the local branch were present[59] – the *F.I.O.M.* leaders wanted to avoid being accused of betrayal yet again. The industrialists refused to modify their conditions, and so the new negotiations proved equally unsuccessful. Furthermore, the only initiative which the workers could take, collecting funds to support the locked-out workers, also proved useless, as the Chamber of Labour, with all the subscribed funds, was ransacked and burned down in a Fascist attack during the early hours of 26 April.[60] This disaster made further resistance impossible, as the lock-out had by this time continued for three weeks and had followed a long period of short-time working.

Having collected almost 9,850 signatures, Fiat reopened its doors on Monday, 2 May, to those labourers, storekeepers, cleaners, etc., who were willing to accept the 'undertaking'. On the first day, few workers braved

[56] *Ordine Nuovo* 14 April 1921.

[57] Prefect of Turin to Ministry of the Interior 15 April 1921 (in *State Archives* cit., 1921, b.64).

[58] Prefect of Turin to Ministry of the Interior 19 April 1921 (*ibid*).

[59] *Ordine Nuovo* 20 April 1921.

[60] *Ordine Nuovo* (*edizione straordinaria*) 26 April 1921. Some of the factories that had continued work, such as Lancia, Scat and Spa, were briefly occupied by the workers as a sign of protest. These occupations caused numerous sackings of the ring-leaders (*Ordine Nuovo* 30 April 1921).

the picket lines;[61] but on Wednesday, 4 May, when the gates were opened to the metal-workers themselves, the Prefect reported 5,000 workers back at work in the main Fiat factory alone,[62] despite all the appeals of the local branch of *F.I.O.M.* On 6 May the local branch was forced to concede defeat, and order the formerly locked-out workers back. One of the conditions posed by Fiat had been the election of new Internal Commissions, and this was doubly essential as most of the former Communist Commissars had been dismissed. The new Internal Commissions, Fiat announced, would be elected directly by the workers, not by the Workshop Commissars, who would cease to exist.[63] The lock-out was, therefore, an unqualified success for the Fiat management. They succeeded not only in reducing the surplus labour force,[64] but also in dismissing most of the important Communists and in ending the Factory Council system. The employers' achievement during the General Strike of April 1920, when they had won a similar struggle, was confirmed, this time permanently, by the Fiat lock-out of April 1921.

The new elections to the Internal Commissions produced few surprises. The Communists were deterred from putting forward their own candidates, as they feared that any candidates who presented themselves would be sacked. They therefore put forward famous public figures, half in jest, half in protest – Pietro Balocco, a recently condemned local murderer, was a candidate at the main Fiat works. Where this was not done, as at Accaierie Fiat, an electorate of 700 produced 200 abstentions, 262 blank papers, and 79 spoilt papers.[65] In these circumstances the members of the new Internal Commission were mainly Socialists. The Workshop Commissar system disappeared, although Fiat appointed a *fiduciario* in each workshop to deal with petty complaints.[66]

The Factory Councils never revived after this lock-out, and propaganda on their behalf largely ceased.[67] Nor was it the end only of the Councils, for they had been the stronghold of Communist strength in Turin. The new Internal Commission elections, and the dismissals of prominent Communists, were a great blow to the party's chances of playing a

[61] None at the main Fiat works: thirty only at Brevetti Fiat, and ten at Fiat Lingotto (*Ordine Nuovo* 2 May 1921).

[62] Prefect of Turin to Ministry of the Interior 4 May 1921 (in *State Archives* cit., 1921, b.64).

[63] *Ordine Nuovo* 6 May 1921.

[64] By 2000, according to M. Abrate, *La Lotta Sindacale nella Industrializzazione in Italia* cit., p. 349; by 2600 according to V. Castronovo, *Giovanni Agnelli* cit., p. 290.

[65] *Ordine Nuovo* 25 May 1921.

[66] *Ordine Nuovo* 21 May 1921.

[67] Although the Committee of Study on the Factory Councils survived in Turin, and issued the occasional hopeful manifesto, e.g. in *Ordine Nuovo* 2 September 1921.

significant role in the labour movement, or of securing any real degree of working-class support. The Communists and Workshop Commissars were purged with the tacit consent of the Socialist-led *F.I.O.M.*, which survived for some years as the only effective workers' organisation among the Turin metal-workers.

Was the Communists' defeat inevitable? Probably; for the Turin Factory Councils were in a very weak position after the Occupation of the Factories. Yet undoubtedly they made mistakes. Perhaps it was right to reject work on munitions early in 1921 – but it meant more dismissals, when unemployment was already high. Perhaps it was right to reject the idea of Fiat becoming a Co-operative in October 1920 – but it meant Communist workers being sacked six months later. Perhaps it was right to accept a new 'collective' (instead of individual) piecework and bonus system from 1 January 1921[68] – but it meant that skilled men earned less than before. Perhaps it was right to keep the national *F.I.O.M.* out of the Fiat dispute for so long – but it meant that the Communist factory organisation took all the blame for defeat. At the end, Gramsci wrote one of his finest pieces of journalism, 'Men of Flesh and Blood';[69] but it was a funeral oration for the whole Factory Council movement.

The local results of the General Election on 15 May provide some measure of the Communists' weakness at Turin. In the city of Turin, they secured a mere 12,509 votes (16.45 *per cent.*), as compared with the Socialists' 22,323 (29.35 *per cent.*). Two Communist deputies, Misiano and Rabezzana, were elected for the nineteen-member constituency of Turin province. Gramsci's name had appeared on the Communist list as first preference choice, yet he came fourth in preference votes, and was not elected.[70] For Gramsci, the elections confirmed that the Communist Party was 'not yet a party of the great masses'.[71] He hoped it would become one, as workers became disillusioned with Socialist reformism, but the fact

[68] V. Castronovo, *Giovanni Agnelli* cit., p. 287; and Gramsci's 'Gestione Capitalistica e Gestione Operaia', in *Ordine Nuovo* 17 September 1921 (now in A. Gramsci, *Socialismo e Fascismo* cit., p. 341). The new system was clearly intended to cause divisions among the workers, but had been accepted in late 1920 'since there were Factory Councils in existence to exercise a real and immediate control over all the capitalists' initiatives.' (*ibid.*).

[69] 'Uomini di Carne e Ossa', in *Ordine Nuovo* 8 May 1921 (now in A. Gramsci, *Socialismo e Fascismo* cit., pp. 154–6).

[70] Misiano received 52,893 preference votes; Rabezzana 52,177; Gagliazzo 51,733; and Gramsci 48,280.

[71] 'Risultati', in *Ordine Nuovo* 17 May 1921 (now in A. Gramsci, *Socialismo e Fascismo* cit., 166–7). The Communists had 16 seats in the new Parliament, compared with the Socialists' 123; they had received 4.6 *per cent.* of the national vote, the P.S.I. winning 24.7 *per cent.* cf. *Annuario Statistico Italiano*, 2a Serie, vol. viii, 1919–21 (Rome 1925), pp. 168–9.

remained that by May 1921 the Factory Councils were finished, and Gramsci's political activity was confined to a small party with no mass support. The next chapter will discuss how that party had come to be founded, and why Gramsci's role in it was so limited.

CHAPTER ELEVEN

The Road to Leghorn

THE foundation of the Italian Communist Party in January 1921 was not caused solely by the 'Occupation of the Factories' the previous September, but it was greatly stimulated by it. Left-wing militants throughout the country railed against the Socialist Party's failure to seize power. They proclaimed that the revolution had been betrayed; the pure in heart should band together, and throw out the ungodly. But who were the ungodly? The reformists and the Trade Union leaders obviously qualified, enmeshed as they were in the Giolittian 'system'; but what of the maximalists, still after all the bulk of the Socialist Party? Had they betrayed the revolution or not? If so, were they redeemable? Should they be persuaded to come in, or should they be ruthlessly excluded from the ranks of the righteous? The debate continued for several months, and the events of 10–11 September (see pp. 168–9) were endlessly analysed. In the end, the founding of the Communist Party reflected the split in the labour movement that had emerged during the occupation. A minority of militants set up their own 'revolutionary party', while most Socialists, more sceptical and perhaps more disillusioned, remained attached to their comfortable older traditions.

The urgent necessity for a Communist Party had, of course, been proclaimed by Bordiga's 'Abstentionist Faction' in 1919, and the abstentionists' National Conference at Florence in May 1920 (see p. 123) had called for a Constituent Congress of a new party, to be held immediately after the forthcoming Second Congress of the Third International.[1] The new party envisaged by the Florence conference would have been formed on the narrow basis of abstentionism – the conference even called on the central committee of the Abstentionist Faction to set up 'an anti-electionist faction within the Communist International'.[2]

[1] *Il Soviet* 16 May 1920; see also 'Theses of the Communist Abstentionist Faction of the *P.S.I.*', in *Il Soviet* 6 and 27 June 1920.

[2] *Il Soviet* 16 May 1920.

However, in August 1920 Bordiga went to Moscow, and was persuaded there to ditch abstentionism. This was a curious episode, and details are still obscure. The Second Congress of the International (July–August 1920) roundly condemned abstentionism. Lenin's *Left-wing Communism – an Infantile Disorder* had been written in April 1920 especially for the Congress, and was partly directed against Bordiga.[3] On the other hand, Lenin and Zinoviev were anxious for a new, disciplined, well-organised Communist Party to be founded in Italy, as elsewhere – even though they thought initially in terms of reorganising the existing Socialist Party and expelling its reformists, rather than in terms of a 'minority', 'leftwards' split by the most militant groups of Italian Socialism. The Congress therefore approved stringent 'Conditions' for a party's membership of the International. They included expelling the reformists, and Filippo Turati's name headed the list of 'notorious opportunists' denounced in Condition Seven. The Russians assumed that Serrati would agree to rid the party of its reformists, and even elected him on to the executive of the International. But Serrati was cautious. By this time he did not believe that revolution was imminent in Italy; if anything, reaction was more likely, and the reformists would be needed to defend the people.[4] He expressed willingness to expel the reformists eventually, but in his own time; and he was certainly not going to allow the Russians to dictate policy to him. All this gave Bordiga his opportunity. He was in Moscow in August 1920 – in the right place at the right time; and he was just the man the International was looking for. Energetic, resolute and sectarian, he at least would have no hesitation in expelling the opportunists. Abstentionism had to go, but in return Bordiga was allowed to take on the supreme task, creating a Communist Party, almost on his own terms. His shrewd proposal, that those who voted against the 'Conditions' at a party Congress should be expelled, was accepted by the International and became the 'Twenty-first Condition'. Serrati had been warned. The International's blessing on Bordiga was no doubt conditional. Zinoviev still hoped Serrati and the maximalists would come round at the last minute, and if they had done so Bordiga would not have remained undisputed leader for long. Bordiga knew this perfectly well, but he had to make some show of working for a broad base of maximalist support, since that was what the International wanted.

[3] J. W. Hulse, *The Forming of the Communist International* (Stanford U.P., 1964), pp. 161–4; E. H. Carr, *The Bolshevik Revolution 1917–23* (Penguin Books, London 1966), vol. iii, pp. 181–6.
[4] P. Spriano, *Storia del Partito Comunista Italiano*, vol. i (Einaudi, Turin 1967), p. 76, quotes Serrati's comments at a meeting with the International's leaders in Moscow on 10 August 1920.

The 'Occupation of the Factories' made this balancing act much easier. The militants' resentment against the maximalists' 'betrayal' was intense. In Turin, the local Socialist Party branch called public meetings to discuss a new party, because 'the present executive committee believes that the greatest and best result of the movement that has just ended is that it has demonstrated the indispensable necessity of setting up a Communist Party in Italy'.[5] Similar meetings were held in local Socialist Party branches in Milan on 28 September,[6] in Savona, and throughout the country. Even the Socialist Party Directorate, meeting in Milan at the end of September, bowed to the storm and voted seven to five in favour of accepting the 'Twenty-one Conditions' and expelling the reformists *immediately*.[7] The vote encouraged the International in its belief that a 'majority split' was probable; but Serrati remained editor of the party's newspaper *Avanti!*, and could therefore continue his campaign for retaining the reformists. It soon became clear that the bulk of the Socialist Party accepted this line. After all, the post-occupation depression worked both ways. It made the militants seek a strong disciplined Communist Party, committed to revolution; but it made more moderate Socialists sceptical, more likely to close ranks around the old Party and its glorious traditions. Individual maximalist notables might defect to the nascent Communist Party, but the Socialist rank and file held firm. Bordiga and his General Staff of former abstentionists were never in any serious danger of being overwhelmed by new recruits.

Serrati's arguments deserve closer analysis, for his position was on the face of it untenable. He was a member of the executive committee of the Third International, yet was refusing to carry out the policy of the 'Twenty-one Conditions', on the grounds that the Conditions needed to be 'interpreted according to the historical and environmental conditions of the country, which is permitted by the International in the case of other countries.'[8] He urged that the Italian reformists, unlike those of other countries, had *not* betrayed the proletariat during the war and therefore

[5] *Avanti!* (Turin ed.) 10 October 1920.

[6] For a report, see the Prefect of Milan's telegram to the Ministry of the Interior on 3 October 1920 (*State Archives*, Ministero dell' Interno, Direzione Generale Pubblica Sicurezza, Affari Generali e Riservati, 1920, b. 74).

[7] For details of this meeting, see A. Lepre and S. Levrero, *La Formazione del Partito Comunista d'Italia* (Riuniti, Rome 1971), pp. 309–14; L. Cortesi, *Le Origini del Partito Comunista Italiano* (Laterza, Bari 1972), p. 250; and P. Spriano, *Storia del Partito Comunista Italiano* cit., vol. i, p. 84. The majority of seven were: Terracini, Regent, Tuntar, Gennari, Casucci, Marziale and Bellone; they were opposed by Baratono, Bacci, Giacomini, Zannerini and Serrati.

[8] This phrase was used in the maximalists' motion put to the Leghorn Congress. See *Resoconto Stenografico del XVII Congresso del P.S.I.* (*Livorno 1921*) (Ed. *Avanti!*, Milan 1962), p. 441.

were *not* counter-revolutionary.[9] Whatever might have happened in
September 1920, there had been no betrayal in 1915. This was a very
sound argument, for the *P.S.I.*'s popularity *did* rest firmly on its record
in the war, and for many ordinary workers a man's attitude to 'interventionism' in 1914–15 was still the test of his revolutionary virtue in 1920.

Serrati also thought it foolish to abandon the party's network of
Co-operatives, Trade Unions and local administrations, and they could
not be run without the reformists. Local government was a particularly
important issue, for new Commune and provincial councils were being
elected in October and early November. This was no time to split the
party. Moreover, Bordiga's reputation for abstentionism was bound to be
unpopular at election time, especially since *Il Soviet* on 3 October called
for a boycott of the local elections.[10] In fact, the elections were a success
for the Socialists. The party won a majority in 2,162 Communes (out of
8,059 in Italy)[11] and in 25 of the 69 provinces; and the new Socialist local
councillors looked forward to transforming local government. It is not
surprising, therefore, that the rank and file stayed with the Grand Old
Party, particularly as mayors had some police powers. As Paul Levi wrote
to the International in January 1921, 'This fact implies an immense
opportunity for bringing in arms and doing undercover work.'[12] Control
of local government was important, whatever happened. It might help in
organising revolution; or if there was a right-wing reaction, mayors
could call out the Carabinieri to defend the workers. Perhaps most
important, Socialist local Councils meant that Peasant Leagues and
Co-operatives would be used for public works, and that the effective
Union closed shop for agricultural labouring jobs would be maintained.
In 'red' provinces like Ferrara, where Socialist Labourers' Leagues were
strongest, jobs were scarce and 'control of employment was the pivot
around which the labour movement turned'.[13] The Communist Party
made few recruits there.[14]

The economic recession beginning in the autumn of 1920, and the

---

[9] *ibid.*; and see the open letter sent by the Directorate of the *P.S.I.* to the International, published in *Comunismo* 15 October–15 November 1920.

[10] L. Cortesi, *Le Origini del Partito Comunista Italiano* cit., p. 241.

[11] *ibid.*, pp. 267–8.

[12] P. Levi to Executive Committee of the Communist International 20 January
1921, quoted in M. Drachkovitch and B. Lazitch, *The Comintern: Historical Highlights*
(Pall Mall, London 1966, for the Hoover Institution on War, Revolution and Peace),
p. 282.

[13] P. Corner, *Fascism in Ferrara* (Oxford U.P. 1975), p. 86.

[14] According to L. Bagnolati, only about 60–65 adult socialists, plus about 90
members of the Socialist Youth Federation, joined the Communist party. *Le Origini
della Federazione Comunista Ferrarese* (Levi, Ferrara 1976), pp. 33–4.

serious attacks on labour organisations by Fascist squads, only confirmed the need for Socialist Party unity. Whatever he might say in public, Serrati by this time was sceptical about an Italian revolution, and even more sceptical about Russian promises of food shipments in the event of an Allied blockade of Italian supplies. The Red Army was in retreat from Warsaw; and where would Italy's coal come from, if not Cardiff?[15] Moreover, Serrati had clearly been shocked by his visit to Russia for the Congress of the International. The Prefect of Milan reported Turati as saying that Serrati 'set out for Russia boiling and came back freezing'; and the Socialist deputy Nofri told a meeting of maximalists at Milan that Serrati had informed Lenin (of all people) that 'the situation in Russia is not Socialism, nor Communism, but real anarchy.'[16] Thus Serrati's policy was not so inconsistent as it appeared. Perhaps he had no real choice. Most maximalists and party members would not have followed Serrati into the Communist Party in any case; nor would Bordiga have welcomed him.[17]

For Bordiga had enough problems already – persuading his abstentionist friends to drop abstentionism, reassuring them that the new party would be largely theirs, yet keeping the door half-open to the maximalists and other groups, so as to please the International. The old abstentionist tradition of sectarianism died hard. In Turin, where the local abstentionists had lost control of the party branch in August (see p. 143), they published a resolution in early October welcoming all those who wished to see the implementation of the Twenty-one Conditions into the Abstentionist Faction, and proclaiming that 'the Faction proposes to be the nucleus of the future Turin branch of the *P.C.I.*, and appeals to all those who, in order to co-operate in the implementation of the Twenty-one Conditions, accept unconditionally a rigorous discipline imposed by a Directive Committee'.[18] Clearly Boero and his abstentionist colleagues were hoping to regain control of the local party branch from the 'Communist Electionists';[19] and they were certainly unwilling to abandon their ideal of a

---

[15] P. Spriano, *Storia del Partito Comunista Italiano* cit., vol. i, pp. 96–7. See also a report of Serrati's speech to the Milan Socialist Party branch, sent by the Prefect of Milan to Ministry of the Interior 17 December 1920 (in *State Archives* cit., 1920, b. 66, 'Movimento Sovversivo: Milano').

[16] Prefect of Milan to Ministry of the Interior 6 October 1920 (in *State Archives* cit., 1920, b. 66, 'Movimento Sovversivo: Milano'). For Serrati's unhappy time at the Second Congress, see J. W. Hulse, *The Forming of the Communist International* cit., pp. 201–4.

[17] G. Berti, 'Appunti e Ricordi 1919–26', in *Annali dell' Istituto Giangiacomo Feltrinelli*, anno VIII (1966), p. 84.

[18] *Avanti!* (Turin ed.) 10 October 1920; *Il Soviet* 17 October 1920.

[19] Even as late as June 1921, almost six months after the *P.C.d'I.* had been founded, the Turin abstentionists were still denouncing 'the many opportunists who may

small splinter party committed to abstentionism, if doing so meant accepting the dominance of their 'Electionist' rivals. However, Bordiga was already committed not to set up a new party solely from among the members of his own faction. He told the Turin abstentionists that they were calling, in effect, for an Abstentionist Communist Party, which the International had forbidden.[20] The episode showed that local jealousies and antagonisms were real, and might easily hinder large-scale adhesions to what had always been a self-consciously 'minoritarian' group.

If this was true in Turin, where the abstentionists had often worked closely with other groups, it was even more true elsewhere. In Arezzo, an abstentionist stronghold, the local abstentionists proclaimed 'a purge of the party is ineffective and impossible. It is necessary to found the Abstentionist Communist Party'.[21] Indeed, the 'Abstentionist Faction' of the *P.S.I.* remained in being right up to the Leghorn Congress in January 1921, when the Communist Party was founded, and it was the nucleus around which the new party was formed. The only other national organisation to adhere to the new party was the Socialist Youth Federation, which was also dominated by the abstentionists.[22] The Youth Federation was quite important, for it ensured that the Communist case would be put in local branch debates throughout Italy, and it provided many of the Communist Party's militants in the next few years – Polano, Longo, Berti, Secchia, Montagnana, Silone; but obviously it could not by itself be the basis of a new party. Apart from the Youth Federation, the new party was able to attract some of the leading maximalists (notably Bombacci and Gennari) who often brought their supporters with them; and it also absorbed the former '*Ordine Nuovo* group' in Turin.

This absorption was ironic. As has been seen, it was the Occupation of the Factories that had finally convinced Gramsci (and Togliatti) of the need for a new party (see p. 174); yet Bordiga completely disagreed with the Turin view that the occupation had represented a golden opportunity for revolution. *Il Soviet* had succeeded in making no mention of the occupation in its editorial columns throughout September, and in early October Bordiga published a tart criticism of the whole *Ordine Nuovo* movement: 'we observe that among the Electionist Communists – even of the extreme Left, even those who are finally convinced of our old thesis that the Social-Democrats must be expelled – there is almost nobody

enter our new party', and were in favour of the continuation of the Abstentionist Faction as such, within the new party (*Il Soviet* 1 June 1921).

[20] *Il Soviet* 3 October 1920.
[21] *Il Soviet* 3 October 1920.
[22] See the 'interventi' of L. Polano (pp. 33–9, especially p. 35) and of E. D'Onofrio (pp. 78–9) in *La Frazione Comunista al Convegno di Imola* (Riuniti, Rome 1971).

who has not been heterodox on the question of Factory Councils, and especially on the setting up of Soviets.'[23] Moreover, Bordiga and Gramsci had very different views about what the new party would be like. Gramsci still expected it to attract most of the former supporters of the P.S.I., so that it would be a broadly-based party with mass support.[24] So the *Ordine Nuovo*'s adherence to the new party was based on some curious misunderstandings. And there was, of course, no question of the *Ordine Nuovo* joining as a group. Gramsci was still an isolated figure, Terracini had become a convinced Bordighian, Tasca joined up reluctantly and immediately became a 'Rightist' Communist.[25] There was even less question of the *Ordine Nuovo* joining as an organised 'faction'; as Gramsci remarked in 1925, they had never created a faction even in Piedmont, let alone nationally.[26]

Yet clearly Gramsci and Bordiga reached some kind of understanding in these months, and it may be unfair to speak of 'absorption'. I have noted how Bordiga had slapped down the Turin abstentionists' hopes of dominating the Communist Party in Turin (see p. 202), but the row simmered on for several weeks. Togliatti, as secretary of the local party branch, called for a 'fusion' of 'sincerely Communist elements' into a 'compact homogeneous and combattive bloc', and appealed to the Turin workers to help the branch executive 'with complete loyalty' to form one.[27] This was an obvious appeal to the local abstentionists to come into the Communist Party under 'Communist Electionist' leadership. In mid-October Gramsci and Terracini went to Milan for the foundation meeting of the 'Communist Faction' (see below, p. 204). On 23 October a further appeal to the abstentionists by the local party executive appeared in the Turin edition of *Avanti!* At this time both Gramsci and Togliatti were carefully emphasising how good the 'Communist' record of the Turin Socialist Party had been, and how Lenin himself had praised Gramsci's article 'For a Renewal of the Italian Socialist Party' at the Second Congress of the International (see p. 141).[28] On 31 October the provisional Central

[23] 'L'Internazionale Comunista e la Situazione Italiana', in *Il Soviet* 3 October 1920.
[24] 'La Frazione Comunista' in *Avanti!* (Turin ed.) 24 October 1920 (now in A. Gramsci, *Ordine Nuovo*, Einaudi, Turin 1955, pp. 420–3).
[25] Tasca's memoirs of these years, *I Primi Dieci Anni del P.C.I.* (Laterza, Bari 1971) are remarkably silent on his reasons for joining the Communist Party.
[26] 'La Situazione Interna del Nostro Partito ed i Compiti del Prossimo Congresso', in *L'Unità* 3 July 1925 (now in A. Gramsci, *La Costruzione del Partito Comunista*, Einaudi, Turin 1971, p. 70).
[27] *Avanti!* (Turin ed.) 10 October 1920; P. Spriano, *Storia del Partito Comunista Italiano* cit., vol. i, p. 89.
[28] Gramsci recalled this episode in 'Cronache dell' Ordine Nuovo', in *Ordine Nuovo* 9 October 1920 (now in A. Gramsci, *Ordine Nuovo* cit., pp. 488–9); Togliatti did so in his speech to the party branch on 25 November – cf. *Avanti!* (Turin ed.)

Committee of the 'Communist Faction' met in Turin (instead of Milan),[29] and it seems likely that the meeting was held there in order to settle the row and in order to persuade the local abstentionists to co-operate with other Turin Socialists. Eventually, and reluctantly, most of the abstentionists came round. By 25 November a Regional Committee of the Communist Faction had been set up in Piedmont, consisting of Gramsci (representing his still extant 'Communist Education Group'), the abstentionist Parodi, and Terracini of the Electionists. The Turin branch of the Socialist Party held formal pre-Congressional meetings at the end of November to discuss the coming split. There was no sign of dissension from the abstentionists at these meetings, and the branch eventually provided a majority for the Communist position of 249 – 84.[30] The successful motion praised Factory Councils, and saw the Communist Party as being formed by winning over workers in the factories and Trade Unions.[31] Bordiga was willing (or was persuaded) to allow the party in Piedmont to be *Ordinovista*; in return Gramsci supported Bordiga at the national level.

What brought most of the various 'Communist' groups together – in Piedmont and elsewhere – was their detestation of the pseudo-revolutionary traditions of the maximalists, the great prestige of Lenin and the International, and the tireless activity of Bordiga. On 14 October a meeting of prominent left-wingers took place at Milan to discuss the formation of the new party.[32] Predictably, they drew up a manifesto calling for the expulsion of the reformists, and for the party to change its name to the 'Communist Party of Italy'.[33] The manifesto also promised

26 November 1920, and P. Togliatti *Opere*, vol. i (Riuniti, Rome 1967), p. lxxvii. They were obviously both anxious to refute Bordiga's argument that the International had not really supported the *Ordine Nuovo* position after all ('L' Internazionale Comunista e la Situazione Italiana', in *Il Soviet* 3 October 1920).

[29] *Il Soviet* 11 November 1920.

[30] *Avanti!* (Turin ed.) 28 November 1920. Nevertheless, the Turin abstentionists later resumed their campaign for abstentionism and against opportunist infiltrators, and Bordiga had to condemn them again in *Il Soviet* 6 January 1921 (A. Lepre and S. Levrero, *La Formazione del Partito Comunista d'Italia* cit., pp. 346–7).

[31] The motion is summarised in P. Spriano, *Storia del Partito Comunista Italiano* cit., vol. i, p. 101.

[32] For this meeting, see *Il Soviet* 17 October 1920, and *Avanti!* (Turin ed.) 21 October 1920. It was attended by Bordiga, Gramsci, Terracini, Repossi, Fortichiari, Polano, Misiano and Bombacci.

[33] *Il Soviet* 17 October 1920. Giuseppe Berti has argued that Bordiga chose this name, rather than 'Italian Communist Party', to emphasise that the Italian party was a section of the International, based on the Twenty-One Conditions, not a mere national party with national policies (G. Berti, 'Problemi di Storia del P.C.I. e dell' Internazionale Comunista', in *Rivista Storica Italiana*, anno lxxxii (1970), pp. 148–98, at p. 173).

changes in party organisation, with greater centralisation and more emphasis on the work of 'Communist groups' within Trade Unions and factories. The thorny question of abstentionism was settled – the new party's 'participation in General and local elections would be of a type completely different to that of former Social-Democratic practice, with the sole objective of carrying out propaganda and revolutionary agitation, and in order to hasten the collapse of the bourgeois organs of representative democracy.'[34] This manifesto, which was signed by Gramsci and Terracini of the former *Ordine Nuovo* group, made no mention of Factory Councils. The Milan meeting, setting up the 'Communist Faction', was the first practical move in the formation of the Communist Party, and it was already clear that Bordiga's views dominated the nascent party nationally.

The only serious challenge to this domination came from Emilia, not Piedmont. In mid-November a group of maximalists in the Bologna area, led by Anselmo Marabini, issued a manifesto calling for the Italian Socialist Party to be won over to Communism without the need for an immediate split.[35] They urged that all maximalists should join the 'Communist Faction', and they proposed that the Socialist Party should be renamed the 'Socialist Communist Party of Italy'. Their main concern, of course, was to avoid a damaging split on the party's Left, and to preserve the Peasant Leagues, Cooperatives and the rest that the Socialists had built up over the years; and it was no coincidence that this was felt to be especially urgent in Emilia. This group – called the Marabini–Graziadei group, after its leading members – controlled about 200 party branches in Emilia, and its efforts to secure a reconciliation between Socialist traditions and the Third International were an important attempt to win mass support.[36]

Bordiga was, and remained, distinctly hostile to this group. It was bad enough having to take in maximalist notables like Bombacci and Gennari, without this last-minute attempt by unreliable 'Rightists' (especially Graziadei) to swamp the party.[37] At the formal inaugural Congress of the

---

[34] The manifesto signed at Milan was published in *Il Soviet* 17 October 1920. cf. also P. Spriano, *Storia del Partito Comunista Italiano* cit., vol. i, pp. 91–2; and A. Lepre and S. Levrero, *La Formazione del Partito Comunista d' Italia* cit., pp. 338–9.

[35] For this manifesto, see A. Marabini, 'La Circolare Marabini-Graziadei', in *Lo Stato Operaio*, anno IX, n. 10 (1935), pp. 662–72.

[36] Giuseppe Berti (in 'Problemi di Storia del P.C.I. e dell' Internazionale Comunista' cit., pp. 180–81) argues that the Russian ambassador Vorovski was behind the Marabini–Graziadei manifesto. According to Berti, Vorovski was very friendly with Graziadei, and both men thought it would be disastrous if the new party fell into the doctrinaire hands of Bordiga.

[37] L. Paggi, *Gramsci e il Moderno Principe* (Riuniti, Rome 1970), vol. i, p. 335.

'Communist Faction', held at Imola on 28–9 November, Bordiga's
'Abstentionist Faction' held a meeting separately from the other groups,
and even tried to exclude the Marabini–Graziadei group altogether.[38]
The situation was only saved when Gramsci made a politic speech
appealing for party unity. By this time a total of 430 Socialist Party
branches supported the 'Communist Faction' (not including the 200-odd
that supported Marabini–Graziadei).[39] Nearly all were in Northern or
North–Central Italy. Most of the delegates at Imola were not former
abstentionists, but Bordiga retained his control of the Faction's organisation, and the final resolution had a strong Bordighian tone. It omitted
any mention of Factory Councils, but 'Communist groups' were to be
set up in all working-class organisations.[40] Thus the Turin motion passed
only two days previously was forgotten. Whatever might be the case in
Piedmont, at national level the *Ordine Nuovo* group had to accept abstentionist leadership. So too did the various dissident maximalists, and the
Marabini–Graziadei group, which joined the new party in January 1921;
most of its members soon formed an influential right-wing faction within
the Communist Party of Italy.[41]

It was becoming clear that the new Communist Party would be a
'minority' party, although the International continued to hope for a
majority right up to the last minute. Even on 9 January 1921 Zinoviev said
that Serrati's supporters would vote for the Communist resolution;[42] and
Georgi Dimitrov actually wrote to his wife from Leghorn itself, while the
Socialist Congress was on, that the ordinary maximalists would abandon
Serrati.[43] But the bulk of the maximalists held fast to the Socialist Party.

[38] The Communist Faction's official journal, *Il Comunista*, sternly declared that
'the Congress is called for official representatives of groups set up within branches of
the *P.S.I.* on the basis of the Manifesto-Programme of the Communist Faction.'
cf. R. Zangheri's *intervento* (esp. p. 112) in *La Frazione Comunista al Convegno di
Imola* cit.

[39] *Il Comunista* 5 December 1920; *La Frazione Comunista al Convegno di Imola* cit.,
esp. pp. 112–14; A. Lepre and S. Levrero, *La Formazione del Partito Comunista d'Italia*
cit., pp. 339–43; L. Cortesi, *Le Origini del P.C.I.* cit., pp. 264–7; and report of Sub-
Prefect of Imola, sent by Prefect of Bologna to Ministry of the Interior 6 December
1920 (in *State Archives* cit., 1920, b. 81).

[40] The resolution was published in *Resoconto Stenografico del XVII Congresso del
P.S.I.* cit., pp. 441–5.

[41] A tradition that has survived to this day in Emilia, especially in the Bologna area.

[42] At a meeting of the Executive Committee of the International, reported in
L'Internationale Communiste March 1921. cf. P. Spriano, *Storia del Partito Comunista
Italiano* cit., vol. i, p. 105; and K. Shirinya, 'Lenin e la Formazione del P.C.I. – Nuovi
Documenti Sovietici', in *Critica Marxista*, anno VIII (1970), n. 6, pp. 107–29, at p. 115.
In early December Serrati had asked to meet Zinoviev.

[43] T. Detti, *Serrati e la Formazione del Partito Comunista Italiano* (Riuniti, Rome
1972), p. 53.

The split finally occurred in January 1921, at the XVII Congress of the Italian Socialist Party at Leghorn.[44] It was an unseemly Congress, full of angry recriminations over lost opportunities. The Comintern's representative, Christo Kabakchev, was irreverently known as the 'Papal Legate'; as he mounted the rostrum, he was greeted with ironic shouts of '*Viva il Papachef!*'.[45] Gramsci wisely did not speak. He was still detested by many as an 'interventionist', and it was a *Communist* delegate, D'Amato from Rome, who distributed leaflets libelling him as a war volunteer.[46] Paul Levi's last-minute attempts at mediation between the Communists and the Serratians failed. Out of a total party membership of over 200,000, 58,783 votes were cast for the Communist motion, 98,028 for the 'Unitarians' (i.e. the maximalists), and 14,695 for the reformists.[47] The Turin federation provided 4,518 of the Communist votes, and the party was also strong in Alessandria (4,104), Trieste (4,462), and Florence (4,003).[48]

When the voting figures were announced, the Communists walked out of the hall, adjourned to the nearby San Marco Theatre, declared the Communist Party of Italy founded, and elected their new officers. The fifteen-man Central Committee consisted of five former abstentionists, seven maximalists, two from the *Ordine Nuovo*, and one from the Youth Federation.[49] The Communist Party of Italy was founded, therefore, on the basis of an alliance between former abstentionists, the former *Ordine Nuovo* group, some disillusioned maximalists, and the former Socialist Youth Federation. Paul Levi thought the new party was too disparate to

[44] For the Leghorn Congress, see *Resoconto Stenografico del XVII Congresso del Partito Socialista Italiano* (*Livorno 1921*) (Edizioni *Avanti!*, Milan 1921, reissued by Edizioni *Avanti!*, Milan 1962); J. M. Cammett, *Antonio Gramsci and the Origins of Italian Communism* (Stanford U.P., 1967), pp. 141–55; L. Cortesi, *Le Origini del P.C.I.* cit., pp. 281–302; and P. Spriano, *Storia del Partito Comunista Italiano* cit., vol. i, pp. 108–21.

[45] P. Spriano, *Storia del Partito Comunista Italiano* cit., vol. i, p. 111.

[46] G. Berti, 'Appunti e Ricordi 1919–26' cit., p. 34. D'Amato also tried to prevent Gramsci's election to the Central Committee of the new Communist Party.

[47] *Resoconto Stenografico del XVII Congresso del P.S.I.* cit., p. 408. There were 981 abstentions. A week later the Socialist Youth Federation also passed to the Communists, adding a further 50,000 nominal members (*Ordine Nuovo* 1 February 1921 claims 54,000; P. Spriano, *Storia del Partito Comunista Italiano* cit., vol. i, p. 119, says 35,000, but this figure seems too low considering that the Socialist Youth Federation had 55,313 members in 1920).

[48] *Ordine Nuovo* 21 January 1921.

[49] Bordiga, Grieco, Sessa, Tarsia and Parodi; Belloni, Bombacci, Gennari, Misiano, Marabini, Fortichiari and Repossi; Gramsci and Terracini; and Polano (*Resoconto Stenografico del XVII Congresso del P.S.I.* cit., p. 451; G. Berti, 'Appunti e Ricordi 1919–26' cit., p. 63; R. Alcara, *La Formazione e i Primi Anni del P.C.I. nella Storiografia Marxista* (Jaca, Milan 1970), pp. 68–9.

be viable, although he admitted Bordiga was resolute and energetic.[50]
The party's leaders were certainly inexperienced. Bordiga himself was
aged thirty-one at Leghorn, Gramsci just thirty, Terracini twenty-five.
It was easy for the Communist Party's enemies to portray it as a group of
young doctrinaires, dominated by foreign bullies, and Kabakchev's
hectoring speech at Leghorn confirmed this impression. The party
was founded by men who rejected the older Socialist traditions, and
perhaps they often veered over into rejecting the older Socialist
generation.

Moreover, the Communists had only eighteen deputies, no Trade
Union organisations or Agricultural Labourers' Leagues; it controlled no
Co-operatives or local administrations. It was too small, as the International soon realised. The vote at Leghorn exaggerated its real strength;
in April 1922 Gramsci estimated there had been about 25,000 adult
Communists represented there, not 58,783.[51] Only a minority of Socialists
were still 'revolutionary'; by this time the Revolution had obviously
Failed. The original sin of the Italian Communist Party was sectarianism,
and it was only the later years of anti-Fascist resistance that transformed it
into the mass political movement that Gramsci had envisaged as late as
October 1920.

Gramsci's silence at Leghorn was symbolic of the very limited role the
Ordine Nuovo group had in the national party. The new party did not
adopt any kind of Factory Council policy, and the majority of its leaders
had actively opposed such proposals throughout the previous year. The
Turin movement was represented on the party's Executive Committee
only by Terracini (henceforth a strong supporter of Bordiga), and on the
Central Committee only by Terracini, Gramsci and the abstentionist
Parodi. Given the strict discipline in the new party, the *Ordine Nuovo*
could not continue for long with its Factory Council propaganda against
the wishes of the majority of the party's leaders, and against a background of mutual recriminations and general demoralisation among the
workers.

In short, the results of the Leghorn Congress were unfortunate, both for
Gramsci's concept of a mass working-class movement, and for his ideal
of a coherent political party with mass support. He consoled himself with
the thought that at least something had been saved from the wreck of

[50] Levi's report to the Executive Committee of the Third International 20 January
1921, in M. Drachkovitch and B. Lazitch, *The Comintern–Historical Highlights* cit.,
p. 281.
[51] In a speech to the Communist Party branch in Turin 5 April 1922, reported by
the Prefect of Turin to the Ministry of the Interior 8 April 1922 (in *State Archives*,
Min. Int., Dir. Gen. P.S., Aff. Gen. e Ris., 1922, b. 88 'Partito Comunista: Torino').

Italian Socialism,[52] and that the split was guaranteed success at some future date. At other times he was more pessimistic, and in 1923 even wrote that the Leghorn split had been the 'greatest triumph of reaction'.[53] Of course, it was not the foundation of the Communist Party that he regarded as a disaster, but its timing – the split had occurred at least a year too late for successful revolution to be organised[54] – and above all its failure to attract the majority of Socialist workers. The great promise of September 1920, when it had seemed as if the Communist Party might be formed as a result of Factory Council activity in the factories, had failed to materialise. In reality, the foundation of the new party served to confirm Gramsci's isolation, and make him dependent on Bordiga for any future political influence.

[52] L. Paggi, *Gramsci e il Moderno Principe* cit., pp. 336–40; P. Spriano, *Storia del Partito Comunista Italiano* cit., vol. i, p. 102.

[53] A note published in P. Togliatti, *La Formazione del Gruppo Dirigente del Partito Comunista Italiano* (Riuniti, Rome 1962), p. 102. Mussolini agreed. On 10 January 1921 the Prefect of Cremona reported that the Fascists would leave the Socialist Party Congress in peace 'given that the Fascists foresee that the split in the Socialist Party is necessary and will benefit them' (Prefect of Cremona to Ministry of the Interior 10 January 1921, in *State Archives* cit., 1921, b. 89).

[54] 'Socialisti e Comunisti', in *Ordine Nuovo* 12 March 1921 (now in A. Gramsci, *Socialismo e Fascismo*, Einaudi, Turin 1966, p. 103).

The Legacy of the
Ordine Nuovo

AT first sight the *Ordine Nuovo* movement ended in complete failure. By 1921 the Revolution had obviously failed, and the Factory Councils were crushed. Gramsci and his colleagues had made plenty of mistakes, and had proved inadequate leaders during critical periods. Disillusionment prevailed, and Gramsci himself was unpopular. The whole 'productivist' aspect of the movement was discredited by the recession and by mass unemployment; and the Factory Councils had been defeated on the key issue of 'controlling' dismissals of skilled men.

Perhaps the defeat was inevitable. The movement reflected the peculiar characteristics of Turin, the only 'proletarian city' in Italy, a city very different from others in its economic and social structure.[1] Hence its vulnerability. The *Ordine Nuovo* movement presupposed continuous 'workers' power' in Turin, the continued ability of workers in Turin to exert effective pressure on employers and on their own national leaders.[2] In the post-occupation gloom, and especially when the industrial recession hit the city in the last months of 1920, the *Ordine Nuovo* movement was lost. Even before this happened, the Turin movement had failed to win over the national labour organisations; as Giuseppe Berti put it in 1935, it was 'enclosed in Turin, like sardines in a tin'.[3] Perhaps Gramsci's insistence on the close relationship between 'productivism' and 'revolution' was meaningless elsewhere.[4] At any rate, it proved impossible for the proletariat to become the 'leading class' in Italy through a Factory Council movement in Turin.

Apart from its isolation in Turin, there were three main inter-related

[1] 'Torino', anonymous article in *Ordine Nuovo* 1 January 1921.
[2] L. Paggi, *Antonio Gramsci e il Moderno Principe*, vol. i (Riuniti, Rome 1970), pp. 315–16.
[3] 'Come sarde in barile'. G. Berti, 'Il Gruppo del Soviet nella Formazione del P.C.d'I.', in *Lo Stato Operaio*, anno XIII (1935), n. 1, pp. 53–70, at p. 65.
[4] F. De Felice, in *I Comunisti a Torino* (Riuniti, Rome 1974), p. 16.

weaknesses of the movement (and perhaps of other such movements, at different times and places). Firstly, there was the probability of provoking reaction by employers or by the repressive institutions of the State, and I discuss this aspect at length below. Secondly (and acting as a partial cause of the first weakness), there was the *Ordine Nuovo*'s failure to organise and *discipline* shop-floor militancy. Gramsci was always very aware of this problem, and of the likely consequences of failure. In the 'Theses on the Trade Union Question', written for the Second Congress of the Communist Party in March 1922, he declared that 'the industrial autonomy of the producers must have the immediate aim of ending the strikes and agitations that are today preventing normal production by firms.'[5] Nevertheless, his movement became associated not with industrial discipline, but with constant short stoppages and frequent long ones (April 1920, September 1920, April 1921), with seizure of factories and industrial sabotage. In many parts of Italy the syndicalists took over, and their rhetoric and Luddism discredited the Factory Council movement (as well as helping to discredit Giolitti's compromises). If the Factory Councils had managed technological change successfully, if they had been seen to embody 'class self-discipline' and 'productivism', all might have been different. They failed to do so. It was obviously difficult to instil 'producers' consciousness' when skilled men's jobs were threatened.[6] In practice, the Fascists proved much better than Gramsci at 'making the trains run on time'.

The third and most important weakness (again acting as a partial cause of the first) was that the *Ordine Nuovo* movement, like similar movements elsewhere, could so easily be diverted into 'reformist' channels. This weakness was revealed by the Tasca and Schiavello schemes in the summer of 1920 (see pp. 135–6 and p. 131), in government proposals for 'Trade Union control' of industry, and – most seriously of all for Gramsci – in the proposal to turn Fiat into a workers' Cooperative (see pp. 181–2). Even more significantly, there was the possibility of being 'absorbed' into a generic anti-Fascist front, interested mainly in preserving 'bourgeois liberties'. Gramsci fought hard against this danger; he was an activist, a left-wing revolutionary, not a sceptical political realist. Even in 1925, he was not interested in preserving 'bourgeois liberties'. That was not what the Communist Party had been formed to do, and for the party to resign

[5] The 'Theses' were published in *Ordine Nuovo* 31 January – 19 February 1922 (now in A. Gramsci, *Socialismo e Fascismo*, Einaudi, Turin 1966, pp. 499–518; the quotation is at p. 513).

[6] cf. C. S. Maier, *Recasting Bourgeois Europe* (Princeton U.P. 1975), p. 585, on the problems involved in adopting 'the centrality of work experience as a (revolutionary) political rallying point'.

itself to such a limited aim would simply be evidence of passivity and scepticism.[7] The 'Theses' for the Third Congress denounced those right-wing Communists (including Tasca) who held that the Communists should be the 'left-wing' of an anti-Fascist coalition: 'This is the expression of a profound pessimism concerning the revolutionary capabilities of the working-class.'[8] There was something to be said for Gramsci's view. After all, the vital questions throughout the Fascist regime were: who would gain power when it fell? and who would lead the industrial workers? Arguably it *was* sensible for the Communists to keep their distance from the other anti-Fascist groups. Gramsci certainly thought so, at least until his imprisonment in 1926.

Yet, despite its failure and isolation, and despite its evident weaknesses, the *Ordine Nuovo* movement was important. It made some contribution to the collapse of the Liberal regime in Italy in 1922, and it also had considerable influence on the later history of the Italian Communist Party – a party which has, ever since, shown remarkable awareness of the 'three weaknesses' outlined above. I shall now consider each of these aspects in turn.

1. The Rise of Fascism

Did the Factory Council movement, by frightening the industrialists, contribute to the rise of Fascism in 1921–2? The answer seems to be: yes, but not much, and not directly.

Many industrialists *were* seriously frightened in the autumn of 1920 – but not by the Factory Council movement. It was the 'Occupation of the Factories', and above all the measures taken by the Giolitti government to achieve a peaceful solution to it, that alarmed the respectable bourgeoisie (see pp. 170–1). To take just one example, Motta, a director of Edison's, and President of the Milan Tramway Company, was described by the Prefect of Milan in March 1921 as being

> in continuous contact with the other industrialists, and notoriously opposed to the draft Bill on control over factories. It is said that he, like the other industrialists, spends large sums on propaganda, especially in the press, against the draft Bill itself, although it has not yet been

---

[7] See Gramsci's reply to Piero Sraffa's letter (which had advocated an anti-Fascist front) in *Ordine Nuovo* 1–15 April 1924 (now in A. Gramsci, *La Costruzione del Partito Comunista*, Einaudi, Turin 1971, pp. 177–81). cf. also M. L. Salvadori, *Gramsci e il Problema Storico della Democrazia* (Einaudi, Turin 1970), esp. p. 175.

[8] Thesis no. 26, now in A. Gramsci, *La Costruzione del Partito Comunista* cit., p. 501.

possible to make sure of this. At the Regional meeting of the Lombardy branch of the *Fasci di Combattimento* on the 20th of last month, Ferrari, acting as spokesman for the above-mentioned Motta, deplored the actions of the Government, and explained that the industrialists supported the Fascists in order to fight against the Government and hinder its activity, harmful to their interests.[9]

The industrialists were well aware that 'Trade Union control of industry' was totally distinct from the Factory Council movement.[10] They had no need to worry overmuch about the Factory Councils, which after all were important only in Turin, and even there Agnelli of Fiat proved perfectly able to cope with them on his own. But 'Trade Union control' isolated the industrialists in opposition to government and labour alike, and it was a great shock (see p. 180). Perhaps one Motta does not make a Fascist movement; but it may be argued that much of the financial support given to the Fascists by industrialists stemmed not so much from the employers' fear of any possible revolution, but from the feeling that the *government* of the day was harming their legitimate interests. As far as the employers, at least, were concerned, the threat came from above, not below.[11]

This picture naturally needs some qualification. Many industrialists – notably Agnelli of Fiat – remained hostile to Fascism;[12] they did not want to antagonise their workers unnecessarily, and saw the Fascist squads as a potential long-term danger. Many other industrialists were indifferent. Certainly the conservative reaction during the winter of 1920–1 was not 'Fascist', more a worried attempt to maintain 'law and order' and to put pressure on the Giolitti Government. The Turin Industrial League gave

[9] Prefect of Milan to Ministry of the Interior 7 March 1921 (in *State Archives*, Ministero dell' Interno, Direzione Generale Pubblica Sicurezza, Affari Generali e Riservati, 1921, b. 71). Motta was elected deputy on the Fascist *listone* in 1924, but later that year became a prominent opponent of Mussolini; see R. De Felice, *Mussolini il Fascista*, vol. ii (Einaudi, Turin 1968), p. 87.

[10] The 'Memorandum of the Italian Industrialists' Confederation on the Movement for Control in Italy and on the Evolution of the *C.G.L.*'s Thought' (in *C.G.I.I.*, *I Consigli di Gestione*, Milan 1947, vol. ii, pp. 47–65) emphasises this point.

[11] On the financing of Fascism, see R. De Felice, 'I Primi Elementi sul Finanzia-mento del Fascismo, dalle Origini al 1924', in *Rivista Storica del Socialismo*, n. 22 (May–August 1964), pp. 223–51; idem, *Mussolini il Rivoluzionario* (Einaudi, Turin 1965), pp. 658–62; idem, *Mussolini il Fascista* vol. i (Einaudi, Turin 1966), pp. 121–2, 289–96; and Adrian Lyttelton's acute comments in *The Seizure of Power* (Weidenfeld & Nicolson, London 1973), pp. 208–17. On the more general issue of the relationship between the industrialists and Fascism, see especially R. Sarti, *Fascism and the Industrial Leadership in Italy* (University of California Press 1971), and P. Melograni, *Gli Industriali e Mussolini* (Longanesi, Milan 1972).

[12] V. Castronovo, *Giovanni Agnelli* (U.T.E.T., Turin 1971), pp. 303–6.

H

21,000 *lire* (and 'lent' a lorry) to the local Fascists for the General Election of May 1921,[13] but they also financed other right-wing candidates (the Ex-Servicemen's Association received 23,500 *lire*), and most of their efforts went into securing preference votes for their 'own' parliamentary candidates, Gino Olivetti and Giuseppe Mazzini.[14]

Moreover, the Fascist reaction was far stronger in the *rural* areas of the Po valley than in the industrial North. There were good reasons why. In some 'Socialist' areas, the local land-owners' position had been destroyed by labourers' closed shops and Socialist control of town councils.[15] In the South, peasants and landless labourers had illegally occupied some of the uncultivated *latifondi*, and conservatives throughout Italy noted nervously that post-war governments did not prevent these attacks on established property rights. A government decree of September 1919 ratified occupations of certain types of land in certain conditions, and ordered Prefects to expropriate uncultivated land and hand it over to the peasants' cooperatives for four years.[16] The onset of local elections in October–November 1920 persuaded all the 'constitutional' parties of the need to countenance occupations in order to win the peasant vote. The clerical Popular Party had the most incentive for such a policy, as it was the most likely candidate for the peasant vote, and it was also the party in the best position to act, as one of its members, Micheli, was Minister of Agriculture in the Giolitti government. Accordingly, a government decree of October 1920 gave permanent (as opposed to four years') guaranteed tenure to the Southern peasantry, thus encouraging land reclamations and improvements, and discouraging excessive exploitation of the land.[17]

The decree on land occupations coincided with a more militant phase among the Catholic Trade Unionists of Northern Italy. On 2 November 1920 the Catholic Union of Labour denounced the share-cropping agreement for 1920–1, and announced its intention of negotiating a new agreement;[18] and in November 1920 a new system was due to come into effect in Upper Cremona, whereby every large farm was to be managed by an administrative council consisting of two peasants and one repre-

13 M. Abrate, *La Lotta Sindacale nella Industrializzazione in Italia* (Angeli, Milan 1967), pp. 362–3.

14 *ibid.*, pp. 343–4.

15 See P. Corner, *Fascism in Ferrara* (Oxford U.P. 1975), and F. Snowden, 'On the Social Origins of Agrarian Fascism in Italy', in *Archives Européennes de Sociologie* n. 2 (1972), pp. 268–95.

16 E. Pratt Howard, *Il Partito Popolare Italiano* (La Nuova Italia, Florence 1957), pp. 188–201.

17 *ibid.*, pp. 263–4.

18 F. Catalano, *Potere Economico e Fascismo 1919–21* (Lerici, Milan 1964), p. 212.

sentative of the landowner.[19] The landowners in the North and Centre of Italy blamed the Popular Party, and the government, for the Southern land occupations, and feared that the same disaster might occur in the North. It was bad enough for the Popular Party to organise the peasantry into Unions, but it was far worse for the party to control the Ministry of Agriculture and to issue decrees ratifying the seizure of land. Even the *Rettore Magnifico* of Rome University was outraged, and complained bitterly in public: 'we are in a state of anarchy, not merely *de facto* but imposed by the authorities, against the law.'[20] Micheli's bill in January 1921, guaranteeing agricultural jobs until the end of 1922, was the final straw, and it unleashed rural Fascism against a government and a State which appeared to be bent on destroying the position of the landowners in Northern and Central Italy.

Thus the Giolitti government alienated vital groups among the ruling classes. The government was too weak, too close to the reformist Socialist Trade Unions and the Catholic Peasant Leagues, apparently too anti-business and anti-landowner. Labriola, at the Ministry of Labour, blundered on, producing various alarming schemes. In October he told Giolitti that a National Council of Labour, elected by Trade Unions and Employers' Associations, should help draft legislation on economic and social issues.[21] In November he actually introduced a bill on these lines, although the Council was to remain purely consultative. He informed the conservative readers of the *Nuova Antologia* that:

> there are only two possible outcomes of the current industrial chaos – the cannon or the *New Order*, inexorable repression à la Horthy ('ten years of peace'), or courageous experiments with new forms, new forms which will not make men any happier, but may manage to restore order to society – and society needs order as much as it needs bread.[22]

Labriola soon became a public embarrassment, and indeed the Giolitti government in early 1921 made a series of hasty concessions to the industrialists (e.g. tariff protection, dropping the bill on 'Trade Union

[19] *ibid.*, pp. 213–18.
[20] F. Scaduto, 'Occupazione Abusiva dei Terreni in Sicilia', in *Nuova Antologia* 16 January 1921, p. 165.
[21] D. Marucco, *Arturo Labriola e il Sindacalismo Rivoluzionario in Italia* (Fondazione Einaudi, Turin 1970), pp. 272–5. The National Council of Labour would replace the existing consultative Supreme Council of Labour, founded in 1902. There had been many proposals in 1919–20 to convert this latter body into a legislative organ on economic and social matters. See International Labour Office, *Studies and Reports*, Series B, no. 9.
[22] A. Labriola, 'La Dittatura del Proletariato e i Problemi Economici del Socialismo', in *Nuova Antologia* 16 November 1920. The italics are mine.

control', allowing the taxes on 'excess profits' to be paid over a five-year period), but by this time the damage had been done. Fascism had risen, and much of the blame must rest with Giolitti.

However, Labriola's words show that the *Ordine Nuovo* contributed something to the outcome. Gramsci's constant arguments about 'producer-consciousness', his emphasis on the need for new institutions to embody 'Socialist legality' in an industrial society, indeed the whole Factory Council agitation in Turin, had a big impact on men's thinking, often in ways of which he himself disapproved, and often in ways that reflected the *weaknesses* of the movement. Perhaps the *U.S.I.* syndicalists would not have been so ready to occupy factories if it had not been for the previous months of Factory Council agitation. Perhaps the plans for 'Trade Union control' – the ill-fated Giolittian 'solution' to the 'Occupation of the Factories' – would not have emerged so readily in early September without the previous debate around the Tasca and Schiavello plans, themselves a response to the *Ordine Nuovo*'s ideas. Even if the 'Occupation of the Factories' had not happened, the *Ordine Nuovo*'s campaign would have had to be 'absorbed' somehow, probably through schemes for 'pseudo-control' and by granting Trade Union bodies greater powers on the shop floor (and perhaps nationally). The appointment of Labriola as Minister of Labour in June 1920, and the ideas he was expressing in July, show the way Giolitti's mind was working. These schemes would have alienated the industrial managers from the Liberal government in any case, although of course the occupations intensified their shock.

The 'Fascist alternative' method of securing labour discipline was to expel trouble-makers, to slow down industrial expansion, to freeze existing privileges (including those of some industrial workers) via tariffs, autarchy, cartels, etc., and to buy off unrest by welfare schemes, organisation of leisure pursuits and the like. The labour Unions (or Fascist syndicates) had an important task in this scheme, that of 'mobilising' and 'representing' workers' interests *within* the existing system, in a *subordinate* role. The reformist Socialist Unions in the *C.G.L.* were perfectly willing to carry out this task, and had done so before 1914; they remained 'available' for some time even under Mussolini, who kept open his links with the *C.G.L.* at least until 1924,[23] and who granted, at least on paper, many of the reformist demands in his Charter of Labour in 1927. But Mussolini did not need the *C.G.L.* The war had shown that Giolittian concessions to the Unions were unnecessary. Introducing his labour legislation to Parliament in 1925, Mussolini put the point forcibly:

[23] R. De Felice, *Mussolini il Fascista* cit., vol. i, pp. 380–6, 474, 613–18.

I consider the nation in a permanent state of war . . . just as during the war . . . disputes in the workshops were not allowed, and there were conciliation bodies to prevent them, and the results were satisfactory because there were no suspensions of work, so through these [new] organisations we are achieving the maximum national efficiency of production.[24]

Although the Fascists paid lip service (especially early on) to 'productivism' and to rule by technocrats, they had no interest in workers' self-management or 'producers' autonomy'. The Internal Commissions elected in the factories were abolished in 1925, and in 1929 even the Fascist syndicates failed to instal workshop *fiduciari* to monitor labour agreements. The syndicates were territorial bodies only, and within the factory managerial authority was unchallenged.[25] Yet the Fascist syndicates succeeded in their main tasks, where Giolitti and the *C.G.L.* had failed, because the Fascists maintained the bourgeois order more *visibly*. For many years the 'military-industrial' system worked well enough. There was surprisingly little labour unrest during the Fascist period, and none that could not be 'absorbed'.[26] But 'military-industrial complexes' sometimes find it difficult to cope with real wars. When production began to matter – when munitions became desperately short in 1942–3 – the Fascist industrial system revealed its weaknesses. New militant factory bodies sprang up to reassert 'producer autonomy'; the new anti-Fascism of 1943 was centred on the factory, indeed on the Fiat factory in Turin.

2. The Italian Communist Party

I have shown in Chapter Eleven that the *Ordine Nuovo* movement played a minor part in the formation of the Communist Party. Its members were divided among themselves during 1920; none of them was in Moscow for the vital Second Congress of the International; they had concentrated on a campaign for Factory Councils, not a new party, until almost the last minute; and Gramsci and Togliatti both had an 'interventionist' past that

[24] Speech of 11 December 1925, quoted in R. De Felice, *Mussolini il Fascista* cit., vol. ii, p. 269; also in B. Mussolini, *Opera Omnia* (ed. E. and D. Susmel, 35 vols., La Fenice, Florence 1951–63), vol. xxii, p. 37.

[25] cf. A. Aquarone, *L'Organizzazione dello Stato Totalitario* (Einaudi, Turin 1965), pp. 122–3, pp. 232–3. *Fiduciari were* recognised in engineering factories in October 1939, but even then were not allowed to contact managers during working hours.

[26] cf., especially, G. Amendola, *Fascismo e Movimento Operaio* (Riuniti, Rome 1975).

all but discredited them.[27] Gramsci was regarded with particular suspicion, as a 'Bergsonian' idealist; after his polemics against the empty demagoguery of the Socialist Left, it was difficult for him to influence those left-wing maximalists who joined the new party. Even in Turin the 'Communist Electionists' around the *Ordine Nuovo* had jealous rivals among the local abstentionists, and nationally Bordiga's 'Abstentionist Faction' had been a well organised, disciplined group. Bordiga therefore had no rivals, and in the Communist Party discipline was supposed to be strict. Gramsci was on the central committee of the new party, but not on the executive, and his party job as editor of the daily *Ordine Nuovo* (the successor to the Turin edition of *Avanti!*) kept him isolated in Turin. During 1921 his former colleagues dispersed. Terracini moved to Rome, to work on the party executive; Togliatti also went to Rome, to edit *Il Comunista*; Pastore and Viglongo left to work on *Il Lavoratore* at Trieste. The *Ordine Nuovo* certainly provided much of the journalistic talent needed to run the party's three daily newspapers, but initially it provided little else.

And yet the *Ordine Nuovo*'s failure was far from total. After all, Gramsci and Togliatti took over the Communist Party leadership only three years after the Congress of Leghorn. They did so because the International had to find an alternative to Bordiga; but it was the *Ordine Nuovo* movement that had first brought them into prominence, and it was the reputation of the *Ordine Nuovo* that made them 'available' as possible replacements of Bordiga.[28] The movement thus provided the party with its leadership for more than forty years, as well as providing many of the persistent 'myths' that surround the Italian Communist Party to this day. The idea that Fiat is the capitalist firm par excellence, the belief in the peculiar importance of the *Turin* working-class (comparable in proletarian status to the miners in Britain), the leadership of intellectuals from the 'Kingdom of Sardinia', above all the willingness to debate cultural and historical topics, the hostility to congealed orthodoxy and sectarianism – all these features of the Italian Communist Party are characteristically *Ordinovista*. In the long run, the *Ordine Nuovo* movement succeeded – and perhaps the full extent of its success has yet to be seen.

Certainly the search for suitable institutions, that might incarnate

---

[27] G. Berti, 'Appunti e Ricordi 1919–26', in *Annali dell' Istituto Feltrinelli*, anno VIII (1966), p. 25; on p. 34 he also reports Serrati's remarks to Trotsky in 1924, on why the *Ordine Nuovo* group had been unfit to lead the Italian Communist Party in 1921.

[28] For the whole process of how Gramsci became leader of the *P.C.d'I.* in place of Bordiga, see P. Togliatti, *La Formazione del Gruppo Dirigente del Partito Comunista Italiano* (Riuniti, Rome 1962).

'Socialist legality', undermine men's adherence to the bourgeois legal order and form the nuclei of the future workers' State, continued throughout the rest of Gramsci's life. At the Rome Congress of the *P.C.d'I.* in March 1922, he and Tasca produced the party's 'Trade Union Theses'. The section on 'workers' control', written by Gramsci, strongly reaffirmed the necessity for Factory Councils: 'The system of Factory Councils is the concrete historic expression of the proletariat's aspirations for its own autonomy'. He envisaged factory bodies 'controlling' hiring and firing, discipline, wages and hours; a central Council for each industry to plan production, distribute raw materials, etc.; and also a kind of national 'control' of the whole economy, exercised by the workers and other exploited classes. Indeed, 'the struggle for control is, for Communists, precisely the field in which the working-class assumes the leadership of the other oppressed classes in the population, and succeeds in obtaining their consent for its own dictatorship.'[29] These were essentially the same ideas as he had expressed in February 1921 (see p. 188). Despite the evident impossibility of any kind of Factory Council movement at a time of considerable unemployment and of Fascist reaction, and despite opposition from the new party's leadership, Gramsci never finally abandoned Factory Council ideas. Similarly, at the Rome Congress he welcomed the anti-Fascist 'Alliance of Labour'[30] not only in terms of workers' unity against the Fascist threat, but also as an opportunity for unity and political initiatives of all kinds. He hoped it might lead to the workers electing local bodies – 'bodies of an almost Soviet kind' – and these might well be more 'opportune' at that time than Factory Councils, given employer hostility and worker disillusionment.[31]

There was, however, a noticeable *extension* of his thinking in this period. I have shown (p. 182) how Gramsci in October 1920 had opposed the idea of Fiat becoming a Cooperative, on the grounds that the Fiat workers would sooner or later become labour-aristocrats, or rather mere parasites of the Giolittian State, enjoying subsidies ultimately paid for by other less privileged groups. On the eve of the Leghorn Congress in January 1921, he produced what looks very like a personal 'manifesto' for the new

[29] 'Il Partito Comunista e i Sindacati' (Theses on the Trade Unions for the Second Congress of the *P.C.d'I.*) cit., now in A. Gramsci, *Socialismo e Fascismo* cit., p. 513.

[30] For the 'Alliance of Labour', see P. Spriano, *Storia del Partito Comunista Italiano*, vol. i (Einaudi, Turin 1967), pp. 192–215; R. De Felice, *Mussolini il Fascista* cit., vol. i, pp. 219–23.

[31] cf. Gramsci's speech at the Rome Congress, summarised in *Ordine Nuovo* 25 March 1922 (now in A. Gramsci, *Socialismo e Fascismo* cit., pp. 518–20); and his 'L'Alleanza del Lavoro', in *Ordine Nuovo* 21 February 1922 (now in A. Gramsci, *Socialismo e Fascismo* cit., p. 543).

party.[32] Capitalism exploited the backward South as well as the Northern working-class, and it was no use Northern workers seeking to win privileges within the existing State (via reformism, Cooperatives, tariff protection and the like), for these privileges could only be bought at the expense of Southern peasants. The whole novelty of the Communist Party was that it rejected this kind of immoral degenerate policy, and insisted on the historic *national* role of the proletariat. The bourgeois State could only be overthrown by the Northern industrial workers, acting on behalf of the poor Southern peasants, and 'setting up a new system of industrial production serving the needs of agriculture'; only the working-class could 'solve the central problem of Italian national life, the Southern question'. I should stress that Gramsci did not envisage an alliance between Northern workers and Southern peasants *within* the Communist Party. On the contrary, he denounced the Socialists for having always had too many agricultural labourers among their members and voters, and he constantly emphasised that the Communist Party must be a party of industrial workers.[33] But they should be workers aware of national problems. Perhaps Gramsci felt that the 'Turin' phase of his life was over. Although he remained as committed as ever to 'revolution from below', to new mass organisations based initially on the factory, and to the industrial working class as the active protagonist of revolution, henceforth he developed a more 'national', above all a more 'Southern', perspective.[34]

In the summer of 1922 Gramsci left Italy to act as Communist Party representative in Moscow, and he spent the next two years there or in Vienna. During this period Bordiga's quarrel with the Comintern line of the 'united front' became acute,[35] and Gramsci and his former col-

[32] 'Il Congresso di Livorno', in *Ordine Nuovo* 13 January 1921 (now in A. Gramsci, *Socialismo e Fascismo* cit., pp. 39–42). cf. A. Lepre and S. Levrero, *La Formazione del P.C.d'I.* (Riuniti, Rome 1971), pp. 355–7.

[33] For example, in 'Lo Stato Operaio', in *Ordine Nuovo* 1 January 1921 (now in A. Gramsci, *Socialismo e Fascismo* cit., p. 6); in 'Crisi dei Popolari?', in *Ordine Nuovo* 5 January 1921 (*ibid.*, p. 19); in 'Il Manifesto dei Socialisti', in *Ordine Nuovo* 13 April 1921 (*ibid.*, p. 137); in his speech at the Rome Congress of the *P.C.d'I.*, summarised in *Ordine Nuovo* 28 March 1922 (*ibid.*, p. 520); and in 'Le Origini del Gabinetto Mussolini', in *Correspondance Internationale* 20 November 1922 (*ibid.*, p. 529).

[34] cf. M. L. Salvadori, 'Gramsci e la Questione Meridionale', in P. Rossi (ed.), *Gramsci e la Cultura Contemporanea*, vol. i (Riuniti, Rome 1969), pp. 391–438, pp. 550–3.

[35] The dispute had been evident ever since the Comintern's Third Congress in the summer of 1921, but it became acute after Bordiga's 'Manifesto' to his comrades in the Italian party, written in the summer of 1923 (published in *Rivista Storica del Socialismo* no. 23, September–December 1964, pp. 515–21). Much of P. Spriano's *Storia del Partito Comunista Italiano*, vol. i (Einaudi, Turin 1967), and of A. De Clementi's *Amadeo Bordiga* (Einaudi, Turin 1971) is about this subject.

leagues were thrust into the leadership of the Italian party – a party whose ordinary members were still very mistrustful of the whole *Ordine Nuovo* tradition.[36]

Immediately party propaganda began to emphasise the importance of workers' organisations in the factories. In October 1923 Gramsci, still in Moscow, outlined 'our Trade Union policy' as being to gain control of the reformist Unions and the *C.G.L.* by means of activity in the factories. 'Revolutionary groups' were to be set up in the factories to win control of the Internal Commissions, and there should be liaison between the various factories so that the Internal Commissions might be transformed into Factory Councils.[37] The Internal Commissions in the main industrial cities were still being elected by all the workers, not by Trade Union members alone (as had been the case before 1919). Gramsci urged that since under Fascism they were the only workers' bodies of significance left, and since – in his view – they could not be suppressed without ill effects on discipline and production, the party should concentrate its efforts on them: they should be given more important tasks and organised into a national network.[38] In March 1924 he proposed that the *P.C.d'I.* should organise, in secret, a conference of factory representatives from the largest factories in Italy, to study the main political problems of the day and set up a 'central committee of the Italian factories'. Gramsci recognised that such a conference would have largely propaganda value, but

> the central committee appointed will be a useful means of liaison [*tramite*] in many agitations, and will become, if we are able to support it, the embryo of a future organisation of Factory Councils and Internal Commissions, which will become the counterpoise to the *C.G.L.*, in a changed political situation ... The national conference should be followed by local conferences in cities, provinces and regions. In this way the activity of our party groups will be revived and strengthened. Naturally there is the problem that we shall be accused of wanting to form another Union organisation. Hence it will be indispensable to:

[36] cf. Gramsci's letter to Leonetti 28 January 1924 (now in P. Togliatti, *La Formazione del Gruppo Dirigente del Partito Comunista Italiano* cit., pp. 182–3): the Italian emigrés in Moscow were divided into two camps on the '*Ordine Nuovo* question', and there were some bitter quarrels and even real fights on the issue.

[37] 'Il Nostro Indirizzo Sindacale', in *Lo Stato Operaio* 18 October 1923 (now in A. Gramsci, *La Costruzione del Partito Comunista* cit., pp. 3–7). For details of how 'Communist Factory groups' were set up in Turin early in 1924, see the party Circulars sent by the Prefect of Turin to the Ministry of the Interior 7 February 1924 (in *State Archives*, Ministero dell' Interno, Direzione Generale Pubblica Sicurezza, Affari Generali e Riservati, 1924, b. 101: 'Organizzazioni Sindacali comuniste').

[38] See the communiqué of the executive committee of the *P.C.d'I.*, in *Lo Stato Operaio* 3 April 1924.

(1) intensify at the same time our campaign for a return to the Confederal Unions [*C.G.L.*], (2) insist on the fact that there is no question of new Trade Unions, but of a factory movement, on the type of the Councils and of the Internal Commissions.[39]

In 1925 the Internal Commissions *were* suppressed, but Gramsci's search for mass organisations based on the work-place continued. The party's slogans were 'Committees of Agitation' in factories, 'Committees of Trade-Union Defence', above all 'Workers' and Peasants' Committees'. These last were supposed to emerge out of ad hoc strike committees, to operate outside the factories as well as inside them, to be elected by the whole working-class, and to organise popular resistance to Fascism.[40] They had no practical success – the Socialist paper *Avanti!* pointed out in October 1925 that not a single one had yet been set up – but the slogan was continued throughout 1925 and 1926, and they illustrate that Gramsci never abandoned his main strategy, of a 'united front from below', of mass revolutionary action radiating out from the place of work.[41]

Moreover, this period saw serious efforts to organise the Communist Party itself on the basis of the work-place. The policy of factory cells was of course laid down by the International, but Gramsci took it up enthusiastically in 1924–5, regarding it as the main method by which the Party could influence and keep contact with factory workers. In arguing the need for 'cells', he frequently referred back to *Ordine Nuovo* experiences in 1919–20, and did so even in the formal 'Theses for the Third Congress' of the *P.C.d'I.* in 1926.[42] The old arguments and antagonisms on this issue soon reappeared. Bordiga and the Left wing were reluctant to adopt a factory organisation for the party;[43] and their reluctance was shared by many ex-maximalists, especially the 'Third-Internationalists' who had joined the Communist Party in 1924. Togliatti reported in April 1925 that 'only the Turin party federation has yet succeeded in applying

[39] Gramsci to Togliatti, Scoccimarro and Leonetti 21 March 1924 (now in P. Togliatti, *La Formazione del Gruppo Dirigente del Partito Comunista Italiano* cit., pp. 243–4).
[40] 'Che Cosa Sono i Comitati Operai e Contadini?', unsigned article in *Lo Stato Operaio* 2 October 1924.
[41] See, for example, the 'Theses of Lyons', esp. Thesis no. 41 ('La Situazione Italiana e i Compiti del P.C.I.', now in A. Gramsci, *La Costruzione del Partito Comunista* cit., p. 511). cf. also Circular no. 15 to all Federations (April 1925), in *State Archives*, Min. Int., Dir. Gen. P.S., Aff. Gen. e Ris., 1925, b. 102, 'Partito Comunista: Affari Generali').
[42] Thesis no. 30, now in A. Gramsci, *La Costruzione del Partito Comunista* cit., p. 505.
[43] cf. Gramsci's report on the Lyons Congress, 'Cinque Anni di Vita del Partito', in *L'Unità* 24 February 1926 (now in A. Gramsci, *La Costruzione del Partito Comunista* cit., p. 105).

completely the International's and the party's directives on the setting up of cells'.[44] In 1924-5 Gramsci and Togliatti faced the problems of party organisation *as well as* those of mass factory organisations, and they attempted to tackle them both in much the same way, indeed in much the same way as in 1919–20. Gramsci wrote that: 'in fact the problem is still the same one: the problem of the relationships between the leadership and the masses in the party, and between the party and the classes of the working population.'[45] The new leaders may not have succeeded in setting up as many factory cells as they hoped, but they did win over the majority of the party (90.8 *per cent.*) to their views by the time of the Third Congress (January 1926),[46] and they did commit the Communist Party to far less sectarian policies than it had pursued in the past.

Gramsci's educational aims were, as always, an important part of his policy. He stressed that the workers needed to absorb and 'dominate' bourgeois culture, if they were to have the knowledge and self-confidence needed to run society, or if they were ever to replace one vision of the world by another. Furthermore, the working class could not take over unless it produced its own technicians, experts, managers and leaders.[47] Communists must be serious, skilled, disciplined, responsible men, men who could inspire confidence in their ability to manage the economy successfully.[48] Gramsci remained, therefore, attached to 'productivism', to the sober industrial virtues of punctuality and precision; the 'greatest satisfaction a revolutionary could experience' was to visit the Giachero typewriter factory in Turin, run by the workers.[49]

In short, the party's duty was to educate and train future working-class leaders, and in 1925 Gramsci embarked on a series of correspondence courses named 'party schools'. The initiative had little success, because the

[44] 'L'Organizzazione Comunista', in *Ordine Nuovo* 1 April 1925 (now in P. Togliatti, *Opere*, vol. i, Riuniti, Rome 1967, p. 635).

[45] Gramsci to Leonetti 28 January 1924 (now in P. Togliatti, *La Formazione del Gruppo Dirigente del Partito Comunista Italiano* cit., p. 183). He also proclaimed that 'our present programme must reproduce, in the situation that exists in Italy today, the position assumed in 1919–20' ('Il Programma dell' Ordine Nuovo', in *Ordine Nuovo* 1–15 April 1924, now in A. Gramsci, *La Costruzione del Partito Comunista* cit., p. 21).

[46] For the *P.C.d'I*.'s Third Congress, at Lyons in France, see P. Spriano, *Storia del Partito Comunista Italiano* cit., vol. i, pp. 498–513. The text of the discussions in the 'Political Commission' was published in *Critica Marxista*, anno 1, nos. 5–6 (September–December 1963), pp. 302–26.

[47] 'Cinque Anni di Vita del Partito', in *L'Unità* 24 February 1926 (now in A. Gramsci, *La Costruzione del Partito Comunista* cit., p. 96).

[48] 'Il Programma dell' Ordine Nuovo', in *Ordine Nuovo* 1–15 April 1924 (now in A. Gramsci, *La Costruzione del Partito Comunista* cit., p. 24).

[49] 'Gli Operai alla Direzione delle Industrie', in *L'Unità* 18 September 1926 (now in A. Gramsci, *La Costruzione del Partito Comunista* cit., pp. 328–30).

police could easily intercept postal deliveries of the teaching material –
receiving a correspondence course was one of the easiest ways for a
Communist to reveal his political sympathies.[50] Gramsci's journalistic
activity was probably more influential in training and educating the
party's key organisers. He was mainly involved with the daily newspaper
L'Unità. Founded in February 1924, it reached a circulation of 50,000 in
June; by April 1925 this had declined to 23,000, but that was still not a bad
figure in the political circumstances.[51] In addition, the party weekly
Lo Stato Operaio sold about 10,000 copies in the autumn of 1924;[52] and a
fortnightly 'cultural review', named the *Ordine Nuovo*, appeared irregu-
larly between March 1924 and April 1925, with a circulation of around
5,000.[53] These journals were of a high standard, as the original *Ordine
Nuovo* had been; and much of the party's work in 1924–6 was devoted to
keeping them coming out.

Thus Gramsci as party leader in 1924–6 was able to impose on the
Italian Communist Party many of the ideas and methods familiar from
the earlier movement. Although he certainly made errors of judgement,
and although the policies he advocated certainly had their weaknesses, his
achievements were real too. He educated a party. He taught it to work in
the factories, to organise mass activity where possible, to encourage
initiatives by local leaders, to prize cultural and scientific knowledge. He
was an excellent educator, journalist, critic, moralist, inspirer – and, after
his arrest in November 1926, martyr.

This is not the place for an analysis of his famous Prison Notebooks,[54]

[50] cf. the complaint of 'Bendi' in his Circular to provincial federations of the
P.C.d'I. 17 August 1925: 'The first experiment in distributing the hand-outs has
completely failed, despite the enormous expenses we have incurred, because the
Fascist government does not permit any kind of legality to our initiative.' (in *State
Archives*, Min. Int., Dir. Gen. P.S., Aff. Gen. e Ris., 1925, b. 104, 'Partito Comunista:
Arezzo').

[51] P. Spriano, *Storia del Partito Comunista Italiano* cit., vol. i, p. 392; and *State
Archives* cit., 1925, b. 102, 'Partito Comunista: Affari Generali' (party circular of
2 April 1925). P. Spriano (*op. cit.*, p. 451) gives a circulation of 35,000 in April 1925,
but this is contradicted by the party circular above.

[52] *Lo Stato Operaio* 30 October 1924; P. Spriano, *Storia del Partito Comunista Italiano*
cit., vol. i, p. 414.

[53] There were eight issues in all. The circulation figures are taken from P. Spriano,
Storia del Partito Comunista Italiano cit., vol. i, p. 414. Gramsci claimed in August 1925
that it had a circulation of 8–10,000 ('In Italia', in *Correspondance Internationale*
7 August 1925, now in A. Gramsci, *La Costruzione del Partito Comunista* cit., p. 475).

[54] A. Gramsci, *Quaderni del Carcere* (6 vols, Einaudi, Turin 1948–51; critical edition
in 4 vols, edited by V. Gerratana, Einaudi, Turin 1975). In English, *Selections from the
Prison Notebooks*, edited by Q. Hoare and G. Nowell-Smith (Lawrence and Wishart,
London 1971); *The Modern Prince*, edited by L. Marks (Lawrence and Wishart,
London 1957). For a brief outline of my views, see my review of the 1971 English
edition, in *Political Studies*, vol. xx (December 1972), pp. 492–6.

but clearly many of their main themes refer back to *Ordine Nuovo* experience. In prison, Gramsci argued that bourgeois rule depended ultimately on maintaining bourgeois cultural 'hegemony', i.e. the received ideas of a self-confident bourgeoisie, transmitted via control of the media, education, advertising, the Churches and so forth. Gramsci had always been convinced of this – hence his constant interest in 'Communist education' and in the training of working-class 'organic intellectuals'. Moreover, Gramsci continued to believe that cultural propaganda was not enough by itself. If 'bourgeois hegemony' were to be overcome, workers would have to develop their own 'authentic' ideas, in line with their own social experience, and this could only be done through 'practical political activity'.[55] Hence new institutions, permitting mass participation in politics, were necessary, and these institutions would, of course, also help to train the next generations of working-class 'intellectuals'. Above all, Gramsci in prison thought constantly about the 'Revolution that Failed' in 1919–20 (and about other revolutions that failed in sixteenth- and nineteenth-century Italy).[56] His analysis of why revolutions fail is a major theme of the Prison Notebooks, and provided the stimulus for his views on the nature of 'hegemony', of political organisations and parties, and of intellectuals. Much of Gramsci's lasting contribution to European social thought emerged from a critical rethinking of his own past.

After the Second World War Gramsci's Prison Notebooks and Letters were published,[57] and proved to be the best 'party school' the Italian Communist Party ever organised. Togliatti used Gramsci's writings to continue the work of 'Communist education', and opened up the Italian party to cultural and historical debate in a way that was virtually unique. It is ironic that Togliatti did this at the same time as he renounced Gramsci's 'revolutionary' perspective, and at the same time as he pursued a respectable 'anti-Fascist' line that typified the 'third weakness' discussed earlier in this Conclusion. The result is that the 'official', 'national' Italian Communist Party has an ambiguous ideological legacy. It proclaims the 'anti-Fascist' values of Western democracy, and looks back to the Resis-

[55] cf. Gramsci's essay on 'The Connection between Science, Religion and Common Sense' (in A. Gramsci, *Selections from the Prison Notebooks* cit., pp. 326–43).

[56] cf. Paolo Spriano's comments at the Paris conference on Gramsci, reported in *L'Unità* 21 June 1975.

[57] For the Notebooks, see note 54 above. His Letters were first published in 1947 (A. Gramsci, *Lettere dal Carcere*, Einaudi, Turin 1947); and a further edition, with 119 more letters, was edited by Sergio Caprioglio and published by Einaudi in 1965. Further prison letters appear in the Italian Communist Press from time to time, especially just before elections. For a selection of the Letters in English, see A. Gramsci *Letters from Prison*, edited by Lynne Lawner (Jonathan Cape, London 1975).

tance in 1943–5 as to a national liberation struggle; but it also has, as part of its ideological inheritance, the 'unofficial', factory-based, Turin-centred *Ordine Nuovo* movement. The *Ordine Nuovo* has often been an embarrassment, but it is part of the legacy, and it cannot be renounced.

Postscript

IN the Introduction to this book, I tried to show that its main themes were still relevant today; and in the Conclusion, I briefly discussed the influence of Gramsci and the *Ordine Nuovo* upon the Italian Communist Party. In this Postscript, I want to emphasise that the issues raised in this book have been graphically illustrated in two subsequent periods of Italian history – the period of 'Resistance and Reconstruction', from 1943 to (roughly) 1949; and the period of 'Militancy and Absorption', from 1968 to (perhaps) 1972.

The period from 1943 to 1949 is an interesting study in contrasts.[1] During the Resistance (1943–5), the aim of anti-Fascist workers and of the Communist Party in Northern Italy was to minimise, even sabotage, production, at least whenever this could be done with any safety. At Fiat and Spa, about 10,000 vehicles were made in 1944, about 60 *per cent.* of the average production in 1941–3; by the end of 1944 only 11 lorries a day were being built at the main Fiat works at Mirafiori.[2] Clandestine organisations arose – Committees of National Liberation in the factories and in the region; Trade Union Factory Committees, including technicians and clerical staff; and, probably most important, factory Committees of Agitation, representing workers only.[3] These organisations were

---

[1] The literature on this period is extensive. I have found the following most useful: P. Spriano, *Storia del Partito Comunista Italiano*, vols iv and v (Einaudi, Turin 1973 and 1975); G. Bertolo et al., *Operai e Contadini nella Crisi Italiana 1943–4* (Feltrinelli, Milan 1974); G. Amendola, *Lettere a Milano* (Feltrinelli, Milan 1973); R. Luraghi, *Il Movimento Operaio Torinese durante la Resistenza* (Einaudi, Turin 1958); L. Valiani, G. Bianchi and E. Ragionieri, *Azionisti, Cattolici e Comunisti nella Resistenza* (Angeli, Milan 1971); and L. Lanzardo, *Classe Operaia e Partito Comunista alla Fiat* (Einaudi, Turin 1971).

[2] A. Gibelli, in G. Bertolo (ed.), *Operai e Contadini nella Crisi Italiana* cit., p. 90; V. Castronovo, *Giovanni Agnelli* (U.T.E.T., Turin 1971), p. 657; R. Luraghi, *Il Movimento Operaio Torinese durante la Resistenza* cit., p. 256.

[3] cf. R. Luraghi, *Il Movimento Operaio Torinese durante la Resistenza* cit., pp. 132–7, 214–20, 311. The Internal Commissions had been officially restored in August 1943, and also continued to exist.

as 'militant' as possible. They existed in order to foment strikes and go-slows; and in this period 'productivism' was forgotten, except inasmuch as workers prevented machinery or equipment being transported to Germany, or destroyed altogether near the end of the war. The Communist Party supported and in some cases organised the disruption, which was quite compatible with its general 'anti-Fascist', 'national-democratic' policy, and which was often even compatible with good relations between workers and management. This 'militancy' certainly benefited the party, and membership grew rapidly in the Northern factories. There were perhaps a thousand Communists in Turin province in March 1943, and only eighty at the main Fiat works, Mirafiori;[4] by January 1945 there were at least twelve times as many, and the expansion had been almost entirely among the urban factory workers, as Giorgio Amendola complained.[5]

Even so, during the Resistance many members were discontented with the Communist Party's policy – not, of course, with industrial sabotage, but with being part of an anti-Fascist front. In much of Italy the party's intermediate organisers – the 'cadres' – were the same men as in 1925–6, but now aged over forty, and with twenty years of underground activity behind them.[6] As early as January 1944 – *before* the famous *svolta* of Salerno in March, when Togliatti pledged the party's willingness to co-operate with the king's government – the party secretary in Turin reported that 'the line of the national front first, that of the Liberation Committee and of the patriotic war later, are endured rather than accepted'.[7] In fact, the Turin party split in June 1944, and an organised workers' movement known as the 'Red Star', with over 2,000 members, agitated against the employers and in favour of revolution after the war. However, the party's 'anti-Fascist' policy came to be accepted, somewhat grudgingly, but only provided it was going to lead to radical changes later. Most party members attributed greater importance to the clandestine inter-party coalitions, the Committees of National Liberation

---

[4] G. Vaccarino, *Problemi della Resistenza Italiana* (S.T.E.M., Modena 1966), pp. 157–8; E. Ragionieri, in L. Valiani, G. Bianchi and E. Ragionieri, *Azionisti, Cattolici e Comunisti nella Resistenza* cit., p. 314 (for the situation by September 1943 see p. 338).

[5] G. Amendola, *Lettere a Milano* cit., pp. 614–5. R. Luraghi, *Il Movimento Operaio Torinese durante la Resistenza* cit., p. 38, gives 12,000 party members in Turin by January 1945; Aldo Agosti, in *I Comunisti a Torino* (Riuniti, Rome 1974), p. 128, quotes a report by Secchia giving 14,600 members of the Turin provincial federation at that time.

[6] E. Ragionieri, in *Azionisti, Cattolici e Comunisti nella Resistenza* cit., pp. 352–4 (quoting a Slovene Communist's report in March 1944).

[7] A. Agosti, in *I Comunisti a Torino* cit., p. 123.

(*C.L.N.*s), rather than to the official inter-party coalition government, although it can reasonably be argued that the *C.L.N.*s were only as influential as they were because the parties in them were also part of the 'national' government; and even the *C.L.N.*s were often accused of 'inter-classism'.

After the war, the Communist Party's balancing act became a great deal more difficult. Clearly the partisans who had fought in the Resistance, and the Northern party organisations in the factories, had to be rewarded for their success. The Communist Party in Northern Italy remained essentially one of factory workers: at the Mirafiori works of Fiat, there were 7,650 party members at the end of 1945, out of a total labour force of 16,000, and the picture was similar in other large factories both in Turin and Milan.[8] Many Communists were ex-partisans, trained in guerilla warfare, 'militant' in every sense, and very confident that they could create a new society. Moreover, the *C.L.N.*s continued to exist, and had to be supported for a time, since many leading Socialists were committed to them as the basis for a more democratic, 'participatory' regime for the post-war period; and the factory *C.L.N.*s were often responsible for running factories just after the war. Thus the Northern, factory-based Communist Party had to remain committed to some kind of radical change. On the other hand, from a 'national' perspective things looked very different. The party was in the government coalition in Rome until May 1947; Togliatti was Minister of Justice; the policy was to work with other anti-Fascist groups for a more democratic State. The party campaigned for the abolition of the monarchy, and regarded the victory on this issue at the referendum of June 1946 as a major blow for a new kind of State. Great emphasis was also laid on the activities of the Constituent Assembly in 1946–7, and on the drafting of a new Constitution. A Parliamentary regime with universal suffrage and proportional representation, guarantees of civil liberties, freedom for Trade Unions – all this was an acceptable, respectable alternative to the Northern radical demands. These political achievements were real enough in themselves, but in Northern eyes they also ensured the 'continuity' of the State machinery. Henceforth the Communist Party was to be a pillar of Republican legality; but Republican legality was not what many Northern workers wanted.

The party leadership's difficulties were increased by the national need for 'productivism', now called 'Reconstruction'. The shattered economy of industrial Italy had to be rebuilt as quickly as possible, and the Communists were ready to play their part. Battista Santhià, one of the 'Commis-

[8] L. Lanzardo, *Classe Operaia e Partito Comunista alla Fiat* cit., p. 45.

sars' who managed Fiat just after the war, urged party workers at Fiat in December 1945: 'every one of us must feel the responsibility that comes from belonging to the Party that is in the vanguard of the healthy forces of the country, and which has assumed the task of directing the battle for reconstruction . . . we as a Party are the mainstay of reconstruction . . . individuals who do not set a good example at work are not Communists.'[9] 'Reconstruction' had its unpleasant aspects. The party had to preach hard work for low pay, it had to persuade workers to accept piece-rates, and it even had to soft-pedal on 'purges' of indispensable engineers and technicians suspected of collaboration with the Nazis.[10] In practice, it proved difficult to control and discipline the Northern workers and the Northern party; and there were plenty of strikes, violent clashes, occupations and even the occasional partisan band operating in these years.

The best strategy for the party leadership was, as ever, to insist on economic concessions – inflation-proofed wages, no dismissals – and to *institutionalise* factory militancy. This could be done within the official 'unitary' (i.e. inter-party, and largely party-controlled) Trade Union structure, and above all within workers', or joint management-workers', institutions within the factories themselves. There were many such bodies: the *C.L.N.*s in the immediate post-war period, and joint Management Councils (*Consigli di Gestione*) by early 1946, both with some management responsibilities; and Internal Commissions, elected by shop-floor workers, which represented workers' grievances to management. The Communists supported, and often dominated, the consultative Management Councils, on which employers also sat,[11] and relied on them to harness and control worker militancy. The establishment of joint Management Councils made it easier to accept the return of former employers and managers, and at Fiat these two aspects of 'Reconstruction' occurred together, in February 1946.

The Management Councils did prove useful in 'Reconstruction', but as time went on they also aroused employer opposition. As Valerio Castronovo has remarked, the functions of the Management Councils were reminiscent of those laid down for factory bodies in Giolitti's 'control bill' in 1920–1,[12] and they sparked off much the same sort of

[9] L. Lanzardo, *Classe Operaia e Partito Comunista alla Fiat* cit., pp. 650–1.

[10] L. Lanzardo, *Classe Operaia e Partito Comunista alla Fiat* cit., p. 117.

[11] According to Horowitz, there were about 500 Management Councils in 1946 (D. L. Horowitz, *The Italian Labor Movement*, Harvard U.P. 1963, p. 252). The Minister of Industry claimed there were 700, and the Confederation of Industry found 103 firms, and 271 factories, with Management Councils in March 1947 (M. Neufeld, *Italy: School for Awakening Countries*, Cornell U.P. 1961, p. 465).

[12] V. Castronovo, *Giovanni Agnelli* cit., p. 697.

response. In 1946-7, as in 1920-1, industrialists refused to accept that the new institutions might have any real powers, that the worker might be a 'producer', or that the Communist Party might make a valuable contribution in disciplining labour. The rows over the Management Councils' role were bitter and public; and, as in 1921, in the end the employers won. By 1949 the Management Councils had disappeared. Deflation and unemployment, together with the exclusion of the Communist Party from government and political discrimination against shop-floor Communists, showed that workers' cooperation was unnecessary. There were other, more robust, ways of ensuring worker discipline. Naturally, too, the Communist Party in opposition had less interest in 'Reconstruction'. It was tempted instead to mobilise popular discontent, and to rely on the more obvious institutions for workers' 'militancy', the Trade Unions.[13] There was, therefore, practically no organised opposition when the Management Councils were finally dissolved;[14] and although the Internal Commissions remained in being, they were weak bodies that found it difficult even to handle grievances, because of workers' fear of dismissals.

Thus the Italian Communist Party's vocation as a national, respectable, 'productivist' party, able to discipline and channel working-class energies, was postponed for some years. It has revived more recently, because of the complex economic and political crisis that Italy has experienced since the end of the post-war 'economic miracle'. During the 1960s, the pressure built up in the Northern factories. Basic wages were low by Western European standards, and productivity was fairly high. The official Trade Union movements were split on political lines into three Confederations: Communist-Socialist, Christian Democrat, and Social-Democrat-Socialist. They were all weak organisations – it has been estimated that only 26 per cent. of Italian metal-workers belonged to any Union in 1968[15] – they were all virtually absent from the shop-floor, and they were all linked closely to their respective political parties. Moreover, a new unskilled working class had entered the factories. One survey of the automobile industry found that in 1951 unskilled workers formed 35.2 per cent. of the labour force; by 1961 they had risen to 47.9 per cent., and by 1968 to 62.1 per cent.[16] Changes in technology and in work

[13] The most detailed, if somewhat Manichaean, account of these years at Fiat is in L. Lanzardo, *Classe Operaia e Partito Comunista alla Fiat* cit., esp. pp. 459–540.
[14] E. Sulotto, in *I Comunisti a Torino* cit., p. 181.
[15] Bianca Becalli, 'Scioperi e Organizzazione Sindacale: Milano 1950–70', in *Rassegna Italiana di Sociologia*, anno XII (January–March 1971), p. 100.
[16] A. Illuminati, *Lavoro e Rivoluzione* (Mazzotta, Milan 1974), p. 137 (quoting a study by Bianchi and D'Ambrosio).

organisation had reduced the need for skilled men, and had made traditional piece-rate systems meaningless.[17] The new workers came partly from an influx of immigrants, but there was also a 'downgrading' of semi-skilled or even skilled men as they moved from smaller workshops into the big factories, and a general crisis of the old training and apprenticeship system and of the old classification of skills. By the late 1960s the 'ideal' car worker was young, adaptable, agile and tireless – but such workers were more resentful of industrial discipline than their older counterparts, and had far less of a 'Trade Union consciousness'.[18] The Unions failed to adapt to the new structure of the Northern working class, and failed to negotiate effectively on wages, training, hours, job security or intensity of work.

Moreover, this was a period of ineffective 'Centre-Left' (Christian Democrat and Socialist) coalition governments, pledged to social reforms, but impotent in practice to carry them through. In the crowded Northern cities housing, public transport, health services and education all suffered the strains of coping with immigrants whose rising expectations were soon frustrated, just when many local skilled workers were becoming downwardly mobile. No doubt there were other factors at work too. The Vietnam War discredited the liberal ideals of the West. 'Spontaneous' student movements in Italy, and the Events of May 1968 in France, showed what could be achieved by unofficial agitation, and taught a *style* of militant protest – a refusal of bureaucratic organisation and representative government, a reliance on mass meetings and 'assemblies', an insistence on self-management and 'participation' – that had a profound, perhaps even briefly 'hegemonic', impact on Italian labour.

The results were spectacular. In 1968–9 came a series of wildcat stoppages, factory occupations and street demonstrations. It seems that older skilled workers, often with a Resistance past, took the first steps in these agitations – they had a tradition of militancy, and some idea of what to do for greatest effect; but the newer generations soon joined in.[19] Factory and workshop meetings became frequent and, even more significantly, 'delegates' representing 'homogeneous work-groups' were elected on the shop floor. The 'delegates' were elected by all the workers in the work-group, and could be 'revoked' at will by their electors. The 'assemblies of delegates' soon became known as 'Factory Councils', and

[17] cf. B. Trentin, 'Tendenze Attuali della Lotta di Classe e Problemi del Movimento Sindacale di fronte agli Sviluppi Recenti del Capitalismo Europeo', in Istituto Gramsci, *Tendenze del Capitalismo Europeo* (Riuniti, Rome 1966), pp. 162–205.

[18] A. Illuminati, *Lavoro e Rivoluzione* cit., p. 140.

[19] A. Pizzorno, 'Quadro Politico delle Lotte Operaie in Italia', in *Quaderni di Rassegna Sindacale* n. 51 (November–December 1974), p. 105.

replaced the old Internal Commissions. They demanded complete workers' control over the speed, conditions and organisation of labour, abolition or mitigation of the hierarchy of skills in the factory, and, as a corollary, equal pay rises for all. Thus the emphasis was on unofficial factory agitations of a markedly 'egalitarian' kind, often ignoring the traditional (but now outdated) Union hierarchy of skills. These agitations were associated with an 'anti-productivist' ideology, with a refusal of the 'pseudo-rationality' of the industrial system, and with a passionate rejection of the Italian Communist Party's compromises with the boss class.[20] The period 1968–72 was, therefore, a very difficult time for the Communist-led Unions in the C.G.I.L. (Italian General Confederation of Labour), and for the Communist Party itself. The party was faced with serious political activity on its Left flank, even in vital sources of strength like the Northern factories.[21] It seemed unable to attract the intellectual young, or even to retain some of the intellectual middle-aged (e.g. the 'Manifesto group', including five deputies, expelled from the party in 1969).

The Communist Unions, and the party, responded to this threat in the classic manner. Firstly, they secured major rises in the basic wage, upwards of 15 per cent.;[22] and secondly, they again 'institutionalised' shop-floor militancy. The Internal Commissions were soon abandoned. In the less militant factories, trouble was headed off. The Unions took the initiative in calling for 'delegates' to be elected, and most of the 'delegates' were Trade Union members. Where workers were more militant, as at Fiat or Pirelli, the same effect was achieved by other means. The national wage agreements were followed in 1970 by a series of factory-level negotiations on incentives, bonuses, conditions and the like. These negotiations were carried out by the 'delegates' and the Factory Council. They certainly led to more egalitarian settlements, and often to the end of traditional piece-

---

[20] On the events of these years, see A. Pizzorno (ed.), *Lotte Operaie e Sindacati in Italia*, vols i–v (Il Mulino, Bologna 1974–5); vol. vi, which will provide a summary and analysis of the movement, had not yet appeared at the time of going to press. Other useful works include G. Giugni, *Il Sindacato fra Contratti e Riforme 1969–73* (De Donato, Bari 1973); A. Illuminati, *Lavoro e Rivoluzione* (Mazzotta, Milan 1974); G. Salvarani and A. Bonifazi, *Le Nuove Strutture del Sindacato* (Angeli, Milan 1973); T. Treu, *Sindacato e Rappresentanza Aziendale* (Il Mulino, Bologna 1971); and L. Albanese, F. Liuzzi and A. Perella, *I Consigli di Fabbrica* (Riuniti, Rome 1973). There are a number of useful articles in *Sociologie du Travail*, vol. xiii (1971), no. 2, pp. 115–90.

[21] cf. Martin Clark and R. E. M. Irving, 'The Italian Political Crisis and the General Election of May 1972', in *Parliamentary Affairs*, vol. xxv (Summer 1972), p. 212.

[22] O.E.C.D. Annual Report, *Italy* (1971), p. 9, reports 17 per cent. wage rises in 1970.

12

work payments.[23] But, of course, the local Trade Union branches often had to be called in, if only to coordinate the campaigns of various factories, and as time went on and the issues became more and more negotiable (and negotiated), the Factory Councils and the local Trade Union branches came to collaborate more and more.[24]

Despite the talk of 'egalitarianism', Trade Unions and employers insisted that there had to be *some* relationship between productivity and wages. In June 1970 *F.I.O.M.* leaders proclaimed that 'the objective divisions which the organisation of work involves are very clear in the minds of the workers'.[25] In practice, the factory negotiations normally led to job-rotation or job-enrichment schemes, or to new detailed definitions of 'skills' (e.g. the ability to perform a dozen jobs on the assembly line), or even to agreement that the *work-group* should have greater responsibilities and initiative (collective piece-rates, and more 'self-management'). These schemes were attractive to workers, especially as inflation was eating away the value of the basic 'egalitarian' wage-increases; and they were accepted by the more enlightened employers as likely to improve morale, discipline and production.

Thus the Unions, who were far too weak to beat the shop-floor militants, succeeded in joining them. They 'institutionalised' militancy via productivity schemes. Their success was perfectly natural – after all, there is something inherently contradictory in demanding, as the Leftist militants did, both decentralised negotiations and complete egalitarianism. By December 1970 the Communist-led *C.G.I.L.* felt strong enough to proclaim that the Factory Council was the 'basic structure' of a (future) united Trade Union. In July 1972, when the three leading Union confederations signed a 'pact of federation', as a step on the road towards Trade Union unity, they defined the Factory Council as the 'primary Trade Union body, with powers of negotiation at the work-place'.[26] The 'delegates' have become the base of the Unions. They discuss speed of work, conditions, skills, and the application of national agreements; they inform the local Trade Union branches, and bring the Unions and the workers closer together. A survey of Milan industry in 1974 found that only 8.9 *per cent.* of the 'delegates' were not Trade Unionists, and even

[23] A. Illuminati, *Lavoro e Rivoluzione* cit., p. 131, gives the index for the pay of a skilled worker (unskilled worker= 100): in 1968, 134.0; in 1971, 119.5. These figures are for all manufacturing industry.

[24] 86 *per cent.* of factory-level agreements in 1969, and 79 *per cent.* in 1970, were signed by the provincial Trade Union branch, 'covering for' the Factory Council; 8 *per cent.* and 13 *per cent.* were signed by the Factory Council jointly with the local Trade Union (A. Illuminati, *Lavoro e Rivoluzione* cit., p. 177).

[25] A. Illuminati, *Lavoro e Rivoluzione* cit., pp. 152–3.

[26] *Rassegna Sindacale* 30 July 1972.

these were balanced by co-opted members and by 'Trade Union workshop representatives', appointed by the local Unions, who formed 7.1 per cent. of the total number of 'delegates'.[27] 'The [Factory] Council is, in short, the instrument that has institutionalised the presence of the Trade Union in the work-place.'[28] It is all highly reminiscent of the 'Tasca scheme' of 1920, although of course the rhetorical references today are to Gramsci rather than to Tasca. The 'Statute of the Workers' ratified many of these developments, and guaranteed such rights as that of assembly within the factory and paid leave for 'delegates'.[29]

After 1971 attention focused on other aspects of 'institutionalisation'. The Unions claimed that many of the issues that concerned them most – pensions, housing, public transport, structural unemployment, investments – were political questions and could only be resolved nationally, by Parliament or perhaps by some system of national planning. This perspective implies that the Unions should retain their links with political parties (links which are, after all, to be found in other countries, including the U.S.A. and Great Britain), and should engage in constant negotiations with the government. Obviously there are difficulties in this strategy, not the least being that when the political parties are competing, the drive for 'Trade Union unity' among the Communist, Christian Democrat and Socialist Unions is weakened. In practice the Unions had little success in the early 1970s. The main achievements of these years were the abolition of regional wage-zones (in 1969), and increased old age pensions; but in most areas of social policy the political system proved recalcitrant. The reasons were complex, but among them were a general swing to the right in national politics in 1971–2, and a revival of neo-Fascist activity. In the 1972 General Election the neo-Fascist Italian Social Movement gained a million votes, and doubled its number of deputies.[30] Again, the parallel with events fifty years earlier is striking.

This time, however, the Fascist advance was itself 'absorbed', especially by the 'Centre-Right' government of Giulio Andreotti in 1972–3. The Trade Unions have survived as 'responsible' institutions, with their own unchallenged spheres of influence, and are increasingly consulted and

[27] Anna Celadin, 'Delegati e Consigli: une rilevazione a Milano', in *Quaderni di Rassegna Sindacale* n. 49 (July–August 1974), p. 177. 57.6 *per cent.* of the 'delegates' belonged to *C.G.I.L.* Unions, 27.1 *per cent.* to *C.I.S.L.* (Christian Democrat) Unions, and 11.5 *per cent.* to *U.I.L.* (Social-Democrat or Socialist) organisations.

[28] L. Albanese, F. Liuzzi and A. Perella, *I Consigli di Fabbrica* cit., p. 83.

[29] Law of 20 May 1970 n. 300, in *Gazzetta Ufficiale* 27 May 1970, esp. Articles 19–27.

[30] The 'National Right' (neo-Fascists and Monarchists) secured 8.7 *per cent.* of the vote at the 1972 General Election, compared with the 1968 figures of 4.5 *per cent.* for the neo-Fascists, and 1.3 *per cent.* for the Monarchists.

brought into a range of discussions at national, regional and local level. They have many more members than before 1968 – the *C.G.I.L.* claims a 55.4 *per cent.* increase[31] – and above all many more *active* members at factory and local level. However, they have not so far secured major social reforms, nor have they succeeded in uniting, nor – above all – have they broken their links with the various political parties. Trade Union unity ultimately depends on a lasting agreement among the political parties; and like their respective parties, the Communist and Christian Democrat-led Trade Unions are at present betrothed, but not married. They have an uneasy, semi-clandestine and unfruitful relationship, and still await the blessing of Mother Church.

Perhaps the rites will soon be solemnised; or perhaps the whole affair may yet be called off. In the past few years the Communist Party and the Communist-led Unions have retained the adherence of the Northern workers;[32] they have cultivated their reputation for sound administration; they have mobilised opinion against the Fascist threat, and indeed sometimes used it to demonstrate their own revolutionary credentials to sceptical Leftists. Mindful of Chile, they have attempted to conciliate businessmen and bishops, judges and generals. In short, they have acted respectably, and have become, in the Italian jargon, 'co-involved' and 'co-responsibilised' – *ma non troppo*. In the 1976 Parliamentary elections, the Communist share of the vote rose from 27.1 *per cent.* (in 1972) to 34.4 *per cent.*; their claim that no stable government is possible without them became even more credible. If the Communists do come to share power, they will do so partly because in 1968–72 they defeated 'anti-productivism' in the factories, and because they absorbed the Factory Councils into the official Trade Union structure. Such is the ambiguous legacy of Gramsci's Revolution.

[31] From 2,461,297 members in 1968 to 3,827,175 in 1974 (*Rassegna Sindacale* 23 February 1975).
[32] The Communist Party's vote rose in the Northern cities in 1972 – in Milan by 3.2 *per cent.*, and in Genoa by 3.1 *per cent.*

SELECT BIBLIOGRAPHY

I have kept this bibliography to a bare minimum. I hope readers will not be inconvenienced. They should find adequate bibliographical information in the footnotes: full details on each work appear on the first occasion in each chapter that it is cited. There is an excellent and up to date bibliography on this period of Italian history, listing about 500 titles, in A. Lyttelton, *The Seizure of Power* (Weidenfeld & Nicolson, London 1973), pp. 515–26. A complete bibliography of works on Gramsci (up to 1967) was compiled by Elsa Fubini, in P. Rossi (ed.), *Gramsci e la Cultura Contemporanea*, vol. ii (Riuniti, Rome 1970), pp. 477–544. The most complete bibliography of works on Italian labour history is to be found in Ente per la Storia del Socialismo e del Movimento Operaio Italiano (Opera G. E. Modigliani), *Bibliografia del Socialismo e del Movimento Operaio Italiano* (Rome and Turin 1956–68): vol. i, Periodicals, in 2 Parts; vol. ii, Books and Pamphlets, in 4 Parts.

Archive Sources

The most frequently consulted primary sources have been in the Italian State Archives (Archivio Centrale dello Stato) in Rome. The files of the Ministry of the Interior have been the most useful, especially the various series of the Direzione Generale Pubblica Sicurezza, Divisione Affari Generali e Riservati, which consist mainly of Prefects' reports from the provinces and reports from police informers within the Trade Unions and the Socialist Party. I should mention also the Serrati documents in the Partito Nazionale Fascista, Mostra della Rivoluzione Fascista files (b. 139–142). Full details of the other files consulted in the State Archives are given in the footnotes.

Other important archival sources used are the Archive of the Communist Party, at the Gramsci Institute in Rome; the Tasca and Rigola archives, at the Istituto Giangiacomo Feltrinelli in Milan; and the Correspondence of Piero Gobetti, at the Gobetti Centre in Turin.

Newspapers and Periodicals

A full list of Italian labour periodicals for the 1892–1939 period is given in Ente per la Storia del Socialismo e del Movimento Operaio Italiano (Opera G. E. Modigliani), *Bibliografia del Socialismo e del Movimento Operaio Italiano* (Rome and Turin 1956), vol. i, tomo 2, pp. 1004–48 and pp. 1065–99. These journals may normally be consulted at the National Library in Florence, although some were damaged irreparably by the 1966 floods. There are excellent libraries containing this material at the Biblioteca Civile of Turin (which has all the journals published in the city), at the Istituto Giangiacomo Feltrinelli in Milan, and at the Istituto Nazionale per la Storia del Movimento di Liberazione in Italia, in Milan.

Published Primary Sources

A. Gramsci *Scritti Giovanili (1914–18)*. Einaudi, Turin 1958.

—— *L'Ordine Nuovo (1919–20)*. Einaudi, Turin 1955.

—— *Sotto la Mole (1916–20)*. Einaudi, Turin 1960.

—— *Scritti (1915–21)*. Quaderni di 'Il Corpo', Milan 1968.

—— *Per la Verità (1913–26)*. Riuniti, Rome 1974.

—— *Socialismo e Fascismo (1921–22)*. Einaudi, Turin 1966.

—— *La Costruzione del Partito Comunista (1923–26)*. Einaudi, Turin 1971.

—— *Quaderni del Carcere*. 6 vols. Einaudi, Turin 1948–51.

—— *Quaderni del Carcere* (Critical Edition by V. Gerratana). 4 vols. Einaudi, Turin 1975.

—— *Lettere dal Carcere*. Einaudi, Turin 1947.

—— *Lettere dal Carcere* (extended edition by S. Caprioglio and Elsa Fubini). Einaudi, Turin 1965.

—— *2000 Pagine di Gramsci* (edited by G. Ferrata and N. Gallò). 2 vols. Il Saggiatore, Milan 1964.

—— English translations from the *Quaderni del Carcere* are in: *Selections from the Prison Notebooks* (translated and edited by Q. Hoare and G. Nowell Smith). Lawrence and Wishart, London 1971; and also in *The Modern Prince* (translated by Louis Marks). Lawrence and Wishart, London 1957.

—— An English translation from the *Lettere dal Carcere* is in: *Letters from Prison* (translated by Lynne Lawner). Jonathan Cape, London 1975.

G. Berti (ed.) *Annali dell' Istituto Giangiacomo Feltrinelli* a. VIII (1966), pp. 243–1078, publishes many documents from the Tasca archives, but unfortunately the selection starts only in 1926.

G. Bosio *La Grande Paura* (debates of *C.G.L.* and *P.S.I.* leaders during the Occupation of the Factories in September 1920). Samonà and Savelli, Rome 1970.

C.G.L. Resoconto Stenografico del X Congresso della Resistenza, V della *C.G.L.* (Livorno 1921). Co-operativa Grafica, Milan 1921.

L. Marchetti (ed.) *La C.G.L. negli Atti, nei Documenti, nei Congressi (1906–26)*. Ed. Avanti!, Milan 1962.

P.S.I. Resoconto Stenografico del XVI Congresso del *P.S.I.* (Bologna 1919). Ed. Avanti!, Milan 1920.

—— Resoconto Stenografico del XVII Congresso del *P.S.I.* (Livorno 1921). Ed. Avanti!, Milan 1921 (reissued 1962).

P. Spriano (ed.) *L'Ordine Nuovo (1919–20)*. (An anthology from the journal.) Einaudi, Turin 1963.

P. Togliatti (ed.) *La Formazione del Gruppo Dirigente del Partito Comunista Italiano nel 1923–4* (letters and documents). Riuniti, Rome 1962.

P. Togliatti *Opere*. 6 vols. Volume One (1917–26) is the most relevant for this period, and is edited by E. Ragionieri. Riuniti, Rome 1967.

Secondary Sources

Various Authors *I Comunisti a Torino* (preface by A. Colombi). Riuniti, Rome 1974.

M. Abrate *La Lotta Sindacale nella Industrializzazione in Italia*. Angeli, Milan 1967.

R. Alcara *La Formazione e Primi Anni del P.C.I. nella Storiografia Marxista*. Jaca, Milan 1970.

A. Aquarone *L'Organizzazione dello Stato Totalitario*. Einaudi, Turin 1965.

R. Bachi *L'Italia Economica* (annual publication, used for the years 1917–21). Lupi, Città di Castello.

G. Berti 'Appunti e Ricordi 1919–26', in *Annali dell' Istituto Giangiacomo Feltrinelli*, a. VIII (1966), pp. 9–185.

G. Bocca *Palmiro Togliatti*. Laterza, Bari 1973.

G. Bonomi *Partito e Rivoluzione in Gramsci*. Feltrinelli, Milan 1973.

J. M. Cammett *Antonio Gramsci and the Origins of Italian Communism*. Stanford U.P. 1967.

A. Caracciolo (ed.) *La Formazione dell' Italia Industriale*. Laterza, Bari 1969.

A. Caracciolo and G. Scalia (eds.) *La Città Futura*. Feltrinelli, Milan 1959.

V. Castronovo *Giovanni Agnelli*. U.T.E.T., Turin 1971.

F. Cordova *Le Origini dei Sindacati Fascisti 1918–26*. Laterza, Bari 1974.

L. Cortesi *Il Socialismo Italiano tra Riforme e Rivoluzione (1891–1921)*. Laterza, Bari 1969.

—— *Le Origini del P.C.I.* Laterza, Bari 1972.

A. De Clementi *Amadeo Bordiga*. Einaudi, Turin 1971.

F. De Felice *Serrati, Bordiga, Gramsci e il Problema della Rivoluzione in Italia*. De Donato, Bari 1971.

R. De Felice *Mussolini il Rivoluzionario*. Einaudi, Turin 1965.

—— *Mussolini il Fascista*. 2 vols. Einaudi, Turin 1966 and 1968.

G. De Rosa *Il Movimento Cattolico in Italia*. vol. ii: *Il Partito Popolare Italiano*. Laterza, Bari 1966.

T. Detti *Serrati e la Formazione del P.C.I.* Riuniti, Rome 1972.

L. Einaudi *La Condotta Economica e gli Effetti Sociali della Guerra Italiana*. Yale U.P. and Laterza, Bari 1933.

Fiat *Fiat – A Fifty Years' Record*. Mondadori, Milan 1951.

G. Fiori *Vita di Antonio Gramsci*. Laterza, Bari 1966. English translation by T. Nairn, *Antonio Gramsci: Life of a Revolutionary*. New Left Books, London 1970 and Dutton, New York 1971.

P. Gobetti *Coscienza Liberale e Classe Operaia*. Einaudi, Turin 1951.

M. Guarnieri *I Consigli di Fabbrica*. Ed. Il Solco, Città di Castello 1921.

D. L. Horowitz *The Italian Labor Movement*. Harvard U.P. 1963.

Istituto Gramsci *Studi Gramsciani*. Riuniti, Rome 1958. (The proceedings of a conference on Gramsci at Rome in January 1958.)

J. LaPalombara *The Italian Labor Movement: Problems and Prospects*. Cornell U.P. 1957.

A. Lepre and S. Levrero *La Formazione del P.C.d'I.* Riuniti, Rome 1971.

A. Lyttelton *The Seizure of Power*. Weidenfeld & Nicolson, London 1973.

C. S. Maier *Recasting Bourgeois Europe*. Princeton U.P., 1975.

G. Maione *Il Biennio Rosso*. Il Mulino, Bologna 1975.

G. Manacorda *Il Socialismo nella Storia d'Italia*. Laterza, Bari 1966.

M. F. Neufeld *Italy: School for Awakening Countries*. Cornell U.P. 1961.

—— *Labor Unions and National Politics in Italian Industrial Plants*. Cornell U.P. 1954.

L. Paggi *Antonio Gramsci e il Moderno Principe*. vol. i. Riuniti, Rome 1971.

G. Prato *Il Piemonte e gli Effetti della Guerra sulla sua Vita Economica e Sociale*. Yale U.P. and Laterza, Bari 1925.

E. Ragionieri Introduction to vol. i of P. Togliatti, *Opere (1917–26)*. Riuniti, Rome 1967.

R. Rigola *Storia del Movimento Operaio Italiano*. Ed. Domus, Milan 1946.

S. F. Romano *Antonio Gramsci*. U.T.E.T., Turin 1965.

P. Rossi (ed.) *Gramsci e la Cultura Contemporanea*. 2 vols. Riuniti, Rome

1969 and 1970. (The proceedings of the International Congress on Gramsci at Cagliari in 1967.)

G. Sabbatucci (ed.) *La Crisi Italiana del Primo Dopoguerra*. Laterza, Bari 1976.

M. L. Salvadori *Gramsci e il Problema Storico della Democrazia*. Einaudi, Turin 1970.

P. Spriano *Torino Operaia nella Grande Guerra*. Einaudi, Turin 1960.

—— *L'Occupazione delle Fabbriche*. Einaudi, Turin 1964 (English translation by G. A. Williams, *The Occupation of the Factories*, Pluto Press, London 1975).

—— *Storia del Partito Comunista Italiano*. 5 vols. Einaudi, Turin 1967–75.

G. Tamburrano *Antonio Gramsci*. Lacaita, Manduria 1963.

A. Tasca *I Primi Dieci Anni del P.C.I.* Laterza, Bari 1971.

—— *Nascita e Avvento del Fascismo*. La Nuova Italia, Florence 1950. (English translation as A. Rossi, *The Rise of Italian Fascism*, Methuen, London 1938.)

R. Vivarelli *Il Dopoguerra in Italia e l'Avvento del Fascismo*. vol. i. Istituto Italiano per gli Studi Storici, Naples 1967.

INDEX